7—

W9-DIA-696

MIND IN ACTION

MIND IN ACTION

Essays in the Philosophy of Mind

Amélie Oksenberg Rorty

Beacon Press · Boston

Beacon Press
25 Beacon Street
Boston, Massachusetts 02108

Beacon Press books
are published under the auspices of
the Unitarian Universalist Association of Congregations.

© 1988 by Amélie Oksenberg Rorty
All rights reserved
Printed in the United States of America
95 94 93 92 91 90 89 88   8 7 6 5 4 3 2 1

Text design by Dennis Anderson

Library of Congress Cataloging-in-Publication Data
Rorty, Amélie.
  Mind in action.
  Bibliography: p.
  1. Psychology—Philosophy.   I. Title.
BF38.R66   1988   128'.2   87-47876
ISBN 0-8070-1404-4

For Jay Rorty

Contents

Preface

These essays were written over a period of fifteen years. When Deborah Johnson of Beacon Press invited me to publish them as a book, I was initially skeptical of the project. Superficially, at any rate, the essays seemed to cover such a wide range of subjects—personal identity, emotions, allegedly irrational attitudes such as akrasia and self-deception, virtues and practical reasoning—that any attempt to conjoin them in a book would produce a chimera rather than a viable creature. But as I began to reread and to group the essays, I realized that they evinced changes that might charitably be called a development. More importantly, I began to see that there are a set of philosophical beliefs and commitments, as well as preoccupations, that generated the views expressed in these papers. Taken together, they form a point of view rather than a heap of random observations.

I have attempted to express that point of view in the introductory essay, "Mind in Action, Action in Context." An introductory essay of this kind affords the almost embarrassing luxury of articulating the skeleton of a philosophical credo, without fleshing it out, without fully describing the organs and musculature that provide its explanatory functions. Since that credo is a commitment to the primacy of the particular, it may be appropriate that the detailed formulation and defense of the general position are presented in the contexts set by the particular problems that are raised in the individual essays.

The essays in this book focus largely on issues in contemporary philosophy of mind. Because we do not fully understand the import of our philosophic problems without understanding their history, many contemporary philosophic controversies appear to end in impasses that block those who have not tracked the archeological layers of their philosophical history. The participants in such controversies are often talking past each other, using what misleadingly appears to be a common terminology in what appears to be a shared investigation. But despite their superficial agreement, the opponents in such debates are asking different questions because they are mining different strata in the history of the philosophy of mind. The companion volume to these essays, *From Passions to Emotions and Sentiments* (Oxford University Press, 1989), traces part of that history.

Without Deborah Johnson's and Thomas Fischer's encouragement, tact, and editorial acumen this book would not have appeared. Without conversations—sustained, shared investigations—with friends and colleagues, these essays would not have been written. Rüdiger Bittner, Myles Burnyeat, G. A. Cohen, J. Thomas Cook, Helen Daniells, Ronald de Sousa, Jon Elster, Owen Flanagan, Ed Johnson, Barrington Jones, Aryeh Kosman, Genevieve Lloyd, Alasdair MacIntyre, Brian McLaughlin, Ruth Nevo, Calvin Normore, Georges Rey, Jay Rorty, William Ruddick, Richard Schmitt, Laszlo Versenyi, and Stephen White listened to early versions of these ideas, and tried to help me formulate them more precisely. I am grateful to John Compton who once asked me the crucial question, How does your work hang together? I join all these friends in the uncomfortable realization that much still remains to be done to clarify and specify the point of view expressed in these papers.

Several of the new essays in the last section—"Virtues and Their Vicissitudes" and "Three Myths of Moral Theory"—were written as lectures for the Baumgardt Prize. I am grateful to the American Philosophical Association for that award, and to Radcliffe College for its generous hospitality during the time they were written.

The cover illustration—*View of the Dam and Damrak at Amsterdam* by Gerrit Adriaenz. Berckheyde (1638–98)—admirably represents a number of themes that this book explores: the ways that character traits, thoughts, and intentions are expressed in gestures and actions; the fusion of individuality with the stereotypes of social condition; the continuity of animal and human life; the vitality and harmony manifest in activities of friends in thoughtful conversation, of families and citizens busily engaged with one another in the affairs of daily life. There is no architectonic order imposed from above or from below: everything shows the improvisations, the inventiveness of the past. In the seventeenth century, the church spire had ceded its centrality to the activities of the port, but it remained a ghostly presence on the horizon of the civic and mercantile world. The interlocked sets of triangles of dark and light, emerging from, and receding into the background of the picture locate us as observers of the scene, as if we were seeing it from the elevated windows of the Town Hall. Domestic and particular, these events are also clearly part of a larger, cosmopolitan world.

Mind in Action, Action in Context

[Because this introduction is the expression of a credo, it is abrupt, abstract, and simple. Written after the rest of the book was finished, it not only sketches the perspective of the various essays, but also indicates the directions of further explorations. A philosophical approach is tried and tested by using it as a map, seeing whether following it reveals or obscures the terrain it explores: the view I present can best be evaluated by the individual essays. The sections of the introduction roughly correspond to the sections of the volume.]

Is the philosophy of mind a subject? The range of issues it now addresses originally appeared in a set of extremely diverse but highly specific contexts, spread throughout the traditional philosophic disciplines. The heterogeneous set of topics that are now treated as canonic—personal identity, action theory, the relation between psychological and physical explanations of behavior, for example—have been detached from their origins. They were originally problems that arose within the context of specific theories, each designed to address distinctive issues. Analyses of the ontological status and the structure of *psychē* and *mens* have always been essential to philosophical theology and metaphysics; a normative epistemology that claims successful regulative power must give an account of the relation between the capacities exercised in rational thought and other psychological functions; there cannot be a robust ethics, or a serious political philosophy, without a robust social psychology that articulates the conditions for liability and responsibility.

Plato and Aristotle, from whom the philosophy of mind inherits much of its ontology and many of its questions, constructed it at the service of normative epistemology and normative political theory. Plato's analysis of the structure of the mind was designed to establish the possibility of a self-corrective rationality, in principle empowered to form and direct desires and passions. It was in the interest of such an epistemology that Plato attempted to distinguish rational knowledge from mystical insight and technical activity. The model of juridical arguments that gives direct witnesses a special measure of epistemic authority suggested the theory of recollection: the possibility of knowledge depends on the soul's ability to recover the forms it had once directly perceived. But Plato also used mathematical proofs as the models of truth-preserving demonstrations: these suggested that a mind capable of knowledge must be capable of performing purely abstract operations. Since formal relations among abstract schemata provide the primary examples and even the proper objects of knowledge, a philosophical psychology designed to explain the possibility of knowledge must account for the formalizing powers of the mind. Plato's philosophy of mind fused the privilege of the direct witness with the authority of formal demonstration.

For both Plato and Aristotle, the question of whether practical and political activity is rational—and whether it is rational in the same way as purely intellectual knowledge—was a question with political implications in determining the criteria for legitimate rule. The answer to the question, Does rationality have effective motivational power? determines whether political systems legitimized by de facto power or by genealogical myths can justifiably be replaced by political systems in which rulers are selected for their intellectual and psychological abilities to promote a thriving polity. By assimilating practical and political knowledge to intellectual knowledge, Plato limited the class of those qualified to rule to the class of true philosophers. Aristotle could legitimate a different class of rulers: the *phronimos* is rational even though he is concerned with matters of practice, with particular actions rather than with demonstrable general truths.

The conjunction of Aristotle's biological with his metaphysical concerns added another set of problems to the canon of topics for the philosophy of mind. As he conceived the matter, *psychē* is an organizing principle whose activities—those engaged in nutrition, reproduction, perception, motivated action—are shared by other living organisms. But humans also have some psychological activities that are, strictly speaking, the activities of *nous* engaged in certain forms of knowledge. Since these can in principle be abstracted from the rest of psychophysiology, they can in principle be shared by nonhuman intellects. Implicitly, Aristotle distinguishes philosophical psychology—which analyzes the interaction among the various psychophysical activities and investigates the physical realization of psychological activities—from the philosophy of mind, strictly speaking, as the investigation of the structure of the knowing mind. *Phronēsis*, practical wisdom, is meant to integrate *nous* with the psychological activities of desire and perception. But Aristotle's discussion requires, rather than provides, an investigation of the details of the integration of mind and psychology.

The success of these various enterprises—Plato's substituting scientific metaphysics for speculative cosmogony and poetic cosmology, rational ethics and politics for traditional mores and power politics, Aristotle's formulating psychologically realizable canons for valid inferences—depends on whether the structure of the mind is actively rational in the ways that Plato and Aristotle postulated.

Medieval theologians held that making a radical choice between good and evil is the (divinely ordained and divinely judged) fundamental human activity. A theology that interprets psychological egoism as the natural, fallen condition, the consequence of original sin, sets a new complex agenda for the philosophy mind. The conceptual apparatus that medieval theologians inherited from Plato and Aristotle—the ontology of souls and minds, the descriptions of their respective activities and powers—had to be reinterpreted to serve these new interests and preoccupations. The Stoic distinction between those aspects of the mind which, like rationality, are causally unconditioned, and those which, like perception, imagination, and desire, are causally determined, was introduced to account for the possibility of salvation. Some held that divine grace can, in principle, provide a new psychology that entirely reorients the operations of the natural faculties, so that they can freely conform to God's will; others argued that there is a set of motives and habits within the natural condition that can pivot it toward its own reform.

When Descartes made the construction of a demonstrative science the fundamental activity, normative epistemology rather than theology again set the agenda for the philosophy of mind. Redescribing essential human activities, Descartes reconstructed his medieval inheritance, reinterpreting the relation between the divine and human minds. It is now *mens,* as the descendant of *nous,* rather than *psyché* or *anima,* that is the subject of investigation. "I consider the mind not as part of the soul but as the thinking soul in its entirety."[1] For Descartes the possibility of a deductive mathematical physics that explains and in principle predicts sensory experience not only requires distinguishing the mind from the body but also requires distinguishing the will and the intellect from sensation, imagination, and the passions. Once made, these distinctions set the major problems for the philosophy of mind: besides the obvious problems of characterizing the relation between mind and body, there is the problem of explaining how ideas caused by the body—perceptions, bodily sensations, and passions—are integrated with the innate mathematical ideas that are supposed to explain them. What accounts for the unity and identity of any individual mind, and how do the unity and identity of mind differ from the unity and identity of an individual person, composed of mind and body?

Idealism marks the philosophy of mind as the dominant philosophical enterprise, absorbing both logic and metaphysics. For those who believe that the structure of the mind provides the structure of reality, the philosophy of mind *is* philosophy. Kant's transcendental turn, and his assimilating experience to the formation of judgment, gives the philosophy of mind a strong cognitivist direction. Hegel's rejection of the distinction between formal and empirical conditions for experience transformed the Kantian program of the unity of science, and set the stage for the reemergence of scientific psychology. But after Hegel, scientifically oriented philosophical psychology split in two directions. The first, which emphasized organic developmental processes, located philosophical psychology within a biological framework. Neo-Darwinians concentrated on showing how psychological activities are physically realized and integrated with the primary organic functions exercised in survival and reproduction. Do cognitive operations have a special status in modifying or directing other processes? What, besides truth-orientation, are the adaptive constraints on belief? What are the sources and forms of social and altruistic behavior?

Emphasizing the centrality of cognition in integrating the distinctive operations postulated by traditional faculty psychology, Wundt and his followers took the philosophy of mind in the second direction. They attempted to develop a general theory of cognitive processing and to discover the laws of thought. When cognitivism took a linguistic turn, the investigation of the structure of thought shifted to the investigation of the deep structure of grammar and natural languages. The primary task for the philosophy of mind became that of constructing sophisticated information processors that might serve as models for explaining the wide range of cognitive and psychological activities. Some of the issues inherited from normative epistemology—the analysis of representation and reference—remain. Cartesian questions reappear in a new form: Is there a language of thought that underlies the varieties of natural languages? Does thought presuppose consciousness and self-consciousness? Because many cognitive theorists believe that their enterprise is presupposed by virtually all other branches of philosophical psychology, they attempt to provide robust theories of perception, emotion, motivation, and psychological and moral development.

The two post-Hegelian branches of scientific psychology continue to struggle for dominance. Biologically oriented theorists argue that the range of cognitive processes functions within an organism whose activities are directed to survival; cognitivists argue that biological functioning is one instantiation of a more general, schematic informational model. Attempts to fuse or integrate the varieties of post-Hegelian scientific philosophical psychology no sooner emerge than they again fission. Psychology now includes a number of disparate concerns. Social and moral psychology, clinical theory, physiological psychology, and psycholinguistics each has its own methodology and theoretical constructs. So, too, the philosophy of mind now covers an oddly assorted set of investigations ranging from cognitive theory to analyses of akrasia and self-deception.

There are good reasons for this history of diversity, unification, and dispersion. Traditionally, minds were characterized by their patterned, discriminating activities, usually described as conscious or intentional and often taken to be susceptible to introspective examination. But the activities that were attributed to minds—thinking, perceiving, sensing, desiring, imagining, inferring, willing, being emotionally affected—are extremely heterogeneous, each composed of quite diverse subprocesses. Their functions and modes of operation are best explained at specific localized levels. To be sure, the analysis and cross-classification of traditional mental activities exhibit genuine regularities. But those regularities are contextually subscripted: they are relative to the focus and interests of distinctive investigations.[2] Preoccupations with the conditions of rational choice, for instance, select and map variables that differ from those appropriate for investigations of the psychology of survival or that of the social formation of motivational structures. Little, if anything, is added to the explanation of these various activities by the additional claim that they are performed by a mind, or that they are all mental activities, as opposed, presumably, to physical activities. If there were a great ontological table of contents, neither *mind* nor *individual minds* would be likely to appear on the list of independent substances. Indeed, it is questionable whether, in this domain, it even makes sense to project one great ontological table of contents, rather than to construct a concordance of references to distinctive activities. In that index, the entry for *mind* would be marked *"vide: mental activities."* The entry for *mental activities* would list an extremely heterogenous set of items, some cross-classified under the entry for *psychophysical activities*.

To be sure, the regulative program of systematic explanation assures us that however disparate they may be, the range of activities now loosely classified together as mental functions has some sort of coherent and systematic account. The range of various 'mental' activities—classified together for different reasons at different times—must each find a place within some explanatory theory. But nothing about the program of explanation requires that they all find their explanations in the same place, under the same rubric, or even in the same theory. As far as the program of explanation goes, the various traditional 'mental' activities may well be subdivided and dispersed, each subdivision finding its niche in a different place. Some of those activities may only make ghostly appearances on a list of eliminable Oldspeak theoretical constructs.[3] There are, of course, likely to be illuminating regularities mapping and sometimes subsuming classifications across distinctive explanatory contexts. But the integration of all these diverse multiple classified activities might well be accomplished only by a long circuitous route. If a theory of all 'mental' activity were to emerge, it might not be a theory of *mind*, but a theory of X, where X is too general to do much detailed explanatory work.

I. Persons and Personae

Forced options are usually false options

Will there be an entry for *persons* in the great concordance that replaces an ontological table of contents? If so, it would have to be a very complex set of multiple listings, with cross-referenced entries that allow individuals or classes—families, corporations, fetuses, the legally disenfranchised—to qualify as persons by some criteria, not by others. With so complex a system of cross-classification, it does not matter whether we deny that there is a single concept of persons, or recognize that the diversity of criteria for its attribution allows individuals and classes to qualify as persons on radically different grounds. The difficult cases are, of course, practical cases where the legal and sociopolitical treatment of individuals and classes are affected by their classification. The criteria for persons are coordinate with, rather than foundational for, a range of normative political principles, and the criteria for personal identity express rather than provide the grounds for legal principles. Neither can provide a foundational justification for the other, and both are primarily expressed and articulated in the details of the particular practices that serve as their context.

The class of persons and the criteria for their identity are defined by reference to a range of activities that are regarded, often unselfconsciously, as centrally and normatively important to a culture, a historical period, or an investigative context. Of course I cannot here properly trace, but only superficially indicate, some of the history of 'the' concept of persons that locates our inheritance within the particular (and as I believe, primarily normative) issues that absorbed traditional philosophers of mind.[4] Practical and political considerations are brought into play even when—as is the case in the abortion controversy—'the' concept of person is adjusted to conform to theological doctrine or to the wide-ranging implications of scientific discoveries.

The modern Western conception of persons derives many of its characterizations—that persons are reflective responsible agents—from Augustine. But his account appears within a theological frame that defines the primary concerns and tasks of the post-Adamic condition. Augustine held that our basic activities are directed toward integrating the divided and corrupt psyche of the natural, fallen condition, so that we can freely consent to being the agents of God's purposes. Augustine used his analysis of the doctrine of the Trinity—his account of how the three persons of the divinity form a single substantial unity—to explain how persons can be simple unified agents despite the diversity, and sometimes the conflicts, among their faculties and powers. His discussions are constrained by the normative requirements set by biblical texts and orthodox doctrine. But his account of persons as agents directed toward integration and salvation is also indebted to Platonic accounts of the soul's erotic attraction to the form of the Good and to legal and dramatic conceptions of *personae* as agents responsible for the unfolding of events.

When political activity is regarded as the privileged, primary activity, the political definition of persons is detached from the theological context in which it had been developed. Conceptions of persons and their powers are reoriented: philosophic interest shifts from political to legal and to social and communitarian issues. Focusing on the source and grounds for the political contract, Hobbes concentrates on the capacities for prudential, rational choice; Locke locates the legal conditions for personal liability and responsibility in the continuity of memory; Hume analyzes the relation between the self-interested passions and those actuated by the sentiment of justice; Rousseau attempts to reconcile the tensions between individual autonomy and the social formation of character. Kant argues that the possibility of morality depends on the capacity of persons to treat one another with respect, as rational agents, members of the kingdom of ends. Theories of political and social persons focus on issues of equality and rights, and on the social formation and transformation of natural psychological processes.

Some of the apparently intractable debates about persons occur when the concerns of one context are imported to another, in the premature interest of constructing a unified theory, or as a rhetorical move in a political polemic. The appearance of forced options often arises from a misguided attempt to derive decisions from 'the' (illicitly decontextualized) concept of a person. When there are repetitive irresolvable debates about the primacy of competing concepts of persons—as there are, for instance, in the controversies over the justifiability of abortion—the first move should be to formulate the issues that lie behind the dispute, specifying the distinctive sources and contexts of conflicting intuitions. Apparently irreconcilable opponents are often interested in different issues, asking different questions, each assuming that the answer to one question determines the answer to the others. In the case of the abortion issue, for instance, apparently conflicting intuitions on the primacy of theological, biological, or sociopolitical criteria for personal identity might be reconciled by regionalizing their respective dominance. Even if a particular sectarian theology classifies the fetus as a person, nothing follows about the propriety of importing that particular theological conception to legal and political contexts. However detailed and articulated it may be, a theological doctrine does not, by itself, establish the propriety of its dominance in a nontheocratic legal system. The criteria for biological and legal individuation need not coincide; nor need those for theological and social identification.

Concerns about how such a strongly contextualist approach identifies entities across contexts are deflected by refusing to provide a general answer. Since questions and contexts are particular all the way up and all the way down, such questions are given their sense and direction by the particular context in which they arise. The question, How are contexts identified and individuated? is answered by the counter-question, Which contexts?[5]

II. Psychological Activities and the Waywardness of Mind

> The mind is a . . . mode of thinking. There is no . . . faculty of willing, . . . but only this or that particular act of affirmation . . . or negation.
>
> Spinoza, *Ethics* 2. 48–49

By contrast to traditional faculty psychology and its (often unacknowledged) influence on contemporary cognitive psychology, a strongly contextualized approach that emphasizes description rather than reconstruction has a number of independent features. It treats each of the varieties of traditional cognitive and psychological attitudes (beliefs, desires, emotions, decisions, doubts, memories, imaginings, etc.) as:

1. Cross-classified with, rather than contrasted to, physical processes
2. a. Heterogeneous classes with disjunctive criteria for membership
   b. Activities rather than states
   c. Complex activities composed of distinctive subprocesses
3. Actively interdependent and mutually constituting
4. Partly indeterminate, open to further determination
5. Organized in habitual or characteristic patterns
6. Socially structured
7. Multilayered and multifunctional

1. It explores the heterogeneity of psychological activities, without assuming that there is a fixed contrast between psychological attitudes and physiological processes, or between cognitive and noncognitive attitudes. Besides perceiving and remembering, there are varieties of patterned, discriminatory responses that function both as physical and as psychological processes. Their psychological functions often essentially embed their noncognitive or precognitive sources and rules. Such activities as reflex actions, startle and flight responses, emotional bonding, mood and motive responses to odors and colors, and selective patterns of attraction and avoidance can be coded and symbolized, recovered, analyzed, recompounded. In their articulated forms, they can be so well integrated with cognitive activities and operations that they can come under direct voluntary control. One method (among others) of classifying the heterogeneity of psychological activities is to distinguish the ways their propositionalizable contents affect their functions.

a. Some psychological activities function in fully propositional form. (Constructing mathematical proofs, for example.) Explaining their etiology and functions requires identifying their propositional content.

b. Some psychological activities that do not function as propositions can be put in propositional form. (Mental imagery, or attitudes of trust and distrust, for example.) While specifying their logical relations requires identifying their propositional contents, analyzing their causal relations need not.

c. Some cognitive configurations, such as magnetized salience in perception (the dominance of red in the visual field, for instance) or categorial preoccupations in interpretations (the dominance of danger or power, for instance) cannot be formulated propositionally because they do not have truth conditions.

d. Some quasi-cognitive activities (reflex actions or responses to pain, for instance) can in principle be fully specified by physical descriptions, though they can also sometimes function as intentional activities, capable of being modified or controlled by beliefs.

2. Each of the varieties of traditional psychological attitudes forms a heterogeneous class of complex activities which are themselves composed of subprocesses. Beliefs, desires, emotions, fantasies, memories, decisions are each attributable on distinctive grounds.

a. They are heterogeneous classes. 'Imagining,' 'desiring,' 'deciding,' and 'being emotionally affected' (etc.) are umbrella terms covering classes of heterogeneous, cross-classified activities. Differences in the etiology and functions of their subvarieties are often marked by differences in the criteria for their attribution.[6] Notoriously, for example, emotions form an extremely heterogeneous class, ranging from such biologically based fears of charging lions to such culturally specific activities as Sunday melancholy, from red-faced, fist-clenched indignation at injustice to a sense of surfeit from reading too much Proust at one sitting. They are attributed on the basis of gestures and behavior, or patterns of associations of ideas and feelings or on the basis of culturally specific assumptions about typical or natural reactions in standard situations. Similarly, there are marked differences in the etiology and functions of activities traditionally classified as desires: needs, wants, wishes, preferences, fantasies. The criteria for their attribution also vary contextually, ranging from patterned routines of behavior to repetitive sequences of associations or obsessive thoughts. In the context of an autobiography or a psychotherapeutic session, for instance, elaborate fantasies and obsessive thoughts serve as grounds for attributing a desire; but they are not sufficient to establish a motive in a murder trial.

b. They are temporal activities rather than occurrent states. A flash of affection, a stab of jealousy, an inferential leap, a flicker of wild imagining, a moment of conviction do perhaps occur, but even these are standardly individuated and identified as embedded within a larger context of other mental activities. Hume (of all people) put the point nicely: " 'Tis not the present sensation or momentary pain which determines the character of any passion, but the general bent or tendency of it from beginning to end."[7]

c. They are complex. For instance, at least some of the subvarieties of *believing that p* typically involve engaging in some of a number of subprocesses: formulating *p*, considering the range of consequences of *p*, doubting some of them, disconfirming those doubts by tracing their etiology, acquiring the feeling of conviction that *p* is true, habitually acting as if *p* were true, and so forth. Most of the subvarieties of *desiring a* involve (as it may be) envisaging the satisfactions of having *a*, constructing scenarios about how to get *a*, lingering on memories of past experiences of *a*, habitually attempting to secure *a*, and so forth. And so, also, for the various subprocesses that are the constituents of beliefs and desires: 'considering the range of consequences of *p*' involves imaging *p*, formulating a set of propositions that would be true if *p* were true, formulating and disconfirming counterevidence, and so forth. 'Remembering past experiences of *a*' involves imaging past experiences, running through a set of verbal phrases, generating a set of associations, and/or so forth.[8]

3. The traditional varieties of psychological activities are actively interdependent and mutually constituting. The inferential patterns of rational thought, the associative patterns of the imagination, the magnetizing functions of the emotions appear within, and partially individuate and constitute, one another. The distinction among states,

dispositions, and activities is correspondingly relativized: apparently recessive dispositions can affect occurrent activities. Dispositional desires not only affect, but individuate, acts of imagining; emotions not only affect, but constitutively individuate, beliefs and perceptions. Mistrust, for example, changes perception: when trust is lost, a face that had been /seen as alert can come to be seen as shifty. Similarly, a dispositional desire to see a particular Rembrandt can significantly affect and even individuate the interpretation of an obscure passage in Spinoza's *Ethics*, (and vice versa). So, too, childhood memories that are dispositional by standard accounts nevertheless often actively influence and individuate occurrent desires or emotions.[9]

Psychological activities can be cross-classified by reference to their motivating power (beliefs and emotions can be as powerfully motivating as desires, for instance); by the extent to which they are socializable or constitutionally determined; by the extent to which they are susceptible to voluntary control or redirection; by the extent to which their lawlike associations are universal or vary culturally or individually; by the extent to which they serve species survival; by the extent to which they are separable from other activities; by the extent to which they can be self-regulating. Jealousy or the fear of death can, for example, be classified with certain sorts of fantasies in the interest of understanding how cognition serves survival; but in the interest of understanding certain sorts of physiological changes, they can be classified with mood responses to shifts in light intensity.

(There are, to be sure, several types of context-relative classifications. There is a significant difference between contexts that are distinguished by differences in performance operations and those that are distinguished by differences in explanatory interests. The distinction between the contexts of microscopic and macroscopic explanations of cellular structures is an example of the first; that between aesthetic and political contexts an example of a [contestable] interest-relative distinction. Classifications of performance operations can cut across distinctive interest-relative contexts, and vice versa. The context-dependence of classificational schemes does not imply that all contexts are equally important. There are interesting correlations among performance-relative contexts and among interest-relative contexts; their classificational schemes can sometimes be subsumed in lawlike ways. A contextualized approach is prepared to explore the possibility that explanatory interests are hierarchically structured. The question of whether there is an interest-independent hierarchical order among interest-relative classifications is left as an open question.)

4. Most psychological attitudes and activities are, at any given time, partly indeterminate, capable of further specification and individuation.

While a person's beliefs are, for example, sufficiently definite to constrain and sometimes to direct further interpretation and determination, their functions and significance are also continuously further formed and constituted by a variety of social factors, including the minutiae of social interactions. So, for instance, a set of philosophical beliefs (about whether Socrates held that virtue could be taught, for instance) might be specific enough for someone to participate in learned discussions on the subject, giving sound reasons for taking sides in disputes about the matter. Still, without changing her mind on any issue she had previously accepted, a scholar's opinions might become more detailed and specific through discussions with colleagues. Her views might, as she could well realize, have acquired a slightly different articulation or emphasis if she had taken a sabbatical in Berlin rather than Oxford. It is not merely the exchange of opinions that further determines a person's attitudes: sometimes a lifted eyebrow, the look of excitement, a shrug, a bored look, even involuntary facial reactions are also effective. Nor is the social determination of attitudes limited to social events. Even in solitude we are affected by internalized interlocutors whose imagined responses guide our thoughts. Of course a person's initial attitudes set strong constraints on later determinations; constraints of coherence, validity, and truth are also usually in force. But because a vast range of further specifications are logically and psychologically compatible with most of our attitudes, such constraints are generally insufficient for fixing their determination. Which of the horde of compatible individuating specifications of our attitudes appears relevant or natural at any given juncture is often a function of the company we keep.

5. An individual's psychological activities are organized in habitual associative patterns that mark a style of thought. Oldspeak memories, beliefs, emotions typically follow and accompany one another in characteristic ways, formed by the person's psychological history.

6. The pattern of an individual's psychological activities is in part socially structured. To begin with, the categories and associations ingredient in a person's native language enter into the individuation of (Oldspeak) thoughts, images, emotions, desires. Second, psychological activities are formed and directed by social practices, particularly those clustering around early socialization. Third, standard cultural narratives, the canonic works of popular and high culture, set the terms of intelligibility and communication. Expectations about the normal unfolding of events—expectations that structure the standard relevant sequence of psychological activities—are formed by popular songs, epics, sacred texts. The repertoire of common cultural stories and tales contributes to the individuation of psychological activities: they are ingredient in the

content and the typical sequence of (Oldspeak) emotions, beliefs, desires.[10]

7. Most psychological and cognitive activities are multilayered and multifunctional, playing a number of distinctive roles simultaneously. So, for instance, exploring the details of a wish may simultaneously guide a novelist's delineation of a character and serve as a substitute satisfaction of one of her own unrealized desires. An administrator's organizing her daily agenda may simultaneously avoid embarrassing conflicts and express her attempts to reassure herself that she is a real figure in a real world. Sometimes the hierarchical nesting of these multiple activities and functions is determinate, with a dominant activity that regulates the rest. But sometimes the priority is indeterminate. So, for instance, it might be indeterminate whether a particular autobiographical narration is constructed primarily in the interests of self-justification, or of expressing gratitude, or of clarifying primary commitments. Sometimes—as in many cases of akrasia and self-deception—the various functions of such attitudes conflict in such a way as to undermine each other.

Instead of attempting to reconstruct all mental activities on the model of propositionalizable cognition, a contextualized approach investigates the different ways that cognition serves, and is directed by, nonepistemic functions. Sometimes these other functions explain the selection and repetition, the patterned sequences of cognitive activities. Self-protection, self-transformation, wooing, engaging in hierarchical combat often set the umbrella contexts in which epistemically oriented cognition occurs. The contexts set by the overarching activity then provide the best explanation of the details of perception, memory, belief. (Why *this* belief rather than any number of others that might fit the person's epistemic set equally well?) To be sure, the great advantage of propositional reconstructions of psychological activities—formulating even such attitudes as fear or envy as propositional attitudes—is that such reconstructions permit the analysis of ambiguous attitudes and prepare for their truth-functional evaluation. In principle, the contextualizing approach is compatible with the propositionalizing approach. There is nothing wrong, and much that is useful, in logical reconstructions of this kind providing that they do not claim to exhaust the descriptions of psychological activities or to provide the norm for their proper functioning. But it is sometimes more important to determine whether an attitude is harmful, excessive, or fruitful than it is to determine whether it is ambiguous or true.

Because they appear to violate the norms of rationality central to an account of the possibility of scientific demonstration and normative ethics, the phenomena of self-deception, akrasia, and the inappropriate preservation of attitudes (after the beliefs that ground them have changed) present problems for philosophy of mind. Such phenomena are standardly either redescribed, or ascribed to ignorance, error, or some sort of malfunction. But each of these phenomena is itself quite heterogeneous. Some types of self-deception are, for instance, aligned with compartmentalization; others are associated with the rhetoric of self-manipulation; still other kinds of self-deception are functional by-products of latitudinarian criteria for belief. Some types of akrasia are classified with cases of social imitation; others are expressions of conflicts among strongly entrenched habits.

Attitudes that seem mysterious and deviant for a philosophy of mind constructed to explain the possibility of rationality present no particular problems for a strongly contextualized approach. Explanations of activities vary with their classifications; actions that have multiple classifications and that play multiple functional roles have multiple etiologies and explanations. Akrasia and self-deception sometimes appear irrational because the actions that constitute them have been cross-classified. The expression of a wish might, for example, function primarily to strengthen a particular motive rather than to report a determinate psychological state. If it is treated as a report, the wish may be self-deceptive; but if it is treated as a strategy in the interest of self-transformation, it is not. Analysts may be confused by what is useful to agents: transformations are sometimes best effected by being disguised as reports. While individual cases are often irrational in being both illogical and inappropriate to the rest of a person's psychological structures, the popularity of akrasia and self-deception is explained by their functionality. Attempts to eradicate them would greatly limit our psychological resourcefulness.

It would be pretty to think that we could map these various features and orientations of a contextualized approach. We might think that order would emerge from chaos if we could, for instance, show that psychological activities are indeterminate because they are classified across traditional distinctions (between physical and psychological processes, for example) or that they are interdependent because they are complex and multifunctional. But while there are interesting correlations among these various features of psychological activities, it is an open, partly empirical question whether these correlations themselves vary contextually. The contextual approach that emphasizes description rather than reconstruction prefers to leave empirically charged questions open for further investigation, rather than to cover unknown territory with theories that inherit or import theoretical constructs originally introduced for quite different purposes, in quite different contexts.

III. Community as the Context of Character

> Ethics without psychology is science fiction; morality without politics is a bicycle without wheels.

What do we want from a moral theory? Besides characterizing the varieties of well-lived lives, and formulating general principles and ideals for regulating conduct, a moral theory should tell us something about how to get from where we are to where we might better be. While it needn't prescribe a decision procedure for determining every detail of every choice and action, it should, in a general way, be action-guiding: constructing a robust ethical theory requires an astute understanding of psychology and of history. Because moral theories combine practical concerns with idealized evaluations, they must be sensitive to the particular political and socio-psychological conditions in which they are to be applied. A moral theory that recommends political and psychological reforms must also pay attention to the ways in which its proposed redirections can effectively and successfully be brought about, given actual conditions.[11]

Who is the *we* that such moral theories address? It is not *we* taken as isolated individuals, doing the best we can to live well by our lights. So described, our powers are so pitifully limited that we might as well forget about the moral life, or anything else for that matter. The *we* in question is the *we* who are the members (in some cultures, individuals; in others, families) of a reflective community, with a specific history, a specific set of geopolitical problems, a specific demography, with a culturally uniform or heterogeneous population. To be sure, *we* are also members of a species that has certain general problems, tasks, and activities: our needs for nourishment and shelter sometimes place us in competitive relations with one another; our prolonged infancy sets certain patterns, expectations, and difficulties for us. As a species, if not as individuals, we need to reproduce, to nurture, socialize, and educate our young; we need to set patterns for, if not actually to govern, our associations with one another. We also form certain kinds of ideals that are not determined by our problems or the satisfaction of our needs, and while these ideals differ markedly from culture to culture, they appear to bear some resemblance to one another. While most of the problems set for moral theory are specific to a particular community, many are also cross-cultural. We are often in the difficult position of not knowing which is which, whether in recommending this or that virtue or principle to our friends and neighbors, we are speaking to their conditions or from ours.

Many contemporary moral theorists are turning to the advantages of an ethics of virtue over an ethics of rules and principles. Virtue theories typically explore the connections between psychological and intellectual habits and habits of action, analyzing the effects of perceptual and categorial preoccupations on patterns of action. They are attentive to the political and psychological issues surrounding moral education; and they are sensitive to conflicts among ideals, the habits engendered by social structures, and constitutionally based psychological activities.[12]

The virtues are commonly initially identified, defined, and promoted by a range of interests that are sometimes engaged in power struggles to define a culture's ideals and to direct its conceptions of its flourishing. Virtues form a set of extremely heterogeneous traits, traits that are believed to conduce to performing central activities well and appropriately, particularly when those activities are thought difficult to perform, because doing so requires overcoming some natural obstacles.[13] The more complex and heterogeneous the culture, the more varied and potentially conflicting are its virtues; and the more difficult it becomes to distinguish those virtues that serve its needs from those that express its ideals. The more conflicting are the virtues of a culture, the more important it becomes to determine which virtue is appropriate for any given context. The natural move is to locate a master virtue—prudence or *caritas*, good will or a sense of proportion—to determine priorities among the virtues when their actions conflict in particular situations. But there is serious disagreement about which trait can best serve as the master virtue, whether, for instance, it should be prudence or good will, *caritas* or a sense of proportion. In any case, the serious candidates for the master virtue are themselves standardly complex, composed of independent traits whose shifting patterns of dominance can prompt quite different sorts of policies or actions. (So, for instance, prudence can allot priority to considerations that weight the widest range of distribution or to those that weight long-range benefits.)

For these reasons, philosophical analyses of individual virtues tend to move to analyses of the psychology of virtuous persons, to an account of the appropriate configuration of traits in a system of checks and balances. But describing the proper configuration of a system of virtues presupposes a theory of the proper weighting of the activities that constitute the whole lifespan of a variety of well-lived lives. A system of virtues designed to enhance the best performance of the activities of youth or middle age is, for example, likely to differ from one that values the habits and traits required for a thriving old age, particularly because stressing the virtues of youth may sometimes present difficulties in developing those of age, or vice versa. Similarly, distinctive social roles (or distinctive psychological types) may require different configurations of a system of checked-and-balanced virtues. Because these various models of virtue can compete with one another for dominance in forming or directing a culture's ideals, attempts to harmonize them can lead to profound political disagreements.

It is here—in disputes about how to weight the primary activities that constitute the varieties of fully lived lives—that we reach the limits of the strategy of resolving disagreements by distinguishing contexts.[14] These limits seem particularly stark in political cases where individual welfare is affected by decisions about priorities among competing conceptions of the varieties of well-lived and fully realized lives. Which (if any) of the varieties of conceptions of persons—of their virtues, their rights and obligations—should be imported into discussions of the legalization of abortion, for example? Are those who undergo or perform abortions under an obligation to weight certain sorts of moral considerations? Like other such politically charged moral questions, the question of whether abortion is permissible occurs in specific social, economic, and political contexts. It arises in the papal chambers in the summer of 1985, or in the Senate of the State of Massachusetts assembled in legislative session in January 1988. Both the pope and the legislators are presented with expert testimony from clergy, physicians, and social workers. Scholars advise them of the history of interpretations of canonic texts, the Bible, and patristic commentaries or the Constitution and judicial opinions. They are informed of opinions of their respective constituencies, the practices surrounding adoption, the availability of quality child care, the socioeconomic costs of providing welfare for unwed unemployable adolescent mothers, the health risks for all those affected by the decisions. But even when the particular consequences are fully and contextually specified, the pope might well remain undecided and the legislators may well continue to disagree. How should the testimony of the various witnesses—who are sure to disagree among themselves—to be weighed? The evidence from existing conditions might well be a function of existing practices; those conditions might well change with new legislation. In any case, the transitional difficulties that normally attend introducing new practices don't by themselves argue against their propriety or benefits.

In relatively well-defined political contexts, it is sometimes possible to arrive at a practical resolution by agreeing on procedural principles that allow the contending parties to arbitrate their differences, if only by regionalizing decisions. But when a group is willing to sacrifice the continuity of a pluralistic political community for the sake of a particular set of values (those set by specific religious principles, for instance), there may be no context from which to negotiate or arbitrate among competing views.

The fear that the limits of arbitration mark the beginning of sheer power politics is a reasonable fear. It forms the hope that philosophical theories about the conditions for rationality (or criteria for personhood) could be used to resolve intractable political differences. But even if it is naive to trust the political efficacy of rationality, it is premature to despair about the limits of rationality or the inevitable relativity of counterclaims in disputes that appear to end in impasses. It is sometimes helpful to evaluate the significance of opposing policies by projecting and representing the minute, detailed descriptions of the consequences of various principles and policies. At least sometimes, imaginative visualization can be clearer and more persuasive than argument, without being any the less rational for being visual. Because vivid descriptions focus attention on the concrete details that are often ignored by general discussions, they can help resolve uncertainty or conflicts. Gandhi and civil rights leaders successfully used photographic and television documentation as persuasive arguments. Of course a strategy of this kind often slides into rhetoric that can be misused by all sides: like all forms of argument, it must be checked and balanced by critical reflection.

Still, even the most detailed and vivid descriptions of the actual consequences of various policies do not always succeed in resolving genuine indecision or deep political disagreements. It is in situations of this kind that visionaries of various sorts, religious and political reformers as well as those who attempt to express or articulate the traditional ideals and mores of their culture, find themselves moving toward constructing philosophical ethical theories. While the distinction between moral systems and philosophical metaethical theories is artificial, it is nevertheless sometimes useful. Insofar as moral systems articulate the constituents and structures of well-lived lives, they implicitly propose resolutions to moral conflicts. They do not, however, necessarily formulate principles for adjudicating between competing moral systems. Philosophical metaethical systems also articulate principles for arbitrating conflicts between substantive moral systems. At their best, philosophical analyses of conflicts concerning the structure of moral systems should also illuminate conflicts about the structure of moral life, disputes about how to live well.

Unfortunately, metaethical reflections of this kind tend to take on a life of their own. Using the problems of substantive moral theories primarily as a convenient source of examples, metaethical theorists introduce distinctions that function primarily within generalized discussions of the problems of theory construction. Instead of showing how various metaethical proposals about the criteria for valid moral arguments (or about the relations among moral concepts) succeed in illuminating moral conflicts, they move to generalized discussions of moral realism, relativism, and objectivity. Metaethical reflection initially introduced to address problems in moral theory becomes metaphilosophy for its own sake. Removed from its origins or applications, it is in danger of losing its sense. Like other metaphilosophical debates, generalized metaethical discussions recede in dizzying regressions that tend to reproduce the original disagreements in ever more abstract, ever less illuminating or resolvable terms.

Metaethical considerations should not force us to choose between an ethical theory focused on rules and principles, or one focused on character and virtue, or on visionary ideals. Those theories may well be compatible; and the problems that arise in one often have their analogues in the others. Nor need we commit ourselves on the relative priority of the good and the right, as if that could be settled *überhaupt*. (We don't even need to commit ourselves to the priority of the best over the good. Of course, other things being equal, the best appears to be preferable to the merely good. Nevertheless, the best can often be an enemy of the good. Even in moral contexts, the consequences of accepting the good as good enough may sometimes be preferable to the devastation and destruction that can accompany striving for the best.) Because the advantages and disadvantages of all these approaches vary with the immediate context in which they arise and are applied, they cannot be assessed outside those contexts. Nevertheless, because the strong and continued dominance of one type of ethical theory often genuinely affects cultural practices, particularly those centering around power relations, it is sometimes a good idea to follow the method of crop rotation, to concentrate on the advantages of an ethics of virtue when an ethics of rules and principles has long been in the ascendancy, and vice versa.

But who decides when it is time to rotate the crops? Who is the *we* who write moral theories, and what relation do we have to the *us* whom we address? If moral theory is practical, then it is enmeshed in issues of political power: it presupposes, expresses, and implicitly exercises particular power relations, especially those that affect the practices of socialization and the institutions that assure the continuity of cultural values. Besides being uplifting about characterizing the lives it might be well for us to lead, what functions do moral theories perform? In being presumptively action-guiding, such theories propose not only to direct but to constrain what we do; they identify vices as well as recommend particular configurations of checks and balances among the virtues. Since the beneficiaries of the exercise of the virtues or the application of moral principles are manifestly not always the individuals or groups who are exhorted to follow them, the promise lies elsewhere. The benefits accrue to rational beings as such, perhaps, or to future generations and the community at large; or morality is argued to bring its own rewards in the form of some sort of nobility. But whose friends and neighbors, whose descendants are best positioned to be ennobled or to benefit? And who is likely to get left out?

Ethical theorists are often surprisingly unreflective and uncritical about the ways they—the authors of these systems—stand to benefit from the realization of the systems they recommend. Neither the classification of the virtues nor their socialization is politically neutral: such classifications express and reinforce a particular distribution of power; they express a culture's political values. Valuing mercantile over martial traits, for example, or prizing traits exercised in consensus governance over those that are individualistically oriented, has profound consequences on the sociopolitical organization of a culture. Publicly acknowledging and genuinely promoting, rather than ignoring, belittling, or implicitly penalizing traits primarily exercised in nurturing activities affects the status and political powers of those engaged in such activities.[15] Of course the political presuppositions and commitments of virtue theories are often highly principled: they are sometimes not only guided by ethical considerations, but are constructed in order to express ethical concerns. Nevertheless, no substantive ethical theory is indifferent to the location of power, even if—or indeed especially when—it is committed to egalitarian ideals.

These disturbing reflections were meant to be quieted by the attempt to structure ethical systems in universalistic or impersonal terms. Indeed, that was one of the particular, political reasons for casting moral arguments in such a way that they answer the question: What does rationality (and presumably rationality alone) require? That shift—the movement from moral theories grounded in authority or in a revolutionary vision to those constructed from the rational, the impersonal point of view—is itself a claim that membership in the moral community is universally extended to all rational beings. To be sure, criteria for valid moral arguments and for membership in the moral community are neutral on many issues in political theory. Such criteria are standardly compatible with both liberalism and socialism; they have no particular consequences on issues concerning liberty, paternalism, or privacy. Nevertheless, a commitment to a particular model for a rational ethics expresses a position about the proper domain of moral concern, the domain of those who are morally accountable and morally entitled. It is not, for example, compatible with a sectarian or exclusivist ethics whose commands and obligations are derived solely from the exegesis of a sacred text. Criteria for the structures of valid moral arguments that also define the domain of moral agents also express general political views.

It might seem merely rhetorical and possibly even tendentious to classify such positions and presuppositions as *political*. Why isn't the determination of the domain of morality just another politically neutral part of moral theory? In a way, the terminology doesn't matter: indeed, since each presupposes the other, we could well do without the distinction between moral and political theory. It is obvious that political theories have normative import, and that normative political theories have moral presuppositions. It is less obvious, but nonetheless equally true, that moral theories have implications for the legitimacy of specific distributions of power. It is therefore necessary for robust and self-critical moral theories to be reflectively sensitive to the political structures that attend their acceptance. There is no general answer to the question of how moral theory, political theory, and moral and political practice interact. Different theories will reflect and affect practice in different ways in different historical contexts.

These considerations—that moral theories are psychologically and politically laden—do not constitute a charge against moral theory. Nor do they deprive moral theories of critical rational arguments, unmasking them as the disguised expressions of personal or cultural power politics, rhetorically cast in generalized and rationalized forms. They rather constitute a plea for moral theorists to examine the ways that their views presuppose, express, and reinforce their political commitments to a particular distribution of power. The best way to examine these structures is to describe, in great detail, the daily consequences of the practices and institutions they recommend. There is a continuity between philosophical argument and rhetorical persuasion. Like other activities, philosophy requires a set of complex and often opposed virtues: it needs the virtues of precision and clarity exercised in disambiguation and rigorous logical argument; but it also needs the virtues exercised in raising disarming questions to shift the burden of proof and those exercised in presenting vivid and imaginative examples to direct attention to neglected concerns. Which of these intellectual virtues should be stressed and valued at any given time depends on the details of the particular situation, on which issues are dominant and are neglected, on what is at stake for whom.

So much for tasks, lamentations, and pronouncements. Since I have expressed a distrust of metaphilosophy, and a preference for the particular, let this be enough of meta-metaphilosophy. Not only the defense but the sense of these pronouncements must be given by their functions in particular contexts. As we say in Yiddish: *Zum Tisch*.[16]

1 PERSONS AND PERSONAE

FRANCISZKA THEMERSON

Social and political conceptions of persons—conceptions of their powers, rights and limits, the criteria for their individuation and continued identity—derive from conceptions of primary, privileged activities, the activities that are thought to express human excellences and tasks. Attributes believed to be required for performing such primary activities are designated as the essential identificatory properties of persons. The significant powers and limitations of persons in a society focused on spiritual and meditational activity are radically different from those attributed to persons in a society focused on political participation or on scientific advancement, and both differ from the properties thought essential to persons in societies focused on military or civic glory. The philosophical problems concerning the identities of persons vary correspondingly: When Descartes treated scientific demonstration as the primary activity, the ego became mind, and the philosophical problems concerning the person centered on the relation between mind and body. When political participation is treated as the paradigmatic activity, the dominant philosophic problems concerning persons shift to those involving the analysis of the relation between private and public interests and rights. When the self is defined by its economic activity, the philosophic problems focus on issues of rational choice.

The essays in this section explore the uses and abuses of the concept of a person. "Persons and Personae" argues that moral or political principles cannot be derived from the concept of a person because the determination of such principles is coordinate with the characterization of persons. In "The Transformations of Persons," I argue that criteria for the reidentification of persons derives from standard narratives about the shape of a human life; in "Persons, Policies, and Bodies," I argue that the criteria for the individuation and differentiation of persons derives from the social practices defining the unit of liability and responsibility. "Characters, Persons, Selves, Individuals" traces the historical transformations of literary representations of concepts of persons from Greek drama, to medieval mystery plays and Chaucerian tales, through early social novels and their later Romantic transformations, to the disappearance of agency in Beckett's plays.

1   Persons and Personae

Controversies about personal identity have been magnified by the fact that there are a number of distinct questions at issue, questions that have not always been clearly distinguished from one another. Parties to the dispute have differed, often without arguing the case, about which questions are centrally interesting. Some have concentrated on analyses of class differentiation, distinguishing persons from computers, apes, fetuses, corporations. Others have been primarily interested in criteria for individuation and differentiation. Still others have been interested in the criteria for reidentifying the same individual in different contexts, under different descriptions, or at different times. Most philosophers who have been concerned with individual reidentification analyze conditions for temporal reidentification, trying to define conditions for distinguishing successive stages of a single continuing person from stages of a successor or descendant person. Yet others have been primarily interested in individual identification: What sorts of characteristics are essential to the identity of the person, so that if those characteristics were changed, she would be a significantly different person, though she might still be differentiated and reidentified as the same individual? Defining the conditions for individual identification does not reduce to specifying conditions for reidentification because the characteristics that distinguish or reidentify persons (e.g., fingerprints, DNA codes, or memories) may not be thought by the individual herself or by her society to determine her *real* identity. For instance, an individual might be reidentifiable by the memory criterion but not identifiable as the same person, because all that she considers essential to her identity has changed: her principles and preference rankings are different, her tastes, plans, hopes, and fears. She remembers her old principles of choice well enough and so, by the memory criterion, might consider herself the same old person; but by grace or reeducation she can be counted on to choose and act in a new way. Though all these questions are distin-

27

guishable, and though a philosopher may legitimately be interested in one without being forced to treat them all, a particular sort of solution to one problem will certainly influence, though probably not dictate, a solution to the others.

Behind these differences in emphases and interests, there are differences about whether we should concentrate on conditions for strict identity (with the consequence that a biological individual may not remain the same person throughout a lifetime), on conditions of loose typic identity (with the consequence that conditions for identity and conditions for individuation become distinct), or on conditions assuring continuity or survival (with the consequence that the conditions for *significant* continuity or survival still require to be specified).

Also at issue are methodological disagreements about what is involved in giving a criterial analysis. Some of the debates have only incidentally been about personal identity; they have been primarily about whether criteria for identity should provide necessary and sufficient conditions, prepared to meet and resist any possible counterexamples. If we look for necessary and sufficient conditions, puzzle and problem cases loom large in the discussion, as possible counterexamples to the analyses. Consider the problems that arise from Shoemaker's Lockean transplant case: Brown's brain is put in Robinson's head, with the results that Brownson, the fellow with Brown's brain in (the rest of) Robinson's body remembers Brown's experience, identifies Brown's body as "his," expresses Brown's tastes and preferences. To give the question "Who is who?" some force, we might ask who goes home to which wife ("Do you love me for myself alone, or for my beautiful body?"). And if one of them committed a crime, who goes to jail?

Those who are skeptical about the utility of giving analyses of logically necessary conditions see the Brownson case as presenting an interesting curiosity, a fringe case of personal identity. They hold that the strategic conclusions to which we are forced in extremities should not be taken to reveal the workings of these concepts in their standard uses. For them, the real point of such thought experiments is to untangle the various strands in our conceptions, to show that although they normally support one another, they are independent, and can sometimes pull apart.

Thought experiments of this kind are always underdescribed: Suppose that Robinson limps painfully. Won't Brown's passion for dancing the flamenco be affected by the discomfort of expressing it in Robinson's hulking, lumbering body? Suppose Robinson's body suffers from an overproduction of adrenalin: will Brownson's memories take on an irascible tone? How can we establish the identity of tastes and memories under different emotional tonalities? In forcing decisions about such cases for the sake of assuring criterial accounts, we move subtly from analyses of concepts in their standard use to constructions whose application to standard cases become legislative and normative, no longer straightforwardly analytically descriptive. This may indeed be a useful and important enterprise: but legislation should take place openly, so that the many factors that affect the accounts of personal identification—moral and political factors, as well as coherence of accounting—can be brought into play. If we are going to tidy up a concept whose various strands have been pulled apart, we had best be clear about the consequences that our tidying will have on our social practices. The most important of these will affect the redistribution of liability and responsibility, of praise, blame, and punishment.

Perhaps the most significant source of the controversy about criteria for personal identity springs from disagreements about the function that the concept of a person plays in social life as the unit of intentional, responsible agency. Locke distinguished the identity of an individual substance, the identity of a human being, and the identity of a person, remarking that as the concept of a person is primarily a forensic, legal notion, the criterion for personal identity must reflect the conditions for an individual's being a responsible agent. Because he focused on legal liability, rather than social responsibility, he was interested in identifying the past actions of persons. He thus took the condition for forensic identity to be continuity of reflective consciousness, established primarily by memory. Those who are concerned with responsibility for future actions might stress the continuity of preference rankings, character traits, and intellectual capacities that affect rational choice and action. In any case, controversies about conditions for personal identity reflect differences about the conditions that establish an individual as a responsible agent.

Why are we interested in someone being the same person, and not merely the same human being or physical object? One reason is primarily retrospective: we need to know whom to reward and whom to punish for actions performed when "they" were acknowledgedly different in some respects from the present population. But we have more forward-looking reasons as well: we want to know what traits remain constant so that we can know what we can expect from the persons around us. We assign crucial responsibilities to individuals, assume important continuing relations to them in the belief that certain of their traits are relatively constant or predictable. And for ourselves, we are interested in our own identities because we make choices that will affect our futures: we set in motion a train of actions whose consequences involve "our" well-being, without knowing whether we shall have, in the future, the desires and beliefs that now direct our planning.

A society's conception of agency is closely linked to the sorts of actions that are taken as central because they preserve or enhance that society's conception of its proper survival and development. In a society of hunters, cripples are thought incapable of action; but in a society of religious ascetics, cripples may be thought most capable of the sort of action that defines the true person. The range of traits and criteria for identification are open to negotiation by the moral and political reformer. Descriptive analyses of personal identity affect the allocation of obligations and rights; but the analysis of persons is itself affected by the allocation of obligations and rights. When paradigm cases of action are set, the traits that conduce to responsible agency for those sorts of actions are fixed, and the range of agents—corporations, human beings, demon possessors, Martians, or dolphins—is also set. But in times of social and political change, primary activities are relocated (from hunting, to religious meditation, to symbolic communication); reformers recommend an expansion or contraction of the class of persons. Changes in practice go hand in hand with conceptual reconstruction and reform, though it may take several generations for the hands to catch up. New conceptions of actions and agency sometimes relocate the conditions for responsibility and liability. That reformers can negotiate the extension of the class of persons certainly does not make the concept of a person *merely* conventional, if anything ever is. Both changes in practice and in conceptual analysis are argued by demonstrating the capacities of previously extended classes.

II

There is a philosophical dream, a dream that moral and political ideals are not only grounded in and explained by human nature, but that fundamental moral and political principles can be derived from the narrower conditions that define persons. Though sometimes bold and wild dreamers do go so far, this dream does not usually express a metaphysical wish that could be satisfied by analyzing the conditions for reflective subjectivity or the psycholinguistic conditions for the reflexivity of first-person attributions. More commonly, the dream is that normative political and moral principles can be derived from what is essential to the concept of a person.

The strongest version of this dream attempts to use the (initially value-neutral) concept of a person to derive specific rights, principles, and obligations; a somewhat more modest version attempts to use the concept of a person to set constraints on such rights, principles, and obligations; a yet weaker version makes the two notions—the concept of a person and the delineation of moral and political rights—mutually explicative. But all versions of this dream press for a single concept of a person, whose various components form a harmonious structure that could provide adjudication among competing normative claims about what does or does not fall within the domain of the rights and obligations of persons. The press for one well-structured concept that allocates priorities among its various conditions is a demand for a decision procedure to settle disagreements about, and conflicts among, competing values and obligations.

But there is no such thing as "the" concept of a person. This is so not only for the obvious historical reason that there have been dramatically discontinuous changes in the characterization of persons, though that is true. Nor for the equally obvious anthropological-cultural reason that the moral and legal practices heuristically treated as analogous across cultures differ so dramatically that they capture "the concept" of personhood only vaguely and incompletely, though that is also true.

The various functions performed by our contemporary concept of persons don't hang together: there is some overlap, but also some tension. Indeed, the functions that "the" notion plays are so related that attempts to structure them in a taxonomic order express quite different norms and ideals. Disagreements about primary values and goods reappear as disagreements about the priorities and relations among the various functions the concept plays, disagreements about what is essential to persons. Not only does each of the functions bear a different relation to the class of persons and human beings, but each also has a different contrast class.

As inheritors of the Judeo-Christian, Renaissance, Enlightenment, and Romantic traditions, we want the concept of the person to fill a number of functions:

1. The attribution should give us objective grounds for being taken seriously, with respect—and to be taken seriously with respect on grounds that can't be lost through illness, poverty, villainy, inanity, or senility. On this view, the idea of person is an insurance policy. Some think of the insurance as guaranteeing us rights. Others think of it as assuring us a certain kind of regard, that we will be treated as ends rather than merely as means, that our activities will be perceived as centrally rational (or at least reasonable) and good-willed (or at least

well-intentioned) and interpreted by an extension of the principle of charity. For some, the special status of persons is justified by some set of properties: persons should be respected because they are capable of critical rationality, or because they are free inventors of their lives, or because they have divinely donated souls, or because they can be harmed, frustrated in living out their life plans. For others, specific rights cannot be justified by or derived from the essential properties of the class of persons, because such rights are among the essential properties of persons. For yet others, claims to rights can only be based on the general social and political benefits that such rights might bring.

Among the Hellenes, the contrast class for this notion was the class of slaves and barbarians. Among Christians, the contrast class is that of unsouled beings. For Kantians, the contrast class is that of nonrational beings, incapable of understanding the laws of nature and unable to act freely, from the idea of the laws of morality. This conception of the class of persons intersects, but is not identical with nor subsumed within, the class of human beings: Martians and dolphins might be persons, as might intrapsychic homunculi.

2. Sometimes the respect and rights of persons are assured by law: persons are defined as legal entities. The legal concept of a person is meant to assure, first, liability. This is a retrospective function, defined by the conditions for presumptive agency: bodily continuity, memory, *mens rea*. (The contrast class is made up of those with defective conditions for agency, for example, the insane and the senile.)

Second, the legal concept of persons ensures legally defined responsibility. This is a prospective and regionalized function that defines specific duties and obligations. Such responsibilities are often institutionally defined: sometimes the legal person's duties and responsibilities are contractually fixed, with explicitly articulated sanctions for default or violation; sometimes the obligations are defined informally by commonly accepted practices and sanctions. In such cases, liability is carried by the legal entity, rather than by the individuals—for example, trustees, corporations, guardians, boards of directors, banks—who act as its officers. (The contrast class includes minors and, still in some places, women.)

Third, the legal concept guarantees specifically defined citizen rights and duties. This is a function that empowers a designated class of individuals to act and speak on behalf of the State. They are, as Hobbes put it, its "artificial persons." Polities accord specific rights and duties of participation in decision-making, representation, governance. Indeed, this is one way political systems differ: by the different ways they distribute the power and the right to act or speak in the person of the State, as an agent of one of its constitutive institutions. As the frontispiece of Hobbes's *Leviathan* graphically demonstrates, the king of an absolute monarchy is the embodied person of the State. If the State is composed of families or clans, rather than of individuals, those families or clans are the person-citizens of the State, and their heads or elders speak and act for them. Similarly, representatives of state-defined political institutions (the judiciary, the legislative body, city officials) act in the person of the State: their decisions personify the official acts of the State. When the Pope speaks *ex cathedra*, he speaks as the personification of the Church; the voice of Parliament is the voice of the people; "We the People"—citizens casting votes on public issues or selecting their representatives—are expressing the views of the person(s) of the State. Even though their rights and welfare are under the legal protection of the state, the disenfranchised—etymologically, the unfree—are the subjects or wards of the State rather than citizen-persons entitled to act or speak as the person of the State. Whether the class of citizen-persons coincides with or is a subset of the class of those who are legally liable is, of course, a political and even an ideological issue. (The composition of the contrast class is usually under contention and may include, for example, aliens, slaves, exiles, and fetuses.)

Neither the Kantian regulative principle of respect nor the Christian idea of the immortal soul have any necessary connection with the legal function of the idea of person. Respect for the person doesn't entail any particular legal rights; nor does the assurance of legal personhood assure social or moral respect. Furthermore, each of the distinctive legal *personae* might well select different grounds for the attribution of personhood. For instance, an individual can claim some citizen rights (the right of *habeas corpus*, for example) without satisfying the conditions for liability. Nor need a legal person be accorded all the rights of citizenship: universities do not, as such, vote or receive social security. The conditions for prospective responsibility are regional and relative: whether an individual or a group is designated a legal person is characteristically a political, and sometimes an ideological, issue.

Some legal theorists argue that no single concept of a person can— or should—be used to derive the wide variety of legislative and judicial policies required to give appropriately differentiated treatment to the varieties of legal *personae*.[1] They maintain that moral and legal practices contextualize and regionalize the status of a person: a fetus is, for example, accorded the status of a legal person in some contexts and for some issues, but not for others; a corporation has the legal status of a person for some purposes, for others not. We should, they hold, draw our inclusionary and exclusionary classes contextually, following our

sense of what is morally and judicially appropriate, rather than attempting to derive our legal practices from a sharply—and, they suggest,
arbitrarily—defined class of persons. ("First come the practices of right
and wrong, and then come definitions and classifications.") The question
of whether there are several distinctive legal concepts of a person, each
with its own pragmatically defined domain, or whether there is one
concept, with distinctive pragmatic applications is an idle question, since
neither legal theory nor legal practice are affected by the answer.

There are, of course, dramatic cultural variations in the criteria for
agency, variations in the legal conditions that define persons. The class
of liable and responsible persons can, for instance, exclude individuals
in favor of groups of individuals (clans or families), or the heads of such
groups (the chief patriarch), intrapsychic homunculi, demonic possessors. It can be treated as an all-or-none classification, or as a matter of
degree. It is often difficult to determine how to diagnose such cultural
variation. Do these differences represent disagreements about the proper
analysis of the concept of a person? Do some cultures lack the concept,
or do they have an analogous construct? Do some cultures lack what we
consider a legal system, or do they locate their legal system in a different
network of institutions? There may be no fact of the matter: exigencies
of theory construction rather than ontology may determine whether we
can legitimately project our concept of a legal person to analogous bearers
of liability and responsibility, or whether we should decline the attribution to individuals whose agency is defined within radically different
schemes of liability and responsibility.

3. The idea of a person is also the idea of an autonomous agent,
capable of self-defined and self-defining choices. There are at least two
versions of this idea. The first is primarily negative and defensive,
concentrating on the desire to fend off external interference: *Noli me
tangere,* or in Amerispeak, "Don't tread on me, buddy." The second is
primarily positive and constructive, concentrating on capacities for
self-determination. Both the negative and the positive idea of autonomy
emphasize critical rationality and independent evaluation. A person is
essentially capable of stepping back from her beliefs and desires to
evaluate their rationality and appropriateness; she is also capable (at
the very least) of attempting to form and modify her beliefs and desires,
her actions, on the basis of her rational evaluations. (The contrast class
would thus comprise the mindless, the nonrational, the dissociated.)

The idea of autonomy, whether negatively or positively defined, also
emphasizes imaginative creativity. Because their decisions and actions
are intentionally identified, and because they have latitude in transforming, improvising, and inventing their intentions, persons can, in a

number of significant ways, form the worlds in which they live. There
are two dimensions on which such formations take place: the political
and the visionary-poetic.

For the first, since the social and political domain is constructed, it
can be reconstructed, if only a piece at a time. To be a person is to
participate actively in public life, forming or at least modifying the social
and political policies and institutions that significantly and effectively
shape life. (The contrast class: the masses, whose opinions and actions
can be manipulated.)

For the second, by choosing or constructing systems of values, persons
create the categories that structure and interpret their world, that form
their ambitions, hopes, and fears. Since they determine what is important
and significant, their interpretations structure both what they see and
what they do. (The contrast class: the dependent, the fearful, the timid,
the unimaginative.)

These aspects of the idea of autonomy mark differences in two faces
or moments in Enlightenment political theory. The first stance is defensive: it is designed to protect the person from what is perceived as
tyrannical or unjust political or epistemic authority. This concept of a
person stresses negative liberty and minimal government. There is some
correlation, but no necessary connection, between the defensive boundary conception of the free person and the conception of the person whose
critical and rational capacities are primarily exercised in scientific discovery or poetic creativity and only secondarily in defense against error.

Although the Enlightenment concept of a person began with the Christian conception of a person as defined by his free will, his capacity to
affirm or deny God's law, autonomy shifted from the freedom of the will
to the rational power of independent critical judgments of truth and
falsity. When the old order loses its authority, the emphasis on persons
as autonomous judges preserving and protecting individual boundaries
is replaced by an emphasis on autonomous legislators generating new
social structures and practices. Negative liberty gives way to positive
liberty; minimal government gives way to a government charged with the
formation of citizen values. Protection against error gives way to the
power of constructing a systematic science, and eventually to the power
of the imagination in constructing a world through poetic language. There
is some correlation, but no necessary connection, between the concept
of a person as a constructive, self-determining legislator and the concept
of a person as primarily a creator. The movement from the earlier defensive to the later constructive conceptions of persons correlates in a
very rough way with the movement from early Cartesian Enlightenment
conceptions of the independent, inquiring, rational self, free of the claims

of dogmatic doctrine, to late Enlightenment Romanticism, with its emphasis on positive liberty, political reform, and poetic creativity.

The conception of persons as deserving respect is sometimes rooted in the conception of a person as capable of self-definition. But of course both the rational and the creative dimensions of the idea of the self-defining person (in its negative and positive forms) leave individual claims to personhood empirically contingent. If claims to respect are based on the capacities for autonomy, we're in deep trouble. Constitutional and sociopolitical contingencies affect the likelihood of an individual actually (rather than notionally or potentially) developing her capacities for critical rationality; similar contingencies determine whether she is actually (rather than notionally) capable of creative self-determination. Has the individual been well nourished and nurtured, well educated and well formed? Or has she suffered irreparable traumas that make autonomy practically impossible? Logical or notional possibility is not helpful here: aardvarks, baboons, and caterpillars might notionally be capable of autonomy. It might seem as if this concept of a person provides grounds for normative political claims. Precisely because certain kinds of political structures are required to actualize otherwise only notional claims to personhood, there is a prima facie obligation to structure political systems in such a way as to allow the best development of the capacities for critical self-determination. Unfortunately, many extra premises are required to substantiate this claim, premises about the primary and the proper functions of the obligations of political systems. The obligation cannot follow solely from the requirements for personhood. (This conception of the class of persons intersects, but is not identical with or subsumed within, the class of biologically defined human beings. The contrast class is composed of all those incapable of self-correcting and self-legislating critical reflexivity.)

Christianity is, for once, surprisingly open and generous. If part of the point of the concept of a person is to assure respect, it is wiser not to rest one's hopes on such fragile and vulnerable capacities as those for autonomy or creativity. Maybe a divinely assured immortal soul— or even just a divinely assured soul, immortal or not—would provide more secure grounds for respect. To be sure, standardly, conditions for rationality and autonomy are regulative rather than empirical: we might take comfort in the principle that every rational being *ought* to be treated with respect. But it takes unusually good luck to get that regulative principle realized under harsh circumstances, just when it is most needed. Respect may be well-grounded without being well-assured. What recourse do the unrespected have when they most require respect?

Moral indignation? Righteousness in the eyes of history—itself a politically variable matter—is not reliably effective in assuring entitlements.

More recently, the Christian conception of persons as endowed with a free will capable of affirming or denying God's law has been redefined: the rights of persons are accorded to all those capable of suffering, those whose naturally formed life histories can be harmed, shortened, frustrated. Whether the sentient are self-consciously aware of the natural shapes of their lives, whether they form plans and expectations (the transformation of the idea of the will as legislator), matters less than the fact that their lives can be painful or unfulfilled. It is the sheer fact of sentience that qualifies an individual to the rights of persons.[2]

4. Social persons are identified by their mutual interactions, by the roles they enact in the dynamic dramas of their shared lives. There are several varieties of this conception.

The idea of a *dramatis persona* as the bearer of roles in a dramatic unfolding of action has its source in the theater. A *persona* is the mask of an actor cast to play a part in developing a narrative or a plot. Essentially meshed with others, the social person's scope and directions are defined by her role in a complex course of events, involving the interactions of agents whose varied intentions modify the outcomes— and indeed sometimes the directions—of one another's projects. While the dramatic conception of a person is only indirectly linked to the concept of a person as entitled to respect, or with that of a self-defining individual, it bears some kinship to the idea of a person as an agent, as the source of liable and responsible action. When *dramatis personae* are in principle able to predict their effects on one another's lives, their intentions can carry moral or legal weight. (The contrast class includes whatever is inert, without the power of intentional action. Since inanimate objects and events—volcanoes, wars, famines—can forward or redirect dramatic action, they are sometimes personified; but they are accounted persons only if intentional action is attributed to them.)

Some psychologists introduce a normative notion of a person as capable of taking others seriously, capable of entering into mutually affective and effective relations. To be a person is to acknowledge the reality of others, living in a commonly constructed world, actively and cooperatively sharing practices. Some psychologists attempt to connect the social with the respect-based definitions of persons, treating them as mutually supportive conditions.[3] But there is not necessarily a link between the two conditions. On the one hand, respect might be grounded in the idea of (a divinely donated) soul, whose sociability is contingent on the identity and roles assigned to it; on the other, some conceptions of sociability might valorize a type of intimacy that minimizes respect-across-individual-boundaries. Such a manifestly culture-bound concept of personhood can easily come into conflict with the (equally culture-bound) concept of the ideal person as capable of radical autonomy. (The contrast class in this instance is made up of dissociated personalities and psychopaths.)

There is a presumptively ontological, prepsychological version of the concept of persons as essentially formed by their relations to others. It perceives the person as constituted, formed by "the look of the other." According to this theory, consciousness is initially unreflective, without a sense of self; it acquires an image of itself—an image that comes to form the person's somatic sense of self—by seeing itself mirrored in the eyes of others. We form one another's identities by the act of mutual mirroring, mutual regard. A person's life is constructed from, and constituted by, such interactive formative relations. Though there may be normative claims about how we *ought* to regard one another, the conception of a person as interactively emergent neither entails nor is entailed by the conception of a person as entitled to respect or to specific legal rights. (The contrast class: nonconscious beings, beings incapable of self-conscious reflection.)

Associated but not identical with the psychological condition is the honorific attribution of personhood. Some individuals are accounted *real* persons: "She's a real mensch!" But although the capacities for autonomy (rationality or creativity) might be ingredient in the qualifications for being a *real* person, in contrast to the usual humanoid, they are not sufficient. Indeed, a partisan of the concept of a person as an autonomous creator might well be disqualified as a real mensch-person. On this view—to be sure a view not widely shared as definitive of the concept of a person—*real* persons are generally distinguished by fortitude and reliability, by their presence, their style and individuality, often combined with compassion and a humorous sense of proportion, an ironic recognition of human frailty and finitude. (The contrast class: the psychopath, the creep, the jerk, the whine, the brute, the Neanderthal.)

5. The concept of personhood is also used to sketch the norms for the appropriate shape and structure of a life. Those who identify persons by a characteristic life history or life plan require an account of a standard—or maybe not so standard—shaping of a life, one that goes beyond biologically determined patterns of maturation and aging. This view originally derives from the Christian conception of the soul, whose life and choices move it toward salvation or damnation; it is a descendant of the definition of persons as constructors of their fates. The emphasis shifts: the person is first identified as the author of the story, then by

the activity of story construction, and then simply by the emergent content of the narrative.[4]

There are two versions of this focus. The first, which postulates a fact of the matter, can give an account of how a culture can malform and misdirect lives, as well as misunderstand the processes by which it shapes typical life stories. The second might be characterized as the "It's all up to us" version, with the "us" referring either to individual free spirits or to the members of a self-defining community.

While the narrative conception of personhood is compatible with the definition of persons as autonomous, it neither entails nor is entailed by that conception. A person's life story need not be autonomously constructed; nor need it provide grounds for respect. Even more dramatically, the conditions for autonomy need have no bearing on the shape and events of life histories, which are, after all, contingent and heteronomous. In a Kantian framework, for example, the conditions for autonomy are purely intellectual: they neither affect nor can be affected by the contingent narrative of a life. Nor is the possibility of reflective subjectivity essential to the construction of a life story: a life can have the shape of a well-formed narrative without its subject experiencing anything like first-person inner subjectivity. It is the convenience of theory construction rather than brute ontology that determines whether the narrative condition for personhood requires further qualification. As it stands, the view that a person is one who possesses a life story seems to allow any subject of a narrative history to qualify even if that subject is not conscious of itself as a subjective center of experience. An individual might have a life story without being subjectively aware of it, and certainly without being self-consciously reflective about her shaping of it. Yet if the unadorned narrative condition of personhood allows mice and mountains to qualify as persons, the additional requirement of active subjective reflection seems too strong: it appears to disqualify individuals who might, on moral or political grounds, qualify as persons. The capacities for active subjective reflection—for constructing life plans—might turn out to be consequences of, rather than presuppositions for, an individual's qualifying as a social and political person.

The contrast class for the conception of persons as characterized by life stories is difficult to define. Everything temporal can be construed as having a life story, even a life story with a normative form. This criterion allows squirrels, a particular patch of pachysandra, and the Mediterranean basin to qualify as persons because they have life stories with a beginning, middle, and end. If we attach the further condition that persons must be capable of reflecting on, if not actively forming, a life story or a life plan, the contrast class is no easier to define. Who has the capacity for the autonomous construction of a life plan? Should the class include individuals who in principle might acquire the capacities for reflective agency, for constructing and following a life plan, if they could be accorded the status of persons? How are such counterfactual claims evaluated in holistic systems?

6. The biological conception of an individual is sometimes taken to provide the foundation or basic structure of the concept of a person. Biologists want a concept that will provide (a) the unit of genetic individuation and (b) *conatus*: the determination of growth and immunology, the energy and direction of action, reaction, and defense.

Persons are, among other things, self-sustainers and self-starters. The biological account of organic independence provides the practical origin of the more far-reaching notion of autonomy. But the concept of an organic individual does not necessarily provide a sharp distinction between human beings and other species, let alone between persons and other sorts of organic entities. Whether there is a subclass, a variety of human beings who can be designated as persons by virtue of a special set of standardly inheritable properties is a matter for empirical determination. If rationality marks the class of persons, are the various properties and capacities that constitute rationality biologically fixed, genetically coded? How do the conditions for reflective critical rationality described by Kant and Frankfurt function in the organism's system of action and reaction, expansion and defense? If self-determination marks the class of persons, are those properties and traits that constitute an individual's capacity for self-determination biologically fixed, genetically coded? How do the various capacities for creative self-definition affect a person's constitution? We are a long way from having a reasonable speculative theory, let alone a sound research program, connecting the moral, political, and legal notions of persons with the biological notion of a reproductive, self-sustaining, defensively structured organism.

It has been argued that just as women and blacks were once excluded from the class of persons on presumptively biological grounds, so too we are now misled by superficial speciesism to exclude dolphins and mammals. But we are a long way from an account of the criteria for appropriate classification: what formally identical or analogous constitutional structures qualify nonhumans as persons? Why should baboons but not robots qualify? Or Martians but not crustaceans? While empirical considerations are relevant (do dolphins have central nervous systems?), they cannot settle the questions of whether corporations and robots only qualify as persons by metaphorical courtesy, while dolphins and chimpanzees qualify as full members by an appropriate corrective extension

of the class. When is a batch of wires a central nervous system and
when is it only an analogue? When is an analogue good enough? When
is it all too good? When does behavioral similarity qualify for literal
attribution? What are the criteria for identifying biologically based behavioral similarity? Both the arguments for excluding corporations and
the left hemisphere of the brain and the arguments for including robots
and Martians depend on normatively charged conceptual analyses. Since
similarities and differences can be found wholesale, other, further considerations are required to select the features that demarcate the class
of persons. What considerations select the capacity to feel pain, rather
than for rational thought, as the criteria for the class? Indeed, because
the classification has significant political and social consequences, we
should not be surprised to discover that conceptual analyses of biological
functions—particularly those presumed to affect intentional agency—
are strongly, though often only implicitly and unselfconsciously, guided
by moral intuitions, ideology, and taste. Controversies among socio-
biologists about drawing relevant analogies between humans and other
animals—their hierarchy or altruistic behavior, their protection of property—should make us suspicious about attempts to support policies
concerning the rights of persons on what are allegedly purely empirical,
biological considerations. (The contrast class comprises inanimate
objects.)

    7. Psychometaphysicians have a notion of the elusive, ultimate sub-
ject of experience, the 'I' that cannot be reduced to an object, even
though it can treat itself objectively, as the focus of introspection and
investigation.[5] But this 'I' can be diachronically discontinuous: the subject of "sequential" experiences need not be strictly identical. And even
synchronic subjects of experiences need not be united: every aspect of
a complex act of awareness could, in principle, have its own subject.
The subject who is aware of the acute pain of loss need not be identical
with the subject who is at the same time aware of the shifting pattern
of light on the leaves of a tree. Or at any rate, the transcendental unity
of apperception (if there is such a thing) does not necessarily provide
specific closure to what is, and what is not, included within the bounds
of such a presumptive unity. The limits of the domain of experience
cannot be set by the subject of a transcendental unity of apperception
without circularity.

    In any case, there are a number of distinctive construals of subjectivity
as the condition for personhood, and while each has quite different
consequences for the concept, none has any necessary consequences for
morality, or for political or legal theory. The 'I' that is the subject of
experience serves as the contrastive notion, but the various contrasts

are not isomorphic. The person as the 'I,' the subject of experience, has been identified with the interior or internal perspective in contrast to the external; with the subjective in contrast to the objective; with the subject-of-experiences in contrast to its experiences; with rationality and the will in contrast to causality and desire; with spontaneity and creativity in contrast to the conditioned; with the decision-maker and agent in contrast to the predictor and observer; with the knower or interpreter in contrast to the known or interpreted; with reflective consciousness in contrast to the content of reflection; with mind in contrast to body.

Although each of these juxtapositions marks quite a different contrast, each is guided by the intuition that persons are capable of bearing a unique reflexive, reflective relation to themselves, a relation that somehow shapes them. Persons are sometimes characterized as capable of having a distinctive set of experiences—ego-oriented attitudes of anxiety, remorse, pride, guilt—that originally give rise to the idea of the self. But the reflective 'I' can reject or identify with these ego-oriented attitudes as easily as it can with its body or its habits. It is no more identical with any set of "existential attitudes" than it is with any of its more externally defined attributes. The *act* of reflecting on an attribute or attitude, asking "Is that *me*?" ("putting the self in question"), is always different from the attitude or attribute itself, even if the attitude reveals— as anxiety is said to do—the precarious position of the 'I' as the act of self-constituting reflection. Being anxious is one thing; being the act that identifies with anxiety is another. Both are different from something-perhaps-a-nothing-I-know-not-what, or a simple soul beyond experience, or a pure act of reflection that constitutes itself. All these—different as they are from one another—are far from the original starting point of the 'I' as a being whose experience, and especially its experience of itself, is *sui generis*. None of these reflexive attitudes carries specific political, legal, or moral consequences. In *Notes from the Underground*, Dostoyevsky's dramatic explorations of the subterranean destructiveness of the endlessly ironic self-mirroring self-consciousness demonstrate that even rational, self-critical reflexivity can assure neither sociability nor morality; and it can destroy self-respect. (The contrast class: objects, those incapable of self-conscious reflection.)

III

The variety of functions that 'the' concept of a person plays—the variety of conceptions of personhood we've sketched—cannot be plausibly combined in a single concept. At most, one might settle for a heterogeneous class, defined by a disjunction of heterogeneous conditions. Even if some rough construction of a denominator common to all these notions and functions were proposed, that conception would be so general that it could not fulfill—nor could it generate—the various functions performed by the various regional and substantively rich conceptions.

But this stark conclusion seems premature. Perhaps we can characterize persons by attempting some sort of synthesis of our various conditions: *A person is a unit of agency, a unit that is (a) capable of being directed by its conception of its own identity and by what is important to that identity, and (b) capable of acting with others, in a common world. A person is an interactive member of a community, reflexively sensitive to the contexts of her activity, a critically reflective inventor of the story line of her life.* Surely this is a parody of a characterization. The conditions only cohere if one doesn't look too closely. It is not clear whether these conditions are conjunctive or whether they are nestled. After all, the conditions for strong autonomy might well on occasion conflict with those for strong sociability. The conditions of critical rationality might well on occasion conflict with those of poetic creativity. The conditions for personhood—and indeed the class of those qualifying as persons—are quite different if critical rationality dominates over sociability, rather than sociability over the capacities for critical rationality. Societies that weight these capacities differently differ dramatically; and sometimes ideological or political issues determine the weighting and priority of the various conditions.

Might the metaphysical notion of a person be primary, in a way that would settle these questions of priority? Primary to what? A universalistic metaphysical notion can constrain, but it cannot select or determine the priorities among competing politically and ideologically defined persons. If the metaphysical idea of a person is rich and robust enough to generate political consequences, it is already charged and directed toward those consequences. If it stands neutrally above those consequences, it is unlikely to be rich enough to do the work done by the various strands in the concepts of persons. The concept of the referent of first-person attributions or the concept of the subject of experience might be a precondition for the political or moral uses of the concept of a person. But even that is questionable: it is not conceptually necessary that the bearer of rights be capable of reflexive first-person attributions.

The notion of a human being is a notion of a biologically defined entity; the notion of a person is, however, normatively and sometimes ideologically charged. It expresses a view about what is important, valuable about being creatures like us, in having this or that set of significant traits and properties. Such creatures need not belong to our biological species. Martians or Super-robots could be persons; organically organized families and clans might qualify, as could intrapsychic demons, homunculi, or consciences. For some, this notion designates a natural kind: there is a fact of the matter about what ought to be important and significant to us. For others, we are that natural kind whose primary attributes are plastic: within limits, we are self-legislatively self-defining, even self-constructing, creatures.

But even those who think of persons as self-defining creators of their identities do not agree about the extension of this class. For some, self-determination is a matter of individual volition; for others, only historical communities with self-perpetuating practices can be considered self-determining. For some, *all* individuals, no matter how pathetically mal-formed, however constitutionally or socially deprived or deformed, are equally the creators of the stories that are their lives. No matter what story one tells about one's life, that story *is* one's life as a person. For others, only Nietzschean self-creating and free individual spirits, the solitary ones who transcend the herd and the conventions of the herd, are capable of self-definition. For others, only cultural and political communities can define or create themselves: individual persons are self-legislating only as members of a community defined by shared in-teractive practices, which define the boundaries and the essential traits of persons. On this view, the definition of persons is implicit in the practices that express and reproduce the community's cultural forms, especially the practices of parenting and education and the distribution of legal and political power.

These reflections on "the" concept of a person seem unsatisfactory: all we have is a complaint inspired by vulgar forms of Wittgenstein-ianism, that shifts the burden of analysis. Instead of dispatching yet another vexed philosophic issue, counseling Quixotic philosophers to stop looking for a nonexistent essential definition of persons, we should perhaps more modestly end with an account of the many different reasons we have wanted, and perhaps needed, the notion of a person. These are, after all, honorable desires, as philosophic desires go. We have, in a sketchy way, explored some of the reasons that philosophers and legal-political theorists want the concept: those reasons are given by the heterogeneous list of functions—some of them rhetorical—that the con-cept has played. The Procrustean tactic of cutting limbs to fit an arbitrary, if elegantly designed, form neither illuminates nor gains anything: it limits rather than enhances an understanding of the various functions of "the" concept.

It is of course possible to legislate one central notion of a person, and to fend off strong contending candidates for definition. Such leg-islation might express a moral or an ideological victory; if it is widely

accepted, it might even succeed in being a culturally self-fulfilling prophecy. But it would not on that account alone constitute an insightful
illumination into the nature of persons. Such legislation about the essential character of persons expresses rather than grounds or legitimates
our moral and legal principles. But significantly, the deep fissures and
conflicts that are central to moral experience, and that make their way
into the complexities of legal practice, are reintroduced among, and even
sometimes within, the various functions of the concepts of persons. We
do not even have the luxury of assuring ourselves that at least the concept
of the person is coordinate with the concepts of moral and legal practices.
At best we can say that the tensions and conflicts at the heart of moral
and legal practices are reflected in, and sometimes clarified by, tensions
and conflicts in conceptions of persons.

Why, then, is there such a metaphysical longing for one concept?
(Or is it a longing for one metaphysical concept?) Perhaps the explanation
is that the various functions the concept plays are each unifying functions: "the" locus of liability; "the" subject of experience; "the" autonomous critical reflector or creator. Since these various functions are
unifying functions, there might be a strong temptation to look for their
unified source. But this is an elementary error, on a par with illicitly
extracting and then detaching an existential quantifier from its proper
nested location. A desire for unity cannot by itself perform the conjuring
trick of pulling one rabbit out of several hats: a transcendental unity of
the concept of person, unifying the variety of distinct, independently
unifying functions that each regional concept plays.

Our reflections leave our conclusions open: we might conclude that
there is no such thing as the concept of personhood, that there are only
highly regionalized functions that seemed, erroneously, to be subsumable
in a structured concept. Or we might conclude that the various functions
of the concept are sometimes at odds, that the concept of a person cannot
function to provide decision procedures for resolving conflicts among
competing claims for rights and obligations because it embeds and expresses just those conflicts. Nothing hangs on the choice between these
conclusions because neither political practice nor philosophic theory is
affected by the outcome. For all practical and theoretical purposes it
doesn't matter whether the concept of a person has multiple and sometimes conflicting functions, or whether there is no single foundational
concept that can be characterized as *the* concept of a person. As long
as we recognize that such appeals are, in the classical and unpejorative
sense of that term, rhetorical, we can continue to appeal to conceptions
of persons in arguing for extending political rights, or limiting the exercise of political power. The success of such rhetorical appeals depends

on whether the proposed concept expresses some of the active values
and practices of the audience.

Another metaphysical longing remains unsatisfied. But of course that
doesn't mean that we shall be freed of metaphysical longing, nor even
of this particular metaphysical longing.[6]

2 The Transformations of Persons

In the *Odyssey*, Menelaus tells Telemachus as much as he knows of Odysseus's wanderings. He reports that Odysseus, wanting to learn the end of his travels and needing directions for returning safely home through the dangerous seas, captured Proteus and held fast to him, though Proteus transformed himself into a bearded lion, a snake, a leopard, a bear, running water, and finally into a flowering tree. Proteus eventually wearied, and consented to tell Odysseus something of what he wished to know.

Presumably Proteus remained himself throughout these transformations; he may have chosen them; certainly his knowledge remained unaffected. Since Odysseus held fast to him throughout, the physical changes were apparently changes in a material object remaining in roughly the same place. But there are also tales of divinities who disappear in one place and reappear, in a different form, in a different place. Unless we invent spiritual or nonmaterial bodies to support these changes, the personal identity of such divinities rests on the continuity of their psychological properties.

But such radical physical changes are precisely the sorts of transformations that occur to divinities or fictional heroes. It is, after all, built into our conceptions of divinities and heroes that they are exactly the sorts of beings whose activities cannot be explained in the usual ways. King Arthur shades away from history and into legend at just that point where he is regarded as capable of the sorts of transformations that we cannot ourselves perform, transformations that do not fall within the canon of our explanations of the normal changes of embryos to infants, infants to adolescents, and so on, with graceful stopping places, to senility and the grave. The fictions in which the careers of divinities and heroes are told grasp minimal threads of plausibility by such phrases as "scientists somehow transplanted," suggesting that an explanation hovers in the wings; but that explanation stays in the wings, and there is a stop to our prying.

Under what circumstances might we imagine that an ordinary human being could undergo Protean changes and remain the same individual human person? If Omega Whirlpool, a very ordinary fellow, who has never been known to do anything the slightest bit unusual, one day disappeared without the aid of a mad scientist, and, exactly where he had been, drinking tea, there appeared the body of his cousin Anemone, complete with what seemed to be Omega's memories and character traits, we wouldn't (to put it mildly) know what to say. It is not, I think, logically impossible to imagine such changes; but by the time we have filled in the details of what might be required to make sense of them, we shall have diminished the dramatic power of the examples, and brought back into play the familiar constraints that ground the continued identities of persons in the network of our social practices and scientific theories. To show that this is so, I shall consider the criteria we use to determine whether Anemone is Omega, rather than a distinct individual who shares Omega's essential traits. I begin with the familiar argument that the criterion of psychological continuity presupposes identifying the same physical agent. In part 2, I argue that the converse is also true: the criterion of bodily continuity presupposes a criterion of psychological continuity because it requires an account of the range of normal intentional action. In the last two sections, I pour oil on troubled waters by showing that the political and social implications of the mutual dependence of the two criteria are not disastrous, but beneficial.

I

One might suppose that Omega is the final authority on his identity. But of course there may well be Omega-impersonators, and if we have any doubts about whether he is the same, we shall be likely to doubt the identity of the person who reassures us. Recognizing the marks of psychological continuity will not completely settle our doubts. If Anemone, speaking in Omega's voice, reports memories one might suppose privy only to Omega and his girlfriend, we may wonder how Anemone acquired information about matters that seemed so private. It would be surprising if we concluded that Anemone was Omega. Multiplying psychological capacities—adding character traits, intentions, hopes, and sentiments to memory—will not conclusively establish identity. Because most of these psychological characteristics require a body, our difficulties will be increased: How does the nostalgic lusty smile that Omega always has when he hears the Goldberg Variations look on Anemone's face? All this will only leave us puzzled as to how Anemone could have got hold of Omega's intellectual capacities and character traits. Being puzzled, we shall treat these as general traits that might be instantiated in different particulars in slightly different ways.[1]

Or we could refuse mystification by advancing a detailed causal account, establishing the continuity between Omega's original experiences and Anemone's present psychophysical equipment. But such a causal account may be too easy to establish. For suppose that Omega is attached to a black box, a perpetually recording encephelographic angel, so that every tone of his experiences is a set of vibrations in the box; Anemone's body is wired to the box, and her vocal cords and facial expressions are so wired as to do the appropriate things at appropriate occasions, that is, roughly to do and say what Omega would have done and said in those situations. Suppose in short that the causality condition for the continuity of memory and psychological traits is met. In the face of such glibness, we shall not know whether to count Anemone's reports as legitimate memory reports or to count them as causally descended from memory reports. It is still open to us either to declare Anemone and Omega one person or to conclude that Anemone's memory reports bear the same relation to Omega's experiences that Omega's reports of his grandparents' experiences bear to those original experiences. Which of these alternatives we choose will, among other things, depend on our views about what constitutes *one* organism.

I want to rehearse, briefly, the familiar difficulties of the memory criterion, by way of drawing a moral about the problems that come from taking any psychological criterion independently of the complex social practices that are the breathing space of our concept of persons. If we separate the memory criterion from the whole panoply of other psychological activities, and also separate psychological activities from the behavior and actions of whole (that is, bodily) persons, we shall have as much difficulty establishing the identity of memory reports and of psychological traits as we have establishing the identity of persons. How are we to determine that two memory reports of putatively the same experience, differing from one another as memory reports are wont to do, are indeed of the same experience?

Ever since Butler criticized Locke, it has been no news that each thing is what it is and not another thing. From this follows Butler's equally pregnant observation that if we are unsure about the identities of persons under different descriptions, we shall also be likely to question the identification of possibly distinct memory reports.[2] Once suspicions of legitimacy are aroused, family resemblances will not quiet doubts about the propriety of descent. Reported memories are (to be sure) directly causally connected with the experiences they describe, and what is at least as important, no memory qualifies as a memory unless it is veridical.[3] But every reported memory is an interpretation of the original experience: memories as they live and breathe come in phrases and visualizations rather than in propositions. They are emotionally charged, infused with fears and desires: one cannot separate the purely cognitive or verifiable aspect of what is remembered from a vast array of other tonalities of what is imagined, fantasied, hoped.[4]

Memories are known by the associative company they keep, by the occasions that surface them, and that have in the past surfaced them. When we remember, we do not count back to the appropriate bead on a thread; remembering is more like looking at Thai silk damask, whose colors and patterns shift when the light changes or when we move. Focusing not only selects, it also blurs. Where does the reproduction, the straight report, leave off and the recasting begin?

This is not to say that complex interpretative psychological activities cannot be analyzed propositionally and evaluated as reasonable or as false. It is in analysis and not in experience that the verifiable core is separated from the complex connotations and desires that also constitute remembering. But in disputed cases it will be just this interpretation that is at issue.

Of course to make sense of veridical memory, we must suppose that the phenomena of remembering can somehow be recast in propositional form. It must be in principle possible to determine in relatively neutral language what *did* happen (though perhaps not just exactly what happened). Unless we have a *conceptual* distinction between genuine memories and reconstructions, we shall lose the concept of memory altogether.

Certainly whatever difficulties attend recasting the complex phenomena of remembering also attend casting focused and interpretatively charged judgments of experience into propositional form. The indeterminacy of memory reports is in part due to the indeterminacy of descriptions of experiences. Reports about experiences can be put into propositional form; but they do not come neatly chopped up, distinguishable from one another by their truth conditions. Identifying the same event under different descriptions is a general problem, not specific to memory experiences.

These difficulties might be thought to be difficulties in applying the psychological criterion, rather than in the criterion itself. While this hedge seems right, there is surely something suspect in a criterion whose application is not only difficult, but question-begging in disputed cases. If we are unsure about whether Anemone is Omega, we shall not be sure how to recast her interpretatively charged rememberings into verifiable propositions. It might be thought that this difficulty could be bypassed by a condition that a memory contains just that set of beliefs and knowledge that was contained in the original experience, and no more. All the rest is later accretion, inference from the core memory. But in the puzzle cases, the line between core and accretion is disputed.

To be sure, interpretatively charged memories would not be used in teaching someone what it is to remember, or to give examples of high standards for exactness in remembering. But what is necessary for the logic and ethics of remembering is one thing, and what is involved in tracking down ordinary unguarded remembering quite another.

In practice, some of the problems that derive from extending Butler's criticisms of Locke are taken care of by conservative principles of good sense and simplicity. If we multiply persons, we have to accept the burden of explaining the surprising continuity of memory, character traits, preferences, and so on. In many disputed cases, proclaiming identity is simply an inference to the best explanation. Given some discontinuity, the appearance of new or distinct entities may be harder to explain than postulating the continued existence of the same one (e.g., it might be more difficult to explain Anemone's appearance *ex nihilo* than it would be to explain how Omega came to look like Anemone). We pick identity or difference by a criterion of simplicity, conformity to known regularities, explicability by current scientific theories, adaptability to the large network of social practices. We make the inference to the best explanation.

It is important to realize that the psychological criterion is often insufficient in normal and not merely in fictional cases. When the psychological criterion fails to provide clear-cut answers, we tend to turn to the criterion of physical continuity. If senile Omega's memory is so defective that he cannot distinguish his memories from his fantasies of Anemone's experiences, we can say that he is in one sense the same and in another not. And we can do this, as I shall later argue, without multiplying entities or making the case undecidable.

We shall regard senile Omega as the same individual, even if he has undergone dramatic psychological changes, if we have scientific theories, often expressed in a body of common beliefs and practices, that attest to the continuity of changes in one entity. If, over a period of time, Omega has become virtually unrecognizable, not the same sort of person at all, we may regard him as the same individual, though no longer the same person.

The primary function of establishing the identity of persons is to provide us with grounds for allocating responsibility and liability in a stable way.[5] We distinguish and identify persons by the characteristics, or patterns of characteristics, that we can expect from them. Of course we know that physical and psychological changes occur in the course of an individual's lifetime; as long as these changes fall within an established pattern, we count them as changes within one person. Knowing the patterns of senility, we consider Omega the same individual, though he is no longer the same personality, and cannot be treated in the same way. Because the standard cases of change are explicable, we allow the criteria for 'individual', 'human', 'person' to run side by side, and to demarcate the same entity. But as the primary function of each of these terms is different, insisting on their extensional coincidence in all contexts may cause strain.

Children who have not yet reached the age of maturity are not, legally speaking, persons: they cannot enter into contracts, are not liable, etc. Of course they are individual human beings, and because we know that children generally grow up to become responsible agents, we count them as persons. And certainly to make sense of the changes in attribution, we have to identify the individual who was a child and is now an adult. If there are theories about patterns of changes in an entity, that entity must somehow be identifiable. If we judge senile Omega a changed person, we must have a way of identifying the individual who has changed. The arguments that an overlapping continuity of traits is sufficient for reidentification are familiar; there is no need to rehearse them.[6]

Now what are we supposed to conclude from these meandering observations? The surprising moral is, I believe, that there is a sense, though far from the intended one, in which persons are identified by their interpretative memory reports: persons and their memories are mutually constitutive. But when we flesh out—as we must—the memory criterion with all that is required for its application, we discover that it includes a criterion of continuous bodily identification, as well as a host of other psychological capacities—imagining, anticipating, desiring, fearing. If we pay attention to the content of memory reports, including as they do perceptual and physical experiences of all sorts, we must introduce a criterion of physical identification in order to apply the memory criterion. We shall then have a criterion that stands to the original bare version of the memory criterion as a human being stands to a computer flow chart. When the memory criterion is fully developed with a fleshed out account of all that is involved in remembering, it has been radically transformed. Properly extended, it no longer differs radically from the criterion of bodily continuity when it is properly extended. If I succeed in establishing this claim, then we shall see that several of the most popular senses of 'identify'—which I have so far blurred—are mutually dependent. Establishing criteria for the numerical distinctness of persons is in practice not separable from defining essential characteristics. Furthermore, although the criteria for identifying individual human beings and identifying persons normally march together, they may sometimes fall apart. But obviously nothing I have yet said entitles us to this conclusion.

II

Can there be Protean changes in Omega's body? The criterion of bodily continuity cannot, unfortunately, rush in bold and bare, uninterpreted, to provide a foundation for identifying numerically distinct individuals. For one thing, we require an account of the normal range of changes in a *human* body, someone who is capable of responsible agency, who has beliefs and desires, makes choices, tries and sometimes fails to enact his choices. The criterion of bodily continuity itself requires interpretation.[7] We could pare down the bodily criterion so that it becomes a matter of establishing spatiotemporal continuity. But that criterion gives too much: spatiotemporal continuity has no joints. If we want to establish the distinctness as well as the continuity of individuals, we shall have to specify what sort of individuals we want identified.

If Omega changes into a lion, we still might have an account that connects Omegalion's physical properties with the psychological characteristics essential to his being a person. But if we want the bodily criterion to establish the continuity of the same person, then even a lion's complex central nervous system doesn't determine whether he has Omega's happy lustful leer on hearing the Goldberg Variations or whether he has the characteristic bodily tone that Omega's happy love affair with Anemone has given him. All this might be accommodated in various ways: some properties can be discarded as genuine but nonidentificatory; others may conceivably be transposed to the lion. But when Omega changes into running water or a flowering tree, we shall have trouble. The story that establishes continuity will have to become more and more fanciful, constructing ways in which water can speak, flowering trees make decisions. It is difficult enough to construct scientific explanations of speaking lions with human memories. Bridging current biology and any account of speaking water would require explanations we cannot even begin to imagine.

The criterion of bodily continuity steps in to support flagging psychological continuity, but it does so having already absorbed some general form of the psychological criterion. To see that this is so, we need only reflect on the sorts of bodily changes that do lead us to say that a person is no longer the same, or no longer exists.[8] We have detailed accounts of the transformations of Omega's body after his heart and lungs stop functioning. The continuity of Omega's physical changes to dust and ashes is as well established, and probably more clearly understood, than the continuity of changes that follow infant Omega to his senility. It is because we have not only an account of bodily continuity, but also one of an organic body, that we draw the lines we do. Not just any old organism will do for personal identity. We require one that fits our conceptions of the conditions for agency, with intentions, memories, relatively enduring character traits, recognizable sentiments, the whole kit and caboodle required for the attribution of responsibility and the assignment of social roles. It should now be evident that the interplay between the various criteria is quite complex: it isn't that one criterion is applied, and then, when a problem arises, we retreat to a more fundamental level, gradually jettisoning the more complex characteristics of persons, until we are left with the bare minimum, which gives our real criterion for identity. For if we jettison the complex characteristics, we are left with a body rather than a person. This is not to say that persons are not bodies, or that they are entities of another sort, but that bodies are the very *least* of what persons are.

III

It might well be objected that this free and flowing appeal to the normal lines of explanations of causal continuities, permitting mutually supportive, benevolent, and protective alliances between the psychological and bodily criteria for identity, at best represents a woolly relativism. Oracular remarks about how persons, their memories, and their bodies are mutually constitutive might be thought the sort of pernicious obscurantism that disguises logical confusion. For it might be thought unpardonably unprofessional to move, as I have so far done, between the strict and philosophical sense of 'identification' as providing criteria for the numerical distinctness of persons, to the loose and popular sense that allows, without even pausing to blush, something as vague as "what is essential to being the sort of person one is." The various senses of identity must be disentangled: unless we have some way of picking out the unique entity who allows or refuses hospitality to various descriptions, however subtle or mutually supporting they may be, we are babbling.[9]

Before trying to meet this objection, a few general observations may be helpful. Many of the controversies about the criteria for personal identity are generated by parties who are trying to capture quite different sorts of entities. Those who think that a criterion for personal identity ought to give a principle of individuation are bound to object to any criterion, however rich and resonant, that does not provide a uniqueness condition. Certainly neither the memory criterion nor other versions of the psychological criterion provide a uniqueness condition: they isolate general and repeatable traits. Attempts to individuate uniquely either shove us back to continuous spatiotemporal location, or make every characteristic a defining one. To give spatiotemporal continuity joints, to pick out a continuously existing *person*, requires specifying the *sort* of individual whose spatiotemporal continuity is to be demarcated.[10] The second alternative, making every characteristic definitive, has an ancient and honorable tradition.[11] But while it may give an analysis of identity, it does not give a criterion for solving the problem cases, fictional or normal. The intuition that some traits are more essential than others is usually reintroduced elsewhere. While these moves may help with the indexical problem, they do not give an account of the concept of personal identity that underlies our practices of allocating responsibility and determining liability.

Because those who disagree about criteria for personal identity often have different conceptions of what a proper answer would be, and on whom the burden of proof should lie for giving a fuller answer, this is a fruitful area for the waste of philosophic lust in action, with the participants standing on widely separated grounds, directing their attention to mirror images of distant lands. Since the issues that would bring the opponents face to face have all the attractions of quicksand, I shall only touch on the distinctions between types of criteria of 'identification', just enough to cover myself against the charge of carelessness.

We need to distinguish criteria that give:

1. Class differentiation: What distinguishes the class of persons from their nearest neighbors: baboons, robots, human corpses, person-stages?
2. Individual differentiation: What are the criteria for the numerical distinctness of persons who have the same general description?
3. Individual reidentification: What are the criteria for reidentifying an individual as the same person in different contexts, or under different descriptions?
4. Individual identification: What sorts of characteristics identify a person as essentially the person he is, such that if they were changed he would be said to be a different person, though he might remain differentiated and reidentifiable as the same individual? We must distinguish two perspectives:
    a. The external perspective: What sorts of characteristics are treated by observers as essential?
    b. The internal perspective: What sorts of characteristics are central to an individual's conception of what is essential to him, so that he would consider himself a different person in their absence?[12]

It might be thought that some of these criteria are to be determined by straight conceptual analysis, with just enough attention to the data to give the analysis something to go on. It might seem, for instance, as if criteria for species identification and individual identification could be read straight off from the phenomena, as the characteristics of species are defined in biology. But when the evaluation and interpretation of institutions hang in the balance, it is unlikely that we shall be able to look at the phenomena and, even with the clearest of insight, read the answer straight off.[13] Upon the concept of personal identity hang the social functions of allocating responsibility for socially necessary tasks. However personal identity is defined, it will demarcate the unit of agency: the analysis of the nature of persons will be used to justify the distribution of rights and duties; principles of political obligation and privileges will be derived from, and will in turn support, accounts of the powers and limits of individual persons. For this reason alone, it seems unlikely that the definitional problems will be on a par with similar taxonomic problems in the natural sciences. Even the most apparently straightforward distinctions will carry political and moral consequences in their wake: for instance, whether we forbid or condone the dismantling of individual persons. Of course these consequences will not be logically entailed by the analysis of the criteria for personal identity. But a philosopher's commitment to a conception of a just social order will quite properly influence his analysis of the nature of personal identity and vice versa. Assessing the losses and gains of changes in social practices, as well as estimating the ramifications of effecting changes, is a legitimate part of the analysis of personal identity. A philosopher is not an ideologue; but ignoring the political consequences of an analysis is not a mark of objectivity. If we refuse to consider these consequences because of the serious logical difficulties of circularity and regression, we shall also cut ourselves off from what is most significantly at stake in evaluating proposed definitions. Instead of controversies, we shall have impasses.

We have been given good arguments showing that the question, "Is it the same or different?" is incomplete until we specify the same or different *what*. In the case of persons, we need to go even further, realizing that the question, "Is it the same or a different person?" is incomplete until we specify what is at issue. It is for this reason that the criteria for numerical distinctness and reidentification cannot be as neatly separated from the other criteria of identification as we might have wished. Our interest in the various criteria for identifying persons does not crop up as a bit of vulgar or even delicate curiosity about the number of entities that fall into this bizarre irreducible class. This is a prime example of the way descriptive metaphysics is rooted in practical concerns. Whatever else persons may be, they are the irreducible units of responsible agency. Because in normal cases the various criteria we use in identifying persons coincide with the criteria we use in identifying human beings and those we use for identifying entities capable of intentional agency, we tend to think of these criteria as providing necessary and sufficient conditions for personal identity. But the concept of person plays and has historically played a number of distinct functions: in some contexts, asking for the census count of persons is asking for the number of individual human beings; in others, it is asking for the number of (roughly) rational and responsible agents.[14] Because 'human being' and 'agent' themselves have expanded and shrunk—not always coordinately—with changes in scientific theory and social practice, it might seem as if we were floating, trying to chart a course by sighting on buoys that are themselves unanchored. This might be thought morally and ontologically dangerous, an opportunity for arbitrary legislation or an occasion for sheer confusion. But it isn't. We can only modify—expand or diminish—the extensions of these terms a few degrees at a time, and only by appealing to already accepted meanings and practices.[15] Because the physical and psychological criteria are mutually supportive, and because persons are paradigmatically individual human beings, any change in the meanings of one of these terms will tend to bring the others gradually into line. But there may be times, and contexts, in which the criteria diverge.

To say that there is a sense in which universities are persons because they are legally liable, and a sense in which human beings who have been lobotomized are not, is not to say that senile Omega is a type of university or vice versa. It is simply to say that some of the criteria we use in identifying persons allow us to count universities as persons because they can perform acts that the members who compose them cannot, as individuals, perform. But by other criteria that we use to identify persons, universities do not qualify. (The good they do is not interred with their bones.) That senile or lobotomized Omega is only the same human being he once was, and not the same person, does not mean that Omega ceases to have any moral or legal claims upon us, though it may mean that his rights are quite different from those he had in his youth. None of this means that 'person' is an ambiguous term, as it is applied to universities or to human beings. Though persons are, as Strawson has shown, not reducible to a set of psychological or a set of physical predicates, the term 'person' is nevertheless complex. It can be applied, by extension, to entities that fill some but not all of the criteria for membership. Those applications are not metaphorical, but, within their context, they are unambiguous.

That we have not arrived at a neatly nestled set of criteria should not cause dismay. It would do so only if we had a dream of a philosophical theory that could avoid all regression or circularity, and do so without any bootstrap operations. It would be pretty to think we might proceed in this way, unearthing necessary and sufficient conditions resting on self-evident foundations. If we had such analyses, however, we would have idealized reconstructions of no historical interest; our actual practical difficulties in applying the various criteria would become incomprehensible. They would have to be construed as signs of frailty, failures of intelligence or good will, the fallenness of the practical situation. Tidy analyses in which criteria for numerical distinctness and reidentification don't get all muddled up with other types of identification would avoid circularity, but at the cost of separating the analysis of the concept of personal identity from the social, political, and psychological practices that are its natural home. Whether this would be an improvement is something that cannot be settled simply by showing it to be tidier. Disagreements about the ethics of philosophical arguments generally end with all parties going off in different directions, each feeling holier than thou because they have either been more rigorous or because they have been less fanciful.

IV

The multiplicity of admissible answers to the question, "Is this the same person?" does not multiply entities, nor does it make criteria for personal identity indeterminate. Let me deal with the second point first: If we grant that some of the most interesting borderline cases of the transformation of persons allow legitimate alternative answers in different contexts, it does not follow that there are alternative answers once the context is specified. If senile Omega is in one sense a different person from Omega in his youth, while in another he is the same, it is not up for grabs whether Omega is the same person. Furthermore, if we make the criteria of physical and psychological continuity dependent on a norm of reasonable causal explanation of the activities of a certain sort of complex organism, and connect it to an elaborate set of social practices, it does not follow that all scientific theories and social practices are equally defensible.

We are familiar with societies that extend or narrow the unit of personal responsibility in ways that differ from ours. The unit of personal responsibility is sometimes the extended family, in which biological individuals are regarded literally as members of a larger body.[16] In other societies, individuals are treated as hosts to several persons by demonic or spiritual possession. The actions 'they' perform under possession are considered those of another person.[17] Still further afield, some societies draw the lines between continuous biological individuality differently, and directly link the health of an individual with the welfare of a tree in the forest, treating 'them' as a single biological entity. Together they flourish, together they fail.[18]

If we recognize that the criteria for personal identity are inseparable from a large body of other beliefs about the normal scope of action and causality, it does not follow that we must regard all such theories or societies as equally acceptable or even equally coherent. Whether we should try to adopt or to change any such practices is obviously a matter that would require detailed investigation of the advantages to be gained, some of them moral and aesthetic, as well as the possible hidden costs of grafting new senses on rooted concepts.

A few last remarks on the problem of ontological inflation. There are objections to Locke's distinguishing the criteria for identifying the same body, man, and person on the grounds that this involves an unnecessary multiplication of entities. But recognizing that entities may fall under a number of distinct categories, some of which support each other while others are subclasses under extended descriptions, does not multiply entities beyond necessity since it does not multiply entities at all. Ontological conservatives need have no cause for worry: the class of persons may still be a subclass of the class of bodies.[19] At the same time, antireductionists need not fear a deflationary policy: the analysis of bodies is hardly the whole of the analysis of persons. As events can fall under many descriptions without thereby becoming many events, so bodies may be grouped and regrouped without creating new substances. This is crucially important for the description of entities that are largely cultural or social. Yet choices among possible descriptions need not be arbitrary; even when there are legitimate alternatives, the cost of shifting from one alternative to another may, for a specific society at a certain point in its history, be virtually unthinkable.

Having generated a lot of confusion, let us step back to survey the view. Where have we emerged in determining the range of permissible Protean transformations in Omega? I have claimed that we shall allow that Omega has undergone Protean changes only if we understand how these changes have taken place. That means that the changes must fit our beliefs and practices about the capacities of organic bodies, whose physical constitutions support the complex psychological requirements for responsible agency. These conditions are mutually supportive: determining whether the conditions have been satisfied presupposes some way of picking out the entity that must meet them; but the criterion for picking out that entity is not generally independent of, but will already reflect, our views of normal responsible agency. As scientific theories and social practices change, some of the criteria may diverge from the others in such a way that the class of individuals that are accounted persons by biological criteria does not exactly coincide with the class of legal persons. When this happens, there will be considerable concern about puzzle cases, and there will be attempts to reduce some of the criteria to the status of metaphorical extensions of others. Any such reductions will be Procrustean beds.

If Omega undergoes Protean changes and remains human, his story can be told in biography rather than sacred scripture; there will be biological and psychological theories to explain his transformations. It will be possible to predict the conditions under which it might be reasonable to expect similar changes from Anemone. But in that case Omega's transformations will no longer be Protean: they will not be changes that only a divinity could undergo.[20]

3   Persons, Policies, and Bodies

According to one tradition, persons are distinguished from their nearest neighbors—robots, corpses, clever chimpanzees—by the capacities required for rational agency.[1] An extension of this view distinguishes individual persons from one another by the policies that guide their choices.[2] The origins of this concept of persons lie in the social practices that require us to assign responsibility and to determine liability: we identify one another by characteristics that determine what we can expect from one another.[3] But legal and social systems differ in the ways they demarcate distinct persons and in the criteria they use to determine the grounds for liability. For instance, liability and responsibility may rest with families or clans, or a chief may be treated as the embodiment of a tribe. A biological individual may be considered to be composed of, or hospitable to possession by, distinguishable persons.[4]

Characteristically, defenders of the theory that persons are rational agents (PRAT) find that they must treat persons as conceptually distinct from human beings and from selves as subjects of experience.[5] Though PRAT begins with a set of social practices that are taken as definitive, analysis produces a term of art, with distinctions that may be finer, more rigid, or more extensive than those associated with the original. For those who hold the accepted and familiar view that persons are biological individuals, talk of individuals as compounded or discomposed persons is at best metaphorical. If such talk is taken literally, it must be mistaken; in any case, it is argued to presuppose a more fundamental view that identifies persons with biological individuals (the 'one person/one body' view).

I want to examine the consequences that follow from taking the capacities for rationality as the criteria for defining personal identity. In part I, I shall ignore the variants of PRAT, and trace its assumptions about the extent to which the needs and desires of persons form a consistent system. I shall argue that if the mark of a person is that he have a consistent rational policy, then the class of persons will not coincide with the class of individual human beings. In part II, I argue

61

that paradigmatic and parasitic cases of persons cannot be distinguished without a program: the concept of persons is rooted in the beliefs and practices that define the actions of biological organisms of a complex sort. The analysis of the criteria for personal identity is vacuous without an account of the various functions that the concept plays in social life and in scientific theories. Finally, in part III, I discuss some of the political and psychological consequences of the view I have defended.

I

What differentiates persons from nonpersons, according to PRAT, is the capacity for reflection on one's wants and desires, along with the capacity to make and enact policies ranking desires independently of their strength or origin.[6] Persons may have conflicting desires, and even more significantly, have conflicts between their desires and their rational policies; but a responsible person is one who evaluates his desires, formulates a system of rational preferences, and consistently tries to act in accordance with his information and his policies, even when these conflict with his desires.

Let us set aside familiar discomforts associated with postulating a free will, suspicions that neither a Kantian conception of rational freedom nor a Cartesian conception of the will are coherent. Battlegrounds over this issue are littered with the corpses of combatants; since there is no lack of diagnoses of the casualties to be expected from the various modes of attack, we need neither enter the lists nor write another post mortem. We can easily reformulate PRAT by contrasting first-order desires with second-order policies, and thus bypass, temporarily at least, the difficulties associated with postulating a free will. PRAT contrasts rational volition with a mechanistic account of the operation of desires, treating them as forces that are quantifiable in strength and direction. Adherents of PRAT disagree on how best to account for the thought component of desire, and how best to analyze the mechanisms by which desires are redirected and refined.[7]

The most obvious drawback of PRAT leaps at once to the surface. A unifying hierarchy of second-order desires and beliefs will either reproduce all the conflicts that appear on the level of first-order desires and beliefs, or, if it is defined so as to avoid that difficulty, it will be too general and unified to accommodate, and certainly inadequate to explain, the various conflicting and even conflicted activities of persons. If the conflicts of first-order desires are not to be reproduced on the level of policies, then second-order policies must rank desires in a system of priorities that are both comprehensive and consistent. But any such system would be so general as to leave the phenomena of conflict behind; what is at least as serious, it could not construct specific resolutions for conflicts, resolutions that could determine action descriptions or guide conduct. If the system of priority rankings remains close to the descriptive level of the policies that actually guide a person's choices and behavior, conflicts will be reproduced on the level of policies as well as on the level of desires. But if it is reconstructed to avoid such conflicts, it will represent an idealized version of a person's policies: what he would choose, if he were a completely rational agent. But a completely rational system of policies cannot provide a criterion for individuation.[8]

PRAT has difficulties distinguishing second-order policies from first-order desires. It might be thought that policies differ from desires in being about first-order desires. But first-order desires for events to take place in the future through one's own agency are also about other desires. My present desire to get up early tomorrow can be construed either as a second-order desire or as a first-order desire. On one reading, what I now want is that when the alarm rings tomorrow morning, my desire to get up should, then, at that point, be strong enough to dominate over my desire to lie abed. But on another reading, my present desire is simply a desire to get up when the alarm rings, and not a desire about a future desire. Are all first-order desires automatically accompanied by a second-order policy: let this desire be enacted? But then first-order desires and second-order policies are isomorphic. If on the other hand, some desires do and some desires do not have policy rights, how is this determination made without generating an infinite regress? The two-level model again collapses into unrelieved isomorphism or moves to an infinite regress.

To attribute a desire to someone is to predict that, other things being equal, he will in the appropriate circumstances behave in a specified way, which he believes will lead to gratification of a specified sort. On this analysis, a desire is a disposition to act; it is either present or absent, and is not evaluatively ranked in relation to other desires. Of course desires differ in strength, measured by the strength of the habit of acting upon them, by their insistence, by their capacity to focus attention away from other apparently relevant factors. They also differ in the degree to which they are, or are regarded by an agent as, genuinely his, and not simply induced in him by social conditioning.

Of course there is an obvious sense in which all our desires are ours, insofar as we act upon them. It is this, my hand, that strikes the match to light the cigarette, however odious I feel smoking to be, and however convinced I may be that my desire is induced by the manipulations of successful advertising. Certainly, if I want to disown a desire, it must in some sense now be mine; but it doesn't follow that all the desires moving me are equally mine.

However subtly they are measured, differences in the strengths of desires do not give us the ordering of a person's desires and beliefs, even if it were possible to map out changes in consequences of acting upon them. Since one can want to strengthen a desire or to be freed of it, the same range of desires can be ranked differently by different policies, quite independently of their strength, as measured by the extent of their ramification, their entrenchment, their intensity, or their being acknowledged by the agent as identifying his character. Not only can we wish to be freed of our strongest desires, but we can also regard our 'best' desires—whether they are strong or weak—as not fully ours, but as the desires of our enlarged, idealized, but not entirely native, selves.

Even if benevolence and omniscience could determine a single rational policy, such a system would not necessarily represent the actual preference scale of the most well-intentioned rational human being, not to mention someone who suffers a conflict of desires.[9] Such a person must, if he is committed to the dominance of rationality over other ideals, attempt to prune, redirect, or redefine his desires when they conflict. But no amount of information can, without a higher order evaluative policy, determine how his desires ought to be reconstructed. Choosing the policy by which desires are to be transformed either generates conflicts on a new level or assumes the resolution it is meant to produce. The decision which picks out 'the best' desires, and makes those dominant, already presupposes the reordering of personality that it is designed to achieve. If a person is faced by a conflict between his desires, or even between his desires and his policies, he is precisely in the position of not knowing what rationality requires of him.

If PRAT has difficulties in distinguishing the level of policies and the level of desires, it does not follow that all policies are simply generalized desires. A system of preferences need not be formulated at the service of a desire, and need not be measured by utilities. In principle, there could be aesthetic or religious policies that rank desires independently of any of the long-range ramified consequences of enacting them. It might be insisted that any such aim must represent a desire, with a system of priorities ranked by the 'utility' of their consequences. Besides misunderstanding the aesthetic or religious point of view, this move only postpones the distinction, which must be introduced somewhere else, between desires for what is pleasurable and useful, on the one hand, and the sorts of motives that can set pleasures and utilities aside, in the name of a good measured by some other standards.[10]

How stable and fixed must someone's policies be, for him to be accounted a person? Frankfurt remarks that a person who has difficulties in formulating clear-cut priorities among his first-order desires must be destroyed as a person.[11] But a disintegrating person is still, at least in some measure, a person: and dissociated persons, even those who have conflicting interpretations of their own memories, whose desires conflict sharply with their policies, nevertheless go through maneuvers toward unification that are recognizably *theirs*.[12]

Frankfurt suggests that a decisive identification of a conflicted person with one (set of) his first-order desires terminates the regress of second-order policies.[13] But we need a time qualifier here: the decisive identification may be made in one context, to be later revoked by a different policy. What's worse, a person may commit himself to several, potentially conflicting policies, half-realizing, sometimes self-deceptively, that some of his identifications must undermine one another. Second-order conflicts may remain latent or recessive; though only latent, they may have the effect of defeating 'decisive' identifications, so that a person's policies often have perfectly predictable consequences that counteract the major lines of identification, though they may suit latent or minor ones. We are familiar enough with patterns of predictable failures and other sorts of self-defeating behavior on the part of highly capable persons. Yet none of these complexities should force us to abandon the concept of person. Unless there were the presumption that such struggles were those of *one* person, we could not even think of this as the phenomena of conflict. The difficulty for PRAT lies in specifying the extent to which a person may be conflicted and sundered, yet for other reasons still be regarded as identifiably the same person, and not merely the same biological individual.

It might be objected that too much is glossed by my free and easy use of 'conflict'. PRAT certainly does not deny that persons are conflicted; it only says that persons cannot knowingly accept contradictory policies without attempting either to reconcile them or to refrain from acting on at least one of them. We may well balk at calling persons who are not discomposed by contradictions entirely rational. But does that mean that we should not consider them as persons, should not treat them as responsible and liable? We may indeed feel disquieted, not knowing where hospitality to contradiction may break out next. But whether conflicts are so formulated that a policymaker must regard them as contradictory already reveals something about his identity. In choosing policies, a person also has some unexpected latitude in determining the logical relations between them. Some, but not all, of the difference between being conflicted and facing a contradiction lies in the way in which a policy has been formulated. Of course PRAT may accept this consequence, and make the capacity to *formulate* policies the criterion of personhood. If it does so, it has shifted the delicate balance between rationality and choice. For whether a person is conflicted or contradictory will then depend on a prior choice, one that is not obviously determined solely by a rational consideration of alternatives.

But these are by no means the sorts of practical problems that should force us to abandon our theoretical hopes. In practice, we do not treat rationality as an all-or-none trait: we hold individuals responsible in some contexts but not others, and we make nice distinctions of degree for different individuals. Versions of PRAT that treat rationality as an all-or-none trait leave us in the awkward position of being unable to hold some nonrational individuals responsible for becoming rational. But the processes of unifying and harmonizing desires requires a wider and more complex range of capacities than are accounted for in the usual analyses of rational evaluation. Or, putting it differently, the processes of rational evaluation are more complex and varied than is usually suggested by the model of rationality given by idealized reconstructions of psychological processes. It is precisely because being a responsible person involves a wide network of capacities that we can hold someone who has some of them accountable for developing others.

Integrative strategies may express one strand of traits in a person, opposed by others with opposed designs. The ascription of unity may lie more in the eye of the beholder than in the person of the agent. The rational integration of desires is not a person's sole task, nor even necessarily his dominant one. It may be the one that is socially useful in (re)identifying responsible individuals. But there is no a priori reason to treat those characteristics as more essential to a person than the voice that bellows in pain, or persistent habits of refusing integration. When the processes of socialization are benign and successful, external and internal identifications may coincide; but they do not do so automatically.[14] That they are delicate and uncertain attests to their conceptual separation. One can, of course, achieve this result by *fiat*, refusing to classify individuals who fail to give priority to their rationally decisive identifications as genuine persons. This move may, however, so drastically reduce the number of persons in the population as to render the concept of person useless in determining to whom to assign responsibility.[15]

PRAT might be saved from this criticism: a person is identified as someone for whom the ideal of rationality *can* be dominant; this need not mean that rationality is actually his dominant ideal, and certainly it does not mean that he is dominantly rational. This reading does save PRAT, but at the cost of making it a more limp and uninteresting theory than was suggested by its original brave flourish. On this interpretation, PRAT gives at best a necessary but not a sufficient condition for being a person. The condition it gives requires, for its actualization and development, a set of physical and social conditions and capacities that are not usually contained in its analysis. When these conditions are supplied, PRAT's analysis of the discontinuity between the ideal of rationality and other levels of mental activity becomes questionable.

Any attempt to deduce the necessary conditions for being a person from the best conditions for reidentifying responsible ones is surely an instance of the sort of philosophical legislation that amounts to imperialism. It would be pretty to think that the conditions for assigning responsibility do in fact serve as the central ideal of persons; but those whom we consider responsible lead more precarious lives than PRAT, even though it allows conflicts, suggests. And it is not a foregone conclusion that all of them are disintegrative. It is at least conceivable, and certainly not conceptually incoherent, that a rational person, as distinguished from a rational will, might search out new conflicts as well as new resolutions. Such processes may well strengthen some of the capacities that conduce to responsible agency, even though they would appear, in the short run, to conflict with rational agency.[16] When conflicts of this sort emerge, the balance of power between the ideal of strict rationality and other ideals is unstable. To say that the very possibility of being regulated by any ideal presupposes the dominance of rationality is to defend PRAT by making it tautologous. What this cannot do, as Kant discovered, is to give us directions for identifying particular responsible persons or particular responsible choices and actions.

II

We are familiar with arguments, as old as Butler's and as subtle as Williams's, that the application of the memory criterion for personal identity presupposes having identified the person whose experiences are remembered; even if memory stands as a necessary condition for identifying a person, it cannot be sufficient, since it requires establishing bodily continuity as well.[17] As these arguments are both powerful and well known, it is not necessary to rehearse them here, or to determine to what extent their claims are somewhat inflated.[18] Similar arguments can be advanced to show that PRAT at best gives a necessary, but not a sufficient condition for personal identity. To identify the same rational agent in different contexts, distinguishing him from others, it is necessary to identify him as a physical agent, endowed with memory, expectations, and other psychological and intellectual capacities, not all of them implicitly contained in the rationality condition as it is usually formulated. The development and exercise of these capacities requires both a complex biological organism and a complex social environment. It is perhaps possible to construe and reconstruct the processes of rational choice as though they took place in a specious present, unsupported by habits of trust and expectation, unjogged by wishes and dreams, uninformed by memory. Certainly we do not now choose or act in this way. If rational agents were disembodied minds whose thought processes consisted of logical inferences without analogical associations, making choices without dreamy fantasies, foreseeing the consequences of their choices without imagining or visualizing alternatives, we would have to revise our conceptions of choice and action quite radically. Either PRAT must include many other intellectual capacities—memory, imagination, perception, perhaps even the formulation of desires—within the analysis of rationality, or it must give an account of the interconnections between the exercise of rationality and these other activities.

For the sake of the argument and without pretending even to have sketched a proof, let us accept it as established that when PRAT is extended to include other faculties and capacities, it will become clear that persons, as rational agents, are bodies, or have bodies, or that they are irreducible subjects of both psychological and physical predicates.[19] But this is not a policy of ontological inflation. It just says that the class of persons is a subclass of the class of bodies. Since the analysis of bodies does not provide an analysis of persons, antireductionists need not be dismayed.

I want to consider how the social practices of assigning responsibility for choices and actions influence our views of the nature of the sorts of bodies persons must have. However the spatiotemporal continuity and discontinuity of biological organisms is defined, so too will follow the lines that identify the same or distinguish different persons. My thesis is that what may, in one society, or in one context, be regarded as a unified incorporated person composed of complex parts can in another be regarded as a sum of distinct but interactive individuals.

Before defending this view against the clear and powerful objections that can be raised against it, it might be useful to have a few examples:

1. 'A' Gahuku-Gama pays retribution to 'his' relatives when 'his' hair is cut off, because 'he' has deprived 'them' of something that is part of 'them', as well as part of 'himself'.[20]

2. Among the Balinese, an individual is initially named by a unique nonsense syllable. Within the family, and in situations involving actions

having effects on the family, he is called by the number designating his sibling ranking. His duties, his privileges, the principles that guide his choices, are determined by his place in a sibling-order. When he assumes offices and duties, his titles *are* his names in that context; he *is* the bearer of that office, the actor of that role. The policies and to some extent even the memories that determine his choices as a bearer of office are entirely distinct from those that guide him as a member of his family. If 'he' keeps the roles distinct, they need not come into conflict; but of course if 'he' tries to conjoin them, 'his' various role-policies can come into opposition. The most significant of his names are those he receives as progenitor: father-of-so-and-so. Beyond that is the symmetrical name *kumpi*, designating either great-grandchild or great-grandfather, without differentiating them. Great-grandchildren are not allowed to mourn for their great-grandfathers, because they *are* the *kumpi* in a new cycle.[21]

3. Amanda's knowledge of Amador's intentions may be as noninferential as her knowledge of her own; she may be so attuned to 'his' states, that moods of which neither 'he' nor 'she' are consciously aware affect not only 'her' desires, but the policies that guide 'her' choices. So fused, Amador and Amanda form a compound person (Amans) whose parts are more closely linked together than are the 'parts' of Amanda to one another when she was not 'part of Amans'.

4. "It was not Hamlet, but Hamlet's madness did this."

These examples show that even if identifying persons presupposes identifying their bodies, a view about the normal sizes, location, and powers of human agents is already presupposed in identifying a particular body as the body of a particular person. This general principle need not be made explicit or brought into play in normal cases of identification. But if there is a dispute, of the sort dramatized by the transplant puzzles, settling it will presuppose agreement about the normal lines of distinguishable physical organisms.[22] Disagreement or uncertainty about whether discontinuity in psychological characteristics or in policies regulating preference rankings demarcates a different person cannot always be settled by turning to the bodily criterion. For in identifying the same *bodily person* (analytically distinguishable, though not necessarily ontologically distinct from the same *material object*), the general view of what properly constitutes continuity or discontinuity in the activities of a biological organism will already have been brought into play.[23] Of course when there is no dispute, no appeal to a general principle will be required. But unless a dispute about identity rests on ignorance or faulty reasoning, it is likely to be symptomatic of a more fundamental disagreement about the general character of complex biological individuals. It cannot therefore be settled by an appeal to the nature of physical agents, or biological organisms.

In its extended version, PRAT requires flexibility in unexpected quarters. If it holds fast to the 'one person/one system of policies' view, there will be unexpected groupings of persons, allowing what had been conventionally treated as distinct biological individuals to be treated, under certain circumstances, as one person. What had been conventionally treated as one biological individual may be treated as several distinct persons. In either case, the parts of the body must be thought to have direct causal influence on one another, within what is considered to be one organic system (as in the Gahuku-Gama and the Amans cases). But such causal efficacy may be quite complex, and the demarcation of one organism may cut across what, in a different theory, would be considered distinct physical individuals. The account of causal efficacy *within one organism* will already reflect theories and practices of responsible agency.

If, on the other hand, PRAT holds fast to the 'one person/one body' view, making the class of persons a subclass of the class of complex biological organisms (however that turns out to be defined), then one biological individual may be hospitable to distinct sets of preference rankings and policies (as in the Balinese case). When these policies come into conflict, an individual may look for a new *persona* to reconcile them. It does not follow that in doing so, he is appealing to an unchanging person—a maskless chooser who stands behind his *personae*. Arbitrators in intrapsychic conflicts eventually become interested parties. Even *in foro interno*, party politics involves shifting alliances and the co-option of disinterested spectators.[24]

Now it is time to turn to the objections: It might be said that all this hospitality to 'cross-bodily' identification of persons and cross-policy identification of bodies must presuppose (re)identifying a physical individual in different contexts at different times. As long as the Balinese reidentify the same individual in various roles and evaluate *his* performances in them, as long as his biography can be traced and questions about which names he has acquired can be raised, then some sort of unified and enduring person, or at any rate, a continuously reidentifiable one, must be presupposed. Talk of psychological fusion, or multiple role identification, or demonic (dis)possession presupposes a person to whom all these are referred, parts of whose continuous story they are, or to whom they belong. It is the individual who is reidentified in various roles, who *is* the person.[25] The Gahuku-Gama who pays retribution to his relatives when his hair is cut off is mistaken; the very grammar necessary to describe *his* action reveals his error. The designations 'his' and 'part of *them*', already distinguishes persons. He does not, for example, pay retribution to his (own) hands, though there is nothing con-

ceptually impossible about his doing so. ("I owe my feet a rest.")
Similarly, however subtle the harmony of the Amans may be, if they
should come to discord, there is no doubt about how they will sort out,
even if Amanda has become all heart and Amador twice as hardheaded.
Their separation cannot make the head(s) go one way, and the heart(s)
another. Two whole and relatively complete persons will go their own
ways.

   This objection can be interpreted as making a physical, a logical, or
a psychological point; none of these, properly understood, need undermine the revised extension of PRAT.

   1. The examples of compounded and discomposed persons might be
said to presuppose one body that enacts all roles, one reidentifiable
material object with a specifiable continuous spatiotemporal location.
When the person is variously identified across distinct biological organisms, or within one organism, *it* does all the policy-making, the maneuvering in the face of conflicts and responsibilities, etc. And if *it* is
to be located, made liable and responsible, it must be located as a
material object, the body (bodies) it is. Now this is quite right, but it
does not at all settle the boundary lines of continuity and discontinuity
of bodies. To say that a person must be identified as the material object
it is, gives no guidance in picking one out, because 'material object' is
too general a term to tell us where to draw the lines that demarcate *same*
from *other*.[26] (Is my hand a distinct material object?) Substituting "organism" for "material object" is an improvement, because we can presumably establish some criteria for reidentifying and distinguishing
organisms. But even that criterion leaves open the question whether, for
example, a family can count as a proper, rather than a parasitic or
metaphorical, example of an organism. Narrowing the bodily criterion
still further, we might take the point of the objection to be that an
individual organic *agent* is presupposed in identifying persons. It is
because he has a recognizable DNA structure, or a unique set of fingerprints, it might be said, that we can reidentify the same Balinese
who plays *his* many roles. In a way, this is right; but when it is so
construed, the condition of bodily identification no longer provides the
precondition for all possible theories and locations of personal identity.
It is, rather, the expression of a set of practices, one that has already
made unique individuals the paradigm cases of agents. If the question
is whether incorporated or discomposed persons are merely parasitic
extensions of the paradigmatic case of a 'one person/one body' view,
then it cannot be assumed at the outset that unique biological individuals
are coextensive with unique persons. That is precisely what is at issue.
Nevertheless, the objection is in one way quite right: persons are, to

say the very least of it, in the class of complex bodies. However the lines of physical agency are drawn, so too are the lines of persons; but this only tells us that they are interdependent notions, not that one presupposes the other.

2. The examples of compounded and discomposed persons might be said to presuppose a single logical subject that is referred to, and reidentified through various descriptions. But this is a grammatical point about all possible predication and attribution, not a special point about personal identity. As a condition for intelligible discourse, it says nothing about what the logical subject of person-predicates must be like. Clouds, solar systems, and vacua are also logical subjects.[27] Granting that if we refer to persons, we must have a judicious sprinkling of pronouns to tie fast the subjects, doing that does not tell us anything about whether those pronouns appear in shudder quotes or whether they are slots for proper names. Nor does it assure us that, in a long biography, the subject of each predication is identified in the same way. When we reidentify a notion through considerable changes in its structure, we do so by reference to some features that remain relatively unchanged, in each gradual contrast. Of course whenever contexts can be meaningfully compared, then some reidentifiable features must be specified, but the features that overlap may be the very features whose significance we consider diminished, and which do not appear in the next comparison or overlap.[28] On this interpretation, the objection makes a valid general logical point, but it does not give us criteria for reidentifying persons. All it does is to tell us that we must have criteria for identifying the subjects whose roles, policies, physical location we judge to be the same or different. But each *particular* such comparative judgment may have its subject, without there being one that is the subject of them all.

3. The examples of compounded and discomposed persons might be said to presuppose a single psychological subject, a continuity of conscious awareness, linking one set of policies, memories, or sensations to one another. It might be said that compounded or discomposed persons are unified or distinct, following the lines of a feeling of subjective unity or individuality.[29] If a Balinese holds himself responsible for filling his roles well, and tries to avoid conflicts by keeping his roles distinct or developing a *persona* to reconcile them, then there must be a subjective awareness of the continuity of consciousness or, at any rate, there must be a continuity of consciousness. If Hamlet disowns his madness, it is after all, *his* madness he must disown. There need be nothing particularly spiritual or high-flown about this "felt unity of consciousness": it can be given a straightforward causal analysis of the sort that has been recently given to perception, remembering, and knowing.[30] Whatever is

a candidate for falling within the consciousness of one person must be causally connected with earlier or with other legitimized experiences of that consciousness. But the causal condition is too generous; it cannot, by itself, settle disputes about whether a causal chain has become so widespread, long, or diffuse that it should no longer be regarded as falling within *one* consciousness.[31] After all, the causal effects of experiences are not confined within one body or one consciousness. (If it were so, the activities of parents, teachers, poets, and political writers would be empty and pointless. We want to convey not only the results of our experiences, but the sense of experiencing them.) Certainly the condition of causal continuity of consciousness requires that there be causal connections between experiences (roles, policies, memories, etc.): but it cannot *by itself* determine the point at which these causal connections become so attenuated that we *must* be speaking metaphorically when we say that 'two people' are of one mind. What of course puts a stop to nonsense in this area is that the psychological condition is firmly planted in the physical condition.[32] It is because we believe that the neurophysiologists will trace direct and continuous causal connections within one central nervous system that we are confident that we shall distinguish metaphorical extensions from paradigmatic cases of causal influence within or between consciousnesses. There are two persons because there are two brains, two complete autonomous biological organisms.

But we have been here before. The psychological condition, supplemented by the physical condition, does indeed strengthen the original arid formulation of PRAT. It does not, however, do this in a way that establishes anything like universal and necessary preconditions for distinguishing or reidentifying individual persons, since it is itself the expression of one view about the conditions of responsible agency. The theory that may one day distinguish direct causal neurological influence within one organism from more tenuous indirect or quasi-influences between distinct organisms will express just that view of personal responsibility that is expressed in our social practices. We can challenge the Gahuku-Gama, the Amanses, and the Balinese who claim the continuity of policies and memories across distinguishable individuals to produce the central nervous system or brain that directly connects the various individuals involved; similarly, we can tell those who disavow and disconnect parts of their memories or policies that there *is* nevertheless a single central nervous system or brain that has registered what they would discard. In doing so, we express one theory of personal agency; we are not however, thereby giving a knock-down, drag-out winner's argument. The opposition can either deny that the identification

of a central nervous system is the relevant feature in the identification
of persons, or try to produce an analogue of a central nervous system
for disputed cases. The move of declaring that analogue a parasitic
extension begs the question.

The psychological form of the objection to incorporated and discomposed persons may take another line. It might be said that persons are,
or have, a yea-and-nay sayer, claiming and assessing experiences. Introspection may indeed reveal such a central self-identifier, though some
individuals may have it more than others, and some societies foster it
while others suppress it. It may claim centrality without having it, and
its identifications may vary radically. If there is a dispute about whether
a set of experiences falls within or outside of that continuous conscious
sense of self, then it cannot be appealed to as final arbiter, especially
if it is unconscious, submerged, or ineffective.

Yet the psychological objection to incorporated and discomposed
selves does, like the others, add something useful and necessary to
PRAT. Continuity of consciousness, whether established causally or felt
subjectively, marches along with personal identity, though it is not
presupposed by it.

III

One might wonder why I have chosen to shoot holes so mercilessly
through a theory that is already a sieve. It is because, among the many
criteria for personal identity, PRAT picks out what is essential to our
concept of persons. Persons are the bearers of responsibilities: they are
legally liable; it is they on whose various capacities we in fact rely. We
distinguish persons from one another by what we can expect from them.
And PRAT is perfectly right that the press of circumstances leads us to
concentrate on the systematic policies of persons. For many practical
purposes it might initially seem as if their other baggage—their memories, hopes, associations—plays little part in our identifying them. The
importance of any characteristic is measured by its contribution to the
capacities for responsible action. So we take psychological traits as
relatively fixed, changing with age and station, but in patterned and
predictable ways.

It might thus be objected that PRAT presents an overly externalized
view of persons, one that forces criteria for identification that are convenient for society, but both inconvenient and untrue of our internal
reflections. This is, I think, a misguided objection to PRAT. And when
we see why it is, we shall understand why the extended version of PRAT,

supported by a criterion of bodily continuity, does not court the dangers of ontological or ethical relativity. The processes by which rational agents evaluate their policies are preserved; the assignment of responsibility and liability does not become arbitrary; even ontology remains intact.

Indeed, when we realize the full significance of identifying persons by their capacities for rational agency, some of the problems of PRAT— the dilemma between the deflationary isomorphism of policies and desires on the one hand, or the heady inflation of ever more abstract policies on the other—are avoided. When PRAT is supported by the criterion of bodily continuity, properly understood as itself reflecting the social and scientific identification of complex biological organisms capable of autonomous reflection and choice, we can avoid being bogged down on the level of desires or dizzied by the vertigo of indecision about ever more general conflicting principles. The presence of others steadies the regressive ladder. Though there is a sense in which persons can be regarded as generating policies autonomously, they do not choose these policies independently of the social practices and current scientific beliefs that are embedded in the ways they formulate their alternatives. When policies conflict, we move outward as will as upward, to resolve them. Though these moves—appeals to the criteria by which the normal lines of responsible human agency are drawn—do not do away with conflicts, they show that the issues that generate conflicts are not arbitrary, and are not always reproduced as we move to more general principles.

Policy decisions are not made in a vacuum, but in contexts where details are available. If deciding whether to strengthen or disown a desire were guided by nothing but the catalog of similarities and differences in the history of a person's branching of traits, it would indeed be an arbitrary choice. Similarly, if philosophic analyses distinguishing between, for example, memories and quasi-memories, or between a past self and an ancestor self, were not really already the expressions of complex social and scientific practices, they would be the rank and empty pronouncements of an emperor talking to himself.[33]

Choices have pasts and consequences. We have been formed by early identifications.[34] The terms in which we conceive our choices are those we have derived from others. We can of course oppose them; when we do, it is usually by levelling one aspect of social priorities against others. We achieve our sense of independence by setting the social conceptions that we have internalized at odds with one another. Independence therefore also travels the path of self-alienation: it moves the zigzag track of the arbitrator who has once been, and will again become, party to general social disputes.

Though PRAT is importantly on the right track, it has unfortunately chosen too narrow a view of agency and certainly too narrow a view of the capacities that are necessary for it. The model of agency and desire implicit in PRAT derives from a simple mechanistic metaphor of forces, inertia, resultants. To these, it diametrically opposes the free activity of rationality. In arguing for the extension of PRAT, I have still talked primarily of bodily agency, stressing the necessity of causal continuity within the movements of one body, even when that body cuts across conventionally distinct individuals. In all this, I've implicitly accepted the same metaphors. But of course bodily movement isn't the only sort of physical agency. Claiming possession or rights or liberties are also actions of persons. Whether they are identical with, or an extension of, physical movements and the laws that regulate them must be the subject for another study, one that moves toward political and economic philosophy.

Composing music and daydreaming may be thought to be marginal to the sort of agency for which PRAT's concentration on reliance and liability is central. But this is a mistake: PRAT must be enriched to give a fuller account of the sorts of activities that are regarded as significant in the assessment of responsibility. Let me just give a bird's eye view of the end of that argument: there is not a list of the activities that gives us the area of responsible action, one that would include political debate but exclude daydreaming. Rather, PRAT must concentrate on those activities—whatever they may be—that come to be historically important in allocating responsibility. The class of actions that are regarded as socially significant will vary as the needs and fears of a society vary. Traits of mind and character that are useful in meeting these needs and resolving these fears will come to be thought of as dominating the account of responsible agency: children will be educated to develop them; their control and exercise will be treated as voluntary. Other traits will recede and be treated as idiosyncratic, not important to the assessment of actions.

I cannot of course substantiate this claim here, but I suspect that PRAT emerges as a strong contender for the analysis of personal identity during periods when our capacities as rational agents seem both powerful and dangerous. I would also suspect that when a society remains homogeneous and stable, when choices seem less dramatic, other aspects of persons come into the foreground as essential for identification: their aesthetic capacities, or religious sensibilities, or physical strength, for instance.

An example may give flesh to these skeletal reflections. Our legal practices in allocating punishment reflect a view of personal responsibility: an individual is tried, judged to be found innocent or guilty; the guilty are punished by fine or imprisonment. If the crime is thought to be excusable in some way, or if its recurrence is thought unlikely, a judge may lighten or shorten a sentence, but the judgment of guilt or innocence is attached to the biological individual. These practices reflect the accepted view that the *whole* individual, and not just the offending traits, bears responsibility for actions. It is, further, the unitary, isolated individual, and not those who may also be responsible for his beliefs and habits, who is liable. But we are familiar with societies that direct punishment to a larger or to a smaller unit than the biological individual, either to an extended family or to the offending trait.[35] But which of these a society does cannot be determined in a vacuum: a change of practice or principles will reflect and effect changes in the whole fabric of social life, and so, too, in the philosophic analyses of personal identity. Decisions that cannot be made piecemeal cannot be made arbitrarily. So, too, philosophical analyses that are not artificially isolated from their social presuppositions and ramified consequences are less likely to generate controversies that are regressive, impasses without arbitration.

4 Characters, Persons, Selves, Individuals

The concept of a person is not a concept that stands still, hospitably awaiting an analysis of its necessary and sufficient conditions. Our vocabulary for describing persons, their powers, limitations, and alliances is a very rich one. By attending to the nuances of that vocabulary we can preserve the distinctions that are often lost in the excess of zeal that is philosophic lust in action: abducting a concept from its natural home, finding conditions that explain the possibility of any concept in that area, and then legislating that the general conditions be treated as the core essential analysis of each of the variants. Such legislation—enshrining general and necessary preconditions as essential paradigms—is tantamount to arbitrary rule. We have not furnished an argument that socially defined entities such as nations, families, and persons, varying culturally and historically in their extensions and the criteria for their differentiation, have a place in a tidy taxonomic tree, neatly defined by genera, species, and varieties. Nor could such a proof be constructed, because there is not one to be had. Because the definitions of such entities change historically, forced by changes in social conditions and in answer to one another's weighty inconsistencies, there are layers and accretions of usages that can neither be forced into a taxonomy nor be safely amputated.

"Heroes," "characters," "protagonists," "actors," "agents," "persons," "souls," "selves," "figures," "individuals" are all distinguishable. Each inhabits a different space in fiction and in society. Some current controversies about criteria for personal identity, for characterizing and reidentifying human individuals, are impasses because the parties in the dispute have each selected distinct strands in a concept that has undergone dramatic historical changes; each has tried to make his strand serve as the central continuous thread. But criteria for reidentifying characters are different from those for reidentifying figures, and both differ from the criteria that identify selves or individuals. The concept of a person is but one in the area for which it has been used as a general class name. There is good reason for this; but we cannot understand

78

that reason until we trace the historical sequence. The explanation of the recent concentration on the criteria for personal identity, rather than character identity or individual identity, is not that it is logically prior to the other concepts in that area, but that it affords a certain perspective on human agency. Before we can see what has seemed central about personal identity, we must trace the history of the notion.

Characters are delineated; their traits are sketched; they are not presumed to be strictly unified. They appear in novels by Dickens, not those by Kafka. Figures appear in cautionary tales, exemplary novels, and hagiography. They present narratives of types of lives to be imitated. Selves are possessors of their properties. Individuals are centers of integrity; their rights are inalienable. Presences are descendants of souls; they are evoked rather than represented, to be found in novels by Dostoyevsky, not those by Jane Austen.

The effects of each of these on us and our political uses of their various structures differ radically. Indeed, we are different entities as we conceive ourselves enlightened by these various views. Our powers of actions are different, our relations to one another, our properties and proprieties, our characteristic successes and defeats, our conceptions of society's proper strictures and freedoms will vary with our conceptions of ourselves as characters, persons, selves, individuals.

I want to give a skeleton outline of some of the intellectual, emotional, and social spaces in which each of these move and have their being, to depict their structures, their tonalities and functions. I shall perforce use the expressions "person" and "individual" neutrally, to designate the entire class of expressions that refer to the entities we have invented ourselves to be, but I shall argue that this usage does not reflect the ontological or the logical priority of those concepts.

Characters

In beginning with characters, we have already leaped some distance into the story: the Greek concept of character has itself already tamed, socialized, naturalized heroes and protagonists. The fate of heroes is their parentage. To be the child of Athene or of the house of Atreus fixes the major events of one's life, determines one's tasks, and even one's capacities to meet them. Yet at the same time the hero is known by his deeds: setting himself superhuman tasks, providing himself worthy of divine regard, his achievements are in the end acts of heroism rather than heroic performances. What was originally a performance of great deeds becomes courage and endurance in the face of fate and chance; what was originally a test of prowess becomes fortitude in the recognition of finitude. As the hero's distance from the gods increases, his heroism comes to be exemplified in his character rather than in sheer glory of his action.

Between the hero and the character stands the protagonist: the one who, through successful and bold combat, reveals his true nature, in ancient terms, his lineage. Such protagonists were often foundlings, whose *agones* with forces that might be thought beyond one of such birth revealed their true powers and thus their parentage. But this subtle shift emphasizes the powers of the protagonist, powers revealed in his *agones*; and it is now these powers that determine who he really is.

Oedipus begins as an epic hero, as the king; but he undergoes a new as well as old *agon*, and so ends by depicting the drama of one who has achieved character. He revealed himself to be not only the king but kingly. He transcended—and fulfilled—his fatal lineage. In comparison to heroes, characters are set in *bas relief*; they *are* their individual powers and dispositions. That their stories are set by oracles and inheritance is less important to their identification than the traits manifest in the ways they fulfill prophecy and work through their inheritance. Both strands are still present, but the order of significance is reversed, the brocade turned inside out.

The characters of speech and writing are the sketches and lines of which language is composed, the elementary signs from which complex structures of meaning are constructed. There is all the comfort and sanity of closure: finite rules of combination and transformation make language, narrative, and social life possible. The qualities of characters are the predictable and reliable manifestations of their dispositions: and it is by these dispositions that they are identified. The elements of character tend to become stoic rather than elemental forces. Theophrastus's characters remain fixed; they are not transformed by the unfolding of events. On the contrary, their dispositional characteristics allow them to be used to develop a narrative or to stabilize the structure of a society. Characters are, by nature, defined and delineated. If they change, it is because it is in their character to do so under specific circumstances. Their natures form their responses to experiences, rather than being formed by them.

In its origins, the psychological theory of character derives traits and temperaments, dispositionally analyzed, from the balance of elements constituting an individual. The psychology of character rests in physiology. Since the elements out of which characters are composed are repeatable and their configurations can be reproduced, a society of characters is in principle a society of repeatable and indeed replaceable individuals. In a world of characters, the criteria of identification are not designed to isolate unique individuals; the criteria of reidentification are not criteria of individuation. What is of interest is the configuration of reliable traits, the range of habits and dispositions, the structure of their interaction under various sorts of circumstance and stress, as they age. The physical constitutions of misers or people with choleric or sanguine temperaments will set the ways in which they develop habits under various sorts of social conditions; within limits, it is their character that determines their responses to social and environmental conditions, rather than these conditions determining their character.

In the theory of character there is no mind-body problem: without reducing either to the other, physical and psychological traits are fused as different aspects of a single organism. Mind is the organization of the living body, whose "parts" are identifiable through their functional activity. What cannot see is not really an eye but only the sort of flesh that normally is eye-flesh. Soul is not a separate substance lodged in the body; it is the living principle, the organic force of some sorts of substances.

Nor do characters have identity crises: they are not presumed to be strictly unified. Dispositional traits form an interlocking pattern, at best mutually supportive but sometimes tensed and conflicted. There is no presumption of a core that owns these dispositions. Some characters are sparsely defined and tightly organized; others flow in complex systems reaching diagonally out of an imaginary frame, with little need for harmony among the main lines of their development. Disharmony among characteristics bodes trouble; it is likely to lead to failure in action, but not to a crisis of identity. Because characters are defined by their characteristics rather than by the ultimate principles that guide their choices, form their souls, they need not in normal circumstances force or even face the question of which of their dispositions is dominant. Of course a character may find himself in tragic circumstances with his dispositions in destructive conflict. When this happens in such a way that no resolution is available, a character can indeed be torn. Sometimes the dispositions he reveals when he is sundered reveal his grandeur; but these resplendent dispositions are no more the core of a unique individuality than are the dispositions that conflicted with one another. The character is the entire configuration, without the traits seen as layers with a core holding them together.

To know what sort of character a person is, is to know what sort of life is best suited to bring out his potentialities and functions. Theories of the moral education of characters have strong political consequences. Not all characters are suited to the same sorts of lives: there is no ideal type for them all, even when, according to some social needs or social theories, they are hierarchically arranged. If one tries to force the life of a bargainer on the character of a philosopher, one is likely to encounter trouble, sorrow, and the sort of evil that comes from mismatching life and temperament. Characters formed within one society and living in circumstances where their dispositions are no longer needed—characters in time of great social change—are likely to be tragic. Their virtues lie useless or even foiled; they are no longer recognized for what they *are*; their motives and actions are misunderstood. The magnanimous man in a petty bourgeois society is seen as a vain fool; the energetic and industrious man in a society that prizes elegance above energy is seen as a bustling boor; the meditative person in an expansive society is seen as melancholic. Such subtle versions of the theory of character as Aristotle's emphasize the duality of habits, showing how habits that can be exercised for good are the very same habits that can effect harm. Only the empowered are capable of either vice or virtue. Two individuals of the same character will fare differently in different polities, not because their characters will change through their experiences (though different aspects will become dominant or recessive) but simply because a good fit of character and society can conduce to well-being and happiness, while a bad fit produces misery and rejection. Both generate characteristic flowering or decay. Societies at war give courageous characters a large scope, good latitudes for power and action; the same character will lie fallow and unused, restless in societies that prize aesthetic or religious contemplation. A courageous man will find his character exercised and his life fulfilled in the former society, but is likely to be regarded and so become a factious and angry man in the latter.

In fiction, characters are dear to us because they are predictable, because they entitle us to the superiority of gods who can lovingly foresee and thus more readily forgive what is fixed. "To be a character" is to maintain a few qualities, nourish them to excess until they dominate and dictate all others. A character is delineated and thus generally delimited. To "have character" is to have reliable qualities, to hold tightly to them through the temptations to swerve and change. A person of character is neither bribed nor corrupted; he stands fast, is steadfast. Of course there are, at all times and places, social and political pressures on people to think of themselves as characters, people of character, whose public performances are reliable. Before the contrast of "inner" and "outer" comes into play, characters are seen externally, their choices and decisions flow predictably from their constitutions and temperaments. There is not a moment when the inner voice speaks while the outer body is silent. Politically, characters are stable, their roles and even their occupations follow from their natures, *are* their natures.

Because characters are public persons, even their private lives can have universal form, general significance. The dramatic character, writ large, can represent for everyman what only later came to be thought of as the inner life of some; it can portray the myth, the conflicts, reversals, and discoveries of each person, each *polis*.

Figures

Figures are defined by their place in an unfolding drama; they are not assigned roles because of their traits, but rather have the traits of their prototypes in myth or sacred script. Figures are characters writ large, become figureheads; they stand at the prow leading the traveler, directing the ship.

Biblical and sacred literature provide the figures of the stories of Adam and Christ, the stories of fall and redemption; the Homeric poems also present their cast. In more recent literature, Charles Williams and C. S. Lewis are, rather self-consciously, trying to revive not only a type of literature but an interpretation of human agency. Like some of Faulkner's people, they present us with figures in modern dress.

Sometimes figures are identified by their occupations. Smithies, for instance, are figures of Hephaestus: a smithy is generally a strong, dark, silent man with a limp, betrayed by his wife, vengeful, moved by inarticulate and smoldering passions. Most figures are not, however, identified by their occupations nor by their social roles. Both their roles and their traits emerge from their place in an ancient narrative. The narration, the plot, comes first: it requires a hero, a betrayer, a lover, a messenger, a confidante. Juliet's nurse is the descendant of Phaedra's nurse and of the maids-confidante in Roman comedy. Of course the figures in Christian dramas—the pilgrim, the tempter, the savior, the innocent—are derived from the biblical stories.

Though figures become allegorical, they were, in their earliest appearances, far from being abstractions. They were fully embodied. Endowed with apparently accidental physical characterizations—Hephaestus's limp, the Nurse's warts and stoutness, the scholar's long red nose—they became vivid, experienced. But far from being individuating, these traits run true to type, even in their concreteness and specificity. These details are not of course meant to represent verisimilitude; rarely is the whole picture presented. Rather, one or two physical details are focused upon, to make a presence salient. Vividness is often taken to be a mark of the real; but it may do so because it is an intensification of the act of attention, rather than a representation of what is visualized. What captures us defines the real for us.

When Miranda is represented as the ingenue figure she is, her experiences will be given order and shaped by her figurative type. An ingenue is someone who finds the marvelous, the novel, in each experience. A confidante is someone whose daily experiences crystallize, shaped by the confidences of the day. She may have gone to buy fish, but what *really* happened was the sharing of confidences.

A figure is neither formed by nor owns experiences: his figurative identity shapes the significances and order of the events in his life. Figures of course become exemplary. In late literary traditions, they are used in the genre of the cautionary tale; like the saints, they present lives to be imitated. Based in fact, they are of course idealizations: that is precisely their function. Plutarch's *Lives* straddles genres: written to depict heroic characters, they were read as presenting inspirational models to be imitated, to guide lives and choices. The stories, the discoveries and reversals, the recognition that lives can be narratively and formally isomorphic set the condition for the possibility of imitation. Autobiographies of revolutionary heroes, the diaries of Che Guevara or letters from Debray, present the same type and have the same function: they are hagiography.

Individuals who regard themselves as figures watch the unfolding of their lives following the patterns of their archetypes. Rather than making their choices following their characteristic dispositions, they regard these dispositions as ordered by an ancestral type. They are Mary or Martha, Peter or Paul. Interpreting their lives by their models, they form the narratives of their lives and make their choices according to the pattern, even sometimes to the point of accentuating some of their physical characteristics, so that they dominate over others.

In contrast with the wholly external perspective on characters, the concept of a figure introduces the germ of what will become a distinction between the inner and the outer person. An individual's perspective on his model, his idealized real figure, is originally externally presented, but it becomes internalized, becomes the internal model of self-representation. Of course in earlier forms, an individual does not choose his figurative type: he is an instance of that type and must discover rather than choose his true identity. But later individuals are thought of as deciding on their figurative identity; with this shift from discovery to choice, we come to the concept of person.

Persons

Our idea of persons derives from two sources: one from the theater, the *dramatis personae* of the stage; the other has its origins in law. An actor dons masks, literally *per sonae,* that through which the sound comes, the many roles he acts. A person's roles and his place in the narrative devolve from the choices that place him in a structural system, related to others. The person thus comes to stand behind his roles, to select them and to be judged by his choices and his capacities to act out his personae in a total structure that is the unfolding of his drama.

The idea of a person is the idea of a unified center of choice and action, the unit of legal and theological responsibility. Having chosen, a person acts, and so is actionable, liable. It is in the idea of action that the legal and the theatrical sources of the concept of person come together. Only when a legal system has abandoned clan or family responsibility, and individuals are seen as primary agents, does the class of persons coincide with the class of biological individual human beings. In principle, and often in law, they need not. The class of persons may include what would, in other contexts, be institutions or corporations. Or an individual human being may be regarded as a host of personae, each of which is a distinct and unified agent, a locus of responsibility for a range of choices and actions.

If judgment summarizes a life, as it does in the Christian drama, then that life must have a unified location. Since they choose from their natures or are chosen by their stories, neither characters nor figures need be equipped with a will, not to mention a free will. Of course they can fail to do what they intend, and can intend to do less than they could perform. But the actions of characters and figures do not emerge from the exercise of a single faculty or power: there is no need for a single source of responsibility. But once there is the idea of judgment, especially if it is eternal judgment with heaven and hell and the whole person languishing there even if it is only a crucial part that has ailed or failed, then all that is various and loosely structured in the practice of assigning responsibility to diffuse character traits must be brought together and centered in a unified system, if not actually a unity. It is then that persons are required to unify the capacity for choice with the capacities for action.

Characters can be arranged along a continuum of powers and gifts, but personhood is an all-or-none attribution. One is either legally empowered or one isn't; one is either liable or not. Degrees of excusability can be granted only after liability is accepted. The Christian theological conception of judgment is obviously rooted in a legal context, one that, in its Roman origins, did not treat every human being as a person. As neither women nor slaves could originate suits, others had to act on their behalf. But of course when women and slaves are not legal persons, they are not persons either. Whatever rights and liabilities they had were theirs by virtue of their being sentient or by virtue of being members of a family. In fusing the legal and dramatic concepts of person, Christianity made every human being with a will qualify as a person, in order to make them all equally qualified to receive divine judgment. With this introduction of a conception of unitary and equal persons, Christianity at one stroke changed both the rule of law and the idea of persons.

Interest in the dispositional traits of characters is primarily social and practical; it is concerned with the allocation of responsibilities. Interest in persons is moral and legal, arising from problems in locating liability. This shift in the conception of agency carries a shift in the focal interest of moral education. In the eyes of God, persons are all alike; there is one ideal type by which all are judged. Of course any complex society must have a variety of roles to be filled: there must be the lives of the bakers and diggers, as well as that of the king. Their virtues and defects in these occupations, like their virtues and defects as sons and husbands, turn out to be incidental to their following the moral law. It is the formation of intention rather than the habits of action that are crucial to the moral education of a person. This separation marks the beginning of the separation of morality from practical life, duty from prudence. When the obligations entailed by social roles are distinct from moral obligations, a person's moral essence becomes completely internal and private. No longer is the internal model derived from the external type: the external type becomes judged by the internal motive.

Personal integrity or disintegration will of course be manifest in the tonality of actions and habits; nevertheless, it is the intention, the capacity for choice rather than the total configuration of traits that defines the person. Here the stage is set for identity crises, for wondering who one *really* is, behind the multifold variety of actions and roles. And the search for that core person is not a matter of curiosity: it is a search for the principles by which choices are to be made.

When the paradigms of persons are actors who choose their roles, a person is a player and worldliness consists of his ability to enact, with grace and aplomb, a great variety of roles. But when the paradigms for persons come from law rather than the theater, ownership becomes the mask of worldliness. The measure and scope of a person, his powers, lie in his ability to transform the lives of those around him. Initially, the powers of persons lay in their rights to sacred and ritual agency; these were tantamount to their political rights as well. But when property determines the right and power of agency and choice, persons become transformed into selves.

The two strands that were fused in the concept of person diverge again: when we focus on persons as sources of decisions, the ultimate locus of responsibility, the unity of thought and action, we come to think of them as souls and minds. When we think of them as possessors of rights and powers, we come to think of them as selves. It is not until each of these has been transformed into the concept of individuality that the two strands are woven together again.

Soul and Mind

Because persons are primarily agents of principle, their integrity requires freedom; because they are judged liable, their powers must be autonomous. But when this criterion for personhood is carried to its logical extreme, the scope of agency moves inward, away from social dramas, to the choices of the soul, or to the operations of the mind. What, after all, is it that is ultimately responsible, but only the will? It is the will that chooses motives, that accepts or rejects desires, principles. To the extent that such activities of the soul or the mind must remain autonomous, unconditioned, free, they are in principle indifferent not only to social class but to physical presence. To find the primary, uncaused cause of action—where that action is to be judged eternally liable—is to look for a simplicity and unity that is its own agency. The shadow of disembodiment that was implicit in the idea of a legal person moves forward, stands stage center: we have a person who is a pure *res cogitans* (or, in the religious versions, one that can survive death).

And it is here, of course, that the mind/body problems loom large, and that problems of individuation are seen as presenting moral and theological difficulties. For the theory of character, there is no expectation of individuation, no need for it. Nor did legal and dramatic persons need to be unique. But souls that are equal in the eyes of God, souls that can be disembodied, souls whose social history is detachable from their nature, have serious problems about choice. Without individual histories, they nevertheless condemn or save themselves. From character as structured dispositions, we come to soul as pure agency, unfathomable, inexpressible.

The Enlightenment version of this view gladly accepted the consequence of minimal individuation. It was an elegant way of assuring universality of rational discourse, even though the investigation began with a private act of introspective, reflective meditation. Mind became the clearest best self: the touchstone to the real, its reflections, the strongest certainties.

Selves

A person's place in society determines the range of his property and his rights in disposing of it; his status is determined not by his capacity to appropriate roles but by the roles that are considered appropriate to him. When a society has changed so that individuals acquire their rights by virtue of their powers, rather than having their powers defined by their rights, the concept of person has been transformed to a concept of self. At first, the primary real possession is that of land, and a person of substance is one of the landed gentry. But when a man's industry determines whether he is landed, the story of men's lives are told by their achievements rather than by their descent. The story of fulfilled ambition is shaped by an individual's capacity to amass goods, by the extent of his properties. The quality of an individual self is determined by his qualities: they are his capital, to invest well or foolishly.

Once an individual's properties and qualities are his possessions, rather than his essence, the problem of alienation can arise. The crises of personal identity center on the discovery of principles that essentially guide choices; the crises of self-identity center on the alienation of properties. Judgments of persons are moral; judgments of souls are theological; judgments of selves are economic and political. Societies of persons are constructed to assure the rights of choice and action; they emerge from a contract of agents; societies of selves are also formed to protect and guarantee the rights of their members. But when the members of a society achieve their rights by virtue of their possessions, the protection of rights requires the protection of property, even though in principle everyone is equally entitled to the fruits of his labors and protection under law.

Jane Austen describes a world of persons on the verge of becoming a world of selves. Her favored characters have a finely attuned sense of propriety, of their proper place. There are of course coarse and vulgar gentry; but an elevated sense of propriety, a sense of the niceties of what is due to each person arises initially from property. To be sure some people of great refinement live in genteel poverty. This marks the transition. Such people are the real gentry: gentry has become gentility. Delicate sensibility is allied with good sense in the avoidance of pretense. In the novel of sensibility we have the seeds of the novel of insight and consciousness; its full growth requires the conception of individuality.

The world that Trollope describes is one that has become a world of selves, many of whom are nostalgic for the world of persons. The property required for stature is no longer land, but an assured income. Rights and the ground of rights become transformed into obligations: an individual is entitled to what is owed to him. Individuals who claim obligations by virtue of their station, rather than by virtue of their qualities appear inflated and hollow; the old order is presented as comic.

The concerns of selves are their interests; their obligations are the duties with which they are taxed or charged. The grammar and the semantics of selfhood reveal the possessive forms. Whatever will come to be regarded as crucial property, or the means to it, will be regarded as the focus of rights; the alienation of property becomes an attack on the integrity if not actually the preservation of the self.

Metaphysical and epistemological analyses of the self make the conscious possession of experiences the final criterion of identity. The continuity of the self is established by memory; disputes about the validity of memory reports will hang on whether the claimant *had* as *hers*, the original experience. Puzzles about identity will be described as puzzles about whether it is possible to transfer or to alienate memory (that is, the retention of one's own experience) without destroying the self. In pathological terms, it is alienists who are charged with the therapy of those who suffer the loss of their identities because they have misplaced or lost their ultimate possession: their memories, whose just assessment is a guide to appropriate responses to experiences.

Societies of selves are liable to rapid social and economic change; they are expansive with the ideology if not the actuality of mobility. Although selves become ranked in a hierarchical order by their power and success, the older conception of the equality of persons remains latently present in the notion that everyone is equally entitled to make the most of himself. The conflict that is latent in this view, between the equal rights of persons and the unequal distribution of property (and therefore, in practice, of rights as well) by achieving selves, becomes more manifest as an expanding society tends to polarize goods, even while improving the general condition.

Metaphysically and epistemologically, the concept of the self also comes into stress. There is difficulty in describing the core possessor, the owner of experiences who is not herself any set of them. One can speak of characters as sets of traits without looking for a center; but it is more difficult to think of bundles of properties without an owner, especially when the older idea of the person as an agent and decision-maker is still implicit. It is presumed that the self as an owner is also endowed with capacities to choose and to act. It is in the search for a concept that will fuse the notion of inalienable properties and principles of rational choice that the concept of self is transformed into the concept of an individual.

Individuals

From the tensions in the definition of the alienable properties of selves, and from the corruptions in societies of selves—the divergence of practice from ideological commitments—comes the invention of individuality. It begins with conscience and ends with consciousness.

Unlike characters and figures, individuals actively resist typing: they represent the universal mind of rational beings, or the unique private voice. Individuals are indivisible entities: initially, they are defined against existing and presumably corrupt societies. Invented as a preserve of integrity, an autonomous *ens*, an individual transcends and resists what is binding and oppressive in society and does so from an original natural position. Although in its inception, individuality revives the idea of person, the rights of persons are formulated *in* society, while the rights of individuals are demanded *of* society. The contrast between the inner and outer person becomes the contrast between the individual and the social mask, between nature and culture.

A society of individuals is quite different from one composed of selves. Individuals contract to assure the basic rights to the development of moral and intellectual gifts, as well as legal protection of self and property. Because a society of individuals is composed of indivisible autonomous units, from whose natures—their minds and conscience—come the principles of justice, their rights are not property; they cannot be exchanged, bartered. Their rights and their qualities are their very essence, inalienable. Society's attempt to assure the development of persons comes to be seen as a possible source of corruption as well. Rousseau describes the dangerous duality of the powers of society: in the dialectic between individuality and community, there is the difficult balance between fulfillment and invasion. Society is at once the benefit and the misery of individuals who remain rudely unformed in nature, but become denaturalized in highly developed society. Rousseauean individuals implicitly give society far more power than the minimal contractual base granted by a Hobbesian person, because they add the right to the pursuit of happiness to the political rights of the protection of life and property.

There were, of course, earlier reforming theories: the moral authority that Luther located in an individual's relation to God only later came to rest in natural law. But that reformer's stance, the clear eye of the autonomy of conscience, universalizes at the same time that it forms an entity. Initially, there was no opposition between the individual and the universal: indeed the individual was the universal's ally against the social. It was through the individual that the universal could be voiced. Individuality, in that sense, has nothing to do with individuation and everything to do with integrity. Here we have the accounts of individuality given to us by Luther and Kant.

But once political and cultural reforms are effected, and the opposition between natural right and social malformation is blurred, once the society composed of autonomous individuals is formed, the individual can no longer define himself *against* a society that purports to be ruled by his voice, each legislating for all. What was only implicit in the idea of autonomy and self-formulation becomes dominant, and the quest for uniqueness begins its way toward frenzy. Initially, one's rightful and natural place is the particular stance one has on the world, the way in which social and historical forces exemplify themselves through the pinpoint of consciousness that is one's perspective, one's own vision. It is then that being an individual requires having a room of one's own, not because it is one's possession, but because only there, in solitude, away from the pressure of others, can one develop the features and styles that differentiate one's own being from others. Integrity comes to be associated with difference; this idea, always implicit in individuality, of preserving one's right against the encroachment of others within one's own society, emerges as dominant. From having been the source of moral insight, the individual shifts to being the self-reliant pioneer, an isolated being hewing out his place in the world, forming the perspective that is an individual's vision of the world. Conscientious consciousness is then the transparent eye that illuminates the substance of social life.

Insight, which was always the primary agency of individuality, becomes clarity of sight: we have Henry James and Virginia Woolf. At first the passion for clarity dominates, and the eye's self-forming action is so wholly absorbed in what it sees that it is all but unaware of seeing. But the pressure of differentiation in consciousness leads to that reflection on inwardness that leads the individual to a unique mode of sensibility. What is seen drops out and the passion for being the seer, eventually the passion for being *this* seer takes over. But when we have a sensibility in quest of a rightful definition, a character whose scope of action is simply to establish the uniqueness of its own perception, when the point of consciousness becomes a light rather than a power, then action is no longer agency, and the order of perceptions becomes arbitrary. From James, we move to Sartre, and from Woolf to Beckett. There is nothing to be alienated; everything could have been otherwise—and remained the same. Such wholly unique individuals become obsessed with the horrors of choice: they come to see themselves as the inventors of their own principles, inventors without purpose, direction, or form. Because they are defined by their freedom, they no longer choose from their natures but choose their identities. But since such choice is itself ungrounded, they are simply the act of choosing; their attempt to submerge themselves in their choices is a necessary act of bad faith.

The rugged indomitable survivors of hardships, the upright representative of social equality against the viciousness of social selves, the members of the Kingdom of Ends, Daniel Boone and Thoreau, figures of moral endurance, have become Molloy and Malone, monologues describing the wintry ending, the fading of the northern light.

The comic and grotesque forms establish the right to uniqueness down to the swirl of the last flourish of a thumbprint. This is the antithesis of figure: the zaniness of an individual soldier in the midst of an insane war: Yossarian in the army or Lucky Jim in academia. The body returns, insistent in its demands, language goes mad.

The comic forms, stretching as always they do toward sanity, cannot reach far enough. In the swirl of achieving individuality, the styles of speech flow loose, fall apart. Experiments with modes of type on a printed page are the representations of differentiated character. At its best, the insanity leads to Universal History again, and the voices of *Finnegans Wake*, each with its own pattern of breathing, blend into history. But it is a history whose forms are so large in scope, aeons and mountain ranges just nearby specks, that the mind swirls and dies of richness just as surely as it did of wintry cold.

Subjects

The tensions within selves and the dissolution of the individual reveals the subject as a field of conflict that distinguishes itself from all of its experiences, without being able to identify itself with anything. Sartre charts the paradoxes of consciousness as that which can only be aware of itself as having this-or-that content, indeed as being nothing else save the content before it, but that is nevertheless distinct from each of its experiences: "Consciousness is what it is not; and is not what it is."

The elusive "I" that constitutes itself by authentically acknowledging the arbitrariness of the experiences that form what identity it has is nevertheless also necessarily caught in bad faith: for even in attempting to identify itself with the pure act of reflection on its own emptiness, it implicitly attempts to reify itself as the act of reflection. When the "I" is not an object of experience, it is not an entity either. The next move is to recognize that the no-thing is nothing; and the move after that is to acknowledge "it" as Nothing attempting to objectify itself. If this sounds perilously like nonsense, that is, Sartre argues, because it is precisely that: non-sense, the absurd without sense. But that is how non-things are.

Consciousness as no-thing is pure act, pure freedom. Because it is unconditioned by its history or circumstances, it freely chooses or rejects its identity. This does not, of course, mean that a thirty-year-old, 300-pound Japanese weight-lifter can choose to *become* a seven-year-old Balinese dancer. The freedom of the subject as consciousness is not the freedom to determine the *en soi*, the fixed character of things that are objectively what they are. Nor is it the freedom of the will: for that is yet another reification. It is the freedom of choice, the freedom of the *pour soi* as nothing save the activity of reflection. In being free to consider himself as different from every detail of his body and history, the 300-pound Japanese weight-lifter is free to identify himself with the seven-year-old Balinese dancer. To be sure, such an identification is psychologically, as well as materially, an act of bad faith: not only is he not a Balinese dancer, but he cannot have the consciousness of a Balinese dancer. But then the decision to identify himself simply and solely as a Japanese weight-lifter is also an act of bad faith. He is the act of refusing or accepting this-or-that identity. But since he is also a Japanese weight-lifter, he would be in bad faith were he to claim he is nothing but his freedom.

The pure act of choice—the act that had been the person's selection of a role-mask, the self's control of property, the individual's political liberties—has become the act of self-definition. But persons are no longer identified by what is chosen—for that is utterly arbitrary—but by the unconditioned act of choosing. Yet since there is no correct way to choose—since neither history, nor physical constitution, nor utilitarian calculation, nor morality can guide choice—freedom and arbitrariness are mutually implied. When persons are self-creating novelists inventing the fictions of their identities, everything in their lives depends on their choices, because they are nothing else but those choices, even though it makes no difference what they choose. There is no salvation and no damnation, no moral fiendishness and no moral heroism. We choose—we must choose—our indignation and outrage: they define us.

Presences

And all along this while there has been The Russian Novel. Novels of a person tell a tale of development, of discovered responsibility, fulfilled or failed. A person's life has a form: it is continuous and unified. Myshkin or Alyosha are not persons: they are presences, the return of the unchartable soul. A Myshkin does not possess his experiences; but he does not choose his principles either. The details of their lives, the content of their experiences could have been quite different, and yet Myshkin or Alyosha would have been the same. They are a mode of attending, being present to their experiences, without dominating or controlling them. This is the antithesis of Sartrean consciousness-as-non-being-trying-to-objectify-itself. It is precisely the absence of willfulness, or choice of roles, of grace or enactment, swirl of action, that makes an

Alyosha present, with immense gravity and density, to his experiences. We can try to give character sketches of them, but we must fail; we can try to project their lives into the future, but they are presences to whom anything can happen. Transparent to their experiences, never holding themselves back, their lives are nevertheless not revealed on any surface. Their powers are always magnetic, always at service, but never centered. Though they are questers, there is nothing incomplete about them. Though others respond strongly to the quality of their presence, to something of the mood they induce, they are not agents. One rarely knows their occupations; whatever it is, it doesn't form them. Their psychological and physical characteristics are incidental to them. Though generally tortured, they are innocent and invulnerable though they may commit crimes of unspeakable horror. The figure of such presences is the Christian, the holy innocent.

Understanding other conceptions of persons puts one on the way of being them; but understanding presences—if indeed there is understanding of them to be had—does not put one any closer to being one. It cannot be achieved by imitation, willing, practice, or a good education. It is a mode of identity invented precisely to go beyond achievement and willfulness. Dostoyevsky paradigmatically, but occasionally Hardy, and (usually unsuccessfully) Lawrence present presences as endowments of grace received beyond striving.

And What Is Left?

What, one might well ask, is the point of this fast trip through history with a slanted *camera obscura*, catching persons in transforming attitudes? The distinctions that I have drawn are forced; most philosophers and novelists blend the notions that I have distinguished. One would hardly find a pure case: Locke tries to fuse the concept of self with that of individual; Kant borrows from everywhere. And of course as the inheritance becomes more complex, it becomes more difficult to separate the various layers, even in a purely analytic way. All of the concepts of identity that I have so briefly sketched remain as undercurrents in our lives, provide the norms by which we judge ourselves and others. Implicitly, they form our conceptions of the principles that ought to guide our choices. Our philosophical intuitions—the intuitions that guide our analyses of criteria for personal identity—have been formed by all these notions: they are the archeological layers on which our practices rest. As is obvious, they are latently in conflict; if we try to be all of them, conceiving of each as having the final obligation over us, we shall indeed be torn.

And society imposes conflicting roles on us as well. We are provided with paradigmatic figures, and at the same time exhorted to be individuals, as if these were in fact easily reconcilable; we intend to become unified persons and also achieved selves, as if these were easily harmonized. And our literature is a hodgepodge of nostalgia as well: much science fiction is an attempt to revive the early idea of individuality, to see figures of stature, half-earthlings of the future, to present a vivid ingenuity that will magically return to us our heroic Promethean selves. We have the nostalgia for Soul, and the depiction of figural identities and ironies of figural identities.

We have our sentimental returns to each of these views as well as our strategies of irony against each. Our literary moves play them off against one another in elaborate shifting patterns. Internally, we play ourselves off against one another in these patterns, sensing ourselves torn because we believe persons ought to be unified.

The concept of *person* now emerges as dominant in philosophic analysis and in social life—with the concept of individuality receding—precisely because these aspects of our history are in conflict, and because when we are torn, we cast about for that concept of identity that shores and anchors principles of choice. And it has always been the concept of a person that has unified action, that was concerned with choice.

Philosophers would very properly ask whether there is not, in all these various strands of agency and identity that I have so crudely sketched, one underlying notion, one that makes the transformation be the transformation of *one* concept? After all, it might be said that this is a history of the concept of person, with implicit guidelines for inclusion and exclusion. We have left out toads and toadstools, have followed the main pull of *a* history.

In a full treatment of this history, we would have discussed the links that connect one moment in the history to another, and have shown how the remnants of the earlier views remain latently present in later versions, sometimes in disguise and sometimes as providing tensed balances to a dominant theme. The important and interesting point is that the details of the transition and of the functions of the archeological traces are always different. Sometimes it is the development of an implicit contradiction that forwards the story, from self to individual; sometimes it is the force of political circumstance, the invasion of a foreign power; sometimes it is the wild invention of a novel, growing its hairshirt in private, caught and carried. There are indeed connecting links. But they are not an underlying substance. The connective and recessive tissue always have their own characters. It is always possible to distinguish the nostalgia for a form from its first appearance, the sentimental from the naive; but the distinction is not always drawn in the same place.

Perhaps one might look for a mock-Hegelian form that characterized all these shifts, the pattern of a dialectic. But Hegel knew that such a form is a mere abstraction; properly speaking the concept is not the form of the dialectic but its whole history, no more, no less. So indeed, there is sense to the objection: there is a concept of a person—there is our present concept of persons, and this (better and more fully told) is its history. So understanding "the" concept of a person is understanding history, just as understanding any particular individual is understanding *his* history.

If the objection demands that we provide an account of the internal unity of this history, of the preoccupations that any theory of persons must satisfy, an account of why the concept changed in the way it did, then it is indeed to the *regional* concept of a person that we turn. The concept of a person was, after all, invented to do just that: when we look for a *unity* of roles, or a single source of change, it is the concept of a person we want. But it would be a mistake to suppose that having analyzed the concept of *person*, we have uncovered the concept from which the others—character, self, individual—could in any sense be derived or unfolded. We have found the concept in that area which required a construction, a location for the unity of principles of choice and the principles of action. Naturally enough, if we try to fuse this concept with those that were constructed to provide continuity of genetic lineage, or to give an account of the patterning of character traits, we shall find just the sorts of puzzles that crop up whenever we have cross-classifications. This should cause no surprise; what *is* puzzling is that it should be supposed that conceptual analysis could, by itself, re-structure and reform these notions so that we could simply discover the "logical" relations among these concepts.

We should use the concept of a person just where it belongs, the area for locating the unity of choice, realizing that we have other preoccupations besides the unification of consciousness in memory or in the principles of choice. For instance, we might do well to focus on the analysis of the development of character traits, to inquire into the ways various traits support different conceptions of responsibility. In doing that, we move away from the agonies of self-definition, of strong personal identification, and turn to thinking about the sorts of traits of imagination and sociability that might be socially and politically beneficial. For this we would do well to concentrate less on persons and more on characters.

The theory of character has other important uses for us. Of all the concepts of persons, it is the one in which psychological and physiological traits are most closely linked. It is around the primacy of psychological and physiological continuity as criteria for personal identity that many controversies center. But more significantly, the outrageously skimpy and forced history of the concept of person that I have sketched is willful and incomplete because in the rush of telling the story, I have disconnected the concept of person from the concept of a human being, a certain sort of organism, not all of whose motives and needs are defined by its conception of itself. Though the concept of a person is, in the larger sense, given by its history, it nevertheless is also closely inter-woven with a nonhistorical concept, one that gives it its natural and biological base. The theory of character is a natural context for the investigation of the connection between the biological base of the concept of persons and its historical transformations.

The issue of whether the class of persons exactly coincides with the class of biologically defined human beings—whether corporations, Ve-nusians, mongolian idiots, and fetuses are persons—is in part a conceptual question. It is a question about whether the relevant base for the classification of persons requires attention to whether things look like "us," whether they are made out of stuff like "ours," or whether it is enough that they function as we take "ourselves" to function. If Venusians and robots come to be thought of as persons, at least part of the argument that will establish them will be that they function as we do: that while they are not the *same* organisms that we are, they are in the appropriate sense the same *type* of organism or entity. Does an entity have to be an organism to be a person? When is a well-organized, self-sustaining entity an organism?

Of course there may be a time when Venusians and robots are called persons by science fiction writers and philosophers and by no one else. The question of the personhood of Venusians and robots becomes serious when we actually start raising questions about their legal rights and obligations. It is a very complex matter: if Venusians and robots come increasingly to be treated as persons are now treated, their inclusion in the class will come to modify our conceptions and treatment of human organisms. Treating ourselves as of the same type as Venusians will gradually and subtly come to affect leading questions and presuppositions about the nature of an organism. But there is no point speculating about what we shall say in transitional periods, and certainly none in legislating in advance what we shall decide. Whether we shall, when the time comes, classify Venusians as persons will certainly depend on what they are like, on whether we like them, and on our political and social preoccupations when the issue becomes a live one.

Humans are just the sorts of organisms that interpret and modify their agency through their conceptions of themselves. This is a complicated biological fact about us. Whether there are other sorts of entities that do this is in part but not wholly an empirical question. The fullest analysis of the concept of person would investigate the biologically adaptive functions of the various cultural grafts: the obsessions with unification and choice, salvation and simplicity, isolated integrity and achievement. From this larger perspective, we might be able to see how the cultural history of the various versions of the concept of a person has been modified by and has in turn modified its biological base.

2 PSYCHOLOGICAL ACTIVITIES

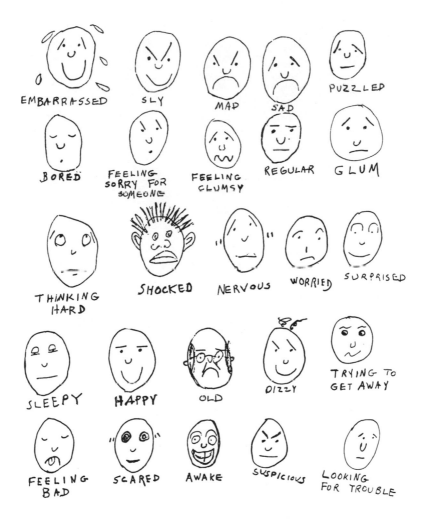

JACOB KOSMAN

Contemporary discussions of the emotions, of desire and rationality, of imagination and choice, suffer from their inheritance: they are shadowed by a speculative psychology originally constructed to provide a foundation for an idealized epistemology. Distinctions between the faculties were designed to substantiate the possibility of an autonomously self-corrective rationality, not only capable of correcting beliefs and inferences, but also (at least in principle) capable of correcting irrational desires and emotions. In this idealized model of psychological activities, the emotions were an embarrassment: on the one hand, they were treated as noncognitive invasions or disturbances; on the other, they were sometimes treated as sound motivational functions, susceptible to a program of rational reform or correction.

The papers in this section undermine the traditional distinctions among the faculties: they present analyses of a number of psychological activities—love, jealousy, the fear of death, self-knowledge—to show that they are all cognitive, motivational, and affective. Instead of treating psychological and intellectual activities as occurrent states, attitudes toward propositionalizable contents, I propose to treat them as processes or activities, individuated, at least in part, by their psychological origins and functions. I also want to trace social contributions to the formation of psychological activities, the ways that the minutiae of interactions enter into the individuation of psychological activities.

5   Explaining Emotions

Sometimes our emotions change straightaway when we learn that what we believed is not true. The grieving husband recovers when he learns that, because she missed her plane, his wife did not die in the fatal plane crash. But often changes in emotions do not appropriately follow changes in belief. Their tenacity, their inertia, suggests that there is akrasia of the emotions; it reveals the complex structure of their intentionality.[1]

I want to examine the strategies we use to explain cases of unexpected conservation of emotions: those that seem to conflict with a person's judgments and those that appear to have distorted our perceptions and beliefs, making them uncharacteristically resistant to change or correction.[2] I shall begin with complex cases, so that we will be forced to uncover layers of explanation that need not normally be brought into play in what are taken to be the standard cases. When people act or react in ways that can be explained by reasonable beliefs and desires, we tend to suppose that these beliefs and desires are the causes of their behavior. We then try to construct our explanations of the more complex cases, using only what was necessary to explain the simple ones. Not surprisingly, we often then find that we are left with bizarre cases at the margins of our theory: self-deception, akrasia, and the irrational conservation of emotions. By beginning with fringe cases, we may find the more complex structures that underlie the apparently straightforward cases but that are difficult to discern when everything is going as we expect. One of the difficulties of our enterprise is that of specifying the psychological principles that rationalize a person's beliefs and desires, his interpretations and responses. When an emotion appears to be anomalous, and its explanation requires tracing its etiology, it is difficult to identify the intentional object of the emotion without constructing its rationale, if not actually its justification. But accurately describing a person's beliefs and attitudes, especially when they involve akrasia or the apparently inappropriate conservation of the emotions, often involves attributing false beliefs, apparently irrational intentional sets.[3] Sometimes it is implausible and inaccurate to explain an inappropriate attitude by attributing a belief or desire that would rationalize it, because the apparently anomalous emotion is embedded in a system of other inappropriate attitudes or false beliefs. Yet explaining a person's condition requires tracing its causal history, reconstructing the details of a ramified, gradually changing intentional system of attitudes, beliefs, habits of attention, and focusing. Constructing the causal history often involves reconstructing a rationale: the problem is to determine at what point in that history to apply some modified version of the principle of charity.[4] Often it is accurately applied only quite far back in the person's psychological history, to explain the formation of prepropositional but intentional habits of salience, organization, and interpretation. It is these that, through later intervening beliefs and attitudes—many of them false and inappropriate—explain the conservation of emotions. When so applied, the principle of charity is modified: it accounts for the coherent appropriateness of the *formation* of a person's intentional system without maximizing agreement on the number of true beliefs. It is not the belief or emotion that is rationalized, but a person's coming to have it.

Emotions do not form a natural class. A set of distinctions that has generally haunted the philosophy of mind stands in the way of giving good descriptions of the phenomena. We have inherited distinctions between being active and being passive; between psychological states primarily explained by physical processes and psychological states not reducible to nor adequately explained by physical processes; distinctions between states that are primarily nonrational and those that are either rational or irrational; between voluntary and nonvoluntary states. Once these distinctions were drawn, types of psychological activities were then parceled out *en bloc* to one or another side of the dichotomies. That having been done, the next step was to argue reclassification: to claim that perception is not passive but active, or that the imagination has objective as well as subjective rules of association. Historically, the list of emotions has expanded as a result of these controversies. For instance, the opponents of Hobbes, wanting to secure benevolence, sympathy, and other disinterested attitudes as counterbalances to self-interest, introduced them as sentiments with motivational power. Passions became emotions and were classified as activities. When the intentionality of emotions was discussed, the list expanded still further: *ressentiment*, aesthetic and religious awe, anxiety and dread were included. Emotions became affects or attitudes. As the class grew, its members became more heterogeneous, the analysis became more ambiguous, and counterexamples were explained away by charges of self-deception.

When we focus on their consequences on behavior, most emotions can also be described as motives;[5] some—but not all—emotions can also be described as feelings, associated with proprioceptive states. The objects of some emotions—exuberance, melancholy—are difficult to specify; such global states verge toward being moods.[6] Still other emotions come close to being dispositional character traits: we speak of vengeful or affectionate persons. But when we speak of a psychological state as an emotion, contrasting it to feelings, motives, moods, or character traits, we focus on the ways we are affected by our appraisals, evaluative perceptions, or descriptions.[7]

The causal history of our emotions, the significant events that form our habits of response, affects our conceptions of their objects. There are three closely interwoven strands in that causal history: (1) the formative events in a person's psychological past, the development of patterns of intentional focusing and salience, habits of thought and response; (2) the socially and culturally determined range of emotions and their characteristic behavioral and linguistic expressions; and (3) a person's constitutional inheritance, the set of genetically fixed threshold sensitivities and patterns of response. Because the social and genetic factors were assumed to be shared or invariable, their effects always appearing within a person's psychological history, we have treated them, when we focused on them at all, as fixed background conditions. But they are essential to the full account, and often critical in explaining apparent anomalies: their contribution to that explanation does not simply reduce to a variant of individual psychological explanation.[8] I shall, however, abstract from the social and genetic factors, and concentrate on the intentional components in the formation of a person's individual emotional dispositions.

Causes, Objects, Targets

Jonah, a newswriter, resents Esther, his editor, whom he thinks domineering, even tyrannical. But as bosses go, Esther is exceptionally careful to consult with the staff, often following consensus even when it conflicts with her judgment. His colleagues try to convince Jonah that Esther's assignments are not demeaning, her requests not arbitrary. Jonah comes to believe he was mistaken in thinking her actions dictatorial; he retreats to remarking that she derives secret pleasure from the demands that circumstances require. Where his colleagues see a smile, he sees a smirk. After a time of working with Esther, Jonah realizes that she is not a petty tyrant, but he still receives her assignments with a dull resentful ache; and when Anita, the new editor, arrives, he is seething with hostility even before she has had time to settle in and put her family photographs on her desk. Although many of the women on the secretarial staff are more hard-edged in mind and personality than either Esther or Anita, he regards them all as charmingly endowed with intuitive insight. He patronizes rather than resents them.

To understand Jonah's plight, we need distinctions. We are indebted to Hume for the distinction between the object and the cause of emotions. But that distinction needs to be refined before we can use it to understand Jonah's emotional condition. In the case of the husband who believed his wife had been killed in a plane crash, the precipitating or immediate cause of the man's grief is hearing a newscast announcing the fatal crash of the plane his wife intended to take. But of course the newscast has such a powerful effect on him because normally such news stories are themselves effects of the significant cause of his grief: her death in the fatal plane crash. Often when we find emotions puzzling, it is because we do not see why the immediate cause should have such an effect.

The significant cause of an emotion is the set of events—the entire causal history—that explains the efficacy of the immediate or precipitating cause. Often the significant cause is not in the immediate past; it may be an event, or a series of events, long forgotten, that formed a set of dispositions that are triggered by the immediate cause. Tracing the full causal story often involves more than locating initial conditions or identifying immediate causes: it requires analyzing the magnetizing effects of the formation of our emotional dispositions, habits of thought, as well as habits of action and response.[9] Magnetizing dispositions are dispositions to gravitate toward and to create conditions that spring other dispositions. A magnetized disposition to irascibility not only involves a set of specific low thresholds (e.g., to frustration or betrayal) but also involves looking for frustrating conditions, perceiving situations as frustrating. It not only involves wearing a chip on one's shoulder but involves looking for someone to knock that chip off. Magnetizing dispositions need not by themselves explain actions or attitudinal reactions: they can do so indirectly, by characterizing the type of beliefs, perceptions, and desires a person is likely to have. Such traits determine actions and reactions by determining the selective range of a person's beliefs and desires.[10] The genesis of a magnetizing disposition need not always lie in an individual's particular psychophysical history; such dispositions are often acquired, along with other characteristically culture-specific intentional sets and motives, as part of a person's socialization. It is because significant causes often produce magnetizing dispositions that they are successful in explaining the efficacy of the immediate causes of an emotion: they explain not only the response but the tendencies to structure experience in ways that will elicit that characteristic response.

In order to understand the relation between the immediate and the significant cause, we need refinements in the account of the objects of the emotions. The immediate object of an emotion is characteristically intentional, directed: it refers to objects under descriptions that cannot be substituted *salva affectione*.[11] Standardly, the immediate object not only is the focus of the emotion but is also taken by the person as providing its ground or rationale. The immediate target of the emotion is the object extensionally described and identified. I shall refer to a person's emotion-grounding description of the target as *the intentional component of the emotion*, to his having that description as his *intentional state*, and to the associated magnetized disposition as his *intentional set*. Of course a person need not be able to articulate the intentional component of his emotions. Ascriptions of emotion, like ascriptions of belief, are inferences to the best explanation.[12]

A person's intentional set may fail to ground the emotion because the target does not in fact have the relevant properties, or because it does not have them in the configuration with the centrality that would ground the emotion, or because it does not in fact exist: the description does not succeed in referring. The difficulties of ascribing intentional states and those of referring in opaque contexts are no more (and no less) devastating in ascribing emotions than they are elsewhere.[13] When an otherwise perceptive and reasonable person widely and persistently mis-describes matters or persistently responds in a way that apparently con-flicts with his beliefs, we first try standard strategies for explaining misperceptions and errors. Sometimes, indeed, we persuade a person that his emotion is unfounded; and sometimes this is sufficient for the emotion to change.

When an emotion remains intractable or an anomalous intentional set persists, we suspect that the emotion is rooted in habits of selective attention and interpretation whose activation is best explained by tracing them back to the significant causes of a magnetized disposition.[14] The causal story of that formation can take several forms. For instance, we might suspect that Jonah resents Esther because he now is, or once was, resentful of his mother. In such cases his mother may be the (acknowl-edged or unacknowledged) target of his emotions, and Esther only the front for that target. But Jonah's mother need not be the explanatory target—acknowledged or not—of Jonah's emotion; she may simply have been a crucial part of the significant cause of Jonah's magnetized dis-position to structure and interpret situations by locating some female figure whom he sees as hostile and domineering, a figure who, so seen, grounds his resentment. Which of the various alternatives best explains Jonah's condition is a matter for extended investigation; we would have to examine a wide range of Jonah's responses, interpretations, and emotions under different conditions. In any case, our best explanatory strategy is: When in doubt about how the immediate target and precipitating cause explain the emotion, look for the significant cause of the dispositional set that forms the intentional component of the emotion.[15]

Habits and Intentional Sets

To see how finding the significant cause can help us reconstruct the rationale of the intentional component of the emotion, we need to examine the composition of the significant cause. An important part of the history of Jonah's condition will show us what we need.

Not only does Jonah regard women in high places with resentment and hostility, but he also suffers from nightmares and, sometimes, from obsessive terrors. Both have a recurring theme: his mother is trying to kill him. Moreover, he loathes scarves, refusing to wear them even in the coldest, dampest weather. No matter what wonderful things have just happened to him, he breaks into an anxious sweat when he walks through the scarf section at Woolworth's. His mother, a gruff, brusque woman, used to swathe him in scarves that she knitted herself. But she always bought the itchiest wool imaginable; and when she bundled him up in winter, she used to tie the scarf with a swift harsh motion, pulling it tightly around his throat. She had never come close to trying to kill him. She was in fact an affectionate woman, but an awkward one. Certainly she was occasionally ambivalent, and sometimes exasperated and angry. It was because Jonah was sensitive to the negative undertones of her attitudes (a sensitivity that had an explanation of its own) that he felt the pressure of the scarf as painful rather than as reassuring or comforting.

To understand what has happened to Jonah, we must examine several components of the significant causes of his nightmares, phobias, terrors. When children remember events as attacks, they may be picking up genuine undercurrents in the behavior of those around them. Adults often behave with hostility without attacking, seductively without trying to seduce. Because children are unable to place the undercurrents they discern in the context of a person's whole psychological character, they magnify what frightens them. But the "fantasy" often rests on something perceived. Perception, magnified or distorted interpretation, and fantasy shade off into one another, often in ways that can only be distinguished with the benefit of theory-laden hindsight.

But let us suppose that what Jonah's mother did would not in itself have been sufficient to form his emotional dispositions. His perceptions of the attitudes that determined her manner toward him are essential ingredients in the causal story of his condition. There were not two events, two significant causes: the tying of the scarf and the tying of it in a way that pained Jonah. In such situations it is often necessary not only to identify the significant cause by an extensional description (scarf tied at speed so-and-so, pressure so-and-so), but also to see it through the eyes of the beholder. When we understand that both components of the significant cause—the scarf tightly tied and Jonah's feeling that tying as painful—are fused in the forming of Jonah's emotional dispositions, we can see how locating the significant cause can help us reconstruct the emotion-grounding description that links the intentional component of Jonah's emotion to its immediate cause and target.

Because the intentional component of the significant cause and the intentional component of the apparently anomalous emotion do not always fall under the same description, it is not always as easy to identify the intentional component of the significant cause of the emotion as, in this post-Freudian age, it has been easy to locate, almost without stopping to think, the intentional object—and even in this case, the explanatory target—of Jonah's emotion. Nor need the significant cause involve a particular set of events that fused and formed the person's magnetized dispositions, the patterns of salience and attention. The causal story is likely to involve idiosyncratic beliefs and associations, many difficult to recover or articulate. In any case, our motto can now be made more precise: When in doubt about the rationale of an emotion, look for the intentional component of the significant cause of the dispositional set that forms the intentional component of the emotion.

But we are not yet through explaining Jonah's condition, for we do not yet have an account of his tendency to focus on the minimally harsh manner of his mother's scarf-tying ways, his interpretating her actions as hostile. It might seem as if we have reintroduced our original problem—the problem of explaining an anomalous emotional reaction—at an earlier stage. Jonah's perceiving his mother as hostile is an essential part of the significant cause of his phobias and his troubles with lady bosses. Nevertheless, if only Jonah and not his brother Abednego has this intentional set, although Abednego was also tightly swathed in itchy scarves, we have not got the significant cause in all its glory: though our explanation is fuller, it is not yet complete.

To understand why the usually perceptive Jonah so misperceived his mother's attitudes, I must tell you more of his story.

Jonah was the eldest of the children. During his childhood, his father the Major was given army leave only to return home for short visits. At an appropriate time after one of these visits, Abednego was born. Since his mother was on her own at the time, Jonah was sent off to stay with his adored grandfather while his mother was in the hospital. Now the truth of the matter is that the adored grandfather loathed his daughter-in-law, whom he saw as a domineering, angry woman, the ruination of his son. Without intending to do so, Jonah's grandfather conveyed these attitudes to Jonah, who at that time was apprehensive of losing his mother's affections. Susceptible to the influence of a figure who represented his absent father, he found in his grandfather's attitudes the confirmation and seal of what might have been a passing mood. His grandfather's perspective became strongly entrenched as his own.

We now have an account of why a reasonable person might, in a perfectly reasonable way, have developed an intentional set that, as it happens, generates wildly askew interpretations and reactions.[16] But have we found a stopping place, thinking we've explained an anomalous attitude simply because we have come to a familiar platitude? Perhaps: that is a risk explanations run; but if we have stopped too soon, at a place that requires further explanation, we can move, whenever the need arises, farther back in the causal story. And indeed, we may want explanations of reactions that are not at all anomalous: we can ask why an accurate perception or a true belief has the form it does, why a person focused on matters *this* way rather than that.

Jonah's persistent and transferable resentment might have his mother as its hidden target, even though it was his grandfather, rather than his mother, who was the significant cause of his emotional dispositions. But causes, objects, and targets are complex. Jonah might resent Esther's commanding ways, yet find himself with a childlike longing for her approval. Esther is the immediate object of both his resentment and his longing: but it is what he perceives as her commanding manner that is the focus of his resentment, and her attention and approval that are the focus of his longing. Similarly, the hidden target of Jonah's attitudes toward Esther may be his mother, but the focus of that target is (his perception of) her elusive and abrupt manner. Understanding the focus of Jonah's attitudes toward the hidden target—the target that was once the object of the emotion that formed his dispositional attitudes—not only explains the conservation of his inappropriate emotions, but also the selection and focus of those emotions. We understand why, for example, Jonah is resentful rather than depressed or frightened, and why he is resentful of her commanding ways rather than of the fact that she is considerably taller than he is. Though the focus of the hidden target is sometimes encoded and transformed, we can in principle reconstruct the rationale of the patterns and the persistence of Jonah's otherwise puzzlingly irrational attitudes.

The principle of charity is now seen to be very general in scope. Characteristically, it is best applied to the intentional components of the significant causes of magnetizing dispositions, where it accounts for a range of attitudes and beliefs (without necessarily maximizing agreement on truth), rather than to individual episodic beliefs. Moreover, its use presupposes not only that we have a certain gravitational attraction toward truth but that we are also endowed with a wide range of psychological dispositions that determine the ways in which we acquire and change our beliefs and attitudes. These dispositions are quite varied: some are neurophysiological determinants of perceptual salience (e.g., red being more salient than gray under standard background and contrast conditions); others are psychological in character (e.g., the dominance order of emotions under standard conditions: fear displacing and reorganizing the emotional field in characteristic patterns); still others are psychosocial (e.g., the effects of mass hysteria or the presence of a schizophrenic on a person's schema of intentional sets). In short, when we try to apply the principle of charity to those places where it best explains and identifies the range of our attitudes, its canonic formulation is so modified as to disappear as a special principle.

But having come to the end of Jonah's story, have we come to the end of an account of how we explain emotions? Our questions seem now to multiply: Will we, in tracing the significant cause to an appropriate stopping point, always still introduce an intentional component of the significant cause? Are we to interpret young Jonah's tendency to take on the intentional set of a figure who stands in a certain relation to him as itself an intentional set? Or do significant causes of magnetizing dispositions sometimes have no intentional component of their own? We do not know enough about the neurophysiology and psychology of early learning to know what constraints should be set on our philosophical theory. In any case, an account of the etiology of the intentional components of emotional dispositions is nestled within a general psychological theory: it is inseparable from theories of perception and theories of motivation. The holistic character of mental life makes piecemeal philosophical psychology suspect.

Since airtight arguments have vacuous conclusions, it would be folly to stop speaking at the point where we must start speculating.

There are good, but by no means conclusive, reasons for recognizing a gradation between beliefs or judgments in propositional form and quasi-intentions that can also be physically or extensionally identified. Let us distinguish

1. Beliefs that can be articulated in propositional form, with well-defined truth conditions.
2. Vague beliefs in sentential form whose truth or satisfaction conditions can be roughly but not fully specified ("It is better to have good friends

than to be rich" or "Men in Islamic countries tend to have sexist attitudes").

3. Specific patterns of intentional salience that can be formulated as general beliefs. (A pattern of focusing on aspects of women's behavior construed as domineering or hostile rather than as competent or insecure might in principle be treated as a set of predictions about the behavior of women under specific conditions.)

4. Intentional sets that cannot be easily formulated as beliefs. (A pattern of focusing on the military defensibility of a landscape, rather than on its fertility or aesthetic composition, cannot be easily formulated as a set of predictions about the benefits of giving priority to military defense over fertility or aesthetic charm. Nor can such patterns of salience be translated straightforwardly as preference rankings. For instance, a painter can focus on patterns of color in a landscape rather than on its compositional lines, but the patterns and habits of his attending are quite distinct from his preferences.)

5. Quasi-intentional sets that can, in principle, be fully specified in physical or extensional descriptions (e.g., other things being equal, painful sensations are standardly more salient than pleasurable ones).

For such intentional sets—patterns of discrimination and attention—the question of whether the significant cause of a magnetized intentional set has an irreducibly intentional component is an open one. Such quasi-intentional components form patterns of focusing and salience without determining the description of that pattern. A quasi-intentional set (patterns of perceptual salience under standard conditions of contrast and imprinting) can be given both physical and intentional descriptions; in some contexts, the physicalistic descriptions can function in an explanation, without any reference to the intentional description. But in other contexts, particularly those that move from functional explanations toward interpretive or rational accounts, the intentional description is essential. Often the intentional and the quasi-intentional component of the significant cause of magnetized interpretive dispositions is ambiguous in this way: we tend to read the intentional component back into the significant cause when doing so helps rationalize the person's responses. But the intentional set that is introduced at that stage often bears a causal rather than a directly logical relation to the magnetized set produced. (The quasi-intentional set that made Jonah prone to adopt his grandfather's interpretations at just that time bears a causal but not a logical relation to the intentional set he acquired as a result of this sensitivity. But the connections between the intentional set he acquired from his grandfather and the intentional set that leads him to see Esther as domineering are logical as well as causal.)

In such cases there are physiological generalizations about the quasi-intentional states under their extensional descriptions. Although the opacity criteria for intentionality do not yet apply, it is useful to recognize that such selective sensitivities are oriented to a stimulus under a description that later does function in its fully intentional form. Holistic considerations influence us: the wider the range and the greater the complexity of behavior that is best explained by the intentional act in its fully intentional form, the more likely we are to treat the significant cause as having that intentional component, even though it need not, in its original appearance, have then functioned in its fully intentional form. (For instance, a child can be frightened by a clap of thunder without initially having an intentional set to interpret such sounds as danger signals. If he is ill and feverish, hearing loud sounds is painful, and, if he is generally in a weak and fearful condition, he can develop a fully intentional sensitivity, becoming frightened of thunder because he has been frightened by it).

Objections

One might wonder: Why do we need these distinctions descending like a plague to devour every living thing, transforming a once fertile plain into a desert? Why can't we explain intractable, inappropriate emotions more simply and elegantly by specifying the relevant belief that fixes the description of the target? Perhaps what explains Jonah's resentment is that he thinks figures in authority are likely to be, or to become authoritarian. Although such beliefs or judgments are occasionally interesting and true, it is sometimes difficult to ascribe the appropriate plausible belief. Jonah does not resent Abe Zloty, the editor-in-chief, though Zloty is far more peremptory than Esther. It seems more plausible to ascribe to him the belief that when women are in a position of authority, they become insufferably authoritarian. But Jonah is a skeptical sort of fellow, who rarely leaps to generalizations, let alone wild ones. Often when we don't understand an emotion, or its intractability, we also don't understand why the person should have and hold the belief that is its intentional component. The belief explains the emotion only by subsuming its intentionality in a more general frame.

But our objector persists, claiming that in tracing the etiology of an emotion, intentional sets and quasi-intentions are unnecessarily complex ways of talking about beliefs or evaluative judgments. If we judge emotions for their rationality, they argue, then some belief must either be presupposed by, or embedded in, the emotion. The correction of emotions generally involves the correction of the mistaken belief.

Certainly many cases do follow such a pattern; and certainly some emotions can be identified by the full-blown beliefs that are also a part of their causal explanation. But the issue is whether the intentional component of an emotion always is a belief, and whether there are emotions that are more properly evaluated as inappropriate or harmful than as irrational.

If the intentional component of an emotion is always a belief, then the conservation of an emotion after a change of belief would always involve a conflict of beliefs. Now this may indeed sometimes occur; but often the only evidence that the person retains the abandoned belief is his emotional state. One of the reasons for resisting assimilating all intentional components of emotions to beliefs is the difficulty of stating what the belief is. There is sometimes no non-question-begging way of formulating a proposition p, where "inserting p in the sentence 'S believes that ——' would express the fact that the subject was in that state."[17]

A person may not only deny having the abandoned belief but (with the exception of the episode in question) consistently act in a way that supports the denial. On the view that emotions always involve beliefs, it becomes necessary to suppose that the person is massively successful in deceiving himself about the conflict between the belief embedded in the emotion and the belief implicit in the rest of his conduct. This is certainly a recognizable and even common phenomenon. It seems implausible, however, to assimilate all cases of the conservation of emotions to cases that involve a self-deceptive denial of such conflicts. No doubt much conservation is to be explained by ambivalence, and at least some ambivalence is to be understood as involving conflicting judgments, with the person deceiving himself about at least one side of a divided mind.[18] But unless the claim is to be question-begging, the conservation of emotions cannot *automatically* count as grounds for attributing self-deception. Characteristically, self-deception involves quite distinctive behavior: signs of facial malaise, frozen features, certain sorts of systematic failures in action.[19]

Even if it were the case that—in a much revised and extended sense of belief—the intentional components of emotions were beliefs, the distinctions we have drawn would have to be reintroduced to differentiate the ways in which a person accepts or uncharacteristically ignores or refuses counterevidence. The phenomena of the conservation of emotion would then reappear as the anomalous conservation of belief. To explain such conservation, we would once again have to return to the ravenous hordes of distinctions between the immediate and the significant causes of magnetized intentional states; we would have to introduce beliefs that could not be attributed in propositional form. Explaining the anomalous conservation of belief, or its resistance to considerations or observations that would characteristically change it, would lead us to exactly the same sort of schema of causal explanation that we use in understanding the conservation of emotions.

There are objections from other quarters. Nowhere does the mind/body problem raise its ugly head with a stiffer neck than in the analysis of the thought component of the emotions. In some cases, it might be said, the significant cause isn't significant at all. It casts no light on the rationale of the intentional component of an emotion because there is no rationale. (In the narrative epilogue at the end of *War and Peace*, Tolstoi describes the emotional condition of the aged Countess Rostoff. She needs, he says—and he suggests that this is also a physiological need—to become angry, melancholy, merry, peevish, to express the cycle of her emotional repertoire every few days. Usually the family manages to arrange matters in such a way so as to give her emotional life an air of appropriateness. But sometimes this cannot be done, and she becomes peevish in a situation in which she is normally merry. Tolstoi remarks that in infancy and old age—and we might add: in adolescence—the apparent reasonableness that we believe really conditions our adult emotional life wears thin, and emotions reveal a rhythm and pattern of their own. Tolstoi does not, unfortunately, go on to speculate whether the independent rhythm of the emotions is merely disguised in our prime, indiscernible beneath our bustling intention-directed activity, or whether it is precisely this difference that makes the emotional life of infants and the senile different from our own, that their emotions are merely coincidentally associated with the appropriate intentions.) When a person suffers from a hormonal imbalance, his emotions have one target after another, none intentionally linked to the intentional component of a significant cause. When we look for the explanation of a recalcitrant inappropriate emotion, there is sometimes no need to look deeply into the etiology of the intention: the state of the person's endocrine system is explanation enough.[20] The best thing to do with this objection is to accept it gracefully. It is after all true.

But we must be careful not to conclude too much. From the fact that the best explanation of a person's emotional state may sometimes be that he suffers glandular malfunction, it does not follow that, under standard conditions, explanations of emotions can be given without any appeal to beliefs or intentional states.[21] Most physicalistically oriented theories fill in their accounts by tracing the causal interaction between the *sorts* of physical states that are associated with being in an emotionally charged condition (generally metabolic states) with the sorts of physical states that are associated with a person's having propositional attitudes (generally brain states).[22] Such physicalists do not, however, claim to be able to identify the propositional content of a person's attitudes solely by reference to physically described brain states. On this view, we would not expect to find strict physicalistic laws distinguishing Jonah's perceiving-Esther-as-Slavic and his perceiving-Esther-as-Semitic.

The hard-core physicalist goes farther: he proposes to identify psychological states as states whose descriptions eliminate all reference to intentional states and their propositional content, distinguishing Jonah's believing Esther to be bossy from his believing her to be vain, by specifying the differences in the brain states that constitute the two beliefs. It seems at the very least premature to present the results of what is an extended and only projected program of research as having provided the explanations we need, especially as zealot physicalists have yet to give us an account of how to proceed with the reductive analysis. So far, all we have are science-fiction stories about possible worlds in which the reductive analysis has taken place, "what scientists somehow discovered" already become part of the popular culture. Until the theory is established, all the physicalist account of the emotions adds to the intentional account is the important observation that, when the best explanation of a person's emotional state is primarily physiological, then raising questions about the causal force of the intentional object may produce arbitrary ad hoc answers. There may be a revealing pattern in the immediate causes or objects of an adrenally charged person's various aggressive angers, but sometimes that pattern is best explained by tracing the effects of chemical changes on perception and attention.

This suggests that, for at least these sorts of cases, the physicalist and the intentionalist accounts of anomalous emotions are perfectly compatible and perhaps even complementary, physicalistically oriented theories explaining why a person is in *that* state, intentionalistically oriented theories explaining why the emotion has *that* intentional object. They appear to be at odds only when both theories get reductionally ambitious: when, denying overdetermination, each tries to explain all phenomena at all levels. Certainly if the intentional accounts deny that a person's hormonal state ever enters into the explanation, and if the physicalistic account denies that intentionality is ever required to explain or identify the emotional states, the two approaches will clash in an unilluminating struggle whose sterility will be masked by the parties goading each other to dazzling displays of ingenuity.[23]

Does it follow that both levels of explanation, the physiological and the intentional, are necessary, but neither sufficient? The situation is (un)fortunately more complex. The physiological and the intentional aspects of our emotions do not enter into all emotions in the same way.

The difference between a distaste for malicious gossip in departmental politics and the terror of waking after a nightmare whose drama one has already forgotten, the difference between nostalgia-for-the-lilacs-of-yesteryear and fear in the face of a powerful danger, are differences in kind.

Some emotions are primarily associated with physical states largely affected by metabolic imbalance: malfunctions of the pituitary or adrenal glands are associated with highly specific emotional disorders, leaving the rest of a person's emotional dispositions relatively intact. Other, quite different sorts of emotional disorders are associated with some sorts of brain damage rather than with endocrinological malfunction.[24] Still other sorts of emotions—such culturally variable ones as nostalgia or Sunday melancholy—seem difficult to associate with any particular physical condition. While the introduction of intentional apparatus seems forced in some cases, the introduction of physiological determinants is forced in others.

Explanation, Change, and Rationality

> We can expect three things from the study of history: the sheer pleasure of knowing particulars; useful precepts for the important matters of life; and furthermore because the origins of things recur in the present from the past, we acquire the best understanding of all things from a knowledge of their causes.
>
> Leibniz, Preface to *Accessiones Historicae*

The conservation of emotions has its explanation in the conservation of habit, especially of those magnetized dispositions involved in selective attention and focused interpretation. We have concentrated primarily on that aspect of a person's psychological history which explains the formation of his characteristic intentional habits. But social and genetic factors also contribute to the causal story; the full account of the conservation of emotional habits would have to introduce these determinants as well. The three layers of explanation—the individual, the social, and the genetic—are closely interwoven. A person's constitution—his threshold to pain and to various sorts of stimuli, the structure of his glandular and nervous systems—affects the development of his intentional sets, his habits of interpretation and response. Constitutional factors (for instance, metabolic rate) influence the social roles and settings in which a person is cast; this in turn also affects the formation of his intentional sets. Sociocultural factors structure the interpretations of a person's experiences: a range of emotional responses is formed by such interpretations.[25] The full explanation of a person's emotions requires not only an analysis of the causal contribution of each of the three strands but also an account of their interactions.

(But what goes without saying may need to be said: we would not be misled by talk of interaction, layers, or strands to suppose that we are dealing with distinct variables whose causal interaction can be traced. What is treated as a variable in a theory need not be independently variable in fact. At this stage, we are still using metaphors; we are not yet entitled to suppose we have detached them as a technical vocabulary. "Biological limits" or "constraints" to sociocultural variation, physiological "determinants" of psychological or intentional processes, cultural "forms" of biological "givens"—all these expressions are borrowed from other contexts. Our vocabulary of the "interrelation" of these "domains" is crucially in the formative stage; talk of separate but interwoven explanatory strands must be treated as provisionary to a developing explanatory scheme—heuristics without ontology. We have here a clear example of the encroaching constitutive character of early terminological raiding. Perhaps eventually, by tracing these sorts of borrowings, we shall be able to see the rewards—and the costs—of theft that cannot be distinguished from honest toil without the benefit of a program.)

It might be thought that my suggestion that emotions are not only explained but often also identified by their causal histories must be either trivial or exaggerated. No one would deny that we require more than the immediate occasion to understand the exact shades of Jonah's resentment: the images and thoughts, sensations and anticipations, the evocation of associated emotions that constitute just *that* condition. But it doesn't follow that we need a causal account to identify his condition as a case of resentment, and to explain it by his perception of Esther.

Certainly emotions are often identified in a rough way without tracing their causal histories; one need not always know why a person is angry to recognize his condition. The contexts in which they occur, their expression in speech and behavior, are sufficient to identify them; their immediate contextual causes are often quite sufficient to explain them. There is, however, a rough and unexamined but nevertheless quite specific folk psychology that stands behind and informs such standard explanations.[26] The explanatory strategies that I have sketched make explicit the stages and assumptions embedded in our ready and quick contextual identifications of emotions and their intentional objects. It is because we supply the standard causal history of emotion-types that we readily identify tokens of that type.

But instances of emotion-types differ markedly from one another in their origins, their expressions in speech and action, and in their psychodynamic functions. To bring order into these heterogeneous classes, we need a much finer taxonomy of the varieties of, for example; anger, melancholy, envy. Such a taxonomy can be constructed by distinguishing varieties of causal histories of the intentional component of these emotions. Differences in the characteristic causal histories of their intentional components help to explain why different instances of the same emotion-type often have different tonal and behavioral expressions. But we have been too impressed by the multiplicity of instances of emotion-types, and so have tended to distinguish different instances of the same type by the differences in their *particular* intentional objects. Certainly if we want an account of their individuation, especially in cases of overdetermination, this is necessary.[27] When we identify and explain a particular emotion without tracing its etiology, however, we are implicitly classifying it as a standard instance of a *variety* of the emotion-type; in doing so, we are relying upon the characteristic causal story that distinguishes that variety from others. If we thought that the causes of a person's condition conformed to none of the standard histories, we would doubt the attribution.

If this analysis is correct, then an account of how people succeed in changing emotions that they judge inappropriate or irrational closely follows the more general explanation of how people change their habits. The difficulties involved in bringing about such changes—the deep conservation of emotional habits—make the claims that emotions are choices or voluntary judgments seem implausible.[28] Sometimes—rarely—it is possible for some people (a happy few) to take steps to restructure their intentional sets, to revise their emotional repertoire. Sometimes secondary emotions—emotions about emotions—play a crucial role in such transformations. For instance, someone who thinks that the objects he fears are indeed dangerous may nevertheless reasonably judge that he is too afraid of being afraid. He may think that he should not go as far as he does in order to avoid situations were there is only a remote possibility of danger. It is this secondary fear ("We have nothing to fear but fear itself") that impels responses the person might judge inappropriate; and it is this, rather than the first-level fear, that he might wish to change. Or it might go the other way: a person might underwrite a second-level emotion, and wish to change its first level.[29]

Shifts in emotional repertoires can often take quite subtle forms: someone might wish to check the standard expression or behavioral consequences of either a first- or a second-level emotion without wishing to change the habits or intentional set of having it. Although some tendency to action, often taking the form of posture or expression, is part of many first-level emotions, it is often possible to restrain or mask the behavior without changing the emotional set.[30] One of the ways of doing this is to distinguish more sharply between the varieties of instances of an emotion-type. A person might learn to discriminate between appropriate and inappropriate responses by coming to see that different instances of the same type cluster together because they have the same causal history. They form a variety defined by its etiology. If he tackles his problem of identifying and overcoming inappropriate resentments separately each time, Jonah is unlikely to make much headway by learning not to resent Esther, and then learning not to resent Anita, and then Sarah, . . . and each and every woman in authority. Because he thinks some cases of resentment are perfectly justified by their causes and objects, he is unlikely to solve his problem by setting himself the task of avoiding resentment altogether. By understanding the special etiology of the variety of resentments of which his resentment of Esther is a particular instance, he can at least begin to be alert to the situations that trigger magnetized dispositions he regards as inappropriate.

The analysis of the causal history of our emotions suggests that judgments of the appropriateness of the emotions must be made on a number of different levels. It may be not only irrational but inappropriate for someone to be frightened of lions in a zoo, but it is not inappropriate to be frightened before one has had time to be reasonable, so constructed that one's fear is not immediately eradicated by one's more considered reactions. It may be irrational for Jonah to take on his grandfather's attitudes without testing them, irrational for him to reinterpret all the evidence that might correct his attitudes. But it is also beneficial for children to tend to absorb the intentional dispositions of the crucial figures around them, even at the cost of generating confusion and conflict. What is maladaptive in a particular case need not be so typically; it may be highly beneficial for habitual responses to domininate rational considerations, and for them to be changed by rational considerations only with considerable difficulty. It is part of the discomforting character of our emotional life that the genetic programming and the social formation of emotional dispositions are not respecters of the rationality or the comfort of individual persons.

6 The Historicity of Psychological Attitudes: Love Is Not Love Which Alters Not When It Alteration Finds

There is a set of psychological attitudes—love, joy, perhaps some sorts of desire—that are individuated by the character of the subject, the character of the object, and the relation between them. Of course, such attitudes can typically be identified without reference to their objects: Mr. Knightly, Raskolnikov, Swann, and Humbert Humbert all love, though Emma, Sonia, Odette, and Lolita are quite different sorts of women. Still, the details of their loves—the dispositions and thoughts that are active in their loving—are radically different in these cases, so much so that each, looking at the others, might wonder whether they really love. When such psychological attitudes are directed to other people, those concerned characteristically want the attitude to be directed to *them*, rather than to this or that trait. "Do you love me for myself alone, or for my yellow hair?" asks one of Yeats's beautiful ladies, and Yeats has a sage reply, truthfully and sadly: "Only God, my dear, could love you for yourself alone, and not for your yellow hair." This concern about the proper object of the attitude is a way of expressing a concern about its constancy or endurance.

The individuation of such psychological attitudes might be thought a consequence of a general metaphysical fact, that relations are individuated by their subjects and objects. But these relational psychological attitudes are not states identified by the functional relation between the subject and some object: a person, a state of affairs, a propositional content. Although for some purposes it may be convenient to treat such attitudes as states, they arise from, and are shaped by, dynamic interactions between a subject and an object. (As slides of frozen cells stand to a living, working organism, so do psychological attitudes construed as *states* stand to phenomena of dynamic interaction.) It is this feature of such attitudes—what we might call their *historicity*—that generates a concern about their constancy and that can, as I hope to show, also assuage that concern. (In calling psychological attitudes *activities*, and focusing on interactive attitudes, I do not intend to classify all of them with voluntary or responsible actions. Interactive attitudes are not necessarily caused by intentions or under voluntary control, even though they are certainly intentional, and sometimes voluntary.) These psychological attitudes are identified by the detail of the narrative of the interactions between the subject and the object, interactions that also individuate the persons involved. Not only are such relational psychological attitudes individuated by their objects, but also the trajectory of the subject's life—the subject's further individuation—is affected by this relational attitude, this activity.

For the moment, I want to set aside the question of whether this characterization defines only a very small class. Because I do not believe passions or emotions form a natural class, as distinct from (say) desires or motives, or some sorts of beliefs and judgments, I shall not even try to determine whether those conditions we now roughly classify as passions or emotions are historical, dynamic, and interactive, and whether their rationality is thereby endangered. I want rather to trace one such interactive attitude through some of its ramifications, to give a sketch of its historicity, showing that far from threatening rationality, it is just this interactivity that shores, though it cannot possibly assure, the sane emendation and corrigibility we want when we try to account for the rationality of such attitudes. I shall take love, rather than joy, desire, indignation, or fear, as an example. We seem to know more about loving than we do about many other psychological attitudes, not because we are more adept at loving than we are at being joyful or indignant, but because, wanting to be loved, we have given thought to what we want, in wanting to be loved. The characteristics that such an examination uncovers are, as I hope to show, historically specific: they arise in particular social, political, and intellectual contexts. The conditions and criteria set on the identification of love reveal the preoccupations of the era.

Although I shall sketch the place of contemporary conceptions of the conditions of love in its historical context, I want for the moment to set aside the question of whether the contemporary forms provide the central and definitory example of love (if there can be such a thing). Though romantic and erotic love are primary examples, they are by no means the only, or even the clearest, examples of this sort of attitude. The kind of love I have in mind is the love of friendship, and sometimes (though in our culture, rarely) the love of parents and children. The account I sketch does not assume that such friendship-love is symmetrically reciprocated or even that it is reciprocated at all. Nor does it assume that there is a strict economy of love, such that its expansion to others automatically constitutes a diminution or loss elsewhere. Nevertheless, although such love is by no means exclusive, it cannot include more people than the lover is able to attend closely. If there is an economy involved, it is the economy of focused, interactively forming attention, one that not only wishes but acts to promote the thriving of the friend.

I want to examine some characteristics of dynamic, interactive, historical psychological attitudes: (1) Their proper objects are a person, rather than this or that characteristic of a person.[1] (2) Such attitudes are permeable; that is, the lover is affected, changed not only by loving but by the details of the character of the person loved. (3) Because such attitudes affect the person, they affect the person's actions. Although some lovers do not act on behalf of the welfare of those whom they love, their not doing so raises a doubt about whether they do truly love. (Parallel: although someone who desires to learn does not necessarily forthwith set about learning, still, not doing so raises a doubt about the desire). (4) These attitudes are identified by a characteristic narrative history. Although there are pangs of love, stabs of fear, twinges of longing, and thrills of joy, these are identifiable as the feeling of love, fear, longing, or joy only within the complex narrative of the living attitude. These psychological attitudes often feature a particular feeling tone that so magnetizes our attention that we tend to confuse it with the dynamic attitude as a whole.[2] But it is the whole history, and not only the focused and highlighted affective aspect, that constitutes the attitude. In the case of love, there is a presumption of some nonaccidental continuity, assured either by the constancy of a particular relation between the lover and the friend or by the character of their interaction.

Let's begin by distinguishing different ways that the continuity of love can be assured, distinguishing its enduring constancy from its interactive historical continuity. When love is constant and enduring, it persists despite changes in the friend's traits, even changes in those traits that first awoke the love and that were its central focus. This kind of constancy is assured only at a very general level: it is directed to the same person, extensionally identified, and the attachment remains at roughly the same level of devotion.[3] If Louis's love for Ella when he is twenty is radically different from his attitude at sixty, has his love been constant? Presumably, constancy can be preserved by defining the object and functional roles of his attitude in a sufficiently general manner. But such generality is unlikely to reassure those who wonder if they still love, when little they desire or do has remained the same.

When Louis and Ella are concerned about the continuity of their loves, they are not only interested in constancy, though perhaps some of their concerns could be rephrased in that way. What might concern Ella is whether it is she who influences or affects the character of Louis's love and whether his delight in her ramifies to affect other things about him. When Ella does not want Louis to love her as Don Juan might have loved Elvira, her concern for his fidelity might be a way of expressing her concern for whether his delight focuses on her rather than on his dazzling gifts as a lover. She wants his speeches, his charming attentions, and his deftly winning ways to be not only directed *at* and *to* her, but to take their tenor and form from his delighted recognition of what is central to her. It is not enough that he gets the color of her eyes right, when he gets to that part of the serenade describing their enchantment. Nor is Ella's worry laid to rest by being assured of his fidelity, assured that Louis is no Don Juan, ranging over variables for his joys as a connoisseur of the subtle and interesting differences between women and their ever so wonderful effects on him. For whatever good such assurance might do her, Ella could be convinced that if she were to die, or if they were to have an irreconcilable falling out, Louis would feel lost, mourn, and only gradually be healed enough to love someone else. But both she and her successor Gloria might be aggrieved that Louis always brings the same love, a love that is contained within *his* biography, to be given as a gift. Presumably Gloria does not want to inherit Louis's love for Ella: she wants Louis to love her in a wholly different way, defined by the two of them. This is a complex and compounded hope: that Louis's love will be formed by his perceiving—his accurately perceiving—the gradual changes in her, and in his responses being appropriately formed by those changes. If Ella and Gloria love Louis, they want the changes they effect in him to be consonant and suitable to him as well as to them, conducing to his flourishing as well as theirs. It is because they want their love to conduce to his flourishing that it is important that they see him accurately and that their interactive responses to him be appropriate.

There is a kind of love—and for some it may be the only kind that qualifies as true love—that is historical precisely because it does not (oh so wonderfully) rigidly designate its object. The details of such love change with every change in the lover and the friend. Such a love might be called *dynamically permeable*. It is permeable in that the lover is changed by loving and changed by truthful perception of the friend. Permeability rejects being obtuse to change as an easy way of assuring constancy. It is dynamic in that every change generates new changes, both in the lover and in interactions with the friend. Having been transformed by loving, the lover perceives the friend in a new way and loves in a new way. Dynamism rejects the regionalization of love as an easy way of assuring constancy: the changes produced by such love tend to ramify through a person's character, without being limited to the areas that first directly were the focus of the lover's attention.

To see how this works out, let's gossip a bit about Ella, Louis, and Gloria. Louis's love for Ella began with his enchantment at her crisp way of playing Scarlatti, the unsentimental lyricism of her interpretation of Schubert, her appreciation of Orwell's journalism. After a while, he found that he was enchanted by traits he'd never noticed or admired in anyone else: the sequence of her moods, the particular way she had of sitting still, head bent when she listened to music. He came to love those traits in her, or her in those traits—he could hardly tell which. He came to appreciate such traits in others because her having them had delighted him. And he changed too, not necessarily in imitation of her, but because of her. An acute observer could discern changes in Louis that had their origins and explanation in his love of Ella, changes that were deeper than those that arose from his desire to please her. Some of these changes might conflict with, and threaten, other long-standing traits. If Louis's interest in Ella brings an interest in medieval music, it brings him into new company as well. The ramified consequences of his new interests are likely to interfere with his Friday night jam sessions with his old friends in the hard rock group. Either his responses to Ella ramify, and he acquires a new taste in companions, or he attempts to regionalize the changes that Ella effects on him. Both alternatives have significant consequences on them, and on him. If his dynamic interactions do not ramify, there will be conflicts between his pre-Ella and his post-Ella self. But if they do ramify, his psychological continuity is loosened by his being formed and reformed by each new friendship. (Of course, such problems are often solved by Louis and Ella sharing important parts of their lives, partners in common enterprises. Sharing their lives and activities assures their both being formed by a common world as well as by each other.) If Louis and Ella are wise, they are careful to avoid the extremes of both regionalization and ramification. Fortunately, this is not wholly a matter of insight and foresight: a person's previous traits resist transformation. If Louis truly interacts with Ella, he cannot become a person formed by and designed to suit her fantasies.

We shall return to the difficulties of regionalization and ramification, the difficulties of abstract constancy and hypersensitivity. For the moment, let us suppose that in this idyllic fairy tale, Louis came to realize that he would continue to love Ella even if she were to lose those traits that first drew him to her and that were still the focus of his joy in her. Even if someone else played Scarlatti more brilliantly, Schubert more discerningly, and had even more trenchant views on the relation between Orwell and Brecht, he would not transfer his love. This does not mean that he would see or love her *de re*, whatever that might mean. Nor does it mean that the character of his devotion would remain unchanged by whatever changes might occur in her. He'd be lunatic to love her at sixty in just exactly the same way as he had at twenty; and he'd be cruel to love her way of playing Scarlatti if her hands had been mangled in an accident. Nor can his love be analyzed by a set of counterfactuals.[4] If she became Rampal's accompanist, he would. . . . If her mother moved next door, he would. . . . If she became paralyzed, he would. . . . If she declared herself impassioned of a punk-rock-schlock electronic guitar player, he would. . . . If Glorious Gloria, the Paragon of his Dreams, invited him to join her in a trip to Acapulco, he would. . . . If this kind of love could be analyzed in a set of counterfactuals, that set would have to be indefinitely large. For there are an indefinite number of changes that will occur and that will affect Louis if he loves Ella.

This explains why even a true historical love might end in dissolution and separation. That it did end would not prove that it had not existed, or that either its permeability or its dynamism were defective. On the contrary, it might be just these that establish—if it is at all sensible to speak of demonstration in this area—that it was indeed Ella that Louis loved, and that he did indeed love rather than swoon. But we have come to a strange outcome. The internal momentum of their interaction—for instance, the consequences of its ramification or its regionalization—might lead to its dissolution. And this might comfort them both: if they parted, it was because they had truly affected one another, and not because Louis's love had accidentally lost its rigidity or acquired a new direction, however slowly or grievously. In such cases, what marks theirs as a historical love that could not endure (though it might have remained constant over appropriate counterfactuals) is not that it was a love *de re* that got transferred to another *rem*, or that their resistance to transference or substitution was expressed by a suitable period of mourning. What marked it as historical was that they had both been permanently transformed by having loved just *that* person. In short, such love is not only individuated by its objects; more significantly, the lovers are individuated by their love. Louis's subsequent history, his new loves, joys, indignations, the details of his continuing individuation—even his love of Gloria—are affected by his loving interaction with Ella. Both the continuity of their love, and its eventual rupture, arose from their interaction.

That dynamic permeability can lead to dissolution should not impel lovers to assure the continuity of their love by preferring constancy assured by rigid nonpermeability. If historical love runs the danger of phasing itself out, constant, rigid, nonpermeable love also has its dangers. If Louis's love is fixed only by his own character, its active expression may not respond to Ella's needs, even though he may be, in an abstract way, supportive. When Ella worries about the constancy of Louis's love, she may be expressing her sense of her vulnerability in the world, the ways that she has come to need and to depend on him for her thriving.[5] Besides expressing a fear of being harmed, a desire for constancy can itself sometimes be harmful: Ella's fears about Louis's constancy might betray a self-fulfilling sense of dependency. She may have come to be so dependent on the responsive sensitivity of Louis's attunement to her, as a supporting force in her thriving, that she has diminished herself, perhaps even muted the very things that Louis originally admired in her. And Louis, initially charmed by Ella's need of him, may for his part have colluded in her dependency. On the one hand, constancy assured by dynamic permeability does not always automatically work to the benefit of lovers: insight and foresight (of a sort that is, unfortunately, acquired only through experience, and even then, only rarely) is required to direct and to prune the modifications that dynamic permeability fosters. Without the tempering of sound good sense, dynamic permeability might simply produce a severe case of *folie à deux*. If Ella knows herself to be affected by the ways Louis perceives her, if her sense of herself—and, so, in a way, the self she becomes— is in part constituted by the way Louis sees her, she wants more than that Louis's love be historical and dynamically permeable. On the other hand, if she hopes to assure continuity by constant rigidity, she may find Louis's love to be a conserving, conservative prison, binding her to continue as the person Louis originally loved or chooses to see in her. Both those who want the sort of sensitivity assured by dynamic permeability and those who want the sort of security assured by a rather more rigid constancy want their friends to be wise, wiser than either a rock or a sensitive chameleon with a skin of litmus paper can be.[6]

It might be useful to ask why we want all this from our loves. There are two reasons, both obvious, both also sobering. Those who are concerned about the constancy and historicity of love are not necessarily self-important or self-obsessed; they suffer the diseases of the time. It is after all rather remarkable that an attitude and an activity that begins in delight, that carries a desire to share the activities of life, and that brings an active wish for well-being should so quickly move to a concern about continuity. The first reason that contemporary love focuses on constancy is that we sense ourselves fragile, vulnerable in the world. In being aware of our vulnerability, we recognize that among the harms that can befall us are those that endanger or erode just those traits for which we are loved. Because those who delight in us seem to vanquish our sense of vulnerability, we think of them as among our strongest protections in the world. And because lovers characteristically want the flourishing of their friends, they often are actively and objectively central to their thriving. Because the continuity of protective devotion is not automatically assured by the permanent individuating effects of inter-action, we want to be loved for ourselves alone rather for our most lovable traits, traits we realize we may lose. Not surprisingly, the idea of in-dividuality and the sense of vulnerability are closely associated. Those who concentrate on the sense of invulnerability that loving delight can sometimes bring, and on the objective protections that devoted lovers often assure, might want constancy and think of nonpermeable rigidity instead of historicity as the best way to achieve it. (The pathological form of this attitude is an attempt to control and to bind the friend.)

The second reason we want continuity is that we are aware of being constituted by the perceptions of others, particularly by the perceptions of those who love or hate us, rejoice in us, fear or admire us. We come to think of ourselves as we perceive they see us. For that reason, it is important to us that our enemies and lovers—the objects of psychological attitudes—perceive us aright, sensitive to the changes in us. Because we crystallize around what they focus, it is important that they continue to love or hate us for what we are—for what conduces to our thriving—rather than for what we were or what they need us to be. (The pathological form of this attitude is failure of integrity, the readiness to abandon parts of oneself.)[7]

This baroque description of the desire for constancy or continuity of historical psychological attitudes might be thought well replaced by a rather more streamlined Bauhaus approach, a functionalist account of psychological attitudes. They are, we might say, identified by their causal roles, by their etiologies and their effects: that is all that is needed to make sense of the different effects of a preference for rigid constancy or for dynamic permeability. But if we favor Bauhaus functionalism about psychological attitudes, we must accept functionalism everywhere. Not only Louis's love but also his beliefs, his perceptions, hopes, and desires are identified by their functional roles. But the functionalist account will not itself explain why Louis's attitudes play their various typical func-tional roles. There is, in a way, nothing wrong with functionalism except that it is radically incomplete: it cannot by itself explain why psycho-logical attitudes have their typical—and typically interactive and clus-tering—roles. (Bauhaus architecture reveals a great deal about how architects solve heating problems; but it does not thereby provide a clear understanding of the needs or even the constitutions of the people who live or work in those buildings.)

Reflecting on why our contemporaries seem to want love to take these forms—why they want their loves to be appropriately interactive and to be enduring—suggests yet another, quite different way that such psychological attitudes are historical. Because the roles that loving friendship play in a person's life vary historically, conceptions of their proper causes and objects and of the behavior that is appropriate to them also change historically. The standard narratives of such attitudes (the usual tales of their dynamic permeability) vary culturally. The story of a dynamic permeable love that I sketched tends to appear quite late and regionally: it arises after Romanticism, after the Industrial Revolution, in a context in which the sense of vulnerability takes quite specific forms. Vulnerable we are, and vulnerable we have always been. But the particular conditions that constitute our sense of our vulnerability varies historically. It takes a particular conception of the course of the life of an isolated individual as something fashioned by that person alone to produce the sense of vulnerability that might seem to make a particular form of love—which after all begins in attentive rejoicing—a protection and a mode of development.

The functional identification of psychological attitudes characterizes their typical causes and effects: to understand why such attitudes as love, indignation, and respect have just those characteristic etiologies and consequences, we need to understand the conceptions of individuality, needs, and vulnerabilities that constitute a typical life. (It is not always needs and concerns that identify the functional roles of psychological attitudes. But because needs and concerns seem to be the primary focus of current theoretical and practical preoccupations, I'll concentrate on them, without being committed to the general view that the functions of psychological attitudes are always defined by needs.) The vicissitudes from which we need protection vary historically: they vary with the sorts of dangers and fortunes that typically arise, with a person's class and condition, with conceptions of individuality.[8] As our conceptions of individuality change, our vulnerabilities change; as our vulnerabilities change, our needs change; as our needs change, our activities take distinctively different forms; as our activities take characteristically different forms, so do our psychological attitudes.

A short and absurdly superficial sketch of the history of changes in the conception of love may help to make this more plausible. Platonic *eros* is a cosmological as well as a psychological force: it has one proper cause and one proper object—the Beautiful Good—that draws us to it. Acting within us as well as on us, it provides the energy and direction of all we do. Although *eros* has nothing to do with individuality or

vulnerability—and indeed is meant to transcend particular individuals—
it is the principle that assures our real well-being. Aristotle's account
of *philia* as a relation among the virtuous, sharing the activities of life
together, each actively wishing the other well and seeing his own virtues
mirrored in his friend, is hardly recognizable as the ancestor of our
notion of loving friendship. The role of loving friendship in that world
was radically different from its role for us. Perhaps because family rather
than friends provided the primary protections against vulnerability, the
philosophical problems concerning *philia* were, for the Greeks, questions
about whether friends are primarily like-minded or complementary and
whether it is better (more beneficial) to love than to receive love. Christian
preoccupations with *eros, philia, caritas,* and *agapē* reflect still different
conceptions of individuality. When it is God rather than kin who determines and secures the shape of a life, the primary questions about
the fidelity of love are whether it conforms to divine intention, whether
it is modeled after Christ's love. Renaissance *amor* brings yet other
transformation: it is the descendant of Platonic *eros*, the active energy
that moves a person to the realization of excellence. The love of Glory,
of the City, of a Lady or Muse are simultaneously passions and the very
springs of action. Because the object draws the person toward it, *amor*
is classified as a passion, a passive condition. Yet the lover's nature is
perfected and fulfilled by *amor* and by the active desires that it engenders. The central question becomes, What is the relation between this
one primary motivational force and the many various desires that follow
from it and that are its expression? Hobbes transforms *eros* and *amor*
into particular desires: the desire for the realization of the Good becomes
a desire for the objects and actions that promote self-preservation and
self-interest. Following Hobbes, but echoing a secularized version of
Platonic Christianity, Rousseau makes an individual's self-love the
source of all his desires. But self-love has a proper and a corrupt form.
Amour de soi is an unselfconscious, noncomparative sense of one's own
well-being in healthful activity; by contrast, *amour propre* is comparative
and depends on a perception of the estimation of others. (Rousseau
would regard the story of Louis and Ella as a story of the fallen condition,
generated by *amour propre* rather than healthful *amour de soi*.) Against
this historical background, Freud's account of libidinal *eros* as the basic
energetic principle, whose social formation and direction provide the
vicissitudes of an individual's psychological history, no longer seems
startling.

Now what does all this mean about the rationality of such psychological
attitudes?[9] Those who would like to make emotional and psychological
attitudes respectable as appropriate sources of action want to assure that

their corrigibility and redirection take the same form as the corrigibility of beliefs. To rescue such attitudes from the seething cauldron of the irrational, they attempt to show that psychological attitudes can be rationally reconstructed on the model of the structure of propositional or intellectual attitudes. But this philosophical reconstruction cannot—nor was it ever intended to—assure that the corrigibility of the propositional content of a psychological attitude is sufficient to secure its psychological appropriateness. Presumably we want psychological attitudes to be corrigible because we want them to serve us well, to conduce to our thriving. Certainly psychological attitudes that can be propositionalized are at least in principle capable of being evaluated for their truth value; and certainly such evaluations are essential to intellectual corrigibility. But correcting the cognitive or intentional core of a psychological attitude isn't the only way of making it more appropriate; and truth isn't the only measure of the appropriateness of a psychological attitude. An emphasis on rational corrigibility does not provide an adequate account of the functional appropriateness of psychological attitudes.

It might be helpful to take an indirect approach to the analysis of the connection between the ability of psychological attitudes to be rationalized and their being well formed to conduce to thriving. In principle at any rate, propositional attitudes differ from psychological attitudes in being affected only by changes in a person's relation to evidence and other epistemically relevant factors. They are not (or should not be) affected by changes in one's character—by whether, for example, one is depressed or elated, angry or affectionate. But some intellectual or propositional attitudes may be historical and permeable in the same way that hate, fear, and admiration can be, and some psychological attitudes can be intellectualized, functioning as if they were epistemic attitudes, generated and corrigible by true beliefs.

Truth-oriented epistemic attitudes and adaptation-oriented psychological attitudes cannot be sharply and neatly distinguished from one another. Epistemic attitudes whose propositional contents remain unaffected by psychological attitudes do not form a class which is typically distinguishable from the class of dynamically permeable psychological attitudes. There are some people who love constantly and rigidly, nonhistorically. The functional role of their love is intellectualized, assimilable to the functional role of propositional attitudes, in that the intentional object of their attitudes is nonpermeable. But there are also people who believe, doubt, and think in a dynamically permeable way. Their cognitive propositional attitudes are psychologized: their thinking, doubting, believing is affected by their psychology, by their character traits, moods, and desires. Even the propositional contents of their epistemic attitudes are dynamically responsive to the nonepistemic features of their attitudes. Psychological associations (puns, visual associations, memories) connected with the cognitive or propositional content of their attitudes affect their propositional attitudes. They do not stand in the same epistemistic relation to someone they dislike as they stand to those whom they like: they cannot hear what that person says in the same way that they would hear just those words from someone they like. They cannot think about what they fear with the same epistemically sensitive attitude as they take to what does not frighten them. It is more difficult for them to evaluate a core belief about what they fear than it is for them to determine the truth of a belief about what brings them pride, and both are more difficult for them to evaluate than a belief about what does not directly affect them. Not only the system of beliefs, but they themselves are changed by their doubts, distrusts, loves. For such people, thinking is, as one might say, psychological, affected by moods, by likes and dislikes.

Still, one might object that this sort of Proustian differentiation of types of believers and lovers does not affect the basic point, that at least knowledge is not psychologically dynamically permeable. Propositional attitudes that have been formed by idiosyncratic associations rather than by their epistemic relation to their propositional contents are disqualified as knowledge claims. However true or appropriate they may be, beliefs about acquaintances that are formed or affected by likes and dislikes are not rational. Still, even if the conditions for knowledge guarantee its immunity to epistemically irrelevant psychological attitudes, the beneficial functioning of such attitudes is not thereby necessarily best assured by their rational corrigibility. Though a propositional attitude becomes epistemically suspect when it is formed by a person's psychological condition (fears, elation, or melancholy), propositionalizing or intellectualizing psychological attitudes need not be the best way to assure sanity and soundness.

What is it then that we want, when we want psychological attitudes to be rational? There is often no one whose inferences are more logical, more formally impeccable, and often there is no one more truthful, than the local lunatic. It is because his impeccable and exemplary truth-preserving inferences do not serve him in the right way that the local lunatic is in trouble. No particular additional truth or inference can help him. His problem is that his rationality cannot guide or form what he does because it is not appropriately rooted in his character. Because we want to avoid the lunatic's troubles, we want more than that our attitudes be corrigible by considerations of truth and validity. We also want them to be appropriately formed to serve our thriving.

The direction we take in assuring the correctness and appropriateness of psychological attitudes may vary, as we focus primarily on their correction or on their formation. If we concentrate on avoiding the harms of malformation, we emphasize rational corrigibility. We are then likely to favor propositionalizing the contents of our psychological attitudes. On the assumption that we at least attempt to free ourselves of attitudes clustered around false beliefs, we attempt to secure the appropriateness of psychological attitudes by assimilating them as closely as we can to propositional attitudes oriented to truth. If, however, we concentrate on developing and forming appropriate psychological attitudes, we emphasize their historicity, attempting to discover the conditions under which dynamic permeability conduces to flourishing.

Rather than assimilating appropriateness and thriving to rationality, construed as preserving truth through inferential sequences, we might construe rationality as itself partially constituted by what serves us well. If the difference between the lunatic and the wise person is a difference in their rationality, then rationality has acquired a substantive as well as a formal condition. If rationality is understood to serve thriving, the rationality of a person of practical wisdom is as much a function of her character—her having appropriate habits arising from well-formed perceptions and desires—as it is from her drawing the right inferences from the right premises. What makes a person rational is not only the logically impeccable character of her reasoning, but what she knows and how wisely her knowledge affects the fine attunement of her actions. Rationality serves the wise person by enabling her to do the right thing at the right time in the right way; it is this that keeps her truth-telling and valid inferences from being inconsequential, inappropriate, blind, stubborn, or silly.

How does any of this help Louis and Ella determine what they require from their psychological attitudes, if those attitudes are to conduce to their thriving? Certainly, if their interactions are to be beneficial, they had better perceive one another accurately. To avoid their responses being formed by mere perceptions of the moment, to avoid the *folie à deux* problem, it is also important that their attunement be appropriate. But how is that to be determined? As we saw, what conduces to the continuity of their love might serve neither of them well, and what conduces to Louis's developing and thriving need not serve the interactive harmony between him and Ella. Although the historicity of their attitudes—their attunement—initially seemed to promise the appropriateness of their responses, there can be difficulties in that promise being fulfilled. The beneficial functions of psychological attitudes seem no more assured by their historicity than by their ability to be rationalized.

Standardly, but not necessarily, rationality, appropriateness, and thriving are interwoven. It is the dream of rational social politics that in the long run these converge even if they cannot coincide. Of course these three conditions can vary independently: the lunatic shows that rationality does not assure appropriateness; the dangers of *folie à deux* show that adaptability and attunement do not assure thriving. Still, such counterexamples do not undermine the presumptive interconnections: rationality (as defined by truthfulness supported by validity) is a central guide to appropriateness, and appropriateness a central guide to flourishing. The separation of rationality from appropriateness produces lunacy; the separation of adaptability from appropriateness produces unhappiness.

Still, how have we spoken to Louis and Ella? It would be a mistake to think we've left them in a sound as well as a safe place. Even if they are assured of the connection between rationality, appropriateness, and thriving, they have yet to discover just what these require of them in particular situations. How dynamically permeable should Louis be without endangering his integrity or joining Ella in a case of *folie à deux?* How ramified or regionalized should his responses be? What *does* rationality require? What *would* constitute thriving? How are the thriving of Louis, Ella, Louis-and-Ella to be appropriately weighted when they seem to go in different directions?

We've left them just where they were: in the continuous, delicate, and delicious balancing acts of their lives. But that is just exactly where we should leave them. It is only the details of their particular situation that can determine what would be rational, what would be appropriate, what would constitute (whose?) thriving. No general philosophical conclusion about the presumptive connections between rationality, appropriateness, and thriving can possibly help them determine just what corrections rationality recommends or requires as appropriate to their condition. It can't even help them determine whether their sensitivities are sound or pathological, insufficient or excessive, let alone whether they should ramify or regionalize their responses to one another, to balance integrity with continuity in such a way as to conduce to thriving. The confluence of rationality, appropriateness, and thriving cannot help them to determine the directions in which rationality or appropriateness or even thriving—taken singly or coordinately—lie. And that is as it should be. Our task cannot be to resolve but only to understand the quandaries of Louis and Ella. Since their condition and its problems are historical, that is, particular, their solutions must be particular.

7   Jealousy, Attention, and Loss

Otto is deeply attached to Deborah: his sense of well-being as the person he takes himself to be is in part formed by what he takes to be her perceptions of him. But he believes that Deborah's attentions have swerved toward, and indeed to center on Chayim. Otto knows that Deborah is loyal: she will not abandon him or their children. Knowing her, he suspects that she will be rather more meticulous though perhaps more abstracted in her care of all of them precisely because she has come to be absorbed in Chayim. But Otto senses that her relation to him will be defined by her own self-respect and her habits rather than by her attentive perception of him. Otto's days are consumed with researches into the exact character of Deborah's encounters with Chayim, his nights are spent in dreams and fantasies of the details of their joys in one another's company. He envisages scene after scene of their happiness. Otto is wracked by jealousy; he loses all sense of himself; his steady behavior becomes erratic and arbitrary. He no longer seems the same man.

What does Otto's jealousy presuppose? In what does it consist? Where does it lead? Certainly Otto fears a loss: but he need not fear losing Deborah or Deborah's love in order to be jealous. He might, as it turned out, stand in the same formal relation to Deborah as before: she might continue to share his bed and board, his life, as ever she did, and perhaps with more forebearing kindness than before. And yet he is jealous. Is it then the loss of her love that he fears? No, because in some cases Otto might well have retained Deborah's love, even though her attentions concentrated on Chayim. (And, as we shall see, in other circumstances he might be jealous of someone where there was no love at all.) Perhaps he might fear that the character of Deborah's love would change, that she might come to love him as one loves a kindly friend, rather than in that wholly absorbed way that she loved him when first they came to know each other. Yet Otto might know that even if Deborah had never met Chayim, the character of her love would certainly have changed from its early youthful form. But yet he might nevertheless fear that her present comfortable love would change still more radically.

135

With Chayim in the picture, Otto might fear that Deborah could not retain any continued sense of her life as being intertwined with his. Even when jealousy is a fear of the loss of love, the loss must have a special cause. After all, Otto might have feared the loss of Deborah's love because she was forced to move away, or because she altered in some profound way, or because she became dangerously ill. Jealousy requires that the loss be experienced as someone else's gain: that there is a direct transfer.

The transfer is characteristically made to another person, but it can also be directed to a cause or an occupation. Otto might have been jealous of Deborah's relation to her law practice, jealous of her devotion to legal researches, and to the welfare of her clients, thinking that the attention she gave them could only come as a diminution of her devotion to him. But Otto's jealousy of Deborah's work need not be a jealousy of her love of her work, her research, her clients; it depends rather on his belief that her attention to her legal practice deprives him of attentions he requires.

Jealousy need not involve love at all. Otto might be jealous that Diana, his favorite chess partner—the person whose regard for his chess playing has confirmed his sense of his unique capacities and style as a chess master—has found a new and favored chess partner. He believes that Diana now regards Clara with the centrality of attention as a chess player that she once gave him. Diana's playing with Clara has cast a pall on Otto's sense of his gifts: he imagines the delights of their chess strategy session, the elegance of their developing interactive style. If he were envious, he would concentrate on Clara's gifts, comparing his unfavorably to hers. If he were envious not only of Clara's gifts but of the attention she receives from Diana, he would compare his situation unfavorably with hers. His envy is transformed to jealousy, when he considers the transfer of attention as a deprivation of an important part of his personality, one that impels him to obsessive thoughts about the rival relation. The fantasies of envy focus on another person's *properties*, and one's own comparative lack of them, but the other person is not believed to have those properties at one's own cost. Even though one loses by the comparison, one is not the loser because of the comparison. The fantasies of jealousy focus on a person's *relations* to another. Of course such relations can be considered properties, and the pattern of a person's envy shows his beliefs about what properties assure the sort of attention he wants. But the relation became the subject of jealousy rather than envy only when another's acquired relational-property is perceived as one's own direct loss.[1]

Yet the sense of such deprivation does not always generate jealousy: it can also generate sadness, longing, or discontent. A person is jealous only when the perceived deprivation makes him doubt himself, forces him to reassess his style or ability or power in a way that generates obsessive thoughts of the rival relation.

Because the focused attention that recognizes and constitutes a set of aspects that an individual takes to be central to himself is also a crucial feature of love, it is natural, but nevertheless mistaken, to assume that jealousy presupposes love. When we find ourselves jealous, fearing to lose a formative attentive regard, we often erroneously take ourselves to love. Often it is only jealousy that reveals the character of our attachments. But we can become attached to a special sort of attention, an attention upon which we depend, without depending on love. There are, after all, many forms of attention that are not necessarily loving. There is for instance, nonloving sexual concentration, which often also has a strongly obsessive character.[2] One of the reasons that jealousy so often focuses on sexual relations is that sexual attention is just about the most focused and concentrated form of attention we experience. It is, moreover, one that can reawaken our earliest experiences of the sort of physical attention that sustained our existence in infancy and that formed our somatic sense of our selves. It is because intensely focused attention is a central feature of both love and sexuality that they tend to go together and that we often move from one to the other, back and forth. (Those who attempt to free themselves of sexual jealousy may therefore find that they must diminish the importance of individually focused sexual experience as part of their sense of their own identity. Either they diminish the importance of sexuality as such to their sense of themselves, or they generalize sexuality, without focusing on the individuality of their partners as a crucial part of the importance the activity has for them, or they identify themselves as samplers and connoisseurs of varieties of individuals, avoiding sexual bonding with any one of them.)

But why should the extension or diversion of focused formative attention generate a fear of loss? It is because such attention has the psychological and the physiological character that it does, that any redirection is perceived as a loss by the original recipient. Certainly there is some economy in love: one cannot love a great many people all at once, either singly or conjointly. But within the limits of the expansion of attention to the details of persons' lives, a shift of love within a small group does not require readjustment to the whole field. Parents do not find that they love their elder children the less, when they have more children, although they certainly find they can give them quantitatively less attention. We come to know that we need not lose love, when our lovers also love elsewhere. It may be a difficult lesson to learn, but sometimes we can recognize that we are better loved, because we are not the only persons on our lover's mind. This is not only true for love: the economy of a large number of psychological attitudes shifts at a critical limit between large and small numbers, at just that point where the capacity for detailed attention can expand no farther.

It is a difficult complication in our loves, that while the capacity for loving can grow by its exercise (especially its happy exercise), one of the preconditions for love *is* subject to a zero sum economy. That condition is the singling out of focused attention. It is, after all, not merely any random glancing attention that is at issue, but an attention that has a special focus on the individual character of a person, a concentration on some traits that, by virtue of being attended in a special way, come to be thought of as centrally constitutive. The thought is that the person regards certain traits as centrally defining his personality and believes that he could not retain those traits outside of the particular attentional relation.

In concentrated attention, a person may project some tangential characteristics, or attend some relatively peripheral features of a person's personality structure. But since loving attention also requires an interest in the beloved's real welfare, it requires attempting to discover what the beloved is really like to determine the conditions for the best development and exercise of the person's central features. When the lover's attentions are active in forming and crystallizing the beloved's personality, the lover is also careful to attend to the real structure of that personality, not foisting or projecting an identity that, by becoming constitutive, will so conflict with the rest of the beloved's character that the person cannot flourish. We do indeed help to create those whom we love: but we do not do it from whole cloth. And that is why the lover who is essentially concerned for the welfare of the beloved takes care that his constituting attention is appropriate to the real traits and the tonal character of the person whom he loves.

Because concentrated attention is such a crucial feature of love, it is natural to confuse the two, and to suppose that the presence of one entails the presence of the other. But the economic logic of the two are distinct: a loving care for what is central to a person's flourishing is not an all-or-none activity subject to a zero sum economy. What *is* such an activity is that part of loving which requires completely focused attention. Such attention is a precondition for loving: but it need not accompany every moment of loving activity.

The paradigm for such attention, that sets the model and expectations for later extensions, is direct gazing. That is how, as infants, we first experience attention and that is how we first experience the possibility of its loss, when the attention that was directed to us is turned away. At that level, anyone's gain must be our loss. We have strong evidence that the development of an infant's ego requires this sort of attention: a child's coming to have a sense of himself as a center of consciousness and of agency depends on his having received attention that centered on him as an individual capable of consciousness and agency.[3] Even more strikingly, some of the detailed characteristics that the developing child comes to take as essentially his, characteristics that define the tonality of his consciousness and the style and direction of his agency are those that centrally attending persons see in him. Gradually, of course, it is not merely parental figures on whose forming attention ego development depends, but also teachers, friends, lovers. "Look at me!" does not stop when one leaves the playground. Nor does that closely related cry, "Catch me if I fall!"

Jealousy need not be experienced as a special sort of feeling, as a pang, or a twinge.[4] An adult may indeed be jealous without feeling so, his jealousy taking the form of obsessive imagistic thoughts of the rival relation, without his being reflectively aware that these thoughts indicate his jealousy. Sometimes there are strong inhibitions against jealousy, not only against its expression but against feeling it. Many parents treat their children's jealousy as if it were a sort of vice, and such children, fearing their own jealousy, learn to deny it in various ways, sometimes by repressing it by ostrich behavior and sometimes by sublimating it. When it is strongly repressed jealousy can be turned to forms of self-destructiveness or more directly vindictive behavior. When it is sublimated, it can lead to the development of strong competitive traits that make a person a visible bearer of characteristics that are likely to attract the sort of focused attentions they require.

But though adult jealousy need not be experienced as such, our earliest experiences of jealousy did involve painful feelings, sometimes the pain of great anxiety. Early experiences of focused attention were also associated with being-attended-to, and there is a natural tendency to fear the loss of sustaining being-attended-to with the threatened loss of attention. Infantile jealousy is an experience of the sort of losses that do in fact genuinely jeopardize the ego.[5] In their most extreme form, they generate anxieties of being abandoned by those whose physical attentions are required for the most basic level of physical well-being. At a somewhat later stage, they involve anxieties of the loss of that sort of facial attention and interaction that is a condition for the development and formation of the child's sense of its own ego. But early experiences of jealousy remain latent in us all. If the development of a person's ego suffered setbacks (and for most of us surely it did), then later incidents of jealousy often evoke undercurrents of unresolved earlier anxieties, even when we are functioning quite well and are reasonably aware of our securities.

Many fears of adult jealousy are quite realistic: a person may genuinely fear to lose prized characteristics that depend on the continued attention of others. Even well-formed autonomous adults can be changed by the loss of characteristics that can only flourish through the attention of another person, and some through the attention of another particular person. It is difficult to sustain a sense or oneself as witty or humorous or sexy unless one is continuously so perceived. And there are forms of wit and forms of humor that require very particular interlocutors for their exercise.[6]

Other anxieties of jealousy—that the loss of even important traits must involve annihilation or the complete disintegration of the self—the anxieties that are evoked by reawakened infant fears, are quite irrational. Nevertheless, irrational or no, jealousy can, when it is experienced as a feeling, involve intense vertigo, like that of fainting or a loss of consciousness, or a sense of strong disorientation and disassociation. Sometimes this sense of annihilation is histrionically magnified by the jealous person, who then seems actively complicit in extending the damage already effected by the transfer of attention. There is a dramatization of the extent of the real damage to other parts and aspects of the ego, and acting out of the sensed destruction. (This often resembles the behavior of children who, devastated by some small damage to a favorite toy, then completely destroy a plaything that seemed still quite suitable for play. This strategy of identifying with the oppressor, taking on the active role of the destroyer to finish off the job, can have the strengthening benefits that any active affirmation of the self can convey; but these benefits are obviously of a not very promising or enduring kind. Such strategies undermine more than they bolster.)

A person might fear the loss of just this sort of defining attention and neither feel, nor be, jealous. He might, without having repressed or sublimated jealousy, directly become depressed or withdrawn or feel self-pity or deny the original relation. The fear of the loss of focused attention is a jealous fear only when the sense of danger to an aspect of one's identity generates a set of obsessive scenario-constructing thoughts. These thoughts generally involve the construction of vivid stories, with the jealous person as a voyeur of an endless series of vignettes that cause him pain.

Jealous thoughts are characteristically (though not necessarily) highly imagistic. Even a person whose thinking is in other contexts not particularly imagistic (consisting rather in phrases, schematic inferences, word associations, and relatively abstract thoughts [whatever they may be!]) nevertheless tends, when he is jealous, to construct fantasies of a highly visual sort: he becomes a sort of voyeur even when the content of the imagery is not particularly sexual. The earliest forms of jealousy may explain these later structures. Infant jealousy is experienced when a parental figure, on whose attentions ego development depends, looks away, focusing elsewhere in such a way that the child does not easily regain the original attention. The first experiences of jealousy actually do involve the jealous person as a witness of the redirected focus of attention: we learn jealousy by *watching* that redirection, experiencing it as our loss. If a parental figure is looking at Chayim, he is not looking at Otto. The child learns of the new relation by *seeing* it take place. It would seem natural that later experiences of jealousy would recreate that structure in fantasy and in thought. Perhaps, too, jealous imaginings tend to be so visual because what is lost is precisely the sense of being *seen* in a certain way. So the content of the fantasies might well involve the visual attentions that the rival received.

Not only is jealous thought characteristically imagistic: it is also highly obsessional. Even persons whose visual thinking does not ordinarily tend to be obsessive do, in jealousy, often obsessively run through scenario after scenario.[7] One might speculate that the obsessive character of jealousy comes from its being an attack on the ego. Whatever strategies a person has developed in the defense of the ego come into play here. There are two ways in which the obsessive character of jealousy tends to exert itself: one is in the *need to know*, the endless tests and investigations and spyings that are so characteristic of jealousy. The other is the *need to visualize*. Both obsessions seem to make the jealous person less passive, less helpless because he is actively engaged in investigating or in imagining. It is as if he joins in the agency of his jealousy, and by being active in it, changes the character of his suffering, even when he actually increases it by doing so. His then becomes an active rather than a passive suffering. Since the fears of jealousy evoke anxieties of infantile helplessness, activity may somehow assuage the sense of annihilation: there is even often a tone of exhilaration that enters into the imagistic investigations.[8] It is one thing to be annihilated by others, quite another to be annihilated as the result of one's own frenzied activity. Even the jealous person's recognition that it is often precisely his obsessive investigations that precipitate a transfer of attention that might not otherwise have developed does not usually deter him. There is an obsessive desire to bring things to a head, to have the worst revealed and perhaps even brought about. Even when it is also accompanied by ostrich behavior of denial, jealousy can be embedded in, or sometimes trigger off a larger, more general project of self-destruction.

Following a suggestion of Sartre, it seems plausible to interpret the obsessive character of jealousy as a way of attempting magically to return to the center of the world.[9] Both the need to know and the need to visualize appear to allow the jealous person to regain control as playwright, director, manipulator. In his thoughts at least, the rival relation becomes his creation, the work of his mind. By being active in its construction, in the determination of its tonality, he is not merely passive and helpless. But these investigations and imaginings make the jealous person vulnerable to additional pain when he actually sees the rival relation, and sees it as having tonalities and characteristics that he himself has not succeeded in inventing in the course of his jealous imaginings. He then suffers the loss of the magic control that he had temporarily achieved by being the only begetter of his jealous imaginings.

Well, then, there is Otto, endlessly imagining Deborah and Chayim at kibbutz festivities, gazing into each other's eyes. He is obsessed with images of the strong intensity of Deborah's attention to Chayim as he rises to speak at the weekly meeting of the production planning committee. Not every jealous person has the same scenarios, but each person tends to have a characteristic set, a pattern whose variations reveal the concerns that his attachment to the person's attention has served. If that attachment defined the character of his sexuality, he will envisage the rival relation in sexual scene after sexual scene. But it will even be more precise: for what may matter to Otto is not simply the fact of some sexual situation, but its tonal character as urgent, tender, prolonged, playful, aggressive, or athletic. Indeed, the tonality may in some cases dominate the actual sexuality, so that what comes to be significant to the person's self-definition and therefore the concern of his jealousy is not so much the fact of sexual intercourse (about which he may be relatively indifferent), as the tonality of the psychophysical relation. What can be at issue is not so much the actual character of Otto's relation to Deborah, but how its (imagined) tonality endangers the focus of Otto's sense of himself.

For instance, if Otto's relation to Deborah formed him as a certain sort of intellectual, the two sharing speculative investigations, then his jealous thoughts of Deborah and Chayim will focus on their being engaged in absorbing intellectual discussions or investigations. If Otto thinks of himself as essentially a truthseeker, his thoughts and fantasies may center on his discovering the truth of Deborah's relation to Chayim. In general, the details of the thoughts and fantasies that are such a large part of jealousy reveal the forms of Otto's characteristic uses of thought-in-the-services-of-defense, as well as the details of the ways in which Otto's relation to Deborah have formed his conception of himself.[10]

But surely one might think of all this as overdone? After all, someone can be jealous of a distant person: an adolescent might be jealous of a rock star's attentions to a movie star. One need not be in a real relation to feel jealousy; one need never have had what one takes oneself to have lost. But when that happens, the person is likely to have fantasied an absorbing relation between himself and the rock star. His jealousy is contained within a fantasy in which he has realized some attentive relation between himself and the distant figure. This sort of fantasy can also occur with people whom one knows. A figure who plays an objective role in one's life can be fantasied as providing a forming attention. The person can be real, and the effect real, but the forming attention only fantasied. The person can then be jolted by jealousy, and even jealous vertigo at the feared loss of something that, although it never existed, did indeed form some aspect of their sense of themselves. If a person has neither had, nor imagined themselves to have had, what they feel as a deprivation, their condition is one of longing rather than jealousy. But since this sort of longing generally generates fantasies of attachment, it usually moves toward jealousy. Because medical situations, especially psychiatric ones, involve the sort of concentrated focused attention on traits that the patient regards as crucial to his well-being, patients are often in a fantasy attachment to their physicians. It is this that is thought to facilitate the operations of the mechanisms of transference in psychoanalysis. And it is for this reason that medical practitioners try to protect themselves and (as they imagine) their patients by adopting a formal and impersonal manner.

Some people are especially prone to fantasy attachments, and others especially prone to fantasy losses of either real or fantasied attachments. Such people have generally been deprived of crucial attentive attachments, or suffered their loss at crucial stages of ego development. They come to expect attachment dependencies or to foresee their vulnerability to the redirection of attention. Their sense of their own reality contains a sense of its own fragility.[11]

There are a number of serious objections to our discussion. It might be argued that in order to explain at least some of the phenomena of adult jealousy, it is often quite unnecessary to postulate an elaborate account of the etiology of such jealousy in childhood history. This theory might be thought to deal primarily with pathological cases, where a person's jealousy is not adequately explained by the situation that engenders it. A person might quite realistically fear the loss of a particular attention, and quite realistically fear that the loss of such attention might cause him to lose important goods. Such losses may affect a person's sense of well-being, without generating a fear of the loss of some important aspect of oneself; and certainly they need not awaken childhood traumas.

On the surface, this objection seems absolutely right. Not every adult jealousy awakens childhood experiences; some adult jealousies are entirely realistic and can adequately be explained by the situations in which they occur. Nevertheless, our account is an account of the etiology of jealousy, and not merely of its pathological forms. Part of our answer is metatheoretical. In general, the explanation and analysis of the pathological forms of an emotion or attitude should not import principles of a radically different character from the explanation of normal phenomena. The pathology of attention and emotions involve an imbalance of just those ingredients that are at work in the normal condition. Pathological jealousy is generally also occasioned by present and real fears: it differs from the normal cases only in that the person has a lower threshold to such fears, and that they also have a lower threshold to the evocation of older fears. Their adult jealousy is more likely to trigger or evoke early fears of abandonment. Our susceptibilities to the pathological evocation of ancient anxieties tends to vary with our vulnerabilities: such thresholds can vary markedly at different times in a person's life, in different sorts of social situations.

The childhood origins of jealousy are of theoretical significance for another reason. While it is true that there are perfectly realistic grounds for a person fearing to lose some important benefits from the attention of another, there is a question about what makes such fears *jealous* fears, rather than apprehensions, predictions, forebodings. Not every fear of the loss of attention that is gained by another person is a jealous one. The roots of jealousy in infant fears of abandonment distinguishes jealousy from other fears: but of course not every case of jealousy activates such fears.

Moreover, childhood jealousy need not be dramatic. A child can be momentarily jealous of the attention received by some sibling, without going through any crisis of identity. Nevertheless, a child's ego—its strength and the directions of its identifications—fluctuates enormously in the processes of its development. Issues of just distribution are the focus of jealousy as well as envy: they give a child the sense of its dependency and vulnerability. A child who has experienced arbitrary or inconsistent attention, especially if favorite siblings are played off against one another, may become chronically jealous or resentful. While standardly jealousy is a reactive emotion, it can become a magnetizing disposition, which structures and sometimes creates the conditions that elicit it.

Etymologically, "jealous" is linked to "zealous": both involve an attentive regard for what is close to oneself. One can jealously guard one's reputation, zealously carry out one's duties. Whatever is the subject to jealous or zealous alertness is bound with one's sense of oneself: one's defining possessions, one's uprightness, one's public face.

Jealousy is an emotion that has distinctive varieties: but there are several ways that these varieties can be classified. One is to distinguish the consequences or secondary attitudes that jealousy triggers. Since jealousy is one of the emotions that has a perceived danger to the self at its center, it generates various strategies of defense. Varieties of jealousy can, then, be mapped according to these strategies and their characteristic etiologies.[12] For instance, some jealousies are attended by depression or withdrawal, others by anger or thoughts of revenge. Still others by an intensification of the original attachment or by intellectualization; others by frantic activity, or with frenzied competitive behavior. The choice among these strategies seems to be influenced by early ego-defense moves in the face of instinctual vicissitudes.

Another way to characterize varieties of jealousy is to distinguish the tonality of the attentive regard that then comes to constitute the character of the person's relation to himself. For instance, early parental attention may be strongly accompanied by anxiety, or by impatient resentment. Even when the attention is loving, its character and direction can be quite variable. The attention can involve joy in the child's activity and alertness; or it can be strongly directive and teacherly; or it can involve an identificatory concentration on traits the parental figures take to resemble their own, eliciting narcissistic or hostile and aggressive reactions. The undertones and associated emotional embedding of attention will then also accompany the adult's own expectations: his later attentions will tend to have similar (or opposed) undertones, and he will seek out the attentions of those whose attitudes have similar (or opposed) forms, almost as if he didn't believe that attention was really *attention* unless it was also accompanied by these other characteristics.

Finally, we can characterize the varieties of jealousy by the varieties in their characteristic causes. So we can distinguish sexual jealousy and its various forms from jealousy in situations of competition for esteem, and so on.

Each of the varieties would be recognizable by their characteristic patterns of obsessive imagery, by the details and structure of the scenario narratives, by the varieties of expressions in posture and gesture that

are manifest in jealousy, and of course by their characteristic consequences. But all the varieties of jealousy depend on a contextually
determined state of a person's ego. A set of events that would spring a
person's characteristic jealous responses at one time might not elicit
them at another, depending on the previous contrast experience, his
physical condition, and his expectations. When a person has recently
had ego-building experiences, he is less likely to be subject to fears
that the transfer of attention requires revision of his own attributes than
he would be if he had just suffered other setbacks to his sense of himself.
Unfortunately, we seem to be so constituted that one ego defeat tends
to make us prey to more, less able to slough them off. A person who
has just suffered inroads on her job or who has been ill is more likely
to be sensitive, if not actually hypersensitive, to the directions of her
husband's attentions than she normally is when she is in a less vulnerable
condition. Of course the contrast effect is not the only operative deter-
minant of threshold: a person's expectations, some of them formed by
very early experiences, and many of them culturally fixed and conveyed,
would also condition his responses.

Is jealousy always damaging? It seems that jealousy is unavoidable,
if only, ironically, from the psychophysical character of biocular focusing
and attention. But are the griefs and fears it causes us always and only
damaging in our development? The damages are obvious; the benefits
less so. In the first place, our patterns of jealousy can teach us what we
take to be our central traits. It is such experiences as jealousy and our
reflections on their patterns, rather than simple introspection, that are
the best indicators of the details of our images of ourselves. By also
revealing the forms of our attention-dependencies, jealousy can be the
first step toward evaluating their directions and appropriateness. Once
we recognize our basic attitudes to ourselves, we can in principle either
confirm or reject these attitudes. Not that such confirmation or rejection
automatically affects our emotional attitudes! The principles of the conservation of emotions are too strong for that. Yet the strategies of self-
knowledge can develop a position and a *persona* whose activities as
investigator and evaluator can in principle sometimes so strengthen the
ego that it becomes less prey to the vulnerabilities of the transfer of
attention. In any case, the revelations of the patterns of one's images of
oneself through such emotions as jealousy can also reveal the preferences, needs, and principles that are at work, guiding our choices and
decisions. For the aspects of personality that are at work in fixing our
attachments and fears are not isolated: they are expressed in our ordinary
decisions and behavior as well as in the more regional experiences of

jealousy. Unmasking the structures of our jealousy can show us how we operate in other contexts.

Jealousy can be a great teacher in other ways as well. Sometimes if a person is thrown back upon himself by the loss of attention he discovers that he can become autonomous in his self-regard. (Children, for instance, often emerge from sibling jealousy with much strengthened egos, having discovered that they did not depend on parental regard as much as they had feared.) At first such autonomy is an internalization of the attentional attitudes of some parental figures, whose modes of attention persons incorporate as part of their own sense of themselves. (That is why Freud says that a man whose mother has adored him is invulnerable for life.) But ironically, a move toward greater autonomy can only occur if a person has, in other ways, the basis of a relatively stable ego, capable of taking on the strenuous tasks of being one's own audience. (But these are extremely delicate matters: a strongly protected autonomous ego may close a person to the possibility of being further formed by the attentive regard of others. The scars that close a wound protect it against infection: but they can also cause other damages to the organism by taking on a feverish growth of their own.)

At its best, then, jealousy can lead to a person's having a better sense of what is central in his character structure, and developing a new form of autonomy. But like other emotions that concentrate on the self, jealousy raises questions about whether there is, at the core of traits that are central to us, an irreducible *me* that would remain even if the most central traits were altered.

Because jealousy is a painful and disorienting experience, whose obsessive character undermines a person's sense of his capacities and destroys what might be saved or salvaged from attentive relations, one might think that we would try to school ourselves against it. But precisely because jealousy does raise crucial issues of personal identity and its survival, there are strong blocks in the way of our overcoming jealousy.

One of these is the set of mechanisms by which threatening experiences tend to evoke responses over which we have very little voluntary control, the most powerful of these being the mechanisms that come into play with anxieties of abandonment that seems to bode annihilation. Recognizing that these may be irrational and unrealistic does not generally help a person slough them off, although it may help them, on another level, to prevent their spinning into a heady regress of more and more dangerous and self-destructive attitudes. Sometimes it is helpful if the person whose attentions have shifted insists on retaining some sort of (perhaps newly defined) bond with the jealous person, especially when he can focus attentively on traits and capacities that are brought into play in the task of coping with jealousy. But the vulnerabilities and dangers of jealousy do not usually permit such a benign outcome. It is, for instance, common to say to the jealous person "Well, it is true that I am entranced by Chayim's ways of resolving the problems of the kibbutz, but I regard your steadiness and composure in times of trouble as ever I did." But there is the "Catch me if I fall!" as well as the "Look at me!" aspect of attention. Since our vulnerabilities are ever latent in our thoughts, and not unrealistically so, we are always testing our friends and relations for their reliability in countdown situations. Otto will wonder whether Deborah's continued regard for his steadiness will assure her returning from a delightful vacation in Ashkelon with Chayim, should Otto fall ill and require attention. The danger is, of course, that Otto's latent fears of losing Deborah may precipitate illnesses and disasters that would test or reaffirm Deborah's devotion to him.

The resistance to the cure of jealousy has another source. Though, to be sure, we often profit from regarding ourselves as composed of distinct and separable traits, recognizing that we can be esteemed for some, while being pitied for others, still we do have a strong pull toward the unification of our traits, the unity of our persons. There is one level—and sometimes it is strongly a physical level, because we are *one* organism, which thrives or languishes as a whole—on which we say: but what about *me*, not this or that trait that I may so wonderfully and uniquely have? Sometimes indeed we test those upon whose attentions our sense of ourselves depends, by taunting them with deviations, violations, and disappearances of just those traits we take to be centrally constituted by our relation to them. It is perhaps an infantile maneuver, and it is perhaps a maneuver that a truly secure adult rarely plays out, but the infant generally lurks just a few layers beneath the skin of even the most secure adult. While it is true that we could defend ourselves against jealousy by consenting to separate our traits, recognizing that someone can continue to attend some, while being detached from others, there is a strong resistance to this splitting or disassociation of traits.

The core of the second resistance to the cure of jealousy really rests on the first ground of resistance: we connect our attentive-relations not only to those aspects of our selves that they define but to our general dependence on sustenance in situations where we are truly vulnerable and helpless. If we protect ourselves against the ravages of jealousy by the strategy of separating our traits, we run the danger of damaging our sense of the unity and the protection of our persons. Now one might indeed have a metaphysical view according to which that sense of unity and the protection that goes with it are illusions well lost, if only because such a sense generates jealousy and its kin emotions, envy, remorse, guilt.

Whether the sense of the unity of the self and the protections that sense evokes are illusions is a question we must leave for another occasion. It is after all a question that has vast ramifications on the theory of agency and responsibility, on choice and rationality, both in psychology and ethics. Until we discover that the conceptions of the ego that underlie our fears are illusions, we do objectively take ourselves to require the attentions of others for our real flourishing. If such notions are illusions, they seem illusions that beings like ourselves inevitably have; with them go the host of attitudes—jealousy, envy, remorse, responsibility—that are conceptually bound up with them.[13] Even when fears of self-destruction are premature and self-defeating, they are not entirely unrealistic fantasies. Without the attentive cooperation of others, individuality starves, physically and psychologically. Perhaps we would be better off without such an idea of individuality: but the idea that we could do without that illusion may itself be an illusion. The drive to connect our traits in a unified entity ("Could you love me for myself alone, and not for my yellow hair?") comes from the fragility of many of our traits (and not merely from the fragility of their unification). The continuity of attention to the core *me* assuages the fears that our traits alter and disappear as they tragically do in just those situations where we need others most, in illness, in age, and in situations of social ostracism. One of the drives toward the bonding of attention to the underlying *me* is the quite realistic sense that when we most need others, we are also least likely to have the traits that on the surface once bound them to us. The impulse to bind our traits together in one whole person and to feel threatened in that whole, where there are only regional shifts in attention, elicits all the forces that are at work, for good or ill, to aid and to deter the integration and the unification of personality.

Oedipal Jealousy

There is no denying that male children are jealous of their fathers' claims to their mothers' loyalty and attentions, that they want desperately to have exclusive right to their mothers. But it is implausible to attribute affects whose ideational content a child does not yet have back into early psychological sets. Jealous, they are; and jealous of some forms of possession, they are. But possession of what? And if that possession has a sexual dimension, what is its ideational content?

In most societies, the one haven that a male child has, the one place where he is safe to be exactly what he is, without judgment or expectation, without the striving, the competition that is the tragic fate of the male in virtually every relation, is his relation to his mother. This bond is cemented even more closely by her physical attentions to him, her supplying his basic physical comforts and satisfactions. The male child's fear of his mother's relation with his father is his terror that the father will take her into his domain, the domain of the judges. Through her tie with the father, he may lose the one place in the world where he is wholly accepted: physically and psychologically attended and safe. And in fact, at just about the Oedipal phase, the child's fears are realized. The male child that was attended, accepted without demands, comes to receive (from his mother!) demands, expectations, judgment. His mother's attentive regard entirely changes character. Terror ensues. Perhaps if he could have exclusive rights over her, he could return to himself, his kingdom, his world. But he cannot: and so his bitterness and resentment of his mother's treachery sets an undercurrent that remains latent in his relations to the very women from whom he hopes to regain his original haven.

This explains why men are generally more jealous of their wives' sexual fidelity than are women of their husbands'. Men who live, as women rarely do, in a world of endless judgment and comparison, the universal animal terror of the constant hierarchical orderings—a world in which a person's self-esteem is always at stake in every encounter— suffer jealousy in a special way. With rare good fortune, a man can, ideally, hope to recreate in his marriage the conditions of his initial relation with his mother: the relation of unjudgmental, noncomparative attention that combined unconditional allegiance with physical care— the one secure place in the world. Of course the economic structure of family arrangements make that hope elusive: if the husband is unjudged, the breadearner often is. And the recollection of his mother's betrayal— her joining the world of the judges—leaves a man wary, if not actually hostile to, the very woman to whom he is most closely bound. Nevertheless, in a traditional marriage, a man can at least expect exclusive sexuality: if he successfully binds his wife's sexuality, he can hope to win the whole attentive bonding as well. Even if that turns out to be an elusive hope, he can at least expect to be sexually secure, safe from the terrible comparison that is his lot in the world. (It is interesting that prostitutes report that their clients seem to want reassurance of their prowess even more than they want sex.)

But if a man's wife sleeps with someone else, the world returns: there is no haven left. He will be compared, he will be judged in that one place where he was secure, most vulnerable because most himself. What, after all, one might ask, is possession, possession *of*? Why is sex thought to give possession of the body? It manifestly does not: strong sexual ecstasy absents the person. The fantasy is that it may give possession of the person. But what can that possibly mean? It may of course mean the power of control, of physical control, and the control of a person's objective social fate. But why should sexual relations be thought to be the key to such extraordinary power? It is because it is thought to be, and sometimes actually is, an assurance of unconditional, unjudgmental attentive acceptance. The excitement of adult male sexuality comes in part from the hope that sexual bonding will assure him what he had received in infancy from his mother: physical satisfaction from an unjudgmental other. The tragedy is closely related: the satisfaction of such hopes continues infantilism. (This is only one of the reasons that sexual play often also has a strong infantile character.)

But jealous fears are closely linked to the corresponding terror of engulfment. The desire for exclusive possession is paired with a contrary desire: the desire for autonomy and individuality. Most of our basic drives are paired in contraries: the drive to exploration matched with that to withdraw, the cycles of sleep and activity, hunger and satisfaction, the need for companionship and the need for solitude, the cycles of slow and fast pacing of activity. We shall not understand the dispositional character of our motivational system until we trace the self-regulating, self-generating cycles of these paired contraries. To understand how male sexual jealousy operates, it is also necessary to understand its paired contrary fear: the fear of absorption and containment, of engulfment. (The desire—and the terror—of the womb.) There is, then, a cycle in which the male child depends on the nonjudgmental attention of his female yet fears that if he is absorbed, wrapped in that attention, he will lose his powers, his identity in the father's world. The need for activity and daring, for exploration and testing pulls him away . . . and into the dangerous world where he is judged. There is a cycle of forays into the world, followed by a return to safety. But the danger of safety is engulfment and debility; and the danger of individual activity is exposure and judgment. The man turns to the woman with conflicting needs: unconditional acceptance on the one hand, and recognition and appraisal of his individual achievements on the other. He wants, and fears, the return to infantilism: and his jealousy bears the stamp of that conflict.

And the girl child? Characteristically, the love she receives from her father comes much later than the love the male child receives from his mother, and the father's love is not unconditional. An important part of a father's love for his daughter is that she does not—as do his sons—pose a judgmental threat to him. The attentive regard that a girl receives from her father gives her the self-image of a nonevaluative, nonjudg-mental female. That is one of the ways that she is prepared for being a mother, and it is one of the sources of her later compliance and her fears of competing with males. An initial condition of her father's love is that she never enter into competitive relations with him. (And, of course, no father can secure such assurances from his sons; because he identifies with them, he sets them the general tasks of emulation and striving, even while trying to control their relation to him.) A boy comes to regard his mother as a traitress: she withdrew the kind of attention she had once given. But a girl does not experience her father as a traitor: the constraint that marks her relation to her father was part of the initial condition of the relation. And that is why a woman's jealousy focuses, typically, on another woman's ability-to-attract-the-attention-of-the-male, while a man's jealousy, typically, focuses on his wife's-attention-to-some-other-man. It is because a wife's infidelity returns a man to the world of competitive judgment that such infidelity automatically lowers his place in the world. It is for this reason that men are more prey than women to jealousy over sexual infidelity. Because women's social real-ities are fixed by their dependence on male attention, they are more subject to nonsexual jealousy than men are. They also are more likely than men to suffer envy of the traits and properties they suppose would assure them the attentions they think they require.

Female jealousy tends to be directed to matters of practical depen-dence. Even when a woman is strongly bonded sexually, it is rare—and this is evident in polygamous societies—that female jealousy is strictly sexual. Women's attentional jealousy arises from their social condition. A woman's well-being in the world depends on her male's continued attachment to her. If she loses it, every detail of her life—the goods and the respect she can command—is subject to change. Her place in her man's world is her place in the world. In societies where widows depend upon their sons for livelihood and status, women are naturally prone to jealousy toward their daughters-in-law, who represent a clear threat, as rivals for the attentions, the goods, and the services that the son/husband distributes. The daughters-in-law are, in turn, jealous of their mothers-in-law's attempt to control their sons. In such cases the command of attention is clearly a command of sustenance and objective social status.

The asymmetries of patterns of male and female jealousy are closely related to the asymmetries of their affectional bonding. Characteristi-cally, women attach themselves—or, in traditional societies, are at-tached by their parents—to males who are thought their superiors, by whatever the goods the society trades: power, money, wealth, strength, age. Psychology and practicality go hand in hand. But, as long as a female's status and character is not so low as to bring a man shame that he can command no better, he need not particularly care about the character of his female. What he requires from her is not wealth, cleverness, or status, but competent physical care and children. Indeed, a markedly higher status is, traditionally, a potential threat to his command and control of her. For an ambitious man, there is often a difficult choice: whether to improve his status by connecting himself to a family that will provide dowry, lands, and well-placed patrons (thus running the risk of being a lowly figure in his household, a petitioner where he should be lord) or to assure his dominance in his household by making a marriage that can bring him no advancement. In polygamous societies, the problem is often solved by two marriages: the first, to a person of lesser status whose labor advances a man to the point where he can afford a second alliance to a higher-born woman. Characteristically, the pattern of the male's jealousy will then differ for his two marriages.

These social and economic differences also help to explain some of the differences in the imagistic and obsessional thoughts to which men and women are subject. Characteristically, the male does not, after the first stages of an infatuation or bonding, wish to know very much about his women's thoughts, interests, preoccupations. Because the women are objectively dependent on their men, any narration of their condition and their experiences constitutes or implies a complaint the man might be expected to redress. But it is just this dependence that requires a woman to be closely apprised of her man's moods, thoughts, foibles, penchants. Her well-being depends on her intimate knowledge of his traits—and on her ability to use that knowledge. This difference feeds directly into the differences in their respective jealous thoughts: the man is more likely to concentrate on what the woman does and the woman on what a man thinks or feels, as a clue to her own well-being.

It is these political origins of male and female psychological attitudes that Freud and early analysts missed. Virtually all of their analytic patients were thoroughly middle class. But a child who comes to see that the parent, on whose attentive regard his sense of himself depends, is a poor thing in the world, undergoes a terrible and dangerous humiliation. It is, of course, a political, social, and economic humiliation. But it is also—for these matters are by no means independent—a psychic humiliation that affects development. The patterns of adult attachments, their expectations and fears, their jealousies, are affected by such a child's shame and anger at his parents.

Of course a male child generally sees what a poor place in the world his mother has: the social, economic, and often political limitations on his mother's power. That recognition affects his relation to her: he must of course in any case cut off any identification he had originally made with her. But since she was originally also his source of self-esteem, that self-esteem is jeopardized as he sees that her judgment counts for little in the larger world. In coming to have contempt for her, he undermines himself. And as Lawrence has so brilliantly shown in *Sons and Lovers*, when the son is the bearer of the mother's social ambitions, her desperate hopes and ambitions for him leave him in a whirl of confusion. While she has not joined the father's forms of judgment, she has imposed on him tasks whose shape he cannot understand. And on her part, her identification with him leaves her prey to later ambivalences of pride and jealousy at his having a relation to the world, claims on its attention, that she cannot ever have.

The son who sees that his father is as poor a thing in the world as his mother is, suffers a debilitating form of anguish. If he strongly identifies with his father, he fears the possibility of his own success, and the threat that it may pose to the father. But more frequently, the perception of the father's powerlessness makes identification with the father much more difficult. The son must then prove that he is, as his father was not, a powerful man. That is one of the reasons that one often finds, among the socially and politically powerless, a strong and often desperate determination to male powerfulness, and a corresponding intense susceptibility to the need for exclusive possession of the female, a jealousy often more intense than that suffered by those who sense themselves to have worldly power.

Interestingly enough, a father's social and political powerlessness does not affect his daughters as much as it does his sons. Of course it affects them in important ways, simply because the reality of their lives is affected by their father's ability to command the goods of the world. But it does not affect their psychological development in the same way, because their initial judgment of their father's powers was never in question. A daughter's perception of her mother's powerlessness, especially if she has strongly identified with the mother, would induce depression rather than jealousy, even when she sees a mother suffering from a father's infidelities. If she does not strongly identify with her mother, she is likely to be angry rather than jealous or depressed, and to be angry at her mother rather than at her father. Frequently, since daughters who attempt not to identify with their mothers nevertheless on some level do accept the identification, one generally finds that women suffer anxious ambivalence rather than simple anger.[14]

8   Unconscious Affects, Mourning, and the Erotic Mind

"It is surely of the essence of an emotion that we should feel it, that is, that it should enter consciousness. . . . For . . . feelings . . . and affects to be unconscious would be out of the question."[1] As coming from Freud, the view that there are no unconscious affects is astonishing. After all, according to popular understanding, it is Freud who—if anyone—has insisted that a person can love or hate without recognizing his condition. "It may happen that an affect or emotion is perceived but misconstrued. By repression of its proper presentation (i.e., its ideational content), it is forced to become connected with another idea. . . . Its ideational presentation undergoes repression."[2] Certainly Freud's case studies present the best evidence for the persistent and canny substitution of one presentation for another, cases where someone is ignorant, and perhaps even systematically, willfully ignorant, of the true objects of his affects. In some cases one object is substituted for another: the clerk's (forbidden) hatred of his father is expressed by his hating his boss. There also appear to be cases where one affect is substituted for another: sons who hate the father whom they believe they love, fathers whose fears for their daughters' safety are a transposition of their own sexual attachments, colleagues who harbor murderous hatred for one another under the surface of elaborate respect or jovial banter. Even in his analysis of non-pathological cases, in the account of the etiology and specificity of adult love—its origins in the family drama that characteristically fix the objects of love—Freud appears to allow that we can be persistently and systematically ignorant of our affects. What, then, could he mean by denying that there are unconscious affects? Is it a defensible claim within his system? Is it a defensible claim independent of that system?

Although Freud would consider most psychological states that are normally classified as emotions to be affects, his notion of *Affekt* is both broader and narrower than the folk-psychological notion of emotion. It is broader in that it includes conditions that, like irritation, surliness, and excitation, are feelings and sensations that need not have characteristic proper objects. It is narrower in that some basic psychological conditions standardly considered emotions in folk psychology—love, for instance—are, on Freud's classification, sometimes direct manifestations of instinctual drives and sometimes by-products of the frustration of those drives. When love is the direct expression of libidinal energy, it need not be experienced as an affect; if it is felt or is accompanied by feelings, those felt libidinal energies would be physiologically and phenomenologically distinguishable from the longing feeling associated with the affect of love.[3] Freud sometimes treats an affect as an independent, self-contained psychological event with a specific sort of etiology and function in releasing or expressing blocked libidinal energy. But sometimes he treats it as essentially and identificationally conjoined with an idea: an affect is then the felt qualia of the idea, the "charge" of the idea as a dynamic force with a functional role that can be phenomenologically experienced.

Sometimes several problems are better than one: by rubbing them together, one can generate a bit of light. Freud's surprising doctrine on unconscious affects becomes somewhat less puzzling if we put it together with three other surprising views. I want first to try to make sense of the claim that there are no unconscious affects, relating this view to Freud's discussion of the phenomena of identificational mourning. With a fuller account of the Freudian canon of explanation in hand, we can understand Freud's concerns about whether affect-laden memories of childhood seduction are fantasized or real. Finally, we should be in a better position to reconsider whether the presumed submergence of affect during the "latency" period is self-deceptive.

I

Freud's chronicles of the unacknowledged rage of a son against his father, a daughter's denial of her jealousy of her mother, chronicles of (what appear to be) self-deceptive—or at the very least systematically misunderstood—affects, do not, on his understanding of the matter, constitute examples of unconscious affects. Although these psychological conditions are often misdiagnosed, although someone can often be mistaken about the true target or object of her feelings, and can even substitute one feeling for another, she *experiences* her condition affectively. To understand Freud's distinction between an affect, its object, its aim, and its function, we need to sketch one of the mainsprings of classical Freudian theory: the theory of drives. It is an almost ludicrously simple theory, resting on an almost breathtakingly simple image that provides the model—a sometimes Procrustean model—of endogenous action.

Behavior has its origin in—sometimes Freud speaks of it as a man-ifestation of—a set of drives. The most basic, most general drive is that of organic survival: it is expressed in a host of more specific drives, for food, for bodily maintenance, and for protection. Each of these generates and sometimes is expressed in yet more specific, intentionally indi-viduated and identified motivating forces. Although drives have proper satisfactions and proper objects, they are the most general and plastic energetic origins of action. Their energies can be directed and redirected, and the objects that satisfy them are substitutable and fungible. The drive for nourishment has food as its natural object, eating as its natural expression, and digesting as its natural satisfaction. But even in this basic, simple process, satisfying the original drive allows latitude for substitution: synthesized chemicals can serve as food; intravenous feed-ing can bypass the usual forms of eating and digesting. Indeed drives are sufficiently general and plastic to allow even contrary realizations and expressions (*The Antithetical Sense of Primal Terms*, SE 11:153). Hunger can manifest itself not only by imagining elaborate feasts but also by elaborate rituals of refusing food. In themselves, drives are blind. They do not carry their own interpretations: a person need not be con-sciously aware of their aim or objects. All behavior—even such a me-chanical, physically caused behavior as hiccuping— can be given intentional significance by an agent. A person can treat such behavior as if it were voluntary, and thus elicit defensive reactions against for-bidden behavior and thoughts.[4] Although actions are identified by their intentional descriptions, and the same piece of behavior can, under different intentional descriptions, designate distinctive actions, at least some actions have standard or fundamental normative intentional descriptions.

The prolonged, physically and psychologically vulnerable dependence of infancy produces acute psychological problems whose resolutions require, and are expressed in, a vast range of symbolic activities and attitudes. An infant's dependence on those who feed and nurture it generates problems—and images—that center around ingestion and in-corporation. The problems of nourishment are followed by those of mus-cular control, expressed in the struggles for physical and psychological power and mastery.[5] Each of these sets of problems is double-faced: the organism is itself affected not only by the objects with which it interacts but also by its own activity in interaction. Not only the food digested but the processes of digesting affect the organism. This double-faced character of the expression of drives makes activity and passivity co-ordinate: every event experienced as a passive response can also be experienced as an outcome and expression of the organism's own activity.

This Spinozistic inheritance has obvious consequences for Freud's theory of affects: when the natural expression of a drive is blocked, the body undergoes a set of physiological modifications that are experienced as affects, that is, as a set of distinctive sensations. For Freud, as for Spinoza, an affective reaction can be transformed into an active expression of an endogenous drive when the person's intentional description of her behavior connects it to her libidinal energy. In any case, the consequences of organic interaction with the environment do not remain localized at the point of interaction: every modification is the "active cause" of changes that are individuated by their etiology.

These elaborations are consequences of Freud's attempts to combine a mechanistic model with an organic one: his psychodynamic theory borrows heavily from, and attempts to unify, Aristotle's psychology with Hobbes' mechanism. He wants to combine the advantages of Hobbes' functionalistic identification of psychological states with an Aristotelian intentionalist identification of actions. He adopts and develops Aristotle's view that genetically and socially determined psychophysical development—the acquisition of habits of action and of mind—affects the intentionality of actions and interactions. He adopts and develops Hobbes' mechanistic account of motivational energy as a quantum of force with direction and momentum. Following the mechanistic picture, Freud characterizes an organism as a homeostatic system functionally organized to preserve its quantum and balance of energy. The system is constructed in such a way that it discharges the excess energy produced by invading stimuli. Because psychic energy is neither created nor destroyed, substitute channels are found when direct reactions to stimuli are blocked.

On this model, the energetic force of psychological states is distinguishable from their ideational contents. Identifying actions that have been determined by vectorial resolutions of forces does not require reference to their intentionally described energetic origins. Part of our problem in interpreting Freud's claim that there are no unconscious affects is the problem of reconciling an Aristotelian intentionalist with a Hobbesian extensionalist identification of psychological activities— the problem of giving an account of the relation between the intentional object of a psychological state and its functional role.

Identifying psychological states requires four parameters or variables:

a. the impetus (the amount of energy)
b. the aim (the character of the satisfaction involved)
c. the object intentionally described
d. the source

(*Instincts and Their Vicissitudes*, SE 14:126)

Because these identifying factors are independent of one another, transformations can occur in one without affecting the others. So, for instance, the object of a psychological state can be replaced by a symbolic substitute without affecting the impetus; and the impetus can be reconstructed—reapportioned within the psychological field—without affecting the aim. Much of the Freudian canon of explanation consists in the set of rules governing the transformation and substitution of libidinal energy: the strategies of drive satisfaction. For our purposes, the significant rules can be characterized as rules for the transformation of energy and rules for the translation of ideational content. The rules for the transformation of energy are formally elegant, involving simple spatial redirections. The direction of the energy can be internalized or externalized; its charge can be changed from positive to negative; the relation can be active or passive (*Instincts and Their Vicissitudes*, SE 14:126). The rules for the translation of ideational or intentional content are much more complex: they permit idiosyncratic symbolization from sources lying in an individual's psychological history, as well as in standard cultural allusions.

The energetic force of a drive remains constant until it is expressed or discharged. It is directly discharged when it is expressed in the sort of behavior that characteristically brings the satisfaction that is its instinctual aim. When the direct expression of a drive is blocked, its redirections will have an affective charge, no matter what form they take. Dreams, fantasies, symbolic ritual acts, or sublimated activities—indirect expressions of a blocked drive—carry an affective charge that releases the original energy. And it is *that*—the affective charge—which can't be unconscious. Affects are just the by-products, the effects of blocked or frustrated drives. They are a kind of psychophysical explosion, a feeling that expresses and releases the energies of the pent-up drive.

An affect . . . represents that part of the instinct which has become detached from the idea. . . . [It] corresponds with processes of discharge the final expression of which is perceived as feeling. . . . Affectivity manifests itself essentially in motor (i.e. secretory and circulatory) discharge resulting in an (internal) alteration of the subject's own body without reference to the outer world. (*Repression*, SE 14:91, 111)

It is precisely their being felt and experienced that releases the force of the drive, and that identifies the psychological condition as an affect.

We are now in a better position to see why Freud thinks that his examples of unacknowledged hatreds, displaced loves, and transformed angers are compatible with his insistence that there are no unconscious affects. The *affect*—the feeling—is (virtually by definition) consciously experienced as such. But all the surrounding material—the original drive, the object, the direction, even the tonal quality as positive or negative, active or passive, projected or introjected—can be transformed, displaced, or substituted to fit the rest of the person's psychological condition: to avoid what is forbidden, to follow habitual, encoded symbolization, and so on. It is about all of this surrounding material, rather than about the presence or absence of the affect, that a person can be self-deceived. "The ideational material has undergone displacements and substitutions, whereas the affects have remained unaltered" (*Interpretation of Dreams*, SE 14:461).

Sometimes Freud speaks of affects as distinctive, nonintentional psychological states, those that succeed in discharging the energy of blocked drives in a specific way: by felt somatic modifications that have no reference to the outer world. But sometimes he says that all indirect expressions of frustrated drives—even those that, like dreams, fantasies, and ritual actions, are essentially attached to an ideational content—carry an affective discharge. But what distinguishes a direct from an indirect release of a drive, particularly if drives are plastic and fungibly satisfiable? What differentiates the redirected or sublimated satisfaction of a drive from an indirect expression of its frustration? Why introduce affects as special events at all? How do they differ from other forms of release? Why wouldn't fantasies, dreams, and redirected activity be sufficient to release the energy of a drive? And why can't someone be mistaken about whether she is in an affective condition?

As long as someone can deny the translation or symbolization of an ideational content or deny that an energetic drive has been transformed, then affects—individuated by their ideational content—can be as unconscious as anything else. The affect is then not identifiable independent of the ideational content to which it attaches, any more than the ideational content is fully identifiable independent of its etiology. This is the solution that follows the Aristotelian intentionalist strand in Freud's thought. But following the mechanistic, functionalist Hobbesian line—a line that Freud considers necessary for the possibility of the redirection and transformation of psychic energy—requires him to separate the energy of a psychological state from its ideational content. And it is this, the mechanistic rather than the organicist version of his theory of drives, that leads him to insist on the impossibility of unconscious affects.

There is a set of related problems: if the affect just is the experience of discharged energy that had been blocked, then there can be no question of its appropriateness to its object or even to its cause. It is not even clear how qualitative distinctions among affects are identified. To the extent that affects just are "motor discharges," they can be distinguished from one another only by the nonintentional sensations associated with their various physiological conditions. "The release of affects as a centrifugal process directed towards the interior of the body and analogous to the processes of motor and secretory innervation" only allows a nonintentional criterion for the differentiation of affects (*Interpretation of Dreams*, 467–68). But if affects are only identifiable and distinguishable by physically based, nonintentional sensations, then an affect cannot be used to recover a repressed idea. When Freud speaks of the inappropriateness of an affect, or of the singular absence of an appropriate affect, however, he clearly envisages a closer connection between its energy and its content. "If the affect and the idea are incompatible in their character and intensity, one's waking judgment is at a loss" (ibid., 459–61). Indeed only if there *is* a proper connection between an affect and its idea is there a reason to repress or displace the idea, to replace the real with a manifest content. And only if there is a proper connection can an affect be used to "give us a pointer as to how we can find the missing (i.e., the censored or repressed) thoughts. . . . The affect [helps us] seek out the idea which belongs to it but which has been repressed and replaced by a substitute" (ibid.). At least in *Interpretation of Dreams*, Freud means to make the close connection between an affect and its ideational content a pivotal diagnostic and therapeutic tool. Because the affect remains the same when the idea is changed, it can be used to recover the original idea; when the idea is again connected to its original affect, some affective disorder can be corrected. Nowhere is Freud's struggle between the mechanistic-associationistic and the cognitive-intentional views sharper than in the tension arising out of his attempts to explain how an affect that has become detached from an idea can be used to recover the repressed idea.[6]

II

Before the situation improves, it must get worse. It might seem that either every psychological state is affective (because it involves the transformation and redirection of blocked drives) or there are no purely affective states (because drives are always somehow expressed). If every case of successfully redirected energy that requires patterned ignorance and misdescription involves the suppression of material that is also implicitly recognized, then self-deception lurks virtually everywhere. Or self-deception is nowhere, because the mechanisms that explain denial,

or repression, or the censorship of unconscious material do not represent
the activities of the self. There is no such single entity. If on one hand
"the self" is a complex whole, composed of more or less integrated
subsystems, it does not, as that whole, deceive itself: one subsystem
systematically misleads others. If on the other hand "the self" is the
well-developed ego, then there is no self-deception, because the ego is
the subsystem that attempts to integrate all others. If affects are just the
nonintentional sensations consciously experienced as the result of
blocked drives, then self-deception could only consist in an attempt at
verbal denial—a denial manifestly invalidated by the rest of the person's
behavior. But if affects are also identified by their ideational content,
then self-deception can only involve systematic misdescription or mis-
identification of the object of the affect.

Freud's discussion of mourning—and his puzzling failure to connect
two sorts of identificational imitation—provides an illuminating example
of his indecision about how to resolve the problems that emerge from
his views on unconscious affects. In discussing the connection between
mourning and identification, Freud observes that the mourner often takes
on the *persona*—the habits and gestures, intonation patterns, and sometimes attitudes—of the person she has lost. He speculates that this
identification attempts to recreate the lost object.[7]

Though it is basic to the explanatory canon, the term *identity* is rarely
characterized with any precision: it is vaguely used to cover a wide range
of senses. Freud's use of the term can be reconstructed in such a way
as to give us some understanding of what it is for a set of traits, ideals,
and habits to be central to a person's identity. What Freud treats as
structure can be interpreted in dynamic and defensive terms. A trait,
object relation, attitude or belief, concern, or ideal is central to a person's
identity when it is essential to her survival as the sort of person she is.
The preservation and expression of that trait (attitude, concern, object
relation, ideal) is motivationally central: a threat to it directly mobilizes
the strategies of defensive maneuvers exercised in self-preservation,
without requiring any other pleasure-bound, pain-avoiding motivation.
Exercising, enhancing, defending, promoting, and expressing those traits
(etc.) is constitutively and directly motivating independent of any other
satisfactions or ends. As it stands, this rough characterization allows
that someone might be mistaken about what is essential or central to
her identity, either falsely believing that a trait (etc.) is central when it
is not, or falsely believing that a trait (etc.) is not central when it is. At
least some traits essential to a person's identity can be extensionally
identified; sometimes that identification can significantly differ from the
person's own conception of what is essential to her identity, even when

the behavioral expression of the two are the same. Yet understanding the systematic pattern of a person's actions and thoughts requires not only understanding what is effectively identificational (in the sense sketched above) but also her conception of what is essential to her, including active ideals that she tries, but fails, to realize.[8]

Freud does not draw the obvious consequence of his theory: the hidden proper object of mourning is the self that has been diminished or transformed by the loss. The reason he does not draw this consequence is that when mourning is expressed as an affect, it does not have a proper object. The energy released at the frustration or blockage of a drive bears no representational relation to the objects or aims of the original drive; nor does it represent the causes of its repression. Freud does not face the problem whether those forms of mourning that recreate, internalize, and act out the life of the lost object are not experienced or felt as affects. On the one hand, such mourning is surely fused with felt grief. On the other hand, it might seem as if identificational mourning does not conform to the conditions of affectivity: it is externally and representationally rather than internally directed. In that case the fact that the mourner can be systematically unaware of reproducing the lost object, and can even deny the loss, does not disconfirm Freud's claim that there are no unconscious affects. When mourning is expressed by assuming and acting out a lost identity, it is not expressed as an affect. Perhaps Freud can have it both ways: the two forms of mourning—the affective and the behavioral—might be psychologically fused while being analytically distinguishable.

Still there is a problem. Identifying with the lost object, the mourner defends herself by recreating and imitating what has been lost. What was necessary or essential to her identity is magically preserved. This defense must be disguised to be successful, particularly in that, all along, the real but obscure object of mourning is the dear self, whose identity has been threatened by the loss. Following this line of thought would lead Freud to preserve the strong connection between an affect and its object: for it is precisely by imitating and preserving the lost object that damage to the self is avoided. For this process to work successfully, the person must be systematically unaware of what she is doing. For if she were fully conscious of the fiction, she would not succeed in defending herself against the threat to her identity. Presumably Freud would have to argue that insofar as mourning is behavioral, it can be unconscious or self-deceptive; but insofar as it is affective, it cannot be.

The labyrinthine intricacy of Freud's view appears even more dramatically when, after the first account of the phenomena of mourning, he remarks that the mourner's attempt to incorporate the lost object is very similar to the sort of identification and imitation that newly married women make: they often acquire and imitate their husbands' traits, opinions, and gestures (*Mourning and Melancholia*, SE 14). He notes, without developing the matter, that there appears to be an asymmetry in the acquisition of traits when couples live together. The woman tends to identify with and imitate the man; rarely does the man take on the traits of the woman. Surprisingly, Freud simply mentions this as yet another form of identification, without exploring the possibility that far from being an independent phenomenon, this type of imitative identification is an instance of self-deceptive mourning.[9] Why does Freud conjoin the two phenomena without connecting them and without elaborating or explaining his observation? Why did he introduce this phenomenon of wifely imitation in the middle of a discussion of the identificational processes that take place in mourning?

In the course of describing and analyzing this process of identificational mourning, Freud remarks that the choice of a sexual object appears not only to influence the development of the ego of women, but also to affect their character, that is, their identity. There seems, he says, to be an intrusive relation between identification and object-choice. Women tend to imitate and identify with the objects of their attachments even when the cathexis is anaclitic and not particularly loving.

Of course there may be many other explanations for this imitative identification. Characteristically, the woman is socially and economically dependent on her husband. Especially when there is a marked difference in age, the wife is often formed by her husband (see, e.g., Freud's educative letters to his fiancée) and formed for him (see, e.g., Rousseau's highly influential *Émile*). Without being aware of doing so, the women may well be placating or complying with or wooing (those whom they experience as) their superiors. But because there is good reason to think that there is overdetermination in this area, I want to explore the possibility that such imitative identification is mourning, with the affect submerged or denied. Our question will then be; Is the woman self-deceived when she is unaware of, and would deny, her mourning?

Freud believes that we acquire our conceptions and expectations of love from our early experiences: the particular tonal character of parental nurturing serves as the paradigmatic model for all that we later consider to be affectional bonding. Characteristically, the kind of love that newly coupled men receive from their women tends to include the sort of attentive nurturing they received from their mothers.[10] Standardly, men are fed and preened by wives who follow maternal patterns down to the details of attending to clothing. But unless they are narcissistic types, women rarely receive this sort of attention, even when they are well loved. Standardly and conventionally, a man's ardor is greater before sexual partnership is established, while a woman's affections are more strongly bonded afterward. On Freud's account, this difference is a function of the differences between male and female genital development: male genital drives are physically developed in adolescence, while female sexuality only matures with experience. Once the couple are established sexual partners, the man not only receives sexual satisfaction: he also reliably receives the kind of nurturing care on which he comes to depend, and which he associates with love. As long as he receives both kinds of attention, he need not experience any affect of love or longing.

But the woman's story is somewhat different. Although in the best cases, her awakened genital drives are satisfied, her need for nurturance is not. Even though the man provides for her financially, he does not actually tend or attend to her as he did during their courtship. But since the woman also formed her conceptions and expectations of loving bonding from parental nurturing, she experiences her husband's bonding as incomplete. She has lost the man who courted her. This is why many women are puzzled by what seems to them as their husbands' withdrawal, while men are puzzled by what seems to them to be their wives' excessively clinging emotionality. The men cannot understand why their women fail to recognize that love is thoroughly expressed in action and in sexuality, in satisfaction rather than in longing. Freud provides the materials for explaining the phenomena. To the extent that some of her needs for nurturance—needs she associated with physical bonding—are frustrated, the newly married woman experiences longing love as a mode of mourning. To the extent that her sense of herself has been bound up with her husband, her identity is threatened by what she experiences as a loss. She often tries to woo her husband back by what is usually counterproductive clinging—the sort of clinging a child evinces when it experiences the withdrawal of a parent—or, like other mourners, she attempts to identify with, and to recreate, the suitor she has lost. The more helpless she is to express that love effectively, the more powerfully felt it becomes.

If the newly wed wife is mourning, she is usually either systematically unaware of, or self-deceived about, the true nature of her affective condition. She may well have reason to deny that her diffuse longing and its accompanying identificational imitation are varieties of mourning, deflections of her sense of diminished identity. If she finds that her continued expressions of melancholic love distance her husband, she may repress the feeling as well as the expression. Yet her imitative identificational behavior may express mourning, as well as the acknowl-edgment of power. If there are such cases of repression, Freud's denial of unconscious affects must, at the very least, be hedged.

III

Freud's difficult vacillation over the theory of childhood seduction—the problem whether adult reports of childhood seductions are bona fide memories or whether they are fantasies—also provides an argument that Freud should accept rather than reject the existence of unconscious affects.

Setting aside those cases of actual physical seduction, does it follow that all other cases of reported childhood seduction are fantasies based on wish, subjected to the usual set of projective transformations? I believe it does not follow. The very large area that combines reality, interpre-tation, and fantasy provides ample documentation of self-deceptive or unconscious affects.

This, I believe, is a naturalistic story about parent-child seductive interaction. In the course of giving their children physical and nurturing care—bathing them, combing their hair, dressing them and so on—parents often come to form an erotic attachment to their children. Finding them delectable, seductive, they may often have erotic fantasies and wishes of which they are only marginally aware. They might simply wish to extend and prolong their caresses and in an obscure way want to arouse the child to return caresses. Though such wishes and fantasies would normally be suppressed and not overtly enacted, still the parent's arousal may be sufficient to change her or his expression and gestures in a subtle but observable way. An intent that is not expressed in overt action can nevertheless be observably manifest to a sensitive child. A child might not only notice but respond to such subtle changes in the features of an erotically aroused adult. The child would of course not understand the latent intent, because it would have no way of assimilating this to other experiences. The event would present something unknown and frightening, both because it is unknown and because it carries an unassimilable, responding, excited charge. Particularly because the sub-tle traces of erotic arousal sometimes can superficially resemble the subtle traces of repressed anger, the child might find the undigested, uninterpreted, unacknowledged experiences difficult and unresolvable. Frequently repeated, sometimes highly charged, such experiences might be strong enough to produce anxiety requiring working out in dreams and fantasies whose own internal psychological momentum might mag-nify it.

Once the child acquires the categories and concepts of sexual life, new explanations can retrospectively be applied to the unabsorbed eroticized experience. The stories of childhood seduction can sometimes fall in that important area between fantasy and reality: the child has correctly recognized the latent and submerged content of an interaction, and has done so at a time when it cannot mark the all-important distinction between an intention that is overtly expressed in behavior and one that is psychologically real but behaviorally sublimated or repressed. Since the distinctions between mood, intention, and action are learned only gradually, and are indeed always being reinterpreted, it is not surprising that the child confuses a real tonality with a realized action. In the absence of any correcting experience, the adult continues the child's confusion, reporting something that falls between memory and fantasy.

What has this to do with unconscious affects? It suggests, though of course it does not prove, that an adult who has reworked such erotically charged experience is recounting and reporting affectively charged memories that can, but need not be, experienced affectively. Sometimes, indeed, it can be just the very deadpan *absence* of affect in situations that, presumptively, are strongly affect-laden that reveals the person's psychological struggles. If it is genuinely possible to report and behaviorally manifest the absence of affect in situations that appear in every respect to conform to the model of blocked—affectively redirected—energies, it would seem that a person could be self-deceived about whether she is affected, as well as about what affects her.

IV

Yet again, things must get worse before they get better. Before trying to resolve Freud's problems about unconscious affects, let us see what the mystery of latency can contribute to the story.

The apparent blankness of the latency period presents a puzzling lacuna in Freud's account of the psychodynamics of development. Why should there be such a long dormant period at a time of important physical and intellectual change? Following the general dictum that all psychophysical and intellectual changes are psychosexually significant, it seems implausible that this period should be developmentally blank, centered primarily on consolidation. As Anna Freud was later to suggest in her account of intellectual development, thought processes can become affectively charged to express and release psychodynamic conflicts. A child's success in developing a powerful, affective and richly subtle intellectual and imaginative life depends on her being systematically unaware of the psychosexual functions of those processes, of the ways her thought expresses and releases psychodynamic conflicts. But systematic ignorance—patterned repressive discrimination of attention—requires scanning for forbidden material, which involves implicit admission of its import. The success of sublimated activity appears to depend on denials and repressions of affect that are suspiciously like self-deception. And if the intellectualization of libidinal processes and conflicts is not affectively experienced, then not only ideas but also affects themselves can be unconscious.

The latency stage occurs between the end of anal stage and the beginning of the genital stage, after habits of psychophysical self-control and mastery have been developed and consolidated. The activities of the oral stage—introjection and projection, absorption and rejection—have been integrated and expanded onto a larger somatic and psychological field. Before puberty focuses on the issues of genitality, a person's central psychological work consists in developing characteristic intellectual patterns of thought, imagination, and fantasy: it is the period for the formation of psycho-intellectual strategies for elaborating, transforming, and gratifying instinctual processes. The metaphors central to the earlier stages remain: seeing is a way of absorbing and introjecting the world, imagining is a way of mastering and controlling it, speaking and writing are expressions, expulsions, explosions. The eye and the mind become eroticized during the latency stage. What we cannot have, we can imagine. What we cannot destroy, we can deconstruct. It is the stage for the development of thought at the service of defense. But it is also the stage in which thought, imagination, and fantasy come to be sources of—and not merely avenues for—independent autoerotic satisfaction. The child develops habits of categorization and association, characteristic narratives of symbolic thought and action, patterns of substitute gratification. Rituals of play and games form expectations of roles and attitudes: life is seen as combat, adventure, or exploration; one's role is that of leader, follower, or observer; the world affords opportunities or frustrations; events unfold with fateful necessity or largely by accident and chance; other players are comrades or kinfolk, mysterious strangers, allies, enemies, superiors or inferiors, primarily men or primarily women, or indifferently men or women. Communication is largely verbal or nonverbal, direct or symbolic; the tone is playful, devious, ironic, or serious. The primary strategies of defense are intellectual or physical, political or aesthetic. (Of course these alternatives are meant to be suggestive rather than exclusive or exhaustive.)

Why didn't Freud recognize the eroticization of the eye and the mind, of language and modes of communication? Of course in one sense it was he who introduced this idea: thought is a means toward, and eventually itself becomes, a form of gratification: the redirection and satisfaction of instinctual drives. Fantasy and the imagination originally provide substitute gratification; but when they have become eroticized, they provide direct as well as substitute satisfaction. When Freud discusses the eroticization of thought, he dampens the distinction between the energy of a psychological state and its content (*Instincts and Their Vicissitudes*, SE 14). But even though his analyses of scoptophobic and linguistic disorders amply document the eroticization of the eye, language, and the imagination, his commitment to one version of the Hobbesian mechanistic model prevents his accepting the consequences of his insight. In Freud's account of general somatic eroticization, the erogenous zones include the mouth, the anus, and the genitals, but not—except in pathological cases—the eyes and the ears. Freud's continued commitment to the mechanization of the biological model—the buildup and release of energetic charges—explains his surprising failure to connect his theory of the development of erotically charged intellectual processes with his theory of the role of erogenous zones in psychodynamic development.

With considerable strain and some Procrustean cutting, Freud can interpret his theory of the activities of mouth, anus, and genitals within his mechanistic model: the mouth devours and spits, the anus constricts or defecates, and genital tension mounts and is orgastically released. Here the problems of theory become dramatic: what are the criteria for *release*? Do eating and defecating really conform to the excitation-and-release model? Each seems to involve a different model of release. In any case, however wide the latitude of the mechanistic model of excitation, accumulation, tension, and release, the eroticized eyes, ears, and mind do not follow it.

One might attempt to combine the two strands of Freud's theory by distinguishing the phenomenological from the ontological enterprise.[11] A causal, phenomenological account allows the separation of an ideational content from its consequent affect; the Aristotelian conceptual and ontological account conjoins the two. The two are compatible because they involve distinctive types of explanation. This would be a pretty solution if it were true. But does an introspective-phenomenological account really reveal the separability of an affect and its content? The phenomenological feel of affects seems content-bound and variable with the details of the individuation of their objects: someone's affective feelings toward (just this) newborn child are radically different from his affective feelings toward that child when she is six, or ten, or twenty. And these are different from his affective feelings toward his brother's children at six, ten, and twenty. And these again are different from the affective feelings one has toward the children of one's friends. Introspectively, affective feelings are protean indeed: but protean because they are bound up with, rather than disconnected from, their ideational content, which itself varies with the psychodynamic role played by that ideational content.

We can distinguish affect types (rage, love, or fear, for example) from individuated ideas-and-affects identified by their etiology and functional roles (for instance, a child's particular fear of a particular church spire on a particular occasion). The former permit the substitution of objects and allow for functionally equivalent replacements (hate for love, gratitude for envy); the latter do not. Even though an affect type is characterized by associated typical intentional objects (sibling jealousy, for instance), it can be detached from its particular objects (brothers, sisters). The minuet graces of transformations (the change of a charge from positive to negative, from active to passive, from projective to introjective) and the rich thesaurus of translations of objects (the substitutions of sons for brothers, kings for fathers, gloves for mothers, church spires for kings) all take place on the level of affect types. Only on that level is it possible to reidentify the same affect under its transformations and the same content under its translations. But individuated affects are radically transformed by every transformation: someone's horror of a particular church spire is different from his horror of his maternal uncle's beard at a particular time, under particular circumstances. This is not important news: it is a trivial consequence of the discernibility of distinct individuals.

Freud can retain the advantages of the physiologically oriented mechanistic model—the advantages of accounting for the redirection of energy from one content to another—with the advantages of the cognitive model according to which individual psychological states (and the behavior and actions that express them) are intentionally identified. The mechanistic model applies at a general level, the level of typical description: at that level, ideational contents of psychological states are substitutable; indeed it is sometimes just their substitutability that allows them to play their appropriate functional roles. Sometimes psychological states themselves—and not merely their ideational contents—are functionally substitutable. So, for some (but not for all) purposes hate can play the same functional role as love, love the same role as envy. The stringency of conditions for the reidentification of a psychological state varies with the level of detail at which its functional role is described. So, for some purposes, an affect can be identified by its generalized functional role: for this purpose, hate need not be distinguished from love. But for other purposes—purposes that require a more detailed and individuated description of functional roles—the two affects are distinguished. *When the functional role that a psychological state plays essentially requires its having a specific intentional content, then the affective charge of the state cannot be separated from its ideational content. When the functional role of a psychological state can be played without any particular intentional content (and perhaps even without any particular type of intentional content) then it can be identified independently of that intentional content.* Because the criteria for reidentification need not reduce to the criteria for individuation, a psychological state can be identified at different levels of generality for different explanatory purposes. So, for some explanatory purposes, it can be separated from the particular intentional contents that individuate it, and for others not.

When affects are identified independently of their intentional contents—when they are identified by their functional roles most generally characterized—they cannot be unconscious. They cannot be unconscious because at that level of generality, there is nothing to them but their affective feel: no affective feel, no affect. At *that* level of generality, affects are not individuated, not even as affect types: characterized so generally, the functional role of hate is not distinguished from that of love. But when affects are identified by their intentional contents, a person can be as self-deceived about her affect as she can be about its intentional content. If the content is translated or substituted, so can the affect be; if the content is repressed, so can the affect be. One of the attractions of this solution is that it gives us a way of saying that at one level of description—as playing a generalized functional role—an affect cannot be unconscious, but at another level of description, it can be. Is it the same affect that, at one level of generality, is unconscious, and at another level, is not? The answer depends upon the generality of the question. At a general level of reidentification—one that allows the substitution of intentions *salve functione*—the same affect can, under one description, be unconscious, and on another, not. But affects individuated by their intentions cannot be both conscious and unconscious.[12]

9   Adaptivity and Self-Knowledge

Does a person's knowledge of his own sensations, emotional states, intentions, wants, and thoughts differ in form or justification from his knowledge of other people's sensations, emotional states, wants, and thoughts? A full answer to this question should not only chart the advantages and liabilities of self-knowledge, but also explain why some people are better at understanding themselves than others and why a person's talents in self-knowledge are not uniform.

My thesis is that self-knowledge has no special status: its varieties constitute distinctive classes, which differ from one another more sharply than each does from analogous knowledge of others. Being aware of one's pains, if it is knowledge at all, is more like being aware of a trumpet call than it is like knowing what one wants or intends to do; knowing one's own character traits is more like knowing someone else's dispositions than it is like knowing how one presently feels. Understanding the varieties of self-knowledge requires a little help from our friends, from neurophysiologists and endocrinologists, to chart the ways in which we absorb information from different sources, the ways in which the language centers function under different conditions. I shall argue that there is much less self-knowledge than meets the ear, and that many cases of self-knowledge are best understood when they are subsumed under other activities: self-knowledge in the service of decision-making, self-improvement, or sociability. Finally, I shall explore the advantages and liabilities of self-knowledge, arguing that while there are no distinctive problems about self-knowledge, there are distinctive problems about being the sort of creature that is capable of it, capable of treating itself as an object to be understood.

I. Some Distinctions

1. We need to distinguish knowing our character traits, preference rankings, and systematically ordered beliefs from being aware of present sensations, feelings, desires, or thoughts. This distinction is easier and

slicker to state than to work out, because our knowledge of our dispositions surely involves awareness and remembered awareness of present states. Certainly some dispositions are analyzable as states of a very complex kind; and some complex states are not only signs of dispositions, but dispositions of complex kinds. (The present state of a fertilized egg determines its normal development, determines dispositions to respond to specific conditions in patterned ways.) For our purposes, these complications can be left as complications: we need only to distinguish being aware of one's present state, its presented qualities, from one's knowledge of that state as part of a projected pattern, treated as an index of future states, an index that may require considerable deciphering.

2. We need also to distinguish being in a state, for example, being exhilarated, in pain, or tired, from being aware that one is evincing the characteristic signs of a particular state.

Sometimes, but not always, being aware that one is in a certain state is the best indication of being in that state, because the awareness is part and parcel of the state. But when our states are complex, the focus of attention may be wholly on the object, and neither on our state nor our awareness of being in that state. When we focus on the object, awareness is absorbed into sensing; when we focus on ourselves as sensing, we may fail to attend to what we are sensing.

The signs of being in a particular state may range from such somatic symptoms as taut muscles or contracted pupils, to overt behavior such as shrugging, wincing, yawning. Subtler bits of protolinguistic behavior such as sniffling, sighing, hissing, moaning, and the like, are also signs of states. Here again it is easier to plonk down a distinction than it is to work out the details. Somatic states or physical and protolinguistic behavior may be contingently or necessarily part of a state, and so may be either contingently or necessarily symptomatic of it. Although determining whether such behavior is necessarily or contingently related to a state is generally a matter of discovery, it may, in some cases, be a matter of convention or decision. The differentiation of discovery and decision is, furthermore, a matter of degrees, with the blend of discovery and decision different for different states. For instance, though it is unlikely that the connection between wincing behavior and pain is necessary, wincing is probably more tightly connected with pain than giggling is with its state. For our purposes, these important complications can be laid aside; we need only recognize that even when somatic, physical, or protolinguistic behavior is part and parcel of being in a particular state, we can distinguish, conceptually at any rate, the state as a whole from those aspects of it that are taken as its indices, symptoms, or expressions.

3. To be sensing is always to be aware of something. But it is not always the case that when we are sensing, we are focused on the fact that we are sensing; attention may be wholly on the object sensed, and not on oneself sensing. And so we can distinguish, conceptually, at any rate

a. being in the sort of state that can, on reflection or with a shift in attention, be seen to be (to have been) a sensory state; e.g., we may learn to distinguish proprioceptive states that we had previously not noticed (because this would be the best explanation of our behavior, we might want to say that we had been in those states, even though we had not yet learned how to attend to them as sensory);
b. being in a sensory state, that is, aware of external or internal stimuli, affecting either the sense organs or proprioceptive mechanisms;
c. being in a sensory state focusing on or paying attention to some specific aspect of the stimulus or object;
d. being in a sensory state focusing or attending to the fact that one is sensing, or to oneself as sensing;
e. being in a sensory state focusing or attending to some further psychological or physical effects of the sensory state.[1]

The difference between attending primarily to some aspect of one's response to stimuli and focusing on some aspect of the stimulus is a matter of degree; it may sometimes be partly, but is generally not wholly, a voluntary matter. Attention can of course shift very rapidly, and it is sometimes difficult to determine whether, in a short period, it has shifted or whether there were simultaneous, distinguishable layers of attending.

4. We need to distinguish expressions of our states that happen to be in propositional form from bona fide propositional reports of those states. What we want in this area is not so much a distinction as a continuum leading to a distinction. On one side there are sighs, groans, hissings, intakes of breath—some almost straight physical reactions, others more distinctly conventional in character—moving toward straightforwardly conventional expressions, "Ouch," "Ai," "Oi," "Yum." These in turn gradually move toward sentential expressions: "That hurts," "Great!" "Delicious!" Some of these sentences verge on the propositional, but here is where discontinuity appears. All of this behavior, subtly differentiated as it indeed can be, is contrasted with a person uttering a sentence meaning to report what is the case, capable of being evaluated as true or false. Of course the same sentence can be used both expressively and propositionally. In a particular instance, "My neck hurts" may verge toward "Ouch!"; in another, toward a precisely formulated proposition. What is more important, as we shall see later,

is that a sentence may be doing both simultaneously: several speech acts can be performed at the throw of one sentence, and sometimes the various speech acts must nestle in a certain order of intentional priority in order for them all to be brought off successfully.

II. Some Caveats

Let's not bog down here, or anywhere else for that matter, about whether we are talking about physical states or psychological states or psychophysical states. I think we are, in all these cases, dealing with psychophysical states, but explaining that is a different shaggy dog story. An analysis of the privileges of self-knowledge may perhaps, as Descartes had hoped, shed light on the mind/body problem; but if it did, it would only be because it recast mirror reflections from many distinct light sources.

It is a mistake to begin with an initial prejudice in favor of cases of high truth and clarity. If we were to discover that a certain type of self-knowledge were less likely to be falsified, because it was noninferential or in some way self-warranted or incorrigible (or any of that crew), it would not at all follow that such types of self-knowledge give us better knowledge of ourselves as we live and breathe than our less clear and less certain knowledge. It might give us better knowledge of our being-presently-aware-of-ourselves-as-sensing, but the relation of those states to the rest of us would still be uncharted. It is Cartesian simplistic formalism to suppose that what is clearest, or most self-evident, is pivotal in other ways: that it is paradigmatic or foundationally central, or the basis of inferences about more complex self-knowledge. It may well turn out that what we know most clearly and certainly about ourselves is also least central to our character taken as a whole. If understood out of context, such knowledge is likely to be highly misleading, however perspicuous it might be in itself, *in vacuo*.

The claim that a first-person report of a present state is incorrigible or self-warranted *in principle* (rather than in that well-known sense of "incorrigible" that means "corrigible later, when we know more") assumes rather than supports mind/body identity.[2] Such reports are indeed no more corrigible than is the height of mercury in a thermometer or a dog's howling at the moon, because the report is itself (treated or translated as) a state. But treated in this way, reports are no more reports than is the height of mercury or a howl. If they are incorrigible, it is because they are not the sorts of things that could be either true or false.

For good causes, but not logical reasons, these incorrigible utterances have the same sentential form as propositions. Uttered as propositions, they are corrigible claims, genuine reports. Reporting is (at the very least) a triadic, if not actually a quadratic relation: a person reports something (to someone). The use of an utterance, and not its sentential form, determines whether it is a corrigible propositional report or an incorrigible howl. The sentential forms of first-person reports are, I shall claim, typically, and not just occasionally, ambiguous: they best fulfill their various functions by being ambiguous.

Nevertheless, there are good reasons, besides a passion for perspicuity, for beginning self-knowledge by inspecting first-person reports of present states. These relatively clear cases do, as we shall see, play a crucial role in complex knowledge of our complex selves. But that role is not that of a building-block, and self-knowledge is not constructed from our awareness or remembered awareness of present states, as if such knowledge were additive or cumulative, a charting of correlated certified bits of clear and distinct reports.

In being careful not to treat first-person reports of present states as paradigms of self-knowledge, we must also be wary of assuming that the self is a tightly organized system, whose processes are in principle directly available to self-certifying introspection. Though they differ in their choice of initial units of privileged self-knowledge, both Cartesians and empiricists assign favored status to conscious processes as central to the organization of the self. Cartesians postulate a unified mind, as a reflective repository of clear and distinct ideas; empiricists construct the mind from sensory experience. Both assume that the mind forms a single system, capable of being scanned from a single vantage point. By treating the mind as a psychic panopticon they tend to overestimate the integrative power of self-knowledge.

We should not begin with an initial prejudice favoring the simplicity or even the integrated organization of the self.[3] Because our interest in the self is not only ontological, but also practical, we should be careful not to suppose that its integrated organization assures the conditions that make self-knowledge possible. We may well discover that the conditions work in the other direction: that presumptive self-knowledge is used in order to achieve integration. Some forms of self-knowledge have authority because they define, form, crystallize an emergently integrated self, rather than because they most clearly express a determinate and formed system.

III. Feelings: Sensations, Pains, and Emotions

There is much force in the intuition that a person's awareness of his own feelings differs from his awareness of the feelings of others.[4] One doesn't, after all, *have* someone else's feelings, though one may understand them better, and in some cases even be attending to those feelings more closely, than the person who has them.

Normally, pain is a perception of an injury in one's own body.[5] But Siamese twins might have pain receptors in the tissue that connects them, so that the nail on which Joe steps may stimulate pain centers both in his brain and in that of his Siamese twin, Shmoe. Of course, Shmoe's pain would still be his insofar as it registered in his brain, and that brain was distinct from Joe's. But it would be a pain associated with an injury done to a body that, on other grounds (its separability, for instance), we would not identify as Shmoe's. And if adrenalin could be carried through the connective tissue, Shmoe might feel fear generated by beliefs and desires that would normally be primarily attributed to Joe.

This little fancy brings out the point I want to make: determining whether feelings have special status, whether they are perceptions, whether they are the sorts of perceptions that are routed through the language centers, should be left safely in the hands of neurophysiologists and endocrinologists. Some of what has seemed mysterious and problematic about self-knowledge requires an understanding of proprioceptive mechanisms, the dynamics of the various perceptual processes, their relation to other functions of the central nervous system; it requires discovering how changes in glandular functions affect the perceptual and nervous systems as well as locomotion and coordination, and under what circumstances the language centers are active in the perceptual processes.

To be in pain is generally not only to be aware of being in pain, but to have that pain be at the (sometimes nagging) focus of one's attention. It is for this reason that pain reports carry such certitude, and for this reason that we learned to express and report our pains so surely. One can imagine a species for which pain is a perceptual sensation much like other proprioceptive perceptions. Members of such a species might be able to take in pains subliminally, the way we take in unaccentuated features of the visual field or the workings of the digestive processes. While this might be a maladaptive trait, one that would diminish a species's capacity to survive in a dangerous environment, there is some evidence that we can, with some training, come to treat some of our pains in this way. There is also some evidence that we can, with training, become aware of, and control, internal bodily functions that we do not now notice. In any case, the dominance of pain sensations and the possible control of that dominance are to be explained by neurophysiologists.

Though it is a contingent fact that pain is associated with a disordered state of one's own body, it is no mere accident. Though pain is normally accompanied by other sensations that follow upon damage to the body (different sensations, as we come to learn, from different parts of the body), these other sensations are not evidence for the pain, any more (or less) than are the whole set of events that have occurred more publicly (e.g., falling, cutting one's hand). They are all coincident, though not accidentally coincident, features of a whole situation. When various sensations have been frequently or intensely associated in our original experiences (and when our attention has been fixed on their copresence), it is sometimes very difficult for us to learn to separate them out again.

Nor does learning to identify one's feelings involve applying general criteria that were somehow acquired in a different way. We have been misled by post-Cartesian and post-empiricist concerns with what is immediate, noninferential, self-warranted, or infallible, hoping to discover foundational material from which to construct our complex knowledge. What is salient in experience—what is normally presumed to be at the focus of attention—is neither evidence nor criteria for our feelings. Yet it is through the salient features of our experiences, along with them, that we learn to reflect on sensations, to identify them and describe their tonalities.

We learned how to give voice to our feelings at our parents' knees, learned to describe those states in propositional form rather than in wincings, howlings, and kickings in exactly the same way, and very often at the same time, as we learned how to describe the wind's rustling the leaves or the parched earth absorbing rain. Though we learned what the world is like by learning our mother tongue as our mother spoke it, learning what is painful is not learning pain language or vice versa. Correcting our pain reports may indeed require relearning the language, but it certainly does not simply consist of acquiring a better vocabulary.

What happens is something like this: a child falls down and scrapes his knees. His parents, assuming that this set of sensations—of startle and pain, the range of particular sensations that they themselves would find salient in such circumstances—are most central in the child's attention when he whimpers or cries, say, "Oh, you've fallen and scraped your knees. That hurts. It must smart." And out comes the care and the ointment. A child benefits from learning to express his experience, his sensations, in clear and unambiguous reports.[6] There is considerable pressure to express one's pain in propositional form, even when one is in too much agony to be interested in performing a propositional reporting speech act. There is considerable adaptive force in training oneself to do it, by second nature, almost as one winces or limps. Such utterances are not given a truth-functional form because one primarily intends to utter what is true, but because one wants help. If banging a drum would do that more efficiently, we'd bang drums. Our needs take precedence over verification: in such cases, we are interested in truth because it is of adaptive service.

We learn to express emotional feelings the same way as we learn to report pains.[7] Because parents are rarely as well attuned to what might be salient and focal in a child's emotional field as they are to his physical pains, learning to express emotions in propositional form is far less successful than learning to express pains accurately. It is a matter of rare good fortune for parents to be good at attentively describing their children's condition, rather than projecting their own feelings, or (out of mistaken tact) avoiding personal talk about what is taken to be a private matter. A person who in all the usual respects knows his language very well may nevertheless be very poor at knowing his own emotions, even if he has, by reading novels, acquired a rich and subtle vocabulary for emotions. One's knowledge of one's own emotional feelings may be highly specialized, depending on where one's parents were askew. For instance, some parents might be relatively good at understanding the subtleties of children's affections, but very poor, or very threatened, at describing their fears. A child whose parents suppose that every little tumble means pain are planting seeds of hypochondria, developing a tendency to focus on certain sorts of sensations as pains; a child whose parents treat such cases as a piffle are more likely to hatch the sort of stoic who does not feel such sensations *as* painful. Parents who are wildly off, or inconsistent, or given to panic, confuse a child about whether he's right to call what he feels "pain." This is a schizogenic environment.

It is important to notice that learning to describe one's pains, sensations, and feelings is not different from learning to describe anything else. A child learns to express/describe (his reactions to) the wind, magnets, and telephone calls in just the same way as he learns to describe events taking place within himself. In both cases, assumptions are made about where attention is likely to be focused, what features in a situation have salience. Sometimes salience is constitutionally and situationally determined (as with pains and reds) and attention can only be diverted or redirected; but sometimes—especially in early childhood—salience is formed by directing and charging attention. In both cases, gifts in self-knowledge may be highly specialized, only regionally acute.

Someone might object that we have not yet touched on what is really peculiar and distinctive about self-knowledge and self-awareness: that it is our own feelings that are directly and immediately, noninferentially present to us, while our awareness of objects is always mediated through some modification in us, some sensory awareness within ourselves. For the sake of argument, let us suppose that something like this is true, that our experience of physical objects comes to us by a modification of our bodies. It is these modifications that constitute the beginning of our knowledge of the world. According to this view we do not construct or infer the properties of our own sensations; if they are intentional, they are so in a more direct and immediate way than external intentional objects, and so our knowledge of them is of a different sort from our knowledge of physical objects.[8]

When this view gets a full head of steam, it sometimes gets carried to the point of saying that there is a sense in which we only directly know ourselves, and that our knowledge of the world is merely inferred or constructed from basic, fundamentally introspective knowledge. Well, what are we to say to that, even in its more modest forms? In one sense, there is nothing that needs to be said. What is at issue is what is supposed to follow from it even if it were acceptable. Neurophysiologists must tell us whether a difference in stimulus makes a difference in type of aware- ness: whether, for instance, the awareness of smells is a different sort of awareness from the awareness of sounds, both different from the awareness of having eaten too much. In any case, there is a sliding confusion, generating either an infinite regress or skepticism, created by saying that because we know the world through (by) our experiencing it, it is our knowledge-of-our-experiences that constitutes, first, our knowledge of ourselves and, then, through that, our knowledge of the world.

Of course it is built into the grammar and semantics of perceptual language that there be a subject, just as it is built into the attribution of any predicates that they be attributed *to* something. But nothing follows from these physical or grammatical givens: it certainly does not follow that we know ourselves, our complex and total selves, better or more clearly than we know external physical objects. Even if sensing were a form of knowing, it does not follow that awareness of sensations is the clearest form of self-knowledge. The simplicity, salience, strength, or decipherability of a sensation does not seem to be determined by the location of its stimulus. Reds and pains are salient; grays and low-grade infections are not.

IV. Wants and Intentions

Some wants and intentions are associated with particular sensations and feelings: under normal circumstances, a person who wants to eat or sleep is in a particular physical state.[9] We learn to report these wants in the same way as we learn to report our feelings, by hearing our parents chatter about how tired we seem, how (despite our protestations to the contrary) we really want to go to bed. Other wants and intentions are even more plastic: they are not necessarily identified with, or accompanied by, any particular sensation, but are both structured and induced by experience and education. In forming these wants, parents are not always guided by hypotheses about what is focal in our attention; on the contrary, they are trying to induce a set of motivational desires that are not yet strongly developed, trying to produce wants whose satisfactions they believe beneficial to us.

Consider what happens when parents are coping with a child's wants: Joe is beating up Eric. A concerned parent steps in and says, "Stop that. Eric didn't do anything to you, and anyhow, even if you are angry with him right now, you don't want to hurt him; you want to be friends with him." What parents say, and even more important, what they do and how they look, will crystallize a set of wants and desires, define their appropriate objects and actions, and at the same time give a vocabulary for reporting them. But few intentions are created *ex nihilo* by talkative parents. Some, but not all, are specifications of more fundamental needs: whether the satisfaction of such desires also satisfies the more fundamental need is not something that is normally determined solely by the ideology of desires, by what we believe to be satisfactory. An indication that the organizing fit is awry is that a person remains restless, uncomfortable, discontent, even when his sincerely expressed wants seem to have been met. In such cases, it is extremely difficult to know what one wants, precisely because the conceptual vocabulary has been deflected.

What parents once did to us, we eventually do to ourselves. We commandeer wants by expressing them in a reporting tone of voice. Much of our talk about our wants is mimetic in character: we express and reflect what we take to be the wants of those around us, without being committed to the actions that are presumed to satisfy those wants. Shared expressions of desires cement communities: our overriding need to belong to what we take to be well-formed communities, to solidify our place in our society, often leads us to express, and sometimes to acquire, desires that were not initially directly motivating. In expressing such wants publicly, we come to take them to be genuine reports, though initially they were neither true nor false, but only vague and indeterminate. In expressing them, we were neither deceived nor deceiving: we were being sociable.

People who are unsure of the place of present wants in the system of their long-range preferences, or who have come to distrust their expressive responses, often engage in experimental self-manipulation by expressing wants in propositional form, leaving open or bracketing the question of whether trying to get is the primitive sign of such a want. Without deliberately doing so, someone may try out a want for size by speaking it out, to see what happens to him *in foro interno* and among his friends when he treats it as a bona fide want. Often this is an elaborate and indirect way of discovering what was wanted all along; but sometimes this process forms a want that was indeterminate, capable of being specified in a number of ways. ("It's hot; I want something cool. Ice cream. No, ice cream makes me thirstier than ever. Sherbet, strawberry sherbet. No, strawberry is too sweet. Lime sherbet, that's it; that's what I want.") When the feedback is unfavorable, the assertion or expression of a want is sometimes the first step in recognizing that it is not what one wants; when the feedback is favorable, it can be the first step in crystallizing and forming a want. ("The mob is in the streets; I must find out where they are going for I am their leader.") The successful maneuvering of self-knowledge requires that a presumed want be treated as if it were actual.

When a want is initially vague and tentative, with some (but not all) of the conditions for its satisfaction left undefined, the process of playing it out in expressive reports gives direction to actions that will eventually count as primitive attempts at trying to satisfy. In such cases, talk that has the look of self-knowledge—and indeed requires the look of self-knowledge—is also simultaneously doing quite different work. Its truth-functional form is at the service of making satisfactory decisions, in situations where motivational conditions are plastic. Its form is a useful benign camouflage, imitating the standard use of the propositional form. The voice of an authoritative report is required to mobilize energy that would be unmoved, not to mention undirected, by utterances that lack the look of truth.

There are two sorts of cases where the expression of wants is ambiguous, and where it is unclear whether reports are genuinely truth-functional. A person who has not yet identified or correctly described his needs or wants may express them hypothetically, proceeding just as he would in any other investigation, seeing whether accepting these desires as his would have untenable consequences. The more difficult and interesting cases are those where the desire is not yet crystallized, where the uncertainty is not merely a matter of the agent's not knowing his own wants, but of those wants being still partly indeterminate. In such cases, the expression of a desire may become reportive, because it has had a causal role in forming the motive.

Of course if such transformation, manipulation, and crystallization were the only forms of self-knowledge, we would have trouble learning how to reflect on our wants. If all desires were grossly indeterminate, we'd even have trouble making it clear what it is to want something, not to mention what it is to understand one's wants. That there are trans- formative and indeterminate cases of self-knowledge does not argue against there being some cases of clear and assured reports of immediate or long-range desires. I do not want to suggest that there are no clear cases of correctly reporting one's defined wants. My claim is only that the complicated and indeterminate cases should not be treated as deviant forms of the clear cases, or as misleadingly described cases of wholly distinctive processes. [10]

It might be objected that the sort of self-knowledge that is formative rather than reportive should not be called knowledge at all. Ambiguous reports might admittedly not be able to form and crystallize motives without being called self-knowledge. But even if individual self-decep- tion were shown to be psychologically benign and necessary, it cannot on that account be justified as a rational general practice. It would take a very long paper to deal with this objection to anyone's satisfaction. I can only here make some bald assertions: misled by a Hobbesian model of wants and intentions, we have taken motives to be determinate, and treated cases of indeterminacy as cases of ignorance or self-deception. We made this mistake because we wished to make the ideal model of rational choice psychologically descriptive as well as logically normative, on the grounds that we could not insist on the normative character of the model unless it in fact corresponded to psychological processes.

One might suppose that it would always be both rational and adaptively advantageous to be as precise as possible about what one wants, to avoid the encroachment of indeterminate desires. But increased definition may mean decreased adaptivity when it limits the range of substitutable satisfactions. Desires that are defined by a clearly formulated set of conditions for their satisfaction may be frustrated by environmental and social changes. More vaguely formulated, less precisely closed wants can be satisfied by a larger range of objects and actions without having to be redefined. The trade-off between rationality and adaptivity requires balancing out the advantages and disadvantages of vagueness in maxi- mizing satisfactions.

Even a responsible systematic comparison of well-formed desires, an attempt to map presumably determinate preferences, is not always an exercise in self-knowledge. The difference between voicing a present desire and reporting one's considered preferences is not always the difference between self-certified but unevaluated opinion (whatever that may be) and a justified true belief; nor is it the difference between an expression and a report. Political tracts and religious confessions are rich in examples of how self-knowledge, systematic comparisons of well-formed desires, and evaluations of long-range commitments can be used to transform or redirect motives. In such cases, self-knowledge and self-improvement are two faces of a single process, one in which it is essential that the dominance of truth-telling and wishful thinking remain indeterminate.

V. Thoughts

Privileged access to one's own thoughts has seemed the most plausible claimant to the special status of self-knowledge. One might well suppose that such reports as "I am now thinking of Vienna" are self-warranted, if anything is. [11] Even if someone gives way under persistent questioning to admit that in thinking of Vienna they were only thinking that it was a city much thought-of by philosophers in search of recherché examples, still, they *were* thinking of Vienna. Even if it turned out, on prolonged examination, that it was not so much Vienna they were thinking of, as what they associated with Vienna—Baroque architecture and austere philosophy, *sachertorte,* and Authority—they were (among other things, as it turned out) thinking of Vienna.

Nevertheless, a great deal of what passes for knowing what one thinks is really speaking one's piece, responding to situations with an improvised repertoire of appropriate speech acts. When people get together for a good talk, only a small part of what they do when they preface their remarks with "I think that . . ." is properly described as reporting or sharing their thoughts. (Not that they are hiding them, either.) People learn to chatter very much as they learn to play croquet, as part of their activities in making friends, competing for attention, getting on cooperatively or combatively. Having interesting (but not too interesting), true (but not too true), conversation is at the service of these enterprises. It is more like an Ionesco play and the Living Theater than like the high-minded enterprise of drawing consequences from premises. Nor is it irrational, or even arational, of us to use ambiguous sentences, apparently propositional in form, to perform nonassertive actions of other sorts.

A child learns to report what happened during the day, learns to formulate, as part of what happened, what went through his mind. He learns to improvise, imitating the grown-ups, answering questions of the form, "What are you thinking about?" and "What do you think of . . . ?" with an appropriate set of responses. Most of the time answering these questions does not involve stepping back, considering the evidence, and reporting the result of one's investigations in the grab-bag of one's beliefs.

One just answers the question, usually truthfully enough, or at any rate, appropriately enough. As long as they speak sincerely, what people say characteristically is at least part of what they're thinking at the time, what is going through their minds. But it does not follow that what people say represents what, all things considered, they think or believe, what in some sense they are willing to be held responsible for. One intentionally thinks and believes against one's better judgment. There is *akrasia* of belief and thought, as well as action. Just as a passing fancy does not always qualify as a want, so a passing (propositional) thought does not always qualify as belief.

Laying bare one's thoughts on euthenasia, South African investments, or the identity of Hesperus and Phosphorus is much more like giving vent to one's feelings, or enthusing over raspberry ice cream, than our general tact and sociability, our respect for the rationality of others, generally let us acknowledge. It is true that when we hear people say what they think, we find out what sort of people they are, but this is not necessarily because we have found out what they really believe. The connection between what people say and what they think is not necessarily that the former represents the latter: sometimes people discover what they think by reflecting on what they tend to say. It is often possible to say, having just glanced at a friend's face, "I know exactly what you're thinking," in situations where he must perform a complex investigation before confirming our insight.

Of course, we need not put this in terms of what people actually say out loud to each other. The description and analysis hold, also, for what runs through people's heads when they are not saying anything out loud. Molly's monologue in *Ulysses* is a complex set of responses to what she sees, to her recollections and associations, to what she thought the moment before. It is what is on her mind and so, in one sense, it is what she is thinking. But no particular slice of that monologue represents what she really believes or thinks, even at that time slice. (Though it doesn't falsely disguise it either.) It indicates what she thinks (it is what's on her mind), without being exactly what she thinks.

Of course we can examine our expressed opinions and beliefs, asking ourselves what, in all this array, we really do think. This process is very much like examining our expressed wants and desires in order to determine our systematized preference rankings: it is formative as well as reportive, normative as well as descriptive. Systematically discovering what we really think borders on determining what we think we ought to think: we hoist the psychology of our beliefs to a construction of their logical relations, committing ourselves to believing what is entailed by our beliefs, even when in some sense we are not prepared to say whether we truly accept these consequences. What we think is not the sum, not even the ordered sum of what we say in a propositional tone of voice, even to ourselves.

There is no correlation between the complexity or the subtlety of an expressed thought and its being accepted as a justified belief, placed in a systematic relation to others. When mathematicians are doing mathematics full tilt, unselfconscious about matters of proof, when they are thinking mathematics, they speak their minds, stimulated by this or that remark. It is more of a Molly Bloom performance than it might at first seem. Of course mathematicians can step back and ask themselves what they really think about all the mathematics they've said. They may then demonstrate or revise what they first blurted out, just as a responsible evaluation of one's desires may reaffirm or revise one's blurted wants. But many fancy thinkers just run on with their thoughts, without faltering to analyze the justificatory status of their claims or to determine whether they indeed believe what they have said. Such thinkers are often very powerful, steaming full head on, sometimes with considerable originality in constructing intricate fugal improvisations of their basic repertoire. It is for this reason that someone who does elegant and complex mathematical work is not on that account necessarily going to be better than the friendly neighborhood bore at knowing what he really thinks about South African investments, or for that matter, better at demonstrating the Pythagorean Theorem to his own satisfaction. Because much mathematical chatter is still chatter, there is no reason to suppose that mathematicians should be better than most folk at knowing what they feel, or for that matter, what they think.

Still, it might be thought that here at last we have come upon the special status of self-knowledge. The capacity to step back to evaluate one's desires or to determine what one really thinks (i.e., rationally should think) seems a wholly distinctive process.[12] Someone who is capable of systematizing and evaluating his prima facie wants and thoughts might be thought necessarily to be in a privileged position to determine what his thoughts are. It might be argued that there must be some sense in which a person must be able to claim all those desires and thoughts as his in order to systematize them, not to mention evaluating his own right to have them. But what are we to make of schizophrenics who do not recognize the "I" implicit in all their experiences, who dissociate themselves from feelings, desires, and thoughts that might normally be attributed to them, and that manifestly move them? If such cases do not cast doubt on the Kantian claim—and most Kantians would certainly argue that they do not—then the implicit direct ownership of one's experiences and thoughts does not have any implication for privileged self-knowledge. It is a consequence of the logic of experiencing and not a royal road to self-knowledge. In any case, the question of whether the capacity to (attempt to) formulate a (rational) system of one's beliefs and desires is distinctive, whether the activities of reflecting and remembering are distinctive, are questions for neurophysiologists to answer. They must determine whether such rational reflection on the system of experiences that one takes to be one's own is a distinctive psychophysical state, which is integrative because it has a nondistortive access to other physical states. Whether there is a nontrivial panoptical perspective on one's thoughts is as much a question for physiology as it is for transcendental analysis. That there is a perspective from which panoptical regulation is claimed, by no means establishes the validity of that claim.

VI. Images of the Self and Reflexive Attitudes

Does a person have a special epistemic access to her sense of herself, a guiding sense of her primary 'identity' that includes her identifications and ideals as well as a primitive somatic sense of herself? I think not. Whatever special relation a person may have to her sense of herself, that special relation is not one of privileged knowledge. To begin with, a person's reflexive attitudes are layered, composed of distinctive strands acquired in different ways at different times. Sartre gives a plausible and vivid description of how a person develops a preconceptual general somatic self-identification, as awkward or deft, excitable or calm, energetic or lethargic, from her constitution and infantile experiences. Childhood illnesses, the bundling or loosening of limbs—all contribute to this underlying layer of a person's reflexive attitudes, her psychophysical sense of self. Even though this fundamental somatic sense may play a crucial role in affecting the structures and directions of a person's motives and social interactions, it does not qualify as knowledge, because it is rarely conceptualized. If a person develops beliefs about her basic somatic sense of herself, those beliefs may be askew. A hefty, healthy person may think of herself—even experience herself—as frail and vulnerable.

The sense of self that an infant acquires through its earliest social interactions affects, and is affected by, the constitutionally and experientially based sense of self. The tonal character of the ways that early nurturing figures react to the child—their delight or repulsion, the anxiety or ease of their handling—forms a further layer in a person's sense of herself. Such initial physical reactions move toward psychological and social role casting: seen as an intruder or as a welcome guest, at the periphery or at the center of family life, the child is impelled into scenarios that form self-identifications. "You're a bore, a pest" or "You are wonderfully amusing" is conveyed to a description-hungry two-year old. Sometimes such characterizations can become self-fulfilling; but they can also be profoundly misleading.[13]

Cultural structures form further layers in a person's sense of self: one layer is articulated by ethnic, gender, class, age, and racial stereotypes that affect actions even when they conflict with more critically self-conscious motives. Another is formed by a person's conscious and reflective ideals, ideals of oneself as a social reformer, or as generous or intellectually rigorous. Sometimes such ideals are personified in an admired figure who provides a model for imitation.

A person can be unaware of, or mistaken about, the ways in which these various strands in her sense of herself—her somatic self-imagery, her social personae, her idealized identifications—interact with one another. She can also be unaware of the roles that the various strands in her sense of herself play in the formation of the structure of her thought, her motives, and her actions. Though the various aspects of a person's identifications are fundamental to her agency, sometimes to the point of being constitutively self-fulfilling, they are nevertheless also capable of being opaque and misunderstood.

An example may help dislodge the notion that reflexive attitudes represent knowledge of oneself and one's motives, knowledge that prompts or directs appropriate action. Consider David casting an interested eye on Bathsheba. His reflexive attitudes partly individuate his desires. His condition is one of *desire* (rather than an inflammation of the gonads); it is a particular *sort* of desire (an erotic desire rather than *furor poeticus*); and it is *his* desire (rather than one caused by a deviant chain, a wicked spell cast on him by the ghost of Saul). His reflexive attitudes—his somatic sense of himself, his sense of his social entitlements and their limits, his idealized identifications—are central in determining whether and how his condition is motivating. For instance, they make a difference to whether David decides to send Uriah, an excellent soldier and an important ally, off to what is near certain death, for the sake of Bathsheba.

But David doesn't need to form a diagnosis of his condition in order to act as he does. Though his reflexive attitudes are expressed within his intentions and their affective tonality, his condition—his erotic interest in Bathsheba—is standardly already the beginning of action. David could, of course, have investigated his reflexive attitudes, and could have attempted to guide or check his actions on the basis of his discoveries. But the diagnostic or interpretive processes that represent one way of checking or redirecting action, are not necessary in order to begin or instigate it. In any case, the results of a person's investigation into the reflexive attitudes that are expressed in his condition, his motives and actions, are only as good as his investigative astuteness. The success of his actions, or the reform of his habits are not a direct function of the astuteness of that knowledge.

VII. The Advantages and Disadvantages of Self-Knowledge

We are hardly likely to underestimate the advantages of self-knowledge. Aside from the intrinsic pleasures of the exercise of our talents for insight and clarity and the narcissistic pleasure of exercising those talents on ourselves, the advantages of objective detachment—freed from the dangerous tyranny of impulse, capable of evaluating the place of a present desire or thought in relation to long-range commitments—are relatively obvious, especially to philosophers who earn a living by making a profession of their talents for insight and clarity. The capacity for this sort of detachment is a condition for being able to evaluate the rationality of one's long-term convictions and desires.

That rational detachment may be maladaptive in some circumstances is less obvious. Like all dispositions, the capacities for self-knowledge can be brought into play appropriately or inappropriately, beneficially or harmfully. The capacities are indeed adaptive, but it doesn't follow that it is adaptive to exercise them under all circumstances, or adaptive to develop those capacities to their utmost potentiality and power. Any generally adaptive dispositional trait, such as sharpness and keenness of hearing, may become maladaptive if it is magnified or oversensitized. The capacity to respond to shifts in sound in our environment, to identify those sounds, is a highly useful trait. But developing those capacities, hearing ever more subtle sounds, constantly noticing the sound differentiations around us, would be highly damaging to the balance of our dispositions. In the very nature of the process, focusing limits. What we want is the adaptive rather than the virtuoso development of our dispositions, including those exercised in self-knowledge, the self-regulatory rather than the wholly magnetized gifts of response.

One of the reasons that self-knowledge is magnified as a virtue is that it looks like a good candidate for the traits that scan the environment to determine where, at any point, the focus of our attending should lie. But if the analysis we've given of self-knowledge is right, then self-knowledge is not a panoptical power. It seems likely that neurophysiologists will discover that the various homeostatic systems that control the direction of attention are very complex indeed; that these mechanisms

are regional rather than central (for example that what brings a sound
into focus is not the same as what leads us to focus on an awareness of
ourselves hearing that sound).

A person who actively concentrates on his awareness of himself as
feeling, wanting, or thinking, constantly evaluating the rationality and
the appropriateness of his responses, can suffer the disadvantages of
extreme disassociation. His attending to the objects of his experience
is often broken to concentrate on reflective questions. He is likely to
have difficulty holding on to his present thoughts, wants, and feelings,
even though he may become very good at recollecting them in tranquillity
and reconstructing them clearly. Though disassociated, such a person
may be able to produce an impressive and sophisticated account of what
he is doing, descriptions that are not false, but that are no longer on
key. He may, for instance, correctly report the reasons for his wanting
to go to Paris; but because his attention has shifted to the absorbing
question of what he wants, or because he is focused on deflecting fears
and insecurities, or on dazzling his friends with the subtlety of his
introspective gifts, his *wanting to go to Paris* has lost its fervor, its
direction. His desire has been put to uses—to please or to teach—that
may be quite different from the original needs. Indeed such a person
may no longer be primarily reporting his desires, but undertaking a
performance of some other sort, impressing his friends by the subtlety
of his self-knowledge. He has achieved objectivity and plausibility at
the cost of conviction. When it comes right down to going to Paris, the
actions of such persons are often ill-timed, wooden, ill-suited to satisfy
even their manifest desires. Because their attention has shifted from
what they desire to themselves as desiring, they cannot bring off the
appropriate action with conviction or *élan*.

These difficulties are not difficulties in the analysis of self-knowledge;
they are difficulties in being the sort of creature who is capable of it.
Self-knowledge does not require capacities for a special sort of direct,
noninferential, intuitive, panoptical view of oneself; on the contrary, it
requires capacities to treat oneself as an object of knowledge, in the
same way as one treats everything else as an object of knowledge. Crucial
among these capacities is that of redirecting attention, focusing on the
fact that we are in this or that state, wanting this or that, having said
this or that. That we are capable of focusing on ourselves as wanting,
thinking, or feeling, capable of evaluating those wants, thoughts, and
feelings in many different ways, and then further trying to modify or
change our responses, has given us enormous adaptive advantages. But
when these gifts are nourished to excess, they may block the equally
adaptive advantages of being unselfconsciously absorbed in our activi-

ties, resisting the fullest development of self-knowledge, in the interests of the best development of our selves.

But even at its properly proportioned best, self-knowledge is no guarantee of well-formed, let alone wise action. The merit of self-knowledge does not derive from the knowledge, but from the character of the person who has it, from the ways that she is able to use her knowledge well and appropriately. Self-knowledge is only as good as the person who has it.

3 THE WAYWARD MIND

SHELLY ERRINGTON

There is a set of apparently anomalous psychological activities—self-deception, akrasia, the irrational conservation of the emotions, agent regret—that present problems for theories of rational agency. Having put aside the distinctions of faculty psychology, and having placed cognitive, rational, activities within a larger psychological context, we are in a better position to understand why such apparently wayward activities are so common, and why they resist correction. They are, I argue, by-products of common, highly functional psychological activities: their analysis reveals the structures and operations of the self, operations largely ignored by reconstructive, rationalized accounts of psychological functioning.

In "Fearing Death," I argue that while it is formally irrational to fear one's own death, doing so is a natural and sometimes functionally benign extension of our fundamental psychological and intellectual processes. "The Deceptive Self: Liars, Layers, and Lairs" develops the view that the phenomena of self-deception can only be preserved by superimposing two incompatible, irreducible theories of the structure of the self, both of which are necessary to a full account of intellectual and psychological functioning. According to the first—which best accounts for reflexive rational critical evaluation and correction—the self is a panoptical scanner of its activities, capable of successful action-guiding legislation. According to the second—which best accounts for the compartmentalized functions of relatively independent psycholog-

195

ical processes and for the conservation of belief in the face of every slight breeze of counterevidence—the self is composed of relatively autonomous subsystems for which integration is a task rather than a starting point. "Where Does the Akratic Break Take Place?" traces the places where akrasia can occur: it begins with akrasia of perception and belief. "Akrasia and Conflict" discusses the occasions for akrasia, and the ways that standard psychological processes contribute to its operations.

10   Fearing Death

Many have said, and I think some have shown, that it is irrational to fear death.[1] The extinction of what is essential to the self—whether it be biological death or the permanent cessation of consciousness—cannot by definition be experienced by oneself as a loss or as a harm.

Many have said, but I think none shown, that one's own death is nevertheless an evil. Death is the privation of life, and life is (generally) a good, or at any rate a precondition for any experience of what is good. But the absence or deprivation of a good is not, just on that account alone, necessarily an evil or a harm. A harm must be a harm-to-someone; but if the dead are by definition extinct, they cannot be harmed by not existing. Yet even if it is not to be feared, the privation of a good may well be regretted, and regretted before it occurs. One can regret that one will not see the outcome of projects that are important to oneself; that one will not see or know one's distant progeny or the progeny of those whom one loves; that one will be deprived of conversations, friendships, and books that would have given one joy and understanding and that might have made one's life immeasurably happier than it could be without them; that one will not hear the western wind bring down the small rain. But indeed one might regret—and even fear—that one might sustain such losses while one is alive. In any case, regret is an activity of the living, and not of the dead. While one can regret and sometimes fear that there will be a time when one will not have whatever the goods of life may be, one cannot regret that one will be harmed by not having them after one is dead.

But if it is not rational to fear death, it does not follow that we should try to free ourselves from such fear. For while there may be many good reasons for not fearing one's own nonexistence, there might still also be strong reasons for fearing, as well as for regretting one's own death.[2] I shall argue that it is proper to have irresolvably conflicting attitudes toward one's own death: it is inappropriate to fear death and yet it is also inappropriate not to fear it, or to attempt to cease fearing it. Sometimes, when there are reasons for a course, and reasons against it, it is possible to weigh the strengths of the reasons on both sides and to form a judgment about what is best, or most reasonable, all things considered. But in this case, the reasons for fearing death are not commensurable with those for not fearing it: no summary weighted judgment is possible. Both views are categorically valid, requiring full assent. The issue is, then, not whether we should or should not cease fearing death, but rather what attitudes to take toward one's irrational but nevertheless functional fears.

Let us be clear about a few minor issues. Our concern is with death and not with dying or horrible ways of dying. Certainly there is nothing amiss in fearing certain sorts of dying, especially if such fears could help prevent one's dying in those ways. If fear of the horrors of dying from lung cancer (as opposed to a sudden massive coronary thrombosis) could be among the necessary causes of a person's taking steps to avoid that sort of death—her ceasing to smoke, changing her job or residence— then there would be good reasons for her to fear that sort of death. Indeed, a person might judge that it would be wise for her to acquire that sort of fear, if doing so would lead her to take effective safety measures she is otherwise insufficiently motivated to take.

We should also be clear about what sort of fear is at issue, and what it is we fear, in fearing death. Although we shall later turn to other sorts of fears—generalized anxiety, fear without a specifiable object—we are initially primarily concerned with a state of fear, experienced in a specific harm-avoiding way, fear of . . . rather than fear that. . . . Such fears presuppose apprehending an object as dangerous or threatening in such a way that it generates some sort of flight reaction, one that can be checked or overcome, although usually with some difficulty. The specific forms of flight reaction can, as both Freud and Sartre noted, vary greatly. Without necessarily being fully propositional, such fears are intentional. We react to the object only under a certain description, even if we do not have a properly formed propositional belief about the character of the danger or an estimation of its probability.[3]

What, then, is it we fear when we fear death? Perhaps not all those who do fear it fear the same thing. What a person fears, in fearing death, often reveals what the person takes to be essential and prizeworthy in her life. The hidden content—the details—of a person's fear of death reveals her deepest conception of herself and her life.

1. Some fear death as the permanent loss of (what they take to be) the goods of life. For some, the goods of life are the activities of life: the growth and thriving of their children, the joys of their work and friendships, the development and acceptance of their beliefs and com-

mitments. For others, the good of life is consciousness itself, the awareness of the activities of life. For them, the loss of consciousness is the
greatest possible loss, quite independently of the content of experience.
But we can lose these goods—the activities of life, or the conscious
awareness of these activities—in other ways. This form of the fear of
death is then to be classified with the fear of senility, exile, ostracism,
friendlessness, the loss of our faculties, debilitating diseases, madness.
Death represents the limit of all these diminishings and debilities: it
has no special psycho-ontological status except as the irreversible limit
that compounds all these fears.

2. Some fear death because it endangers those they cherish, leaving
them vulnerable or helpless, their condition in the world worse for lack
of a special protection. When a person fears her death will damage her
primary concerns, she fears the harm done to those concerns, rather
than her experiencing such harm. And while in principle someone else
might be more efficient, more effective, and certainly more admirable
than ourselves in forwarding our projects, it need not be vanity but a
perfectly reasonable calculation of probabilities that someone who does
not stand in just our relation to our projects is unlikely to give them the
same care and devotion that we do. But when we fear the harm that our
death might bring, it is the harm that we fear, and not our death, in
and of itself. Such harms would also come if we were incapacitated,
senile, diseased, imprisoned, or exiled.

3. Some fear that the world will go on without their being there to
experience it, to comment on it, to understand and explain it, to joke
about it, and to attempt to improve it by their own lights, even when
they despair of doing so. The drama will continue without their participation, and perhaps none the worse for that. What turns such sorrow
into fear is the thought that all our efforts to live well, our attentions
and dedications were for nothing, that our joys and generosities, pains
and stoic resolutions were all in vain. We may fear that the balance of
our lives was wrong: the fear is a terror that death shows our significant
projects were meaningless, that our lives were idle and pointless, our
enterprises arbitrary.

4. In fearing death some fear that their lives will be assessed and
judged in ways that they can no longer influence. There it is, all one's
life, now taken as a whole and of course found wanting. All possibilities
are closed; one can no longer try to remedy those things that we would
have otherwise, cannot make restitution, ask for forgiveness, and above
all, we cannot have that last explanatory word that would make it all
come out right. But this too is something that might occur during one's
life: with senility, aphasia, and other forms of debility and exile.

5. For some the fear of death is an extreme form of the fear of the unknown. Some fears of the unknown are quite specific: fear of the dark, fear of what lies beyond the boundary of the hearth. Animal alertness to danger often closely resembles human terror; when a rabbit or squirrel is strongly attentive to the environment, its senses are maximally alert, its heart beats violently; the creature is all aquiver. For some animals, being alert to the environment just is being alert to predators and to prey. It seems that for them, to live is to be in a state of fear. For some, the fear of death is a heightened awareness of danger, with extreme generalization of stimulus conditions. For them, death is the symbolic representation of the most vulnerable condition, where a person is abandoned without hope, recourse or help.

All these fears of death seem to be fears of the harms that attend other conditions as well as death. They are fears of what death brings rather than fears of being dead. But evidently there are some who fear death as such, who fear their nonexistence. It is the appropriateness of this fear that I should like to examine: the fear of death as a fear of nonbeing, rather than the fear of the various harms that attend death.

It seems all too easy to show that at least some fears of death—those that implicitly reintroduce a subject to experience its own nonbeing— are irrational because they presuppose an incoherent belief. Similarly, it is all too easy to show that if it is rational to fear or regret losses, it is rational to fear or regret the loss of life. But there are other dimensions for the evaluation of the appropriateness of such psychological attitudes as fear besides that of determining whether the beliefs they presuppose are coherent, valid, or at least justifiable by appropriate canons of argument or evidence. It might be appropriate and desirable to have the capacity for and even to develop the disposition to certain fears, knowing that they will sometimes involve rash and inconsiderable beliefs and actions. One can evaluate the rationality of maintaining and developing a generalized disposition, independently of evaluating a specific exercise of that disposition. There might be rational grounds for acquiring a disposition whose exercise is admittedly often irrational.

But what could be meant by evaluating the appropriateness of an attitude, if not evaluating the truth or validity of the belief it presupposes? Evaluating the functionality of a psychological attitude is one thing; evaluating its rationality is another. An attitude that is highly functional is not therefore automatically rational; nor is a dysfunctional attitude automatically on that account irrational. Besides being intrinsically interesting, the fear of death is also interesting as an example of the various dimensions on which we evaluate the appropriateness and the propriety of psychological attitudes. We shall see why it might be appropriate and even rational to choose to be capable of the sort of fear that has, as one of its consequences, a susceptibility to the fear of death, even when, in some particular cases, that fear is incoherent.

An analogy should clarify the strategy of my argument. Standardly, pain is undesirable; it is a harm to be feared. Yet our constitutions being what they are, we would not choose—it would not be rational to choose—to be incapable of feeling pain. This is not for any dark or Dostoyevskian reason that pain or suffering brings nobility. Suffering and pain can sometimes ennoble some people, but one had better not count on it. Certainly it would be a high-risk gamble to seek suffering for the sake of being ennobled. It is a tragic irony that we are generally not only harmed by whatever causes us pain or suffering, but also harmed by suffering itself, since it tends to engender the further damages of self-pity, hypersensitivity, alienation, and misanthropy. Pain is useful for a much simpler and more straightforward reason than the Dostoyevskian one: it is an important signal that damage is being done, a signal to move away from what is damaging. The victims of Hansen's disease suffer many further damages to their bodies because they lack the danger signals that pain brings.

Of course pain does not always contain or reveal its message clearly or unequivocally. It generally signals that something is wrong, without always signaling what is wrong. Some pains have physical reactions built into them: withdrawing the hand from the fire is standardly part of the behavior of pain-at-being-burnt. But not all signaling pains carry reflex actions with them. It takes experience, intelligence, and a considerable amount of good fortune to read pain signals in the right way. Often pains locate a damaged part of the body; but the source of the damage may be in some other part of the body. And if the cause is some external object, considerable deciphering and even theory may be required for appropriate diagnosis. Nor is the appropriate remedy evident from the pain itself. The element of good fortune in being able to be informed by one's pains is that of having been brought up knowledgeably, acquired an astute lore about the characteristic causes and remedies for various sorts of pains. In any case, it seems clear that without any sentimentality about pain or its ennobling effects (things being what they are, and we being constituted as we presently are), one might well reasonably choose to be capable of pain and pain reactions, to have reasonably sensitive receptors, with reasonably low thresholds. But the safeguarding effects of pain require an aversion to pain, an aversion roughly proportionate to the damage indicated by the severity of the pain. One form that such an aversion can take is fear, especially when fear involves actually beginning to remove oneself from the damaging object, to take motion before one has had time to weigh matters carefully.

It is precisely this precipitous character of basic or fundamental fears that makes them functional in situations that require rapid and relatively undiscriminating global reactions. This suggests that the nonrationality of fear is inextricably interwoven with its functionality. At least some basic fears are expressed in rapid safeguarding action, triggered when something is perceived as dangerous, without its being rationally evaluated in any precise detail. We are set in motion before deliberation takes place. These are fears of clear and present dangers to our well-being, not fears of dawn, or the state of the GNP, potato pancakes, or the song of the nightingale. Some of our basic reactive fears seem constitutionally based; others are acquired, sometimes as part of our socialization in a certain culture, sometimes from individual experience. Even acquired fears can come to have the force of second nature: no particular rational evaluation is necessary to elicit the appropriate reaction. It is enough that the person roughly gauge a situation as potentially dangerous. (Think, for instance, of the quick fearful intake that leads us to brake in order to avoid a collision, even before we determine exactly how probable it is.)

For acquired fears, the question arises: would I undo this fear if I could? Or would I try to ensure that my children and others near or dear also share those fears, reacting to them as I do? It is sometimes rational to choose to be capable of such fears. And in the same way, and for the same reasons, one would choose to be capable of those fears that, among other things, issue in the fear of death. When fearing is the beginning of appropriate safeguarding motion from danger, and when it is the most rapid and efficient motivational assurance of safeguarding behavior in certain sorts of circumstances, then the capacity for fearful reaction is desirable. Though it is not desirable to experience fear, it is desirable to be capable of experiencing it, and to tend to feel it when doing so is the most efficient trigger for moving us out of harm's way.

There are several reasons why such basic fears might be thought undesirable. Though these reasons are distinct, they are psychologically connected. (1) It is part of the very structure of such fears that they lead to relatively unconsidered reactions: they are attitudes whose exercise is in its very nature prone to irrationality because they operate before rational evaluation takes place. (2) The subjective experience of a fearful reaction is, like pain, an unpleasant one to have. If we standardly enjoyed fear or other painful attitudes, they would be highly dysfunctional: our taste for them would lead us to seek out dangerous and harmful situations.

(3) Fear is not only a relatively unpleasant attitude; it is also one that functionally dominates and interrupts other activities. The insistent character of fear, its unpleasantness, and its precipitous character are all part of its efficacy as a safeguarding motive. If fear were a relatively muted pastel sort of emotion that, like nostalgia, stayed in the background of our attention, it would not be efficacious as a reaction to danger. It is precisely because fear is unpleasant, because it is insistent and disturbing, and because it is often prerational in its occurrence and in its effects, that it helps move us out of harm's way. Fear is one of our conservative attitudes, inhospitable to the gambler's calculated evaluations of tolerable risks. Its very essence is a low tolerance for risk, even when the risk is rational. But it is then the very undesirability of the experience of fear that provides the grounds of choosing to be capable of such reactive fears.

We might of course wish we had been constituted in a different way, wish that we had less unsettling and unpleasant sorts of motives or reactions in moving away from danger. We might wish that some of our more considered and rationally evaluative and discriminating motives could move us as rapidly as do fear and other disturbing conditions. What might be rational for us to wish if we were constituted quite differently is, however, a matter for the speculations of science fiction rather than those of philosophic analysis.

Still, there might be considerable leeway within the bounds of our present constitutional structure. Sometimes we can acquire traits that are less disturbing and no less efficient than those associated with fear. But when such a trait—say a certain sort of reactive caution—becomes second nature in this way, when it can operate with the rapidity and motor efficiency of fear, then it seems to lose the fine discrimination of weighed and weighted thought. Precisely to the extent that it involves quick reaction before detailed comparative evaluation, precisely to the extent that it begins motion straightaway, such a dispositional motive becomes liable to inappropriate and irrational use. Any capacity whose operations are functionally equivalent to fear—a capacity activated by the rough gauge of a stimulus, one that sets us in motion before fine evaluative discriminations are made—becomes, just by virtue of the rough rapidity of its operations, subject to erroneous exercise. The principle is this: we are better served by being constituted so as to move (even often move) foolishly and mistakenly from mere shadows than we would be by being constituted so as to fail to move the one time that the shadow is that of a hungry lion. Even if death is not an evil, life is, other things being equal, a good. Better a live jumpy fool, than a prematurely dead sage.

But, one might say, what has this to do with fearing death? All that has been established is that it is rational to want to be capable of fearing certain sorts of harms. Why should it on that account be rational to fear death? If the extinction of life is not a harm, then why should the sort of damage to ourselves that causes death be feared? Certain sorts of painful and debilitating damages to the body might be feared: the fear of being blinded or maimed in ways that make one dependent, and so also prey to resentment, and other similar debilities. But why fear damages that lead to death? One reason is that it is by no means always easy in the moment to distinguish debilitating from mortal damages. However incoherent and perhaps even in itself harmful, the fear of death seems more efficient than an indefinite number of particular fears we would have to have: fear of exposure in very low temperatures, fear of dehydration, fear of this and fear of that. Suppose the question arises, why should one fear—why should one wish to be able to fear—to be up on the 200th floor of a skyscraper, to be there exposed to winds of 100 mph when there is no barrier or retaining wall, to be there wearing the slipperiest of shoes, whose bottoms have been covered with grease, to be there on the 200th floor without a parachute? In itself, that condition is not be to feared. What makes it reasonable to fear going up to the 200th floor of a skyscraper under those conditions is that it would be likely that one would fall off the building, plunging painlessly and perhaps even exhilaratingly to one's death. Without a healthy fear of death, we would have no reason not to go to the top of the skyscraper for the view.

But it might be objected: none of this need presuppose the *fear* of death. Why can't the recognition of danger be a sufficient safeguard? That recognition can be as indeterminate and strongly dominant as is necessary for taking efficient safeguarding measures, without having to be a fearful recognition. At least since Descartes, we have distinguished cognitive psychological attitudes from straightforwardly motivational ones. Certainly motivational attitudes have a cognitive component: they are directed to ends under certain descriptions, they presuppose a set of values, they can only be exercised with perceptual and categorial discrimination. But on the Cartesian map of psychological functions, cognitive attitudes are in principle motivationally neutral. The same cognitive content can be asserted or denied, can be the subject of desire or of aversion. The presumption is that as one can deny or assert or refrain from judging the truth of any propositional content, so the rational person is able to take favorable or unfavorable attitudes toward any state of affairs, as his best reasoning dictates. On this view, such separation of powers is necessary in order to explain why we need not automatically follow our strongest, most entrenched motives. But if recognizing a mortal danger does not entail taking safeguarding measures, such reactive measures are not part of our perception of the recognition of such danger. The view that assures the possibility of opposed propositional attitudes toward the same propositional content requires a set of motivational attitudes that operate independently of cognition and recognition. If recognizing danger doesn't automatically in and of itself generate specific motivational attitudes, something else must be introduced to do that work. Clearly on this view it follows that the recognition of danger cannot as such play the same safeguarding functional role that fear and similar motivational attitudes play.

But even theories that do not separate cognitive from motivating attitudes classify certain sorts of fear as functional. To be sure, if the recognition of danger directly motivates, if reacting to danger is built into perceiving danger, then such recognition could be a functional replacement of fear. But motivationally charged recognition of danger seems no less free from the little disturbances of man, no less disturbing and perturbing than fear. Suppose that for safeguarding purposes the recognition of danger were functionally equivalent to fear. The question would arise, how does that recognition work, as the beginning of the motions of running away, removing the hand from the fire, etc. Does it work because the recognition is felt in a certain way, felt in the way that fear is felt? Or does it work directly, without the intervention of an emotional state, the cognitive state itself beginning the motion of the muscles? This looks suspiciously like an empirical question about the antecedents of various types of safeguarding behavior. It looks like a question about whether a person whose glandular functions were damaged without affecting his cognitive functions could in fact take the same safeguarding measures to perceived dangers as one whose glandular system was in functional order.

At this juncture of the argument, we can only speculate about what would be the appropriate attitude, on each of the various possible empirical outcomes. (Philosophical questions that lead to an empirical turn signal neither the end nor even the interruption of philosophical analysis.) Suppose that the recognition of danger could directly motivate safeguarding measures, without the intervention of any independent motivational attitude like fear, but that it did so less efficiently and effectively than fear. Suppose that such recognition is more discriminating and less disturbing than fear, that it involves fewer unnecessary safeguarding measures that interrupt ongoing projects. But suppose that affectively uncharged reactions to sudden unpredictable dangers are also slower and less effectively mobilized. Then one might wish to be capable of the fears associated with the danger of death, even though there were less unpleasant ways of safeguarding oneself for standard minor dangers that do not require massive rapid reaction. Oddly and interestingly, a person's choice between the dominant capacities of fear and those of more discriminating and calmer recognitions might vary with the sorts of dangers that he would expect to encounter in the standard difficulties of his ordinary life. If his natural environment has a relatively high frequency of sudden mortal danger, he might sensibly prefer the unsettling follies of irrational fear in order to secure efficient safeguarding measures. But if he lives in a relatively controlled environment, whose dangers are normally foreseeable, then it might be sensible to prefer the functional recognition of danger, even if its safeguarding strategies were slower than those of fear.

It might at this point be objected that I have slid suspiciously among several quite distinct kinds of fear: reflex avoidances, heart-in-the-mouth reactions to situations perceived as dangerous, and generalized global metaphysical anxieties about one's nonbeing. The structure and function of each of these fears is quite distinctive. On the one hand, it might seem unnecessary to introduce fear as embedded within or presupposed by certain sorts of reflex avoidances. Such behavior might be adequately explained by reflex action and aversions to pain, without introducing any intentional attitude at all. On the other hand, Epicureans might argue that the propriety of danger-averting behavior does not affect the impropriety of a generalized metaphysical fear of nonbeing.

Before turning to metaphysical anxieties, we should consider whether reflex avoidances and aversions to pain and danger should be classified as species of fear. It is important to distinguish reflex actions that presuppose beliefs or perceptions from those that do not. Jerking one's knee when the patella is struck is quite different from blinking at an oncoming object. But there is also a significant difference between blinking one's eyes at an oncoming object and running in fear from a charging lion. While the former involves some perceptual-conceptualization (that there is an object, not a shadow, and that its motion has a certain trajectory), there need be no set of specific beliefs about the character of the object and its effects. One blinks at the drop of eye-medication as well as at a cinder. But some reflex reactions not only presuppose a belief about what is dangerous: they also contain a specific evaluation about the character of that danger. The details of that evaluation determine the desire or aversion that is part of the person's reaction: it fixes the character of the person's reaction. One does not dodge, but runs away from a charging lion; one neither dodges nor runs away from a tornado in Kansas: one gets into the cellar. It is this class of reflex actions that concern us: those that would not have taken just that specific form of action without specific beliefs about the kind of danger the object presents. Despite the great differences in the range of appropriate reactions and actions, the phenomenologically experienced quality of such avoidances is the quality that is normally the quality of fear experiences. While it is not logically necessary that the person who runs from a charging lion experiences what is standardly called fear, it is characteristic that he does; and moreover, his fearful state is characteristically part of the explanation of his reaction. Since such reactive avoidances are experienced as fears, it seems reasonable to classify them as such, especially as the perceptual-conceptualization that is embedded in such reactions, their intentional component ("this is dangerous"), is the intentional component that is ingredient in fear.

It is true that we could explain such reactions—not all of them reflex actions and not all of them experienced as fears—by other theoretical constructs: by the instinct for survival, or by specific reactions, some of them learned, to specific stimuli. But these solutions raise the further question: what beliefs and attitudes are presupposed by those reactions? Postulating an instinct for survival commits one to a range of theoretical apparatus of instincts, their vicissitudes, their transformations. It is by no means clear that any of the usual advantages of theory construction are gained by replacing "fear" with "instincts to survival," whose operations are far more questionable and baroque than those of fear. What about simply introducing certain aversions instead of fears? But either aversive behavior will be functionally equivalent to fear, or it will not be strong enough to do the explanatory work that is required. As a psychological attitude, aversion in itself is not strong enough to explain massive reactive behavior. Aversion is much more easily controlled and directed, much more selective than the sorts of fears we are discussing. So it is the subclass of aversions that are fearful aversions that are at work. Moreover, we shall either take certain sorts of aversions as primitive—the rock bottom of explanation—or we shall look for some explanation of the selection and direction of our primitive aversions, those that do have an action-component presumptively built into them. Both alternatives lead back to the sorts of fears we have been discussing. Primitive aversions turn out to be not only functionally equivalent to primitive fears, but also to be characteristically phenomenologically indistinguishable from them. Those that direct actions in the appropriate way presuppose the perception of something as dangerous, rather than, say, disgusting or vicious.

We can now turn to the objection that the metaphysical fear of death—*angst* at one's nonbeing—is entirely different from the functional reflex safeguarding reactions we have been discussing. A metaphysical fear of death is the sort that a person might have when there is no clear and present danger, a fear she might have sitting in her study and looking out of the window and brooding on the nature of things. Certainly anxious metaphysical fear is quite different from the sort of functional fear we have been discussing, and it is this fear that might be thought irrational. It is this sort of gratuitous metaphysical fear, surely, that was the subject of Epicurean attack: it is this sort of fear that brings us to foolish enterprises, engages us in pointless activities about whose importance we deceive ourselves. Epicurus argued that if we could conquer the fear of death—and he surely meant the metaphysical terror of nonbeing— then a great deal of our lives would be more rational, calmer, and happier. Our dreadful gravity toward fame, the endless trouble we take to secure ourselves by amassing worthless goods, our undignified servility to people whom we do not respect—all those indignities are, Epicurus thought, superstitious protections against the dangers that bring death. Surely Epicurus is right in at least this: the ramifications of our fears of death are subtle and far reaching. They stand behind and explain other- wise baffling and bizarre activities, activities that would make sense if they spring from, and are directed by, the mistaken belief that they will protect us from death. (Of course there are many other hypotheses that would also explain these activities, many other beliefs that would ra- tionalize this sort of behavior. All that is required for our account is that the Epicurean hypothesis be among the plausible ones: we are only considering whether, if Epicurus is right, and the irrational fear of death explains a great deal of futile and troubled human activity, it follows that we can and should give up the irrational fear of death.) Now on the Epicurean account, if we abandon the metaphysical fear of death we need then no longer suffer the smaller fears: we need no longer fear the heat o' the sun, or the furious winter's rages, or even the intimations of mortality. Abandoning the metaphysical fear of death would free us from the particular superstitious and fetishistic fears that are its consequences.

But even if the fear of death leads to much folly, that does not prove that it always leads to folly, or that it only leads to folly. There might be other good reasons to be committed to such folly. Fetishistic fears and superstitious actions might even be beneficial, despite the care they give us and the false beliefs they involve. One might ask: what else would we be doing with our time? If we did not fear death, would there be a more rational measure of how best to engage our interests and spend our time? Consider the inquiries—astronomy, biology, psychology, the range of agricultural and medical sciences—that on an Epicurean ac- count might have begun with the fear of death. It is of course important that they became independent of their origins: but would they have begun at all without pressing needs and the fears that attend them? (Do we indeed have a notion of psychologically experienced biological need, without a notion of the distress and fear that accompanies the frustration of what is needful to survival? Needs characteristically motivate by being felt, and felt as discomforts. A creature capable of reflecting on what the need signifies, as a signal of a somatic necessity for survival, implicitly has the idea of its death.)

The anxious metaphysical fears castigated by the Epicureans—the scholar's terror of his nonbeing or that of the poet contemplating Chamonix or Mount Aetna—are indeed irrational. We have suggested that these fears are by-products of functional fears. From an extension and improvisation of a Kantian argument we can derive other reasons for thinking that irrational attitudes to death are ineradicable. Kant argued that reifying the soul—treating it as a possible object of experience that can be brought into being and go out of being, something that can be caused and that can have causal effects—is an inevitable but inappropriate metaphysical application of certain rational argument forms. He tried to show that the illicit reification of the soul is built into the structure of reflective inferential thinking, built into the structure of certain sorts of arguments. The structure of a rational argument form is universal in its application, indiscriminate to variations in content. If Kant is right, a mind capable of certain kinds of causal reasoning cannot restrict the use of such reasoning: though we necessarily and properly apply the categories of substance and cause within experience, we inevitably and also necessarily apply those categories improperly to what falls outside the limits of experience. Reifying the totality of experience, illicitly treating it as if it could itself be a possible object of experience, we ask questions that are appropriate only within experience: when, where, and how did it come into being or cease to exist? Similarly we ask these questions about the simple unified soul, the subject of experience reified as what it cannot be: an object of possible experience.[4] These questions are both inevitable and illicit: they are built into the operations of rational inference, and yet are improper and meaningless. If, as Kant thought, reification and the causal and temporal reasoning that accompany it are part of the very structure of thought, then we cannot regionalize or check such thought or the attitudes that are ingredient in it. Of course such reifications and the attitudes that attend them need not be verbally articulated. The person whose reflections have generated metaphyscial terror need not be a poet or a philosopher: *l'homme moyen sensuel* can awaken to the dark night of the soul at four in the morning. The Kantian argument does not claim that everyone actually harbors metaphysical fear, if they would but admit it or focus on it. His argument only shows that the thought which is the core of metaphysical fear—the thought of experiencing one's own nonbeing—is implicit in and presupposed by reflective patterns of transcendental thought, which are themselves conditions for the possibility of experience and rational reflection on experience.

But it might be argued that these improvisations on Kantian arguments at best show the inevitablity of certain sorts of inference patterns: they by no means establish that specific attitudes must accompany such thinking. Couldn't a rational Martian or rational machine draw metaphysical inferences without suffering *angst?* Indeed they could; and nothing is more likely than that they would. But we are concerned with the reactions of rational human beings, embodied as we are. Just as Kant argued that certain natural human motives—the universal desire for happiness, for instance—supplement and accompany strictly rational moral motives, so one would expect that there would be an equivalent set of natural human attitudes that would accompany metaphysical thinking beyond the limits of experience. (For instance, in the *Critique of Judgment,* Kant treats awe as the natural attitude toward the indefinite; and he introduces respect as the appropriate attitude toward the categorical imperative. So a Kantian might well analogously introduce *angst* as the natural human attitude toward nonbeing.)

Is there anything left of the Epicurean view that it is not rational to fear death even though the loss of life is a grief? Certainly everything of the original argument remains: death as such is not be be feared; nothing in that state can bring us harm. Is it then a matter of evaluating the arguments that death is not be feared against the arguments that the fear of death is functional, and in any case ineradicable by creatures constituted as we are, with our sorts of bodies and our sorts of rational capacities and structures? Surely not: the two sides of the argument are not commensurable; they cannot be weighed and summarized in such a way as to allow us to determine what is, all things considered, the rational attitude toward death.

Are we then simply left with the unresolvable opposition, a dilemmatic conflict in our attitudes toward death? There is another way of reading the Epicurean position, a way that brings it closer to Stoicism. The person who has, and recognizes that he has, an irresolvable conflict between regarding his fear of death as irrational and yet inevitable and even functional, can still take attitudes toward his condition. He can take a certain sort of second-order position toward his fear of death, distancing himself from its irrationality, and minimizing as best he can the damaging effects of such fears. But he could at the same time (and not just alternately in a vacillating way) recognize his fear as a natural fact, a consequence of being constituted in a certain way, having certain sorts of rational capacities. Taking this sort of dissociative attitude toward his irrational fear would not necessarily assuage his fear: but it would mean that he was not simply identical with the fearful person. He might then be able to develop distinctive attitudes toward his functional and his dysfunctional fears, perhaps learning how to modify, or at least modify the effects of, his irrational fears, recognizing that there are limits to his control over them. Recognizing the (natural) inevitability of such fears while also dissociating oneself from them can illuminate a conflict that might otherwise have been merely debilitating.

11　The Deceptive Self: Liars, Layers, and Lairs

Self-deception is the best cure for melancholia.

If anyone is ever self-deceived, Dr. Laetitia Androvna is that person. A specialist in the diagnosis of cancer, whose fascination for the obscure does not usually blind her to the obvious, she misdescribes and ignores her symptoms, symptoms that the most junior premedical student would recognize as the unmistakable signs of the late stages of a currently incurable form of cancer. Normally introspective, given to consulting friends on important matters, she uncharacteristically deflects their questions, their attempts to discuss her condition. Nevertheless, also uncharacteristically, she is bringing her practical and financial affairs into order: though young and by no means affluent, she is drawing up a detailed will. Never a serious correspondent, reticent about matters of affection, she has taken to writing effusive letters to distant friends and relatives, intimating farewells and urging them to visit her soon. Let us suppose that none of this uncharacteristic behavior is deliberately deceptive: she has not adopted a policy of stoic silence to spare her friends. On the surface of it, as far as she knows, she is hiding nothing. Of course her critical condition may explain the surfacing of submerged aspects of her personality. Self-deception is not always the best explanation of cases of this sort: sometimes people do undergo dramatic changes, changes whose details have complex but nevertheless straightforward explanations. But let's suppose that Laetitia Androvna's case is not like that. The best explanations of the specific changes in her behavior require supposing that she has, on some level and in some sense, recognized her condition.

To deceive herself, Laetitia need not be lying to herself, need not assert what she believes to be false. Without focusing on what she is doing, she can mislead herself, blind herself, distort or misrepresent her actions, attitudes, perceptions, moods, and tastes. Most effectively, she can direct her attention in ways that subvert what she takes to be her primary attitudes. Such deflections can bear all the hallmarks of intentionality: they are often finely discriminating and patterned; they can be sensitive to the norms of inference and the subtleties of a person's characteristic symbolic codes. In systematically, persistently, and uncharacteristically avoiding paying attention to what is obvious, Laetitia must recognize and scan the domain in order to determine not to look further. Although the phenomena are much richer, I shall focus on cases of straight-out denials of attributable beliefs: these are the hardest cases of self-deception, where the phenomena are most difficult to preserve and to explain.[1]

As is the way with other forms of deception, self-deception multiples. Not only is Laetitia deceiving herself about her cancer: to maintain this deception she is also deceiving herself about her self-deceptive moves, the significance of her uncharacteristic focusing, deflections, denials. If self-deception involves more than being mistaken or conflicted, it seems (on the face of it) to require some second-order attitudes as well: some recognition of the conflicts among her beliefs, and some ad hoc strategies to reconcile those conflicts. If the charge of self-deception is to hold, these second-order attitudes should not themselves be mistaken or conflicted: as tailor-made, trumped-up, ad hoc rationalizing maneuvers, they are themselves deceitful.[2]

The phenomena of self-deception seem, on the face of it, paradoxical. How can a rational person deliberately lie to her present self? Of course she can unintentionally contradict herself, and she can also intentionally and even deliberately initiate a process whose predictable outcome is that she come to believe what she initially disbelieves. But if that process succeeds, she will no longer hold her initial belief. Those who deny self-deception argue that its attributation is incoherent: a person cannot deliberately believe what she takes to be false; nor can she be simultaneously aware and not aware of her beliefs. The phenomena of deflected focusing, inconsequent beliefs and actions, and problematic lack of self-knowledge cannot best be described as involving the strict numerical identity of the deceiver and the deceived, intentionally affirming what is recognized as a contradiction or misrepresentation. If the self is rationally integrated, automatically scanning and correcting its beliefs, self-deception is incoherent.

By contrast, a self that is a loosely organized system composed of relatively autonomous subsystems seems hospitable to the possibility of self-deception. Self-deception is demystified and naturalized, and even to some extent explained, if the self is a complexly divided entity for whom rational integration is a task and an ideal rather than a starting point. Yet despite its intitial hospitality, the second picture of the self also undermines the possibility of strict self-deception. Where there is no presumption of systematic unity, there can be no failure of unification;

nonintegration is not a flaw or failure. After examining the grounds for interpreting the self as a rationally integrated system, and those for interpreting it as composed of relatively autonomous subsystems, I want to save the phenomena of self-deception.

My strategy is guided by an image: standard theories of rational agency represent the self as a city of broad avenues radiating from a grand central square with the federal government buildings, with magisterial façades and elegant capitals. At the center of the city, in the square from which all avenues radiate, are the judicial, legislative, and executive branches of the self: although the governmental functions are distinguished, they are presumed to act from a single set of rules, with clearly defined priorities fixed by a classical conception of rationality. Decisions emanate directly from the center, along the broad boulevards to the outskirts, to the commercial and industrial centers, to the suburbs. Even foreign relations are presumed to be regulated by the same systematic rational plan.

The phenomena of self-deception lead us to a different image of the structures of the self. It is the older medieval city of relatively autonomous neighborhoods, linked by small lanes that change their names half way across their paths, a city that is a very loose confederation of neighborhoods of quite different kinds, each with its distinctive internal organization and distinctive procedures for foreign relations, even different conditions for entry into the federation: a city of guilds, the courts of grand families, religious orders, and old small towns. Imposed over the medieval city there is the grand plan of radial avenues emanating from the center to the outskirts: the rational plan of the city that one can see from an aerial view. But the new main arteries do not necessarily provide the best routes from one part of the city to another, and they do not give the most perspicuous idea of the working relations among the various parts of the city. The radial, radiant city does indeed exist and function over the medieval configuration: our task is to understand how the two cities both serve and block each other's operations. An examination of the strategies exercised in self-deception reveal the various strata and layers of the self, its complex archeology.

Our ordinary practices presuppose that the self is both a rational integrator and that it is composed of relatively independent subsystems. The classical description of strict self-deception arises from the superimposition of two ineliminable and irreducible conceptions of the self. Despite its evaporation under the close scrutiny of each of the two reigning pictures of the self, strict self-deception does nevertheless exist for some sorts of selves, for those who superinpose the radial on the medieval city.

I

A true self cannot deceive itself.

If the self is essentially unified or at least strongly integrated, capable of critical truth-oriented reflection, with its various functions in principle accessible to, and corrigible by, one another, it cannot deceive itself. According to the classical picture, the self is oriented to truth, or at least directed by principles of corrigibility that do not intentionally preserve error. The self is of course engaged in many other activities besides those of amassing or attending to truths or even minimizing the possibility of error. We are busy avoiding or creating trouble, worrying about and enjoying our friends and relations, running for office or at least keeping the scoundrels out of office, being dazzled by the seasons and by paintings of the seasons, enhancing and ornamenting our world and ourselves, wooing, engaging in and trying to avoid hierarchical squabbles, despairing of our lives. But the successful exercise of all these activities is made possible by our capacities for critical reflective rationality, dominant over capacities directed to other intellectual and psychological goods: richness of associational consequences, the joys of amazement, reverence, irony, intensity.

But a dominantly truth-oriented self need not be incapable of ignorance or error, careless and unregulated judgment, failures of attention, illogical inferences, erratic belief, or unrecognized conflict. A complex unified self can suffer all these debilities: but it is in principle capable of being aware of its disorders, and under normal circumstances, their correction requires no additional motivation. Nothing structural stands in the way of integration and everything is actively directed toward it.

Ad hoc irrationality—including putative cases of self-deception— can be given ad hoc explanations, by the intervention of deflecting, interfering psychological causes. When such causes are not *reasons*, the unity of the rational self is not jeopardized by them. Under conditions of opacity, there is nothing mysterious about unintentionally suffering from failures of attention, particularly when—as might happen when a person is tired or ill—it would take unusual acuity to recognize relevant material. Nor is there anything mysterious or illicit about a person finding herself unable to free herself from a particular piece of irrationality. As long as she acknowledges it, she need not be self-deceived, particularly if she follows some sort of principled strategy for attempting to suspend or reconcile her conflicts. It would be enough for her to confess, helplessly, that she is unable to dispel the conflict or correct the failure. (But she could be self-deceived in this very confession.)

But patterned and persistent forms of irrationality, especially those that involve monitoring the material to be ignored, and those that uncharacteristically resist obvious, readily available correction, require more than ad hoc explanations or apologies. Laetitia needs entrenched, finely attuned discriminative monitoring—monitoring that standardly conforms to canons of rationality—to distinguish the symptoms she wants to suppress from those bodily conditions she normally notices. Explaining the phenomena of systematic, discriminative, entrenched irrationality requires postulating interfering systems that, while falling outside the system of supportive reasons, nevertheless also function within the system of rational beliefs and attitudes.[3] Interfering causes appear in a duplicated system of bookkeeping, within the system of rational beliefs and attitudes on the one hand, and as part of an interfering causal system on the other. Distinguishing the belief that rationalizes from the belief that causes without rationalizing assures the independence of functions in the double-entry bookkeeping. But that solution generates problems of its own, determining criteria for the identity of beliefs, under distinctive functions.

Of course sometimes interfering causes can be rationalized, and even justified, by general principled motives or policies. Responsible believers can justify regionalized, contextually distinctive criteria for validity without thereby automatically demoting themselves to erratic believers. It is not necessarily irrational or self-deceptive for thoughts to be guided by fears and wishes: a person might have a justified principle defining acceptable conditions and contexts for such maneuvers. Aware of her tendency to hypochondria, and knowing diagnostic physicians are susceptible to fears of illness, Laetitia might have adopted a general policy of attempting to ignore, or at any rate, to avoid monitoring her physical condition. Her denial of her cancer need not be an unprincipled, ad hod maneuver. It might be rationalized by a justified policy of avoiding occasions for hypochondria. If it brings strong benefits, a policy that allows self-deception as an unintended but predictable consequence can sometimes be the most reasonable policy, all things considered. The self-deception is irrational; the policy that tangentially accords it hospitality, not.

Yet sometimes—and this is what is at issue in determining whether there is bona fide self-deception—the motives or policies that rationalize self-deception and other persistent patterned forms of irrationality are not principled: they become themselves increasingly ad hoc and specialized. In blatantly unacknowledged or denied ways, they conflict with the person's most fundamental epistemic policies. To explain such cases of unprincipled irrationality, the picture of the self that best explains epistemic and practical integrative responsibility gradually drifts from strong to increasingly weakened conditions of unity, transparency, truthfulness, reflexivity.

The simple version of the first picture of active effective critical rationality requires that the self be (1) a simple *unity* dominated by rationality; (2) *transparent*, in that its states are accessible to one another or to a central panoptical scanner; (3) oriented to *truthfulness*, in such a way that its transparency is organized to maximize truths or at least minimize error; and (4) *reflexive* in that the criteria for rationality can themselves be subject to critical evaluation. Attempts to explain patterned irrationality—particularly that kind of irrationality produced by the intervention of functions that unite nonrational and rationalizing psychological causes—weaken these requirements: *integration* replaces *unity, systematic connectedness* replaces *transparency; rationalizing principles* replace *truthfulness;* the condition of *reflexivity* becomes a regulative ideal. The process can be outlined as a series of shifts:

1. The *unity requirement* has increasingly weakened conditions for unification:
   a. The self is a simple unity, with access to all its psychological states. The panoptical center is also a judicial and to some extent a legislative center, capable of evaluating beliefs and forming its judgments accordingly.
   b. In the absence of a central scanner, the self is hierarchically organized, so that its mutually accessible, mutually supportive psychological states form an unconflicted system that maximizes truth.
   c. In the absence of a hierarchical organization, subsystems are cooperatively related; there is a procedure for resolving apparent conflicts between independent functions.
   d. In the absence of a central procedure for resolving conflicts, subsystems are designed so that localized conflict-resolving procedures automatically go into operation when conflict arises.
   e. In the absence of such localized conflict-resolving mechanisms, the system is so constructed that it is not destroyed by conflict: it can operate and survive at lower levels of efficiency and energy, because its various functions are either replaceable or substitutable when the integrative processes are damaged or depleted.

2. The *transparency requirement* has increasingly weakened conditions for accessibility:
   a. There is a central panoptical scanner with direct and immediate access to all psychological states.

    b. There is a central panoptical scanner that can in principle initiate a process to access any psychological state. But sometimes this method is mediated (an intervening process is required for access), and sometimes it is indirect (the content and character of at least some psychological states can only be inferred).

    c. In the absence of a panoptical scanner, mutually relevant and appropriate psychological states are automatically accessible to one another.

    d. The system can continue its basic operations at a diminished level even if its psychological states do not automatically have appropriate relevant access to one another.

3. The *truth orientation requirement* has increasingly weakened conditions for truthfulness:

    a. All psychological functions are cognitive and operate in their propositionalized forms. It is as propositionally formulated reasons that they operate as causes.

    b. Though not all psychological operations are truth-oriented, their independent functions coincide with, and are supported by, the formation of true beliefs in propositional form.

    c. Although they need not function in their propositional forms, psychological operations can in principle be propositionalized in such a way that they can be assessed for their rationality.

4. The *reflexivity requirement* has increasingly weakened conditions for reflexivity:

    a. The content and sequence of thought has a reason that rationalizes it, according to the person's principles in the light of her other attitudes. All general strategies can be rationally justified and corrected. Every critical self-assessment is in principle sufficient to produce an appropriate modification in thought.

    b. Every thought can be critically assessed for its truth and for the appropriateness of the categorical assumptions implicit in its formation.

    In attempting to deal with the phenomena of intractable patterns of irrationality, the first picture gradually drifts toward the second, unity moves to integration; compartmentalization becomes a strategy of integration. It might seem as if that drift could be checked by relativizing and regionalizing integration. But the problems for self-deception remain unaffected. The possibility of self-deception remains exactly coordinate with variations in degree and region: Laetitia could be self-deceived only in those regions where, and to the extent that, she is integrated, truthbound, reflexive.

It might also seem as if the drift to the second picture could be blocked by making the first picture purely regulative. But the descriptive problem would remain: only if and to the extent that the capacities for critical rationality are effectively in working order can self-deception be charged. If those capacities are not actualized, putative cases of self-deception reduce to ignorance, conflict, or error. Where there is no presumption of, or capacity for, rationality, there are no failures of rationality.

II

Nothing is as brilliantly adaptive as selective stupidity.

We would not have survived as the creatures we are if our sole capacities were those of unified transparent critical inquirers; we would not even have survived if critical rationality were our central regulative ideal, dominant over all others. The second picture of the self—the complex survival picture—is generally constructed to explain our adaptive strategies rather than our capacities as responsible believers and agents. On this picture, the mind is not unified, but rather "a problematically yoked-together bundle of partly autonomous systems. Not all parts of the mind are equally accessible to each other at all times."[4] The loosening of the integrative bonds of the self moves to its psychological conclusion: it is to our benefit that relatively independent but integrable subsystems sometimes fail to communicate. Some integrative strategies are local, others generalized and centralized. When there is overlap and replication of functions, there can be tension among the various integrative strategies.

Fragile creatures who survive in highly differentiated changing environments must be able to discriminate between subtly different sorts of dangers and opportunities without being too sensitive to adaptationally irrelevant changes.[5] Though for some purposes a central panoptical monitor is adaptive, we are also well served by autonomous and automatically triggered subsystems. Survival is served by psychological and physical plasticity, as well as by replication and specialized differentiation. Plasticity and replication allow substitutability of functions in cases of damage; diversification and differentiation allow for relatively automatic, unmonitored, highly specific responses. Compartmentalization, self-manipulated focusing, selective insensitivity, blind persistence, canny unresponsiveness—capacities and habits that undermine integration—have enormous benefits. The more sensitive the creature, the more highmindedly rational, the more vulnerable it is to disorientation and debility by attack at one central point.[6] A creature whose critical rationality is impaired by lack of sleep, let alone by the flu, is well served by regionally specific, automatically activated habits.

What are the attractions of being capable of self-deception? The structures and capacities that enable us to manipulate ourselves in situations of indeterminacy allow self-deception as an unintended, tangential consequence.[7] In the interests of generating a self-fulfilling prophecy, we intentionally shift our epistemic policies. We can speak to ourselves as the friendly neighborhood demagogue, cannily conning ourselves to believing that we can do things that are only distantly or marginally within our repertoire. Self-deception is an effective if irrational cure for melancholia. Devoting energies to many of our projects often involves a careful shift of perspective, a refusal to see matters *sub specie aeternitatis*, ignoring the relative unimportance of our various enterprises and projects, shelving doubts and hesitations, setting aside the large corrective perspective. Effective focusing enlarges what is directly present and blurs what is on the periphery: what is blurred falls out of sight, becomes irrelevant. Writing philosophy papers, devoting ourselves to political causes, taking the minutiae of our friends' tribulations seriously, and believing in the futures of our students do not, of course, require self-deceptive manipulation. But it helps.

Trading on the fact that declarative sentences normally assert beliefs, we use them to induce beliefs: on one reading, such sentences express vague intentions, perform non-truth-functional rituals. On another reading, they assert presumptively true beliefs. It is by playing on the ambiguity of these two readings that we can induce the beliefs that serve us well. If we were careful to avoid deceptive manipulative strategies, we would be restricted, unable to act energetically and loyally beyond our initial means. (Yet the capacity to be one's own rhetorician also allows the hypocritical immoralist to congratulate herself on her nobility.)

Just as there are patterns of dominance in visual attention (e.g., red over grey, irregularly moving over stationary objects), so too psychological salience follows strongly entrenched patterns that do not always reflect a person's beliefs and priorities. There is a general correlation between a person's considered priorities about what is important and the patterns of her attention. Magnetizing attitudes—fear, aggression, erotic bonding, bonding to children, actions and reactions to power—are connected with what is important to us and to our well-being. But the strength of those generalized habits of attention can override considerations that are appropriate to specific situations and events. When that happens, a person may not be able to use the material at the periphery of her attention, material of which she is, as we say, marginally aware, to correct magnetized attention. *Being aware of something* does not occur at a single glance, at an instant. It takes place over time; it integrates distinct actions of focusing, scanning, refocusing, and reconstructing a series of interpretations derived from shifting the foreground and the background of attention. Standardly, marginal information corrects the distortions of attention that arise from intensive focusing.

But when a person is afraid or absorbed in love or grief, or concentrated on some form of hierarchical combat, she can fail to integrate the relevant material that is at the periphery of her strong attentive focusing. Sometimes patterns of tunnel vision and salience are constitutionally based; sometimes their origin lies in the person's individual history. Sometimes their import is direct and obvious; sometimes it is indirect, encoded by idiosyncratic associations. Sometimes it is directly motivated; sometimes it is a by-product of functional but unmotivated psychological structures or habits. When attention is strongly riveted, the periphery or background of the perceptual field is not closely attended. Still, a person knows in a general way what is there, and may even know that it provides a corrective to her salient beliefs and attitudes. Even in normal, nonpathological cases, when someone is aware that her magnetized attention does not reflect her general all-things-considered attitudes, what is not salient can seem subjectively unimportant. Though salience and importance (particularly importance for corrigibility) are strongly correlated, they can vary independently. It is this feature of psychological structures that makes both self-deception and akrasia possible.

Another psychological and intellectual strategy that opens the way to self-deception is the inertia of belief in the face of counterevidence.[8] The utility of conservation does not lie in the particular case, but in the general practice of resisting oversensitive criteria for revision and modification of beliefs. Latitudinarian believers develop strongly entrenched habits that work best when they operate relatively automatically and unreflectively. Susceptibility to self-deception is the unintended but predictable cost of the benefits of such psychological strategies. Of course in principle, decently grounded rules for self-manipulative focusing, compartmentalization, and latitudinarian policies of belief are distinguishable from indecent ad hoc policies of convenient blurring. But when the cost of constant, alert scanning is greater than the benefits of the unmonitored application of latitudinarian policies, there is a natural slide from sensible strategies to dangerous self-deception. The habits of compartmentalization and selective focusing are (to our general benefit) usually stronger and more deeply entrenched than the principles that guide, correct, and check them. Even when the occasion makes them

inappropriate, we follow entrenched habits of thought, hiding the behavioral traces that reveal the carefully preserved myopia, the consistent
canny averted gaze. Of course the local irrationality that is the fall-out
of a globally beneficial epistemic policy has a double evaluation. In the
instance, self-deception and irrationality are undesirable, to be identified
and eliminated. But the policy of eliminating occasional local irrationality is, for latitudinarian believers, outweighed by the more general
policy that first offers such irrationality hospitality. The problems are
both theoretical and practical: How can we distinguish a well-grounded
from a suspiciously convenient ad hoc policy? How can we avoid the
natural slide that occurs when we follow a policy that endorses not
monitoring attention?

We've described some of the attractions and operations of creatures
composed of relatively independent subsystems. But we have not yet
characterized the second picture of the self in any detail. On one version
of this picture, the self is subdivided into homuncular subsystems that
are themselves composed of increasingly simple independent subsystems, eventually reaching a level of relatively mechanical subpersonic
specialized proto-intentional functions.[9] On this picture, the self includes subsystems that fix patterns of visual and psychological attention,
whose weighted salience (e.g., fear, eroticism, bonding, astonishment,
competition and combat, hierarchy and domination) may serve long-
range survival, even though they do not always express or reflect individual commitments, priorities, or even welfare.[10] Intentionality begins
with relatively simple preconscious discrimination and ranges through
increasingly complex forms to self-consciously and systematically justified clusters of propositionalized beliefs. Since these routines of intentional activity can occur relatively independently of one another,
intentionality can be a matter of degree.

We can distinguish among the following activities:

1. Pre-intentional physiologically based discrimination (e.g., discrimination between light and dark, sensitivity to heat).[11] While such
discriminative responses are integrated within a person's articulated
system of beliefs, they also simultaneously continue to function pre-
intentionally, relatively automatically.
2. Pre-logical categorial discrimination that, while itself too vague to
be propositionalizable, can be specified by general descriptions (e.g.,
mood responses to colors or to weather). Such discriminations can be
integrated within an articulated system of beliefs, where they often affect
patterns of inference. But they are usually not cognitively corrigible by
counterevidence or argument.

3. Propositionalizable interpretive descriptions of events (e.g., seeing a situation as dangerous).

4. Propositionalized interpretations of situations and events ("This is a cumulus storm cloud").

5. Critically evaluated propositionalized interpretations of situations and events ("In these climatic conditions, a cumulus storm cloud gives a 76 percent probability of rain").

6. Reflexively critically evaluated propositionalized interpretations of situations and events (critical evaluations of the statistical laws predicting weather conditions).

Some psychological activities can function as carriers of information without performing any functions that require their "having the information they bear": though such protological weathervane states conform to some conditions of intentionality, they do not fully conform to conditions of rationality.[12] But those activities, and the information they bear, can also be functionally connected with propositionalized intentional states. They are, so to say, two-faced: under some descriptions they function within the system of rationally corrigible beliefs; under others, they function as causes to modify perception and behavior. While by some standards of rationality, the functions of such subsystems preserve the intentionality of the mental, they are defective by other standards. Similarly, pre-intentional activities that also function in an intentionalized form (e.g., reactions to color, light, and weather) can be arational by some standards, irrational by others. For the explanation of self-deception, it does not matter whether the phenomena of pre- and proto-intentionality reveal that some intentional activity is subconscious or that some conscious intentional activity is subdoxastic. What matters is that some psychological activities fuse a number of different functions, with intentions whose rationality is measured by quite different standards. Relations among the various intentional subsystems affect the relations between the nonrational and the rationalizing functions of intentional actions or inferences. On this version of the second picture, there is nothing unusual about possible conflicts among the various grades of intentional "takes" on the same event or situation. At least some types of self-deception involve a conflict between two independent intentional "takes" on an event or situation when there is a presumption that the two processes should be coordinated.

On this picture of the self, a person's activities—including intentional, voluntary, and even purposive inferences and actions—need not arise from any particular set of motives: they can arise directly from constitutional structures without motivational intervention. Selective focusing and compartmentalization occur whenever the conditions for triggering the operations of the relevant subsystems obtain. A particular irrational inference or action might have several distinctive etiological sources: overdetermination allows a psychological state or an action to be (non-motivatedly) constitutional along one etiological line, while being motivated along another. In principle, constitutionally based and motivationally generated activities might sometimes conflict. There is no particular difficulty explaining the frequency and persistence of what is, on the first picture, simply classified as irrationality. On the first picture, a good deal of thought and behavior is simply classified as erroneous, irrational, conflicted, ignorant. But when irrationality is patterned, and when purportedly rational beings show unexpected resistance to correction, we need an explanation. We want to know not only how it occurs, but why it is such a fashionable indoor sport. Why is it often so highly patterned? And does the pattern explain the attractions it has for us? The first picture does not help us answer these questions.

On the second picture of the self, self-deception is readily assimilated into the failure of integration among systems that are standardly coordinated: it is a natural by-product of functional structures and strategies. Because there is no assumption that the system is constantly informed, let alone self-informed, about its condition, no defensive regression of deception about the first-level strategies is required. Even the capacities for critical rational reflection are subdivided into subsystems. Rule-bound patterns of inference, calculation, "stepping back to evaluate evidence" are analyzed as themselves arising from a variety of relatively independent constitutional, psychological, and cognitive habits. Because psychological and intellectual activities are performed by loosely conjoined subsystems, there is no difficulty in explaining how a person can believe contradictions, can be aware and not aware of herself as holding contradictory views, can adopt conflicting policies and strategies. The phenomena of self-deception are naturalized and demystified on all varieties of the second picture. Since Laetitia need not be aware of the etiology of her beliefs, she might well have persistent and patterned unfounded or malformed beliefs without being implicitly aware of her condition. But it now seems as if this second picture of the naturalized self as a strategic survivor has demystified self-deception so thoroughly that it has evaporated. Starting out by saving the phenomena, we seem again to have lost them. The picture of the self as a loosely confederated system of subsystems, which includes the various activities of critical rationality without giving them centrality, loses self-deception: it has abandoned the identity of the deceiver and the deceived. The left hand is misguiding the right hand, the neck is averting the gaze of the eyes.

But the eyes do not both see and not see exactly the same things in the same way at the same time. If self-deception is incoherent and impossible in the first picture, it is lost in the second. The phenomena of self-deception again turn out to be nothing more than ignorance, conflict, nonintegration, or compartmentalization.

III

Self-deception is a disease only the presumptuous can suffer.

Have our attempts to preserve self-deception failed after all? I think not. Despite the elusiveness of its various forms, self-deception resists evaporation and reduction. We certainly think we can recognize self-deception in others, and we strongly suspect it in ourselves, even retrospectively attributing it to our past selves. If this is illusory, why is the illusion so persistent? Why are the many varieties of self-deception so recognizably and subtly chronicled in biographies, novels, case studies? Why is it the subject of such passionate indignation—and sometimes envy—among friends and enemies?

The reason that we are convinced that there is self-deception is that we cannot renounce either of the two pictures of the self. The classical model of the integrative rational self is the picture that makes sense of systematizing beliefs and attitudes, integrating (even) independent subsystems. Even the weakest form of that model, taken as an active regulative ideal, is essential to our thinking of ourselves as responsible agents and responsible believers. Those committed to and actively capable of rational integration are set to avoid false beliefs, correcting them where possible, suspending judgment when necessary. Responsible agents, like responsible believers, must be able to carry out a rationally structured complex plan of action, giving the capacities for critical rationality not only the authority but also the effective force that reflect the normative power of their rational justification. The strength of the cause must be a function of the strength of the reason. The requirements of responsibility and rationality are not satisfied by assigning the subsystem of critical rationality the weight it would have on a principle of "One subsystem, one vote," or even "Weight each subsystem according to its psychological strength." Even those who take epistemic and moral responsibility to be regionally a matter of degree must treat the capacities of critical rationality as *prima inter pares,* with centrality and dominance in the areas to the extent that responsibility is assigned.

We can't imagine what it would be like to give up this picture of the self. Who would be the "we" who would consider whether, in the interests of truth and accuracy, we should renounce the pretentions of an actively regulative principle of rationality? Even characterizing the self as a set of subsystems seems to introduce a system, distinct from other systems-of-subsystems. There are all sorts of subsystems: which do, and which do not, fall into the rough area of the self? In any case the self is, after all, a biological organism, a body that lives and dies, thrives or fails as one entity. Even when the subsystems do not always work together, even when they actually conflict, still at a minimal level, they are all either alive together or dead together. Organic interdependence provides a presumptive basis for psychological integration.

But from the point of view of the second picture, the claims of the first picture of the self are empty: what is at issue is not the existence, but the character and structure of organic interdependence. Any serious version of the first picture must introduce other capacities besides those of critical rationality: a creature whose only beliefs and motives are derived from the principles of critical rationality would be a very boring and short-lived creature. In the second picture, some of the component subsystems of an organism can be effectively dead while the whole survives. Relying on the details of modular theories of all kinds, the second picture explains our hospitality to self-deception and other forms of irrationality.

Each picture claims to represent the important features of the other, and to save the phenomena neglected by the other. From the point of view of the first picture, the picture of the self as a complex survivor fails to account for the dominant centrality of critical rationality in integrative processes. Even the division of labor among subsystems sets a presumption of their integration. But from the point of view of the picture of the self as a complex naturalized survivor, the first picture suffers from delusions of grandeur. Rational subsystems and their modes of integration may well claim centrality. That is their function and that is their business. Such regulative principles are meant to (attempt to) establish the dominance of rational strategies. But a subsystem, even a centrally important subsystem, claiming dominance by no means thereby establishes the validity of such a claim. From the point of view of the second picture, the first picture is unnecessary: whatever benefits it can genuinely bring can be captured within the second picture. Any other benefits it might claim are illusory.

A modified version of the second picture—one that accords special status to the range of capacities exercised in critical reflection—might seem to save the phenomena of self-deception. But it is a version that effectively superimposes the first picture onto the second, superimposes the capacities for critical rationality onto the system of subsystems, according it legislative as well as panoptical powers. The capacities for critical rationality are allotted independent and dominant status. Themselves causally independent of other subsystems, they can nevertheless modify and correct them. They not only have judicial, but legislative and executive power that enables them to scan and effectively integrate all other systems.

Justifying beliefs and attitudes requires a process of integration whose normative power is not reducible to the system of subsystems that, according to the second picture, compose the self. If the effective normative power of the capacities central to critical rationality had no independent status, the justificatory strength of any rational argument could only be a function of the effective causal strength of the subsystems that formed it. In order to make sense of the self as actively having the power to initiate integration, to evaluate and correct magnetized, persistent perspectival distortions, the power of the capacities for rational integration cannot merely be a function of their causal (psychological) strength in relation to other subsystems that compose the self. The first picture of the self cannot be absorbed into the second; the self of critical rationality cannot just be one component of the system of subsystems.[13] Its power must be a direct function of its rational authority, rather than of the vicissitudes of its psychological and physical history. (But the voice of the second picture says: "What kind of *must* is this? The *must* of a desperate and presumptuously imperious wish?")

Though each of the two pictures claims to represent the other—claims to give an account of what seems right about the other—they remain stubbornly opposed. Both are required; neither is eliminable, neither is reducible to the other. They cannot be reconciled by making one a part of the other. Nor can they be reconciled by characterizing the first as presenting a regulative ideal for rational inquirers and responsible agents and the second as a descriptive account of the self. The rational have, by definition, actualized that ideal: it *is* the way they function. Those committed to the first picture must take it to describe the deep structure of their actual functioning, and not merely as a projected ideal for which they might strive in an irrational way. The process of striving must itself conform to the canons of rationality.

Nor can the two pictures be reconciled by classifying the first as the subjective or first-person perspective of the self, treating the second as representing the objective or third-person point of view. It is not necessary to rehearse the familiar arguments that thought and action presuppose a community of inquirers engaged in common enterprises and practices, requiring the principle of charity in interpreting one another. The first picture gives an objective account of the intellectual and psychological structures that anyone capable of epistemic and practical integrative responsibility must have, whether or not she is experientially aware of herself as having or applying those structures. On the other hand, the second picture can also represent the first-person perspective: as virtually all of Dostoyevsky's novels vividly show, psychological dissociation and disintegration can be phenomenologically experienced.

The apparent intractability of self-deception comes from the superimposition, rather than the subsumption or complementarity, of the two pictures, the two selves. When the first picture is projected onto the second, the self is deceived by itself when its subsystems uncharacteristically, persistently, and systematically resist the correction and integration that is readily available to them. When the two pictures are superimposed, what is (on the second picture) a failure of integration is interpreted (by the first picture) as a piece of irreducible irrationality.

Only those who, despite their effective, actual commitment to the first picture, are actually composed of relatively autonomous subsystems can fail to integrate what they believe. So only a presumptively integrated person who interprets her system-of-relatively-independent-subsystems through the lenses of the first picture of the self, only a person who treats the independence of her constituent subsystems as failures of integration, is capable of self-deception. Not everyone has the special talents and capacities for self-deception. It is a disease only the presumptively strong-minded can suffer. Only to the extent that Laetitia Androvna superimposes the first on the second picture of the self, only to the extent that she interprets the activity of her subsystems in terms of the structures of critical rationality, can she be self-deceived.[14]

12   Where Does the Akratic Break Take Place?

When Mohammed the Mullah first accepted the sage young Fatima as a private pupil to study the Koran, he did not forsee the dangers they would run, dangers to Koranic rules that both took to form their actions. Since Mohammed had studied abroad, his worldly experience should have led him to forsee that despite Fatima's modest decorum and his precautions in assuring a chaperone, their close study together was likely to put their strictly Koranic lives in peril. In him, such a failure of imaginative foresight may well have been akratic, the akratic beginning of a series of other akratic actions. After a time, he and Fatima began to perceive one another—flashing eyes and dark brows, the curve of the head bent over the sacred text—in ways that ill accorded with their commitments to the commandments. Their akrasia was then in their perceiving, their ways of focusing and attending to one another. After the surprise of their passion, they began to form intentions that violated their judgments. Their lapses were not simply lapses between intention and action, their elaborate assignations required nested conditional qualifications: "If your uncle is at the mosque, we'll meet here; but if he is at home, I shall see you at the oasis by the well." Their akrasia was then in the formation of their intentions. Yet sometimes, having formed prudent resolutions, they nevertheless impulsively decided to meet. Their akrasia then fell between resolution and decision, a decision that was still at least sometimes an act of thought requiring further planning to execute. Yet sometimes, their akrasia came between decision and action: having met, and decided against passion, they sometimes acted contrary to their decisions. There is more to their story: but for the time, we have ample material for philosophical investigation.

Let us suppose that in all these cases, Mohammed and Fatima acted as voluntarily as anyone does, that their actions were intentional, falling under descriptions that on some level they took to conflict with their judgments about the preferred course for them in that situation. Let us suppose these are cases of akrasia, if ever there are any.[1] What has gone wrong and where?

We can distinguish:

1. A person's general beliefs about appropriate human aims, what is commanded by God, or required by morality, or conduces to human well-being.

2. A person's commitment to actualize or realize those aims, to instantiate them in his actions, to attempt to be guided by them.

3. A person's interpretation of a particular situation:
   a. His perceptual categorizations: the structuring of what is salient in a situation, at the center of his focused attention
   b. His verbal descriptions and characterizations of his situation
   c. His beliefs about that situation
   d. His emotional responses, as they affect and are affected by, his perceptions

4. A person's forming an intention to act:
   a. A person's forming an *intention* to act, where the intention is conditional on the satisfaction of some antecedents in one isolated piece of practical reasoning directed by one end. "If it is raining, we'll meet at the porch of the mosque."
   b. A person's forming a *resolution* to act, where the resolution is not detached from the comparative practical reasoning that has formed priorities. "Despite all to be said against it, we must continue to meet."
   c. A person's *deciding* to act according to his resolution, where the *decision* is detached from the comparative practical reasoning in which it was imbedded and from which it was derived. The decision is no longer treated as a conditional.

5. A person's acting according to his decision.

These stages on thought's way to action can be regarded as supplementing Aristotle's schema of the practical syllogism: the person's most general evaluations represent the major premise; his interpretation of his particular situation represents the minor premise; his intentions and decisions represent his forming the conclusion of the argument and his action is the consequence of his having drawn the conclusion. These distinctions allow us to locate the junctures where psychological akrasia can occur, in ways that explain the occurrence of behavioral akrasia. When a person commits himself to a major premise that violates his general ends, he might be said to suffer from *akrasia of direction or aim*. When the minor premise is malformed, the person suffers from *interpretive akrasia*. Flaws of inference in drawing the appropriate intention or decision are forms of *akrasia of irrationality*; failure to act from one's decision is *akrasia of character*.

Traditional accounts of akrasia that concentrate exclusively on behavior often cannot explain why and how the person succumbed to
akrasia. While they diagnose the difficulty as a flaw of character leading
to irrationality, they do not specify the aspect of character that has failed.
By distinguishing the varieties of psychological akrasia, we can get a
much more detailed explanation of behavioral akrasia: we can locate the
distinctive psychological and intellectual sources of (specific types of
character failures that issue in) behavioral akrasia. The place where the
akratic break takes place also locates the place where the self-reforming
akrates can best intervene to remedy his condition.

Of course an agent does not generally first form general evaluations,
and then commit himself to them, and then apply his general principles
to particular cases, and then form an intention, then a resolution and
then decision, and then proceed to act. Moreover, his actions need not
be means to realizing his ends; they can constitute or instantiate those
ends. Nor need ends be purposes that are realized in actions: they can
give the significance or the point of acting. The thought that forms the
action can be, as Aristotle said, *in* the action. The thoughts that are
sometimes the reasons for, sometimes the formulations of, and sometimes
the causes of actions need not be at the center of a person's awareness;
and certainly they need not be the result of conscious deliberation.

Now, types and stages of akrasia:

1. The akratic break can appear between a person's general beliefs
about what is good, divinely commanded, morally desirable—his general
principles and ends—and her commitment to guide his actions by those
evaluations. Traditionally this form of akrasia has been characterized as
a debility of the will, and has been allied to sin or vice. Because this
characterization misleadingly reifies the will as a single faculty, it might
be better to describe this form of akrasia as *deflected direction or aim*.
Such akrasia can consist of a person failing to commit himself to follow
what he judges best; or it can consist in his refusing to follow what he
judges best.

In the first sort of case, a person can allow himself to succumb to
lassitude, cynicism, weariness, depression.[2] What medievals called *accidie* or *melancholia*, is—at least for some sorts of agents—voluntary.
Not only is it often a predictable result of more obviously behavioral
actions, but it can also consist in a series of minute psychological
activities: actions of interpretation and decision. The person who fails
to commit himself to a policy of following the course that would realize
his general values and principles need not be radically conflicted: as a
result of actions he could have and still can avoid, he treats himself as
powerless to realize his ends. His conflicts result from, rather than

explain, his akratic powerlessness. Like other akratic conditions, *accidie* or *melancholia* can carry other akratic actions in their wake: having failed to commit or to engage oneself to ends one judges best, a person can—as did Goncharov's Oblomov—form further akratic intentions and decisions.

The second sort of case—refusing rather than failing to commit oneself to follow one's general views about what is best—is the rarest and perhaps only a notional kind of akrasia. Traditionally, it is classified as vice, but it is the kind of vice where the agent knows that his secondary ends conflict with what he takes to be best. A Dostoyevskian character, Goethe's Mephistopheles, can for a time, or at least in principle, decline to serve the ends he takes to represent the Human Good. ("Non serviam." "Let evil be my good." "I will be the imp of the perverse.") Because there is standardly a psychological as well as a conceptual connection between the structure of a person's motives and his primary principles and values, someone who consistently denies his general ends and values in favor of such other goods as freedom, or self-determination, or the contemplative life, will generally tend to elevate these other goods to the status of primary ends, often incommensurate with and sometimes opposed to other human goods. Nevertheless, someone who believes that free self-determination is superior to (say) happiness can akratically commit himself to follow the course he thinks less noble or dignified, taking what he regards as the merely human, lesser course. (In Dostoyevsky's account, the Grand Inquisitor commits himself to the course he thinks incompatible with what Christ represents as the Word of God; he chooses to follow what he takes to be the weaker good.)

Not every radically conflicted person is akratic, and not every kind of akrasia involves radical conflict. A person whose conflicts are unresolved, and certainly a person whose conflicts are unresolvable, will violate at least one of his preferences: but such a person is akratic only when he stands behind, underwrites, avows one side of the conflict, reflexively taking himself to be identified with and judged by his commitment to that side. To be capable of this sort of akrasia, an agent must, as Frankfurt and others have shown, be capable of evaluating his motives and actions, taking second-order attitudes toward his wanton self.[3] But second-order evaluations—stirrings that present themselves as conscience—can sometimes be regarded as remnants of poor social conditioning, and a person can sometimes reflectively favor first-order motives against second-order evaluations. When evaluative attitudes are themselves in radical conflict, the strongly voluntary agent can, as Charles Taylor has suggested, take reflexive attitudes that put a stop to the indefinite regress of reflective nth-order evaluative attitudes.[4] By underwriting one side, he takes a reflexive stance that not only evaluates his motives and reactions, but identifies him as a certain sort of agent, defined by his primary commitments. But it is not enough for reflexive identificatory attitudes to be formed in a Gide-like journalistic way ("Ah, how interesting, *this* is the kind of person I am, fundamentally!") As Alston has argued, for someone to qualify as capable of voluntary action, there is a presumption that such attitudes can modify the person's motivational structures.[5] Ironically, akrasia is among the diseases only the strong can suffer. Among the radically conflicted, only those capable of strongly identifying themselves with one side of their conflicts, and of acting from that identification, can suffer from this sort of akrasia. As long as radically conflicted agents do not primarily underwrite or commit themselves to one side of their conflicts, they suffer vacillation, indecision, vertigo, but not this sort of akrasia.

When the radically conflicted agent underwrites one side of conflicting ends or principles, say, self-determination rather than the happy political life, he need not make that commitment on rational grounds; nor, having made that radical choice or commitment, need he think that following it represents the most rational course. Certainly having underwritten his preference, he will have a reason to act consistently with his commitment; but he need not suppose that reason to be identical with, or justifiable by, what on other grounds he takes to be the summary conclusions of rational prudence. He need not even believe that the details of the actions that would follow from his primary commitment will promote his welfare, as measured by grounds he considers both morally and rationally prudent. Of course his commitment to the preferred course can be formulated as a general rule, and his acting inconsistently with that course is, just so far, nominally or minimally irrational. But by the agent's criteria of prudential rationality—his criteria of benefit—the akratic alternative need not be itself irrational: it can violate his conception of what is most important and best, without violating his conception of what is either morally or prudentially beneficial.

Akrasia originally appeared problematic within the context of theories of moral psychology according to which no one willingly follows a course he takes to be bad.[6] Because such theories not only identify the best with the most rational course, but also deny that there are radical conflicts between incommensurable human ends, akrasia was characterized as a species of irrationality, a lapse from a person's best reasoning about the best course. Davidson, among others, schooled us to see that akrasia is not necessarily a problem of moral psychology, that the best or most preferable course need not be thought morally the best.[7] We can also see that although it is inconsistent with the preferred alternative, the

akratic course is not in itself necessarily prudentially irrational. To say
that the akrates violates his preferred judgment about what is best is
ambiguous between saying that he deviates from his judgment, however
arrived, about the preferred course, and saying that he deviates from a
preferred course that he underwrites because it is the most rational
course.

Mohammed and Fatima's commitment to follow the commands of the
Koran, fall the skies where they may, need not be a commitment that
they regard as either rationally grounded or rationally justifiable.
Whether the details of Allah's commands can be reconciled with the
dictates of rational practical reasoning, whether the Koran exists for the
benefit of the Faithful, whether Paradise is the promise of those who
succeed in living Koranically, are, they believe, beyond anyone's powers
to judge. Not only is following the Koran a principle of necessity beyond
reason, neither rational nor irrational in itself, but also the details of its
commands are not subject to independent rational evaluation. Let us
suppose the Koranic penalty for their infraction requires the most ignoble
possible death for Fatima, while for Mohammed it decrees decapitation
followed by whatever consequence Allah sees fit. And let us suppose
that Mohammed and Fatima live in the heart of brightest Saudi Arabia,
in a wealthy but miserable village where they are the only learned,
indeed the only literate sages. If they accept their Koranic punishment,
they endanger their brothers in Islam: there will be no one to read, let
alone interpret the Law. Let us suppose the Koran is silent on the priority
of the punishment for their infraction and their implicit duties to their
Islamic community. They are strict constructionists; where the Koran is
silent, there is no presumption of legitimacy. Fatima must die, Mohammed must be decapitated. Having studied at Harvard and MIT,
Mohammed sees that rational morality and rational prudence coincide
. . . but on the side he considers the akratic alternative. Although he
has accepted the views of rationality he learned abroad, he considers
his commitment to the Koran to have overriding force: counterrational
though it may be, following the Koran outweighs all rational considerations of moral benefit and utilitarian prudence. Akratically, Mohammed
persuades Fatima that they must not accept the punishments allotted
them by the Koran. Of course, having acted inconsistently with their
primary commitment, they have behaved irrationally. But both regard
their akratic action as the prudentially and morally rational, yet lesser
course.

2. The akratic break can take place between a person's general principles
and commitment on the one hand, and his interpretation of the situation
in which he finds himself on the other. This interpretive form of akrasia

is, as Aristotle and some Stoics suggested, a flaw of the imagination; a person comes to see or interpret his situation and condition in a light that does not conform to his commitment to general ends or principles. His perceptions and interpretations are formed by inappropriate *fantasia*. Interpretive akrasia can take place at a number of points:

2a. A person's perception of a situation can fail to accord with his summary judgments: someone who has repudiated racism might see Caucasians as crude or Orientals as sly. Someone who has repudiated ageism might see the lines of the faces of the elderly as deformations, their motions as disabled. Of course many aspects of perception are not voluntary: there are more constraints on what one sees than there are on how one can move one's body. But at least some aspects of perceptual interpretation are voluntary: and they can conflict with a person's judgment about what is best. As one can voluntarily shift one's focus on gestalt sketches, seeing now a vase, now two women, so one can see the lines on the face of an elderly person as deformations or as marks of stoic and humorous endurance. But there are more obviously voluntary aspects of perception: Mohammed and Fatima might akratically attend to one another's sexually arousing features, instead of concentrating on one another's more scholarly contributions. For some people, at least some aspects of seeing involve *looking for:* when scanning the visual field is a way of answering questions, it is possible to ask different questions; doing so allows quite different aspects of the perceptual field to emerge. One sees differently. Someone might akratically scan a landscape looking for its defensible strongholds or its potential mineral wealth, instead of looking at it—as he believes he should—for its fertility or aesthetic composition. Or someone might scan a social gathering of friends, akratically looking for occasions for advancement or the exercise of power. Scanning, looking for, focusing are activities in which we have (at least in part) been schooled. To be formed by a culture or a milieu is to acquire just such habits: patterns of salience, implicit questions that direct attention. Of course patterns of perception also standardly express a person's general evaluations: it is because the two standardly go hand in hand that the person of practical wisdom can straightway act from what he sees without elaborate calculation or deduction. Because his values form or are expressed in his habitual perceptual patterning, he can act directly from his interpretations. But sometimes, a person can revise his general evaluations—the phenomena of moral and religious conversion are examples of such revisions—without straightway revising his perceptual habits. Someone who can become aware of the selective patterns of his perceptions, the ways in which his preoccupations form his interpretations is then sometimes in a position to modify those patterns to accord with his revised evaluations: he can avoid the interpretive akrasia he would suffer from the discord between his perceptions and his values or principles.

2b. One of the ways it is possible for a person to bring his perceptions into accord with his preferred judgments is to redescribe what he sees. Verbal interpretations are, at least for some, far more voluntary than perceptual ones. For that very reason, interpretive akrasia is much more frequently verbal than perceptual. A person's descriptions of his situation can fail to accord with his evaluations and commitments. He can categorize situations in ways that form expectations that will predictably lead him to act contrary to his judgment. The verbal connotations carried by etymology, by literary and private associations, by contextual expectations, naturally carry presumptive evaluations that influence action. Often in speech, more often in writing, the choice, shading, and informal implications of descriptive expressions can violate a person's preferred judgment. Someone who is committed to nonsexist attitudes can describe the behavior of men and women differentially in ways that prevent his really hearing what women say, in the same ways he would hear those words spoken by a man. What he calls self-respecting behavior in a man, he calls manipulative or demanding in a woman. These differences can lead to different responses and actions: the man requires and deserves respect and cooperation; the woman is to be suspected and resisted. This is one of the reasons that political reformers stress revising and changing the vocabulary of the old regime: banning references to niggers, broads, and old geezers can sometimes be a way of attacking more overt behavioral akrasia that sometimes originates in akrasia of description. The hope is, of course, that it will not only modify the behavior of the akrates but, by modifying the behavior, also change the beliefs of those who had been nonakratically discriminatory.

2c. A person can akratically come to believe something against her better judgment. We do not choose to come to conclusions, and we cannot directly will to believe; but we can sometimes put ourselves in situations where, predictably, we will form specific beliefs because we have used judgments in inferences that we took to be merely provisional. While we cannot directly control the formation of our expectations, we can avoid using judgments that we regard as unsound, in inferences just for the sake of the argument, when we can predict that we are likely to detach the conclusions of such hypothetical arguments, acquiring working beliefs that conflict with our better judgment.[8] Someone who akratically behaves rudely to Swedes may do so because he continues to use a belief he regards as suspect, voluntarily licensing jokes, snide remarks, and the like, in ways that will predictably affect his perceptions and actions. Or someone can akratically cut off inquiry or investigation, knowing that if he pressed on he would revise his beliefs. Or a person can direct experiments—experiments of all kinds, not only laboratory experiments but thought experiments—selecting, describing them, and conducting them in ways that will predictably reinforce questionable beliefs, quite voluntarily avoiding investigations that might jeopardize such beliefs. Often akrasia works as a strategy toward self-deception: a person can be his own home sophist.

Akrasia of belief can be quite extended: it can involve sets of narratives or scenarios that form a person's expectations and strategies of explanations. So, for instance, a person can continue to make decisions by means that he does not underwrite, allowing daydreams to have more weight than he thinks they should. Or he can engage in elaborate patterns of praise and blame, excuses and expectations that do not reflect his judgments about what is praiseworthy and blameworthy. Such akrasia of belief is not limited to individuals in private life: a scientific community or a governmental and bureaucratic elite can be akratic in this way, forming judgments by procedures and habits that they do not underwrite, and that they could modify. Akrasia of belief and self-deception often go hand in hand.

Of course these cases most commonly involve conflict or hypocrisy rather than akrasia of belief. As things stand, only a relatively select part of the population is capable of the sort of self-conscious reflection that can gauge a belief to be provisional; few are capable of predicting the ways that beliefs can be secured or revised; even fewer are capable of setting about deliberately attempting to revise dispositional beliefs that no longer command assent.

2d. A person's emotional reactions can fail to accord with his judgments about what is appropriate to a particular situation, and with his preferred judgment. He might fear someone he does not consider dangerous or hostile, knowing that if he concentrated on, or described the person in a different way, he would cease being afraid. Or he might be vengeful or envious in circumstances he thought did not warrant those reactions, when redescribing the situation could modify his responses. Because emotions are rarely under direct voluntary control, akrasia of the emotions generally follows akrasia of interpretation or akrasia of description; sometimes it follows behavioral akrasia.

It might seem improper to treat an emotional state as akratic: after all, emotions are generally not obviously actions or activities. Yet sometimes being in what is called an emotional state just *is*—consists in—a nexus of minute activities of interpreting, reacting in specific ways, following certain characteristic trains of thought.[9] Even when an emotion

238

THE WAYWARD MIND

is a relatively simple state, the agent can be in that state as a result of voluntary actions. When the whole sequence—the action and its predictable outcome—is akratic, we can elliptically speak of the outcome—the emotional state and the actions that partially constitute being in that state—as akratic, just as, under similar conditions, we speak of someone's being drunk as akratic and consider the actions he involuntarily performs as a result of that condition as actions for which he can be held responsible when he is the sort of person who could have avoided being in that state.

That some emotions are in some circumstances voluntary does not, of course, mean that they all are, or could be. In any case, it is not an emotion type as such—vanity and disdain, or pride and hate—that is voluntary or involuntary, but a particular emotion in a particular context for a particular person. A person who is not able to evaluate or redirect his emotional reactions can suffer conflict or hypocrisy but not emotional akrasia. Nevertheless, because various types of emotions are normally typically voluntary or involuntary in standard situations, we can elliptically distinguish involuntary fears from, for instance, voluntary contempt.

Although the varieties of interpretive akrasia (perceptual, descriptive, belief, emotional) are analytically distinguishable, and although a person can be susceptible to one without being susceptible to others, they are often strongly interactive. In the "The Idea of Perfection," Iris Murdoch describes how a person can come to change her akratic attitudes toward a daughter-in-law whose brash vulgarity irritates her by coming to think of the young woman as spontaneous rather than brash, unaffected rather than vulgar. The mother-in-law attempts to diagnose the juncture where she can most effectively intervene in the interactive psychological activities that have akratically composed and formed her attitudes. It is because we tend to bring our interpretive attitudes into consistent alignment that we have some leeway in changing those that are less voluntary by changing those that are more voluntary. But people differ in the juncture at which such changes have optimal efficacy. These differences give us one way of distinguishing types of agents by distinguishing the ways that different psychological activities function in the formation or determination of their behavioral actions.

3. The akratic break can also take place between a person's evaluation, his commitments and his interpretive stance on the one hand, and his forming a particular intention or decision to act on the other. Akrasia of irrationality involves drawing an inappropriate conclusion from a practical syllogism.

3a. A person forms an *intention* when he proposes to take an action that, under specified conditions, is required by some end to which he is committed. The akratic break take place when the person draws a conclusion inappropriate to the premises of an isolated piece of practical reasoning, performed without comparing ends. Fatima says, "I want to be a good physician, I want the best medical training possible. The university that has the strongest department has accepted me with a generous fellowship for next year. So I think I shall stay here and study the Koran with Mohammed." Of course as it stands, the irrationality and irrelevance of the conclusion is so extreme that we can hardly recognize the patterns of thought as an inference, a piece of practical reasoning. Without further embedding the iceberg tip of this practical thought, we can't identify the problem: it is not clear whether it is an enthymeme, with the crucial ruling premises suppressed; or whether the intention has been akratically formed. The oddity of the inference reveals what is often hidden and unnoticed in most philosophical discussions of practical reasoning. The considerations that are represented as an agent's practical reasoning are, even when intelligibly and validly formulated, the merest surface of a ramified structure of thought, patterns of interpretation, motives—the vast array of psychological functions required to explain the significance, the justification, and the motivational power of the agent's reasoning. The practical syllogism is an elliptically formulated reconstruction of the agent's ends, perceptions—indeed, his character structure.[10] When there is nothing deviant in the way that an agent formulates his intentions, we suppose that the last piece of his practical reasoning represents the whole. We implicitly supply the rest of the missing structure: introducing the standard motives and ends that are characteristic of normal voluntary agents in those sorts of situations. When things go awry, we are at a loss because we cannot attribute the psychological structures that are standardly formative in identifying and determining that sort of action. The behavioral action is then not explicable by the psychological history that is its characteristic ground and rationale. In extreme cases, we may be unable to identify the action.

3b. More commonly, the akratic break occurs in the formation of a *resolution* that expresses a comparative summary of the various considerations relevant to the action. The formation of an intention arises from one line of practical reasoning; the resolution is a summary of weighted comparisons. When, as is often the case, many of the considerations are incommensurable, the person forms a resolution by assigning priorities, by standing behind one set of considerations, underwriting them. But having constructed an elaborate piece of comparative practical reasoning, a person might form a summary resolution that is irrelevant or inappropriate to his reasoning, even though it is still attached to the premises that provide the conditions for acting.

3c. The akratic break can come in *detaching a decision* from the practical reasoning in which it is embedded and which provides its grounds; when it is so detached, the decision is no longer treated as conditional. A person's practical reasoning can lead him to form a summary resolution that reflects his evaluation and commitments; but he can then detach an inappropriate decision. Charitable interpreters tend to suppose that the inappropriate decision is detached from (other) practical reasoning that does support it, or that the person made an involuntary error in computation. But sometimes a longer and more detailed investigation makes the charitable interpretation inplausible: it seems the person has been voluntarily irrational.

One of the reasons akrasia of practical inference is difficult to attribute is that there are two criteria for identifying an intention or a decision. On the one hand, it is presumptively identified by the behavioral action that it typically initiates. Since actions are standardly intentionally identified, standard action descriptions—"going to the bank," "looking for a job"—carry a presumptive description of the agent's intention. But standard intentions are also presumptively embedded in standard patterns of practical reasoning—going to the bank to make a deposit or draw a check; looking for a job to earn a living. On the other hand, a decision is identified by the particular practical reasoning in which it nestles and of which it is the conclusion. So although "going to the bank to draw a check" might describe the *sort* of action a person performs and so locate the *sort* of decision that prompted it, the details of that decision (going to *this* bank, to get *this* amount of money, for *this* purpose) are filled in by the details of the practical reasoning of which the decision is the conclusion. The standard action description provides the initial thin identification; the practical reasoning provides the fuller contextual identification.

Certainly the two criteria for identifying decisions—the agent's practical reasoning and the behavioral action typical of such reasoning— normally coincide. Our social practices would be unintelligible if they did not. Because we can reasonably expect that a person's practical reasoning conforms to standard social norms, we are able to make dependable judgments about the characteristic motives and traits of those around us. By reading off a person's psychological dispositions from what he typically does, we are able to determine the patterns of his practical judgments, his ends, and his interpretive directions. That is how we distinguish friends from enemies and decide with whom to cooperate and whom to combat. But the two criteria can diverge. When they do, it is difficult to substantiate an attribution of akrasia because we can't tell whether the person's action is supported by atypical or appropriate reasoning. For instance, someone might go to the bank in order to gossip with his friend or an anthropologist might look for a job because she is interested in the rituals of socializing the labor force. Such differences in practical reasoning would of course also affect the description of the action: going to the bank to see a friend, looking for a job as a part of a piece of anthropological research. An action that might seem akratic by standard action descriptions may not be when it is identified by its nestling in the structure of the agent's practical reasoning. But overdetermination being what it is, it may be difficult for the agent herself to determine whether her primary intention was formed by the standard normic description of her action or by her particular typical practical reasoning. This is one of the reasons that isolated cases of akrasia are difficult to identify: it is difficult to establish their connections with the person's extended practical reasoning, or to locate the action within the larger context of the agent's ends and commitments, the habits of interpretation that characteristically form his decisions. But there may well be more akrasia of practical and theoretical inference than is commonly supposed. Even when the agent's decision or intention conforms to his practical reasoning, his ends and commitments, he may in fact have formed his decision through a deviant chain that does not conform to his preferred judgments. His decision then only nominally and accidentally coincides with his preference, his judgment about what is best: it is in fact formed by, and because of, principles that he does not underwrite. Despite its apparent appropriateness, it is nevertheless genuinely, but submergedly, akratic.

An action can be akratic under one description but not under another. When an action is described as issuing from interpretations and decisions that are themselves akratic, it need not be nominally akratic in relation to the last bit of reasoning. The action may nevertheless be a case of submerged akrasia, if it violates the agent's primary commitments, and the preferred judgments and interpretations that he underwrites. The extent of akrasia of irrationality is often masked, not only by the difficulties of opacity that are to be expected in intentional contexts, but also by self-deception.

4. For good reasons, akrasia of character that occurs between a person's decision and his behavioral actions has received the closest philosophical attention. The paradigm cases of akrasia have been taken to be those where a person has decided one way about food, sex, going to the movies—and then the hand, the body, goes another way.

Because a person's character includes his interpretive and inferential habits, the varieties of psychological akrasia can be subsumed under akrasia of character, largely defined. A person's patterns of thought not only reveal and express, but also constitute part of his character. His character is, among other things, how he thinks, and vice versa. While cases of akrasia can be described as character flaws that issue in inconsistency and thus in minimal irrationality, describing akrasia in that way does not explain how or why someone who is capable of voluntary action nevertheless in this instance failed to take the course he preferred. The generality of this characterization prevents our understanding of what has happened.

Akrasia of character arises from and is the expression of conflicts among the person's psychological and intellectual traits. Some of these—those that are represented in akrasia of direction and aim—are conflicts between basic ends. But the conflicts expressed in akrasia need not be radical conflicts: what is more interesting, they need not even be conflicts among evaluations and motives. They can involve conflicts among voluntary habits—habits of thought, perception, inference, as well as behavioral habits. To be sure, sometimes conflicting habits reveal or represent conflicting ends. But not all habits are acquired because, or in the service of, the agent's own ends. Some voluntary habits of thought and behavior are acquired quite accidentally. In evaluating the ends that may sometimes be implicit in them, an agent need not make a radical choice between his ends. For instance, the bon vivant who acquired miserly puritanical habits at his parents' knees, but who successfully repudiated the principles behind his puritanical upbringing as soon as he was old enough to understand them, might now and again akratically forgo a present pleasure—buying a basket of fresh strawberries, or taking a pointless saunter by the river—in favor of a stern distant alternative he considers inappropriate. It is also revealing that the akratic alternative need not be the second best alternative: it is often a dark horse among the range of the agent's considered preferences. When Fatima's uncle prevented her meeting Mohammed, her sorrow and frustration led to bizarre akratic actions: against her better judgment, she drove her Porsche through a red light. But breaking the traffic laws of Saudi Arabia was by no means the thing that, next to seeing Mohammed, she most wanted to do.

The attractions of the akratic alternative are often not those it wears on its face, not evident in the intentional description of the action. The course represented by the akratic alternative sometimes has the attractions of presenting a conflicted person with an action outcome. The attractions lie not so much in *what* is done, as in the case of doing that sort of thing, for that sort of agent when he is conflicted. Far from being pathological, the various strategies and habits that pull toward the akratic alternative are standard psychological functions and activities that operate even in the most rationally considered actions.[11] Because such strategies do not require any particular motive to be brought into play, because they are habits of thought and behavior that can operate independently of the agent's current motives, they can alleviate the condition of a conflicted agent who has no taste for conflict, and no approved means for resolving it.

Where, if anywhere, are we after running this maze of distinctions? And what is the view from there?

Distinguishing the varieties of akrasia enables us to distinguish the layers of psychological activities that can conflict. Disentangling the strands in the intentional components and determinations of action enables us to supplement the standard story of how beliefs and desires determine actions in ways that, according to some accounts, can be overcome by acts of rational will. The class of intentional activities that are grouped together under the rubric of beliefs do not of course form a strongly homogenous class: some of them are not even propositional in form. Nor do the motivational dispositions generally classified together as desires form a homogeneous class: the wishes, emotions, moral or religious commitments, wants, needs, fantasies of different types of agents enter into the formation of their actions in functionally distinguishable ways.

The phenomena standardly classified together as *believing* are in fact quite various and diverse. The propositional content that we detach as *the belief* occurs only as an isolatable aspect of a complex series of actions and activities, many of them habitual: attending, focusing, seeing as, classifying, describing as. One might think that it is just this that assures a disanalogy between akrasia of belief and akrasia of action. But I think not. What we standardly think of as *the action* is also only an isolatable aspect of a whole series of actions and activities, many of them habitual.

In both cases, what we might call the bearer—the sentence or the behavior—is intentionally as well as physically identified, and in both cases, the agent/believer's intention presupposes a standard normic description. As a sentence must have a meaning for someone to mean something by it, so a standard action must have a typical normic intentional description for an agent to perform it intentionally. In both cases, the believer/agent can deviate from the norm, but only by standard moves within normic description. And in both cases, different sorts of believers/agents can arrive at their beliefs/actions by distinctive sorts of routes:

the etiological explanation of their beliefs/actions can significantly vary in characteristic ways.

Our catalog of varieties of intellectual akrasia suggests that asserting and denying are sometimes the last of a range of activities that form the content of a belief or decision. One might think that all of this argues against, rather than for, treating believing as the sort of voluntary condition that can be akratic. It might seem as if akratic belief requires akratic focusing, inference, or akratic perceptual and intellectual attention. That seems right. But it is in fact just this that makes it more rather than less plausible that there should be akratic belief. Directing attention, focusing, redescribing, following, and continuing to follow a train of thought can be voluntary.

The role that an occurrent belief—the assertion or denial of a propositional content—plays in thought or in action is largely a function of the way that it has been formed by the rest of a person's intellectual habits. When believing-that-p, is actually thinking-that-p, then believing is an activity. But a person can believe-that-p, without thinking-that-p: even occurrent beliefs can be dispositional. They are then attributed on the basis of what a person is likely to say if asked, to infer if they were to consider, etc. Even when holding an occurrent belief does not consist in thinking-that-p, when believing is a state, a condition, or disposition, a person can be held responsible being in that state, condition, or disposition. Not every voluntary action for which a person can be held responsible is, in the event, immediately and directly controllable or avoidable. All that is required is that the person could under normal circumstances have foreseen what would occur and could have avoided it. "You ought to have known . . . ; you should have remembered . . . ; you surely were aware that . . ." indicate parallels between cognitive states and action outcomes. Even more tellingly, the attribution of responsibility for an action (which in the event is not avoidable) often rests on the attribution of a culpable and negligent ignorance of some sort. Even when a person's belief is not an occurrent act-event of his thinking-that-p, even when his belief (or failure of belief) is dispositional, he can be responsible for his disposition. It is, to that extent, voluntary.

The advantages of distinguishing varieties of akrasia by distinguishing the locations of the akratic break do not stop with providing a sharper, more precise and acute diagnosis of the character flaws of our friends. One of the conditions for akrasia is that the agent be capable of recognizing that he has violated his preferences. Of course that recognition, and as Aristotle says, the regret that characteristically accompanies it, need not be made at every time and every level. Even if the akrates suffers the additional (usually unforgivable) akrasia of giving a fraudulent justification of his akratic action, he must in principle be capable of seeing that what he has done is akratic. If he were incapable of recognizing that his action violates his preferred judgment, then he would not be the sort of person for whom that action is properly voluntary. This condition is a reflexive one. Not only does the akratic agent have preferences, but he must also be capable of recognizing them as *his* preferences. If the akratic action is voluntary, the agent must be capable of avoiding it, not just accidentally avoiding it, but avoiding it because he takes it to be a violation of his preference. Someone capable of akrasia of a particular kind is capable of voluntary action in that domain: this means that he is in principle the sort of person who could have done otherwise. The conditions for akrasia assure the conditions for the self-reformation of akrasia; the precise location of his akrasia locates the place where intervention is optimally appropriate.

On Aristotle's account, it is the agent's capacity for effectively regretting what he has done that explains why the akrates is more likely to reform than the vicious person. But while that regretful recognition may be necessary, it is not sufficient for such self-reforms. And it is just here that our distinctions between the varieties of psychological activities that enter into behavioral akrasia can help the self-reforming akrates. The usual admonitions to exercise rational will are singularly unhelpful. Like the terms *desire* and *belief*, *will* and, even more so, *rational will*, cover a wide array of quite different activities, carried out in quite different psychological domains and in quite different ways, by different types of agents. For some, the *reforming will* consists largely of the exercises of redescription; for others, it consists largely in more persistent and careful, wary attention to inferential procedures, not cutting them short, avoiding hasty detachment of marginally relevant conclusions. For some, it consists in acquiring new habits of attentive focusing; for others it consists in avoiding situations where certain sorts of action-guiding emotions can predictably be aroused. It is just here that the distinctions between types of akrasia can help the self-reformer. The particular juncture where the akratic break has taken place—the location of the person's characteristic psychological akrasia—reveals the optimal leverage for change. Akrasia can take place only where there is voluntary action: locate the precise point of akrasia, and you have located at least one place where there is scope for alternative action.[12]

13   Akrasia and Conflict

Hans is neither a brute nor a fiend. He has nothing against his Jewish neighbors, nor does he have any sympathy for Klaus, the street bully who has donned a uniform and become a Nazi. On his way home from work one night, Hans accidentally runs into a meeting of the party cell; Klaus is haranguing the group: tonight they must smash the windows of all the Jewish shopkeepers in the neighborhood. Although Hans has no taste for this sort of thing, he knows that Klaus and the Nazis are on the rise, that they are ruthless and cunning, and that standing in their way might be dangerous. Nevertheless, it is dark; he knows he has not been noticed; he could slip home without anyone being the wiser about his participation. Yet, having himself nothing against the Jews, no sympathy for Klaus, and no prudent reason for doing so, he stays in the middle of the excitement, follows the gang in following Klaus. Hans, like the others, is an active participant in *Krystallnacht*, acting against his judgment about what would have been appropriate in the circumstances.

Let us suppose that in acting as he did, Hans was acting voluntarily, and that he was not deceived about his beliefs and judgments: he did not harbor some secret hatred of the Jews, or some secret admiration for Klaus. Let us suppose that what he did was a case of akrasia if ever one is.

What has gone wrong, what has happened? Since what did not happen is clearer than what did, let us start there. First, a few terminological remarks. Let's call the course that Hans thinks best, the course that is consonant with his general beliefs and his perception of the situation, that represents his comparative judgment about what is appropriate to the situation, the *preferred judgment* about the preferred course. As we shall see, he need not have reached the preferred judgment by deliberation, or even by a course of reasoning that he underwrites as rational. Let us call the action that Hans performs, the course he takes, the *akratic alternative*.

A person can act intentionally, and even voluntarily, without articulating either his preferred judgment or his immediate intention. His

246

action, its place in the scheme of his beliefs and motives can be at the extreme margins of his awareness. To qualify as akratic, Hans's action must not only be intentional, but voluntary. An action is identified by the intentional description under which the agent performs it; that description can, but need not, essentially refer to his motive or his purpose. For Hans to have acted voluntarily, he must not have been coerced or compelled; there were serious options genuinely available to him; he could have acted otherwise.

I

Now, what akrasia is not:

1. In the eyes of the agent, the akratic action need not have a specific alternative. It is enough that the agent regard the action as deviating from some preferred alternative, whose description can be so general as to cover a large range of possible actions. For his participation in *Krystallnacht* to have been akratic, Hans need not have planned to go to the Bierhaus, or to play chamber music with the Cohens: he need not have formed any particular plans for his evening.

2. The akratic action need not have been second best. Even if Hans had specific plans for his evening, the akratic alternative of breaking the window of the Cohens' printing shop need not have been anywhere near the top of his list of preferences for his evening. The akratic alternative can be a dark horse among the range of alternatives. The rationale that Hans might retrospectively provide to make sense of what he did could rank very low in the structure of his preferences or reasons. The intention that identifies the akratic action does not transparently represent its cause, let alone its rationale. Of course sometimes the akrates can understand, though he does not justify, the causes that pulled him toward the akratic alternative; but he need not be aware of them. Indeed his recognition that he has acted akratically can be masked by self-deception.

3. The akratic alternative need not be wrong or immoral. When it comes down to it, the Mafioso just can't pull the trigger that would kill the Godfather's competitor. "Alas," he thinks, "despite my better judgment, and against my intention, morality has had its way with me." But of course, also, the issue and the situation can be quite amoral from the agent's point of view.

There are interesting but essentially historical reasons for akrasia appearing initially as a problem within moral psychology. The problem of characterizing akrasia arose within the context of the Socratic doctrine that no one willingly takes a course he believes bad. Socrates' view was that if someone takes what seems the worse course, he is either acting involuntarily, from some compulsion, or ignorantly, not really knowing what he is doing, unaware of its consequences. Of course a person might say he knew better: but one might speak so, not really understanding what he is saying, speaking by rote or fashion.[1] Within the Socratic tradition, acting against one's judgment is acting against one's judgment about what is good or desirable: akrasia is a moral problem, with psychological dimensions.

Plato accepts the terms of the Socratic problem, and undertakes to explain why a person might be ignorant of what, in some contexts, might seem obvious. Akrasia, like vice, comes from ignorance; but characteristically akratic ignorance occurs because a person has been waylaid by pleasure. Certain sorts of pleasure have, he thought, the power to make a person forget what he knows, or to keep him ignorant of what is obviously before him. But ignorance and ignorant action are always involuntary.[2]

Aristotle takes the Socratic and Platonic accounts of akrasia to be a denial of the phenomenon: there are, he thinks, genuine cases of akrasia that are not ignorance or compulsion, where a person voluntarily acts against his better judgment, sometimes even knowing that he does so. Yet Aristotle still frames the problem as one about how a person can act contrary to his ends, to his beliefs about what is good. His solution to the problem rests on his differentiating types of knowledge: the akrates might, unlike the vicious person, have correct beliefs about what is in general good; he is, however, ignorant of how a particular situation instantiates or forwards that good, or he irrationally forms an intention inappropriate to his general knowledge and his perception of his situation. Akratic failure is either ignorant perception of the particular or irrational practical reasoning, the person not drawing the appropriate conclusion from his premises.[3] When the agent is capable of voluntary action, that is, when he is the sort of person who can be presumed to know what he is doing in particular situations, when he is capable of reasoning well and acting from his reasons, akratic failures are voluntary. Like Plato, Aristotle thinks that akratic ignorance or irrationality is characteristically explained by the person being misled by some sorts of pleasure: but being so misled does not always constitute being under compulsion.[4] At least for those who are capable of voluntary action, being misled by pleasure is itself a kind of culpable ignorance: it is within the power of such an agent to avoid being misled in that way. While Aristotle thus saves the phenomenon of akrasia, he continues to locate it as a problem within moral psychology, a problem about how someone who is capable of voluntary agency and who has the right ends can act against his conception of what is good.

These earlier formulations of the problem set the terms of later discussions. Even Gnostic and Manichean writers treat akrasia like vice, as a form of ignorance. Except for the fall of Satan, the fallen human condition is simultaneously a fall from light and a fall from goodness. Aquinas's account of akrasia remains Aristotelian. The akrates is distracted; a fantasy captures his attention; a bodily change for which he is responsible affects his perception of his situation, his capacity to reason or to use his reasoning. He fails to consider or to center his attention on what he in fact habitually knows. But Aquinas's diagnosis for akrasia is severe: it is the akrates's concupiscence that sways his imagination and his attention; and this concupiscence is itself caused by the wrong sort of self-love, which is the root of all sin, including the sins of weakness committed through some passion. The ultimate source of akrasia is then original sin: for it is original sin that explains why a person comes to love himself as an end in himself, rather than loving himself as a creature of God. By weakening the imagination and attention, self-loving concupiscence causes the sort of disorder among the faculties in which akrasia consists.[5]

It is only relatively recently that akrasia is treated as a psychological problem that might, in some contexts, have moral dimensions, rather than as a moral problem concerning the employment of psychological faculties. Dostoevsky, Nietzsche, and Freud cast doubt on the doctrine that agents are essentially motivated by a conception of what is good or desirable, and that when they deviate from their better judgment they are drawn by some desire for pleasure. We cannot now assume that all motives are desires *sub specie boni,* and that whatever is seen as *sub specie boni* is, in the end, finally guided by what is seen as *sub specie rationis*.

4. In contrast to the preferred alternative, the akratic alternative need not be, or be believed to be, harmful. The agent can think of the akratic alternative as functionally neutral for his well-being or thriving. Someone committed to following a preferred course even if it harms him might akratically take the safer, less harmful course, regarding his doing so as a violation of his judgment about what is best. It is tempting to assume that when someone acts against common conceptions of prudence, he does so because he has a larger notion of his spiritual good. The presumption is that if someone has forgone considerations of (traditional) prudence, it is because he does not weigh those benefits as the most important or significant for his true thriving. But a person can believe

that the preferred course is intrinsically good or generally desirable, and
yet be under no illusion that following that course will serve him in any
way at all. The philosopher who consents to rule may have good reason
to believe that his own moral or spiritual condition will be worsened by
his becoming a ruler. He may believe that he will be spiritually lessened,
become corrupted and coarsened in just the ways he regards most important. It is only in rhetorically improving tales that martyrs are reliably
ennobled by their martyrdom; and it is usually an important part of the
plausibility of such tales that martyrs die fairly quickly, and that there
is a heaven for their souls. Someone might believe the preferred course
requires becoming a politician, a parent, a religious figure, and see quite
clearly that in all the ways that matter, that preferred altruistic course
will be altruistic to the last exaction. What they do will not ennoble
them in any way, though it will improve their cause. Perhaps posterity
might regard them as noble for what they did; but there would be bitterness and irony in that recognition: the person might think that the
preferred course would be irreversibly harmful to him, though not to
many things that mattered to him. Such a person might then, akratically,
take the less harmful course, the course that is spiritually and practically
prudent; akratically, he avoids the problem of dirty hands, without believing that it is his only serious option.[6]

5. The akratic course need not be immediate or present, while the
preferred course represents long-range future benefits. An elderly or
infirm person who has been accustomed to acting from long-range considerations and who has habitually delayed gratifications might decide
that such a policy is inappropriate, perhaps even unwise, for her present
condition. But it might well happen that despite her judgments about
what would be best, all things considered, despite her new resolutions,
she akratically denies herself the immediate satisfaction of harmless
whims and impulses.

6. The akratic alternative can of course involve a failure to act. The
action can be an action of omission as well as commission.

7. Akrasia is not merely a case of conflicted vacillation. Sometimes
in the press of action, an agent reverses or abandons his judgment about
what is best, and then reverts or returns to his original judgment after
he has acted. But the story of vacillation does not solve the deeper
problem of akrasia. The problem about how an agent can at the same
time accept and reject a judgment about what is best for him to do is
solved. But that problem is replaced by another: how can a responsible
agent temporarily endorse a preference that he on the whole rejects? Of
course if the span of time is long enough, and the new attitude is relatively
stable, the person may have changed his mind, acquired a new judgment,

or learned better. But the standard cases of akrasia are not stable in that way: if they involve shifts, they involve rapid shifts. Yet rapid and constant shifting of judgment about a preferred course is as problematic for responsible and voluntary agency as conflict. The conflicts of temporary vacillation require as much explanation as those that take place within a narrower scope of time.

8. The akratic alternative need not represent desire against evaluation. As that term is usually construed, the person need not desire the akratic alternative. As Davidson and Watson have shown, there is reason and desire, motivation and evaluation on both sides.[7] (Hans might say, as his fist goes through the window of the Cohens' Printing and Book Shop, "I don't really *want* to do this.") The akratic alternative can represent well-developed prudent, practical reasoning or it can represent habit: desire may stand on the side of the preferred alternative.

(In a rough way, we can of course call any psychological state that can motivate a *desire*. But the class of motivational dispositions is both large and heterogeneous: not all the members of that class have the same logical or psychological form as conventionally defined desires. Among a person's motivational schemes are instinctual drives and reactions that can operate independently of an agent's desires, even when they are intentional responses to stimuli-under-a-description; habits and character traits; wishes, fantasies, reflective attitudes, moods and emotions, aesthetic, religious, and moral commitments. The members of the class differ markedly in their characteristic causal histories, their functional roles, their physiological realizations. Some have fixed satisfaction conditions; others are hospitable to a range of substitutable satisfactions; still others have characteristic expressions in action rather than satisfaction conditions. Of course we could do a Procrustean cut: we could lump these various motivational conditions together, formulate them as we formulate desires, and decree that what does not conform to our construction is not a motive. We would have stopped our explanations much too soon, without an account of why an agent has just that collection of beliefs and desires, why motivational systems form characteristic and reliably continuing patterns, rather than arbitrary sequences of psychological states. A Procrustean cut might allow the construction of a theory of something; but it would not be a theory of human agency.)

9. The akratic alternative need not be, or be thought to be, pleasurable. Even when the agent takes pleasure in the akratic alternative, his anticipating doing so need not be the primary explanation of his taking the akratic course. Neither the intentional description of his action, nor its primary motivational explanation need essentially refer to a pleasure-seeking motive, or to a motive whose exercise is in some

way pleasurable. The akratic agent can act from a habit whose exercise is painful or discomforting. Sometimes the akratic alternative is thrilling, absorbing, intense. It is then thought pleasurable only because it is absorbing. But not every exciting or absorbing experience is on that account pleasurable, or contrariwise. Because many of our star pleasures are intense, we mistakenly tend to suppose that intensity is a reliable mark of pleasure. Sometimes the akratic alternative is thought pleasurable not because of any of its primary characteristics, but because it carries the secondary pleasure that following a forbidden course can have. But even when the akratic course is followed because it is forbidden, its attractions are not necessarily those of the pleasure of doing what is forbidden.

The akratic agent is characteristically a conflicted person. Even when the akratic course provides temporary relief for a conflicted agent who does not have strategies for dealing with conflicts, he need not have taken the akratic course in order to reduce the tension of his conflicted situation. And if he did follow the akratic course because doing so reduced the tension of his conflict, it does not follow that he regards that reduction of tension as pleasurable. The intentional description of the akratic action need not refer to its tension-reducing qualities, or refer to them as pleasurable.

10. The akratic alternative need not be irrational. A person might subscribe to a preferred course on what he takes to be nonrational grounds, and deviate from that course in a direction he takes to represent the rational, but akratic, alternative. A person can commit himself to a preferred course because he accepts authority or custom. Sometimes he has taken in or formed his judgment unreflectively, and could only articulate it with considerable difficulty. The agent need not believe that it is rational or wise or even sensible for him to form judgments in this way.

Perhaps an ideally rational agent would only form his preferred judgment by a process that he regards as in some way justified. He might, for instance, think that following the judgments of the Wise Elders or conforming to custom are perfectly reasonable ways to form one's judgments about a preferred course. Though he would not himself have justified his preferred alternative, he would have reached it by a method he thought reasonable. But these conditions are too stringent for agency, let alone responsible agency. A person can subscribe to principles and judgments he takes to be nonrational; he can also believe that the processes by which he came to form those judgments do not reliably ground or justify them. He might be agnostic about whether he was

justified in forming his judgments as he did. But he might also think
that his preference is based on beliefs, and formed by processes, that
he could not underwrite as reasonable, without thinking this was his
only serious option.

A Homeric hero might be committed to guiding his life by considerations of nobility and honor, no matter the consequences for himself
or for his kin. He did not choose such a life on the basis of rational
deliberation, on the grounds that glory and honor represent the highest
goods of human life. But it might happen that political prudence—a
prudence he thought useful, rational—counseled his setting aside the
pursuit of honor for the sake of the safety of his child or his *polis*. Let
us suppose that his heroic code does not absorb such a sacrifice, so that
he becomes all the more honored for having laid aside his own fame for
the sake of his child's welfare. Akratically, he forgoes honor and follows
rational prudence, taking what to him represents the lesser, weaker
alternative.

Of course the hero acted irrationally just in the sense that what he
did is inconsistent with his principled commitments. Nevertheless, he
acted akratically in setting aside what he believed to be the arational
but preferred alternative, in order to follow the course of rational
prudence.

In determining whether the preferred judgment is rational, there would
be a number of considerations.[8] One would determine whether

a. The preferred judgment is coherently and consistently formulated.
b. The preferred judgment is logically or validly derived from a general
   principle or evaluative judgment.
c. The general principle or evaluative judgment from which the preferred
   judgment is derived is not implicitly ill-formed or inconsistently
   formulated.
d. The general principle from which the preferred judgment is derived
   is itself consonant with, and generally supported by, the rest (of the
   system) of the agent's beliefs, motives, and evaluations.
e. The agent's system of beliefs, on the whole, as these things go, is
   true, and his system of evaluative judgments is on the whole, as
   these things go, sound.

In determining whether an action is rational, there would be further
considerations. One would determine whether

a. The action conforms to the agent's preferences.

  b. The agent's preferences are themselves rational (in the various senses
      sketched above).
  c. Among the action's essential causes are reasons that the agent con-
      siders justified and sound.
  d. Among the action's essential causes are the reasons that also formed
      the agent's preferred judgment: he acts from, as well as in accordance
      with, his preferred judgment.

The akratic alternative might be rational by some of these measures, the
preferred alternative by others. Determining the validity of the preferred
judgment might involve a variety of quite distinct criteria for appropriate
rules of derivation. For instance, determining whether our Homeric hero
has violated the code of honor is a difficult and complex matter. Presumably he could not deduce or prove that the prudential course is the
baser alternative. Characteristically, the casuistry that locates individual
actions within a complex moral and social code has its own rationale:
since such codes are often in flux, and since political power often hangs
on the outcome, an action that is regarded as a violation by some, will
be regarded as justified by others.

   Now of course we could assure the rationality of the preferred judgment
by characterizing whatever rules govern its derivation as the rules of
rationality. This move seems less arbitrary if we also combine it with
giving a rational reconstruction of the agent's derivation of his preferred
judgment. After all, we would expect that the psychological processes
by which agents form their preferred judgments might be quite unreli-
able, perhaps even idiosyncratic. The principle of charity might then
be thought to require that we give an account of the sort of justification
that the agent could reasonably give for his preferred judgment, even if
these reasons were not the causes of his coming to hold it. Presumably,
we would limit ourselves to showing that the preferred judgment can
validly follow from premises or beliefs that the agent actually holds. Our
account would rationalize the preferred judgment, from the agent's point
of view. From that reconstructed rationalized point of view, the akratic
alternative would be irrational, in a strong sense.

   But this is no great discovery about the character of akrasia: it follows
directly from the task of rational reconstruction. From this, nothing would
follow about whether an agent, in this instance, was in fact irrational in
following the akratic course. A reconstruction that provides a rational
justification of the agent's preferred course does not necessarily describe
the agent's reasoning or the psychological processes by which he formed
his preferred judgment. To say that if those processes do not conform
to the reconstruction he would be irrational, is to beg the question at
issue. [9]

11. Akrasia is not always in the action itself. An action that is, strictly speaking, in accordance with a decision or intention, may nevertheless be akratic because that intention or decision is akratic. 'Paying attention to', 'describing as', 'forming an intention to' are actions; indeed, they are often voluntary actions. A person can intend, decide, and attend in ways that conflict with his preferred judgment. We can call such akrasia embedded akrasia, to indicate that while the action accords with the person's immediate intention, that intention is itself akratic.

12. There are what we might call cases of submerged akrasia, in which the agent's action appears to conform with his preferred judgment. The agent may hold, and indeed be strongly committed to a belief that rationalizes his action. Yet that belief need not have been the cause of the action; indeed, it need not have entered into the causal history of the formation of the intentional description of the akratic action. The action may have been caused by beliefs and evaluations that conflict with the agent's preferred judgment. The intention that identifies the action does not transparently represent its cause.

This suggests that there is a great deal more to akrasia than meets the eye. It is a condition of akrasia that on some level, the agent recognizes that his action conflicts with his preferred judgment. Apparent conflicts might be resolved by compartmentalization or contextualization: the agent must take the apparent conflict as occurring within the same domain. Of course this can often be masked by self-deception. But self-deception requires awareness of the conflict on some level, and it is on this level that submerged akrasia is recognized.

II

What is left of akrasia after all these demurrings and denials? The akratic agent voluntarily acts against his preferred judgment. Even when they can be given a good rationale, the causes that explain his following the akratic course do not in his eyes justify his doing so. While we can, in standard contexts, identify akratic actions without detailed knowledge of the agent, we do so against the background of theories about normal agency. We implicitly supply what agents normally know and believe, infer, expect, and desire. When the presumption of standard character development does not hold, when the etiological derivation of the agent's intentions is deviant, we reconsider the classification of the action-token, even though an action of that type would be akratic for an agent with a standard structure of beliefs and motives. When we classify an action as akratic we are still implicitly relying on the agent-oriented criterion: we classify the isolated action by filling in presumptions about its conformity to the typical case of akratic agency.

What then explains what the akratic agent did? What sort of person is he?

To be akratic, a person must be capable of voluntary agency. He must be capable of reasoning, acting from his preferred judgment; he must understand the language and culture of his community, the expectations and presumptions of the people who will affect and be affected by his actions; he must know the standard consequences of various actions in his natural and cultural environment. He must have reasonable self-knowledge, know his characteristic patterns of action, his habits, his commitments, his reactions: how he will be affected by this or that course. He must be committed to some relatively clearly defined ends, and to be capable of being guided by these. He cannot change his motivational schema and beliefs with every action: his character must be relatively stable and reliable. As we saw, none of this entails that he has arrived at his preferred judgment by a rational process or by a process for which he can give some rationale. It does not even presuppose that he has articulated his ends or preferences. All that is required is that he be able to reason about the presuppositions and consequences of his actions, to determine which actions would instantiate or support his ends and preferences. He must have standard operating intellectual, emotional, and psychological capacities, being capable of perceiving reasonably accurately, interpreting events in ways that will permit him to act consistently with his ends. This means that he must also be able to correct his judgment when it is appropriate to do so, revising both his beliefs when they conflict and his motives when they are incoherent. Although he must have a stable character, he cannot be so rigid as to be unable to learn.

The standard of normality that identifies agents capable of voluntary action is of course not statistically defined. There is a normic component in identifying the normal agent, in specifying the proper development of intellectual, psychological, and physical capacities. While a society's implicit theory of normal agency becomes constitutively self-fulfilling in many areas (for instance, in the determination of legal and religious liability and responsibility), that implicit theory also makes claims that can be evaluated independently of the practices of the society. While the criteria for identifying normal agents (and thus for identifying those capable of akratic agency) vary culturally, there are also cross-cultural constraints on the appropriateness of at least some of these criteria.

If this rough sketch fixes some of the conditions for voluntary agency, what then distinguishes the character of the akrates? How does he differ from other voluntary agents? First of all, akrasia is characteristically regional, and often temporary. A person who is through and through akratic would hardly qualify as an agent: unless he conforms to his preferred judgment in some crucial areas, he'd hardly survive. What then identifies the akrates in the regions where he is akratic, when he is?

The akrates is characteristically a relatively conflicted person. He sees choices where others have routines that enable them to act directly from their ends and their perceptions of their immediate situations. Not only does he see choices where others have a pattern of hierarchically arranged habits; he sees situations of choice as situations of conflict and loss. (This doesn't mean that a person whose habits are so fixed that he rarely faces situations of radical choice is better off than the akrates. Akrasia is by no means the most serious or worst among our psychological disabilities. In any case, sometimes *not* seeing a situation as requiring choice, or *not* being conflicted, might itself be akratic.)

The balance of the akrates' habits—his ends and his judgments—is such that he can find himself in a situation where the habits and thoughts that led to the preferred alternative are not consonant with the habits and thoughts required to actualize it. Sometimes his habits of perception conflict with his motivational habits; or his intellectual preferences are not securely grounded in his behavioral habits. His second-order habits do not characteristically function to resolve his conflicts in the direction of his preferred judgments. [10]

But not every case of conflict is a case of akrasia. After all, some kinds of conflict are so basic, so radical, that they would prevent a person from qualifying as a voluntary agent. And other sorts of conflict are the condition of moral agents. While akratic conflict divides a person, it does not divide him in such a way as to make it impossible for him to form a summary preferred judgment, behind which he stands, which he underwrites, which he takes to identify him as an agent. Of course a person capable of voluntary agency is capable of standing back to evaluate his motivational scheme and the structure of his beliefs, perceptions, and intentional sets. [11] But it is not enough for him to evaluate his beliefs and actions; it is not even enough for him to have reflexive attitudes by which he evaluates himself by his motives and beliefs. He must underwrite some character traits as strongly *his*, disassociating himself from others that he recognizes as also psychologically and motivationally his. He undertakes to guide his future actions by his reflexive evaluative appropriations, those motives and beliefs with which he identifies. [12]

Reflexive attitudes do not need to be derived from an agent's most cogent reasoning, nor need they underwrite or appropriate all and only those motives and evaluations that the agent judges most rational. This is one, but only one, highly functional type of reflexive identification. While a voluntary agent must be capable of rational inferences, and capable of correcting his beliefs in the light of those inferences, he need not primarily identify himself as a rational agent. He need not take conformity to rationality as his highest value, reflexively appropriating only those judgments that are preferred because they are the strongest survivors of the exercise of his best reasoning. Though they must also be capable of rationality, a Nietzschean, a Koranist, and Kierkegaard's Esthetic Man do not disqualify themselves as agents because they do not commit themselves to follow their most rationally founded judgments.

But we do not yet have an account of an akratic agent. We only know that he is capable of voluntary action, and that he suffers from specific sorts of conflicts between his habits and the reflexive identifications that underwrite his preferred judgment.

How did he come to be that way, and what explains his taking the akratic course? There are many ways that a person can come to find himself in such a debilitated position.

An agent capable of responding appropriately to the potentially conflicting demands of a rich and rapidly changing environment develops potentially conflicting traits. On the one hand, he requires strong relatively conservative habits of behavior and thought, of interpretation and understanding, habits that provide action outcomes even when the person's motivational scheme is indeterminate or fluid. On the other hand, he requires the capacities of critical inquiry, of rational thought that is not formed, determined, or directed by his habits. A voluntary agent requires Tory habits and Whig critical capacities. Furthermore, an agent living in a complex heterogeneous social world requires strong empathic capacities for acquiring the interests and motives of the members of his community. Rousseau and Freud have shown us that the mechanisms that make social cooperation easy and natural are mechanisms that also internally divide a person. Precisely to the extent that a person can empathize with and acquire the interests of the various members of society, to that extent he will be divided. The capacities that help overcome the internal divisions of a genuinely social and empathetic person, the capacities of strong critical and often unswerving autonomy are also clearly necessary. Reconciling narcissistic, empathic and autonomous capacities involves a long-range integrative project for a conflicted agent.

Sometimes the akrates has been unfortunate in ways that lead him to believe that the world does not afford—or does not afford him—alternatives to match those that must be rejected in a choice. On some level he is not convinced that he will have their like again, or anything as

good. He thus finds it difficult to turn from proffered goods, even to
something he believes better. Or he may not believe in his own future;
he can believe, abstractly, that the preferred alternative is not only the
best, but the best for him, yet find his future subjectively unreal. The
risks and probabilities he has calculated fail to carry subjective conviction: they seem abstract or academic.

He may not have learned how to envisage the preferred good, not
have developed the perceptual and imaginative habits that enable him
to attend to it, to see it as vivid. It can seem less real to him because
he does not know how to specify it in detail, because he can only conceive
it schematically. Or he might not know how to conceptualize it in ways
that actually connect it with his strong habits. He has difficulty seeing
himself carrying it out, because he has defined it in ways that are
unfamiliar. Or he may have envisaged it all too vividly: but quite externally, without knowing how to place himself in the situation. He cannot
connect it to his repertoire of habits. His difficulty may be that he treats
his actions only observationally, not having developed the capacities for
internal kinesthetic rehearsal. His practical reasoning carries neither
the habits nor the rehearsal that begins action.

There are many ways that a person's conception and imagination can
come to be so damaged as to produce a sense of debility, powerlessness.
He may have experienced crucial failures or he may have been educated
to be passive in situations of choice; or his early choices may have been
beyond his powers of action, causing him to distrust himself. Or he may
have developed a range of poor habits, mismatched with his desires,
gradually coming to sense himself powerless. Or his strong perceptual
habits may be at odds with his later beliefs, so that his patterns of
attention no longer represent his preferences.

Akrasia has a strongly political dimension. A population can have
damaged powers of imagination, utopianly overdeveloped to generate
unsatisfiable desires, or channeled to unrealistic courses. More commonly, the powers of the imagination can remain undeveloped, stultified,
so that a whole sector of a population remains unable to perceive,
imagine, or schematically define alternatives that they think, in an abstract way, best.[13]

A person can become akratic because he finds himself in a social or
political situation in which he cannot exercise his strongest traits, a
situation in which his judgment lacks scope of action. An exile, a person
alienated from his social milieu, a person who has suffered strong restrictions or restructurings on his actions can find himself debilitated,
his habits and dispositions blocked. The sort of stress that induces a
sense of powerlessness is not always initially intrapsychic. When there

is a failure of fit between a person's traits and his situation, he can develop secondary habits that do not conform to his judgment. (Sometimes, of course, such stresses and difficulties elicit coping traits: a person can discover unexpected, previously hidden, forms of integration. But much more frequently, externally induced stress becomes intrapsychic, especially if a person is strongly empathic, and tends to form self-images by internalizing those that he perceives others to have of him.) Anomie, alienation, subtle victimization, and isolation are seedbeds for akrasia, ambivalence, emotional inertia, and other sorts of conflicted behavior.

Like extreme powerlessness, unusual and unrestricted power tends to generate akrasia. One of the ways in which power corrupts is that it allows unusual scope for the akratic release of the powerful but stressed person. The normal checks and constraints that might add weight to the preferred course are absent. The powerless are often lightning conductors for the akratic actions of the powerful. The conflicted akrates is often canny about the directions of his akrasia, acting against his better judgment primarily only against those too weak to restrain him.

Debilitating conflicts put the akrates in a position where he will lose important goods, no matter what he does. Sensing himself conflicted, distant from the preferred alternative, he turns himself into lower gear and follows the easier course, the course that is assured by relatively automatic psychological habits. While the psychological dispositions that draw him to the akratic alternative solve his problem about what to do, he doesn't in fact follow the akratic alternative under the description that explains his taking it.

What then, above its surface attractions, does the akratic alternative promise the conflicted akrates? What draws him to it against his better judgment? Of course characteristically, the akrates can say something by way of rationalizing the akratic alternative, can explain why his decision did not accord with his intention. But the pains of akrasia are more than those occasioned by the loss of the goods represented by the agent's preference. At least some of the discomfort of akrasia comes from the agent's being mystified by what he has done, rather than from the actual outcome of the akratic course, which can sometimes be quite enjoyable or serendipitous. Akratic actions are often unsettling because their occurrence gives the agent a sense of vertigo about his qualifications as an agent; that is one reason why self-deception often rides on the back of akrasia, to steady the vertigo of a voluntary agent who seems unable to command himself.

There are, roughly, three attractive strategies of akrasia. These are of course not mutually exclusive, nor are they exhaustive. Indeed, they often augment and supplement each other.

1. The akratic alternative sometimes acquires its attractions by its power to dominate the agent's attention: it has more salience for him than the preferred course. It draws and focuses the agent's attention on some feature of the akratic alternative; by filling the experiential field, it drowns out the preferred alternative. The akratic alternative can be dominant by default: a person's preferred judgments may fail to magnetize or hold his attention. There are of course a number of ways in which an alternative can dominate attention: it can be immediately present, filling the visual field; it can have imagined intensity or excitement; it can promise absorbing pleasure. It can be represented in vivid detail, with a high degree of specificity and determinateness. It can be physiologically or psychologically salient. It can represent the satisfaction of a frustrated need. There is of course a continuum between constitutionally fixed, although relatively plastic, patterns of salience and dominance, their strong cultural formation and reinforcement, and patterns of dominance fixed by the vicissitudes of an individual's biological and psychological history. It is not always easy to identify the attention-dominating features of an akratic alternative: their dominance can be symbolically coded, in ways that could only be deciphered by tracing the etiology of the formation of an individual's habits of intentional focusing.

2. The attractions of the akratic alternatives are sometimes those of the familiar, the habitual, the easy course. When the preferred course is perceived as difficult or as distant from habitual action routines, a conflicted agent is often akratically drawn into a strongly entrenched habitual routine, just because it presents an easy solution, rather than because of any particular attraction it has. Any strongly habitual or easy action would have done equally well. The habitual course presents ready-made, relatively automatic action solutions. Perceptual habits of attending and focusing, cognitive habits of structuring or interpreting situations, habits of inference and narrative expectations are as voluntary as many behavioral habits. They often support the akratic alternative against the preferred course.

3. Social streaming can pull in the direction of the akratic alternative: the akrates can follow the charismatic leader, or be influenced by the mechanisms of sympathy or antipathy to take a position or adopt an attitude that conflicts with his judgment, being role-cast into action routines that conflict with the preferred alternative.

These three strategies can all be construed as having the force of attention-focusing habit. In following these strategies, a person exercises psychological dispositions that function relatively automatically; such dispositions are easily triggered. Far from being pathological or compulsive, akrasia often provides a conflicted agent with an action-solution.

It might seem that this account of the attractions of the akratic alternative runs the danger of taking akrasia out of the realm of the
voluntary. But of course habits are not compulsions. A course that an
agent takes because it is easiest does not on that account fall outside
the scope of voluntary agency. Psychological dispositions that pull toward
the akratic alternative are as much a part of the agent's character as
those that lead to his identifying himself with the preferred alternative.
This is why the self-reforming akrates can steal the fires of the akratic
course, learning to transfer the attractions of the akratic alternative to
the side of the preferred course. He can learn to perceive the preferred
alternative in ways that focus and magnetize his attention, or to define
it in ways that connect with his strongly established habits; or to place
himself in situations where social streaming will direct him to the preferred rather than the akratic alternative.

Demystifying akrasia reveals that attractions of the akratic alternative
are those of the most ordinary and common sorts of psychological activities. Far from being pathological, they are automatically and constantly functional, not only in pre-intentional behavior, but also in the
most considered, most rationally considered action. Even when a person
takes rationality to be more than a crucial criterion for the legitimation
of his various ends, even when he takes the exercise of rationality to be
the end with which he primarily identifies himself, it cannot provide the
sole or sufficient principle of choice. It cannot by itself provide the range
of aims and directions required for a recognizably human life. The
Platonic dream of integration is that the direction of rationality will
coincide with the directions of other goods. And perhaps, for a happy
few, they do. But the prevalence of akrasia, self-deception, ambivalence,
and conflict show that the standard story of rational agency requires
strong modification. Not only are human agents more complex and conflicted than the naive accounts of rational agency project, but the various
functions of rationality in agency are themselves often in latent conflict.
The psychological strategies exercised in self-deception and akrasia
operate quite independently of rationality. That, indeed, is precisely
their contribution to rational action: a rational agent could not do without
them. Such an agent would have no focus for attention: his psychological
field would be nonperspectival, without preference. He would be a rational agent, without any reason to act this way rather than that.

The strategies that operate on the side of the akratic alternative are
standard operating procedures. That is precisely their attraction and
power: they are continuous psychological operations that do not require
any particular motive or commitment or preference in order to be brought
into play. The choice of the akratic alternative consists in a person

reverting to lower gear, to relatively automatic psychological functioning. His doing so provides him with a solution to the question: *what to do?* It is in the character of the akrates to be led to that question. The conflicts among his habits require him to make choices, to underwrite some of his motives and ends, and to disown others. The most common fundamental psychological and behavioral functions lead the conflicted akrates to the akratic alternative. Acting from them is not acting from compulsion: acting from them, especially when they are quite specific in their detail, is acting from character. Following them is as voluntary as anything is, even though in following them, the akrates is not following the bent that he underwrites, with which he identifies.

One of the ways that the phenomena of akrasia and self-deception illuminate the shortcomings of the standard model of action as an outcome of beliefs and desires, an outcome that can be overridden by rational will, is that they show how complex and varied the class of motives is. The class of motives is highly heterogeneous; various members of that class function in quite distinctive ways in forming actions, and the conditions for their satisfactions are quite distinctive. Wishes, religious and moral commitments, wants, needs, fantasies, and habits are often standardly classified as desires or wants or preferences. But their respective relations to beliefs are quite distinctive in form; they determine the details of the action outcome in distinctive ways; the formal conditions of their satisfaction are distinguishable. The explanatory description of the actions that issue from each of these—the description that identifies the significance of the action by tracing its etiology—has a different form. In principle, such attitudes can be formulated as reasons and beliefs, as propositionally defined desires by Procrustean moves. Either they are capable of being propositionalized, or off-with-their-heads: they are irrational. While this Procrustean procedure may reveal the structure of the logical justification of our actions and attitudes, it does not reveal the ways in which such intentional protorational motives really function. Even when such reconstructions reveal the structures of the rational reconstruction of our attitudes, they do not by themselves provide the basic premises that are the substance of that reconstruction.

So though the akratic action formally satisfies some motive simply because it is, after all, voluntarily performed, the motive can be extremely general in character: it need not specify a particular desire. But explaining actions—particularly actions that appear deviant—requires specifying the level of generality of the intentional component that identifies the action. Is there a feature about the particular action that sets the satisfaction conditions, or will any action of a quite general similar structural type satisfy? Sometimes an action satisfies a motive simply because the motive is strongly entrenched; but a motive can become entrenched accidentally rather than because it consistently leads to satisfactions. Not all motives are desires *sub specie boni;* nor is whatever is seen as *sub specie boni* so seen because it has been taken *sub specie rationis*.

Standard theories of rational agency trade on important ambiguities in the notions of preference and satisfaction. Because they take satisfactions and preferences at face value, they do not give explanations of an agent's desires; their accounts of motivation are simplistic. An agent's felt preferences$_1$ are what he believes and senses himself to want: standardly, these are desires for felt satisfactions$_1$. Such felt satisfactions$_1$ are defined by their corresponding desires. But since there are also preferences that are not phenomenologically experienced, and since a person can be mistaken about his preferences$_1$, *preference* becomes a theoretical term that encompasses a wide range of motives, only some of which are phenomenologically experienced as such, and only some of whose satisfactions are phenomenologically experienced. Habits, moods, emotions, religious or moral commitments, aesthetic reactions like disgust or admiration and other sorts of character traits are, in the larger sense, motivational. They form a person's preference$_2$ system, and often explain the structure of a person's preference$_1$ rankings.

The psychological explanation of the agent taking the akratic course need not appear, even in disguised form, in the intentional description of the akratic course. What draws the agent to the akratic course is not necessarily the surface description of his perferences$_1$ for the akratic alternative, but the psychological mechanisms—his preferences$_2$—that operate in standard rational habits. These preferences$_2$ can operate without the agent having to act from an occurrent desire, in ways that preserve the voluntary character of the action. When the agent is conflicted or debilitated, he lacks a reigning occurrent desire. So he turns himself into what we might call the lower gear of standard operating procedures, of a large variety of psychological processes, which can all roughly be characterized as habitual because they operate without the intervention of a current desire. Acting on such procedures satisfies preferences$_2$. A satisfaction$_2$ of a preference$_2$ is the state of affairs that represents the realization of a preference$_2$ where that preference$_2$ may conflict with the agent's felt desires, his preference$_1$ rankings.

III

A brief and highly programmatic summary is in order. First, these accounts of the strategies and attractions of akrasia suggest that the picture of a rational agent as someone whose actions are outcomes of beliefs and desires, with a capacity to override these by some act of rational will, requires to be supplemented. The class of beliefs, the class of motives, and the class of acts of will are heterogeneous. They form and rationalize actions in quite distinctive ways.

Second, we cannot neatly distinguish irrational psychological functions from those that are rational. Psychological functions that are in some contexts irrational, or at best arational are necessary to the rational functions. Akrasia is pervasive because it is closely connected to strongly entrenched functional psychological processes. Attempts to eradicate akrasia would jeopardize these processes.

Of course, it does not follow that we can forthwith justify or accept akrasia. Even when we can recognize that akrasia or self-deception can sometimes be the agent's best option, he cannot himself choose that course under a description that justifies it. Although akrasia is not by any means the worst among the psychological and intellectual vices, there is no way of underwriting it in general. Yet is it important to remember that the correction of akrasia can sometimes lead to consistent unconflicted vice or, equally dangerous (though moral), floundering vacillation. Akrasia is among the phenomena of conflict: as such it is potentially dangerous, because conflicted agents are often unpredictable, and at worst quite destructive. But there are worse dangers, and the strongly righteous determination to eradicate akrasia can sometimes lead to strong vice.

4 COMMUNITY AS THE CONTEXT OF CHARACTER

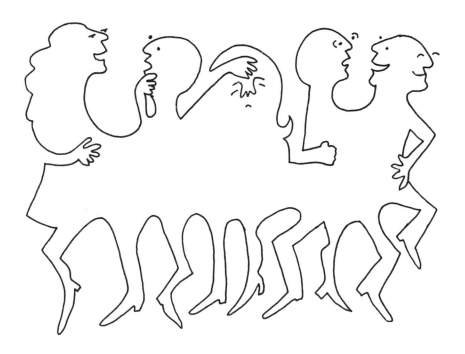

SHELLY ERRINGTON

Contemporary moral philosophers who advocate a return to virtue theories need to examine the political dimensions of moral systems, and to include a range of excellences beyond the traits assured by good will. They also need to expand their conceptions of practical rationality to include the psychology of *phronēsis,* as immanent in perception and the minutiae of action. In "Three Myths of Moral Theory," I sketch a brief history of conceptions of practical reason and analyze the theory of action that appears to be implicit in recent moral theory. "The Two Faces of Courage" analyzes the cognitive components of courageous dispositions. Because presumptively virtuous dispositions can be inappropriately, harmfully exercised, there is a general problem about how to assure the appropriate, proper exercise of various dispositions that constitute the virtues. "Virtue and Its Vicissitudes" examines some traditional solutions to this problem: it presents a critique of the "master regulatory virtue" solution, and proposes to locate individual virtues within a system of character traits that support, and counterbalance their operation. The appropriate configuration of a person's virtues—their patterns of dominance and recessiveness—is, I argue, supported by social and political institutions and interactions. But since community can also corrupt virtue, there is, I conclude, nothing that can assure virtue, though there is much that can promote it. In "Imagination and Power," I argue that the range of a person's power is largely controlled—either liberated or limited—by controlling her imagination. It is this—her conception of what is possible and thinkable—that enhances or prohibits the sorts of cooperative alliances that can redefine practices.

14 Three Myths of Moral Theory

> The rats were devouring the house, but instead of examining the cat's teeth and the cat's claws, they only concerned themselves to find out if it was a holy cat, a pious cat, a moral cat.
>
> Mark Twain

It was Hobbes who did it, and once it was done, not even Kant could reverse it. What happened? Aristotelian *phronēsis*—immanent in perception and interpretation, visible in the tone and manner of a person's action—became reason in its practical application; the relation of thought to virtue, its role in acting well and appropriately, was changed. The diagnosis of the problems of an agent trying to act well and wisely also changed: instead of setting herself to integrate intellectual habits with habits of action, appropriately expressing her intentions and thoughts in her smallest perceptions and gestures, the agent attempts to select the best among competing determinate alternatives, for the best reasons. Practical reasoning becomes either instrumental or formal: it serves, and at most enlarges and directs rather than permeates, the substantive content of a person's perceptions, interpretations, habits, desires, and actions. The agent whose actions were identified within and formed by a community becomes a judge selecting the best alternative; her reasons, which had been articulated within a system of practices, become foundational, selecting or supporting those practices.

There are three ways of contributing to contemporary moral theory. The first is historical: it involves showing how the agent became a judge, how Hobbes transformed *phronēsis*, how prudence became practical reason, and how moral theory was detached from psychology and political theory. Because those who do not understand the past do not understand the present, and those who do not understand the present are doomed to repeat the part, past I—"From *Phronēsis* to the Judicial Model of Practical Reason"—presents a sketch of this history. The second is polemical: it seeks to analyze and correct the relatively crude theory of

271

action presupposed by even the most sophisticated moral theorists, arguing that standard models of rational deliberation oversimplify the ways that reason forms, as well as evaluates, actions. But it is cavalier and unjust to try to present a single diagnosis of the flaws of radically different views, to force them all into one scarecrow to be burnt in effigy. The third way is more modest, but also perhaps more constructive. Instead of attempting a global critique of highly articulated and differentiated contemporary theories, part II proposes to direct attention to a set of neglected phenomena and issues. It contrasts two approaches to moral psychology. The first approach is characterized by three tempting myths: *the myth of justificatory judicialism* is a myth about rational agency; *the myth of eminent domain* is a myth about the special character of morality; and *the myth of apolitical individualism* is a myth about the relation of ethics to political theory. The second approach—the approach that redirects our investigations—is best characterized by showing how it modifies and transforms those myths. But temptations would not lure us if they did not speak to our intuitions and desires. Because these myths present—though they mispresent—partial truths, I'll try to preserve what seems right and appropriate about them, suitably reinterpreted, to suggest how they can be supplemented by a communitarian *praxis*-oriented understanding of action and practical reasoning.

I. From *Phronēsis* to the Judicial Model of Practical Reason

Aristotelian *phronēsis* is a Janus-faced fusion of the intellectual and character virtues: it is the ability to recognize and actualize whatever is best in the most complex, various, and ambiguous situations. Though practical wisdom is of course useful, the *phronimos* need not be motivated to develop or exercise it by considerations of its utility. We are so constituted that we develop and enjoy its exercise, as far as the constraints of our constitution and situation permit. Although *phronēsis* is a set of dispositions to draw well-formed, truth-bound inferences about the vagaries and uncertainties of particular situations, it is also expressed within the most minute habits of rightly ordered salience, habits of perception and interpretation, classification and inventiveness. The man of practical wisdom, magnetized toward appropriate ends, sees what should be seen, desires what is worth desiring, finds solutions to what appear to be intractable problems: he deliberates in such a way as to form well-ordered actions. Because he perceives and categorizes his circumstances in such a way as to recognize the goods that can be realized in the particular situations in which he finds himself, his recognition is easily, smoothly, and above all habitually carried to well-formed, and even elegant action. His desires and his habits are at the very least informed, and at best actually formed by true beliefs, both about what is the case and what is good. The exercise of practical wisdom is not only action-guiding in that it generates appropriate decisions as conclusions of valid pieces of practical reasoning; it is also *effectively* action-guiding in that it generates the actions appropriate to those well-formed decisions.

As it is described in the *Nichomachean Ethics, phronēsis* fuses reason and desire (*orektikos nous* or *orexis dianoētikē:* desiring mind or mindful desire [NE 1139b 5–6]). It combines sound judgment (*orthos logos*) with virtuous character (*ēthikē aretē*; NE 1144b 30ff.). But it is the man, not merely the combination of belief and desire, that is the cause of action. (NE 1112b 33ff.) A person's character explains the pattern of his standing desires, the direction of his deliberation (*bouleusis*) and even some of his beliefs. The details of an action—its being done in the right way, at the time for the right reason, for instance—express the entire configuration of a person's character, his ends, his habits and skills. To be sure, a person can be held accountable—praiseworthy or blameworthy—for voluntary (*hekousion*) actions, even when their formative desires are not intrinsic (*kath' hauto*) to his character, when they do not come from him (*eph'hēmin*) in the sense of being specifications of his ends. For a person to be held accountable, it is enough that he is in a position to know what he is doing, and to be capable of doing otherwise. But a person is responsible in a much stronger sense when he acts deliberately, when his desire (*orexis*) accords with, and is formed by his ends. Because it suggests the outcome of a relatively external and formal inference, *choice* is a misleading translation of *prohairesis*, whose etymological sense modestly designates *that which comes before*. The practical syllogism is a model and reconstruction of the rational formation of deliberate, responsible action, rather than a description of that process. For an action to be rationally chosen, to be the outcome of deliberate *prohairesis*, it is enough that its formative desires follow from the person's general ends.

When there is conflict—and of course even in an Aristotelian world there is conflict—it is not between desire and thought, or between inclination and obligation, but between varieties of thought-defined desires. There is no specific domain of the moral, characterized by its altruism or its impartiality. Practical wisdom is directed toward *praxis*, any kind of practice. The virtues are the whole range of excellences that affect action: some are cognitive dispositions and skills (insight, acute perception, sound inference); others are dispositions of temperament and character that enable us to modulate natural tendencies when their exercise might be undesirable (courage modulates natural and functional fear, moderation modulates the natural and functional desire for plea-surable activity); some are the actualization and exercise of species-defined excellences (the range of traits that are exercised in scientific investigation and in political activity); others are specific to a particular polity (the capacities for mercantile activity in a mercantile polity). None have to do with the Will, because there is no such faculty.[1] When we are conflicted, we are not torn by the large dichotomized conflicts between altruism and egoism, or between principles of morality and the psy-chology of desire and interest. Our conflicts are those between particular thoughtful desires or thoughtful habits that cannot all be simultaneously realized or enacted, because they eventually undermine each other. The resolutions of such conflicts rarely involve denying or suppressing one side, for both sides of intrapsychic conflicts, like both sides of political conflicts, represent functional contributions to thriving. Such conflicts are at least sometimes best resolved by imaginative integrations and reconciliations (cf. NE 1144 23ff. on the role of *deinotēs*, brilliant clev-erness) rather than by abstract selection and denial. Indeed, political or intrapsychic conflicts are seen as occasions for craftsmanly, states-manly solutions that modify and merge distinctive interests. *Phronēsis* includes ingenuity and resourcefulness, inventive initiative, the ability to improvise, as well as the deft execution of traditional and conventional action patterns. To be sure, *phronēsis* is systematic; but it maps priorities by placing them within the context of the whole of a well-lived life rather than by deducing particular decisions and actions from a set of general first principles or ends. Indeed, it is the conception of the whole of a well-lived life—an appropriate configuration of the activities that are essential to a full human life—that shapes the proper taxonomy of ends, rather than the other way around. A sound ranking of priorities derives from an understanding of the proper ordering of the essential activities of a well-formed human life. The characterization of the *telos* of a life—of its proper ends—does not precede, but is part and parcel of, the characterization of its *eidos*, of its nature.[2] *Phronēsis* involves the active understanding of the proper place of what we do—of particular activi-ties—within the larger frame of a well-lived life. Such an understanding is active, in that it guides action, without requiring any further motivation to do so.

 Aristotelian *phronēsis* not only determines an action, but also modifies the way it is performed. The problems of an agent are not only those of knowing what to do. They are also centrally the problems of acting well, in the many senses of that ambiguous expression: acting appropriately, acting properly, and properly acting. Virtues are expressed in the tonality of what we do: acting in the appropriate manner, in the right way at the right time, in the right place. Voice, gesture, expression, all are part of virtue: when an action emerges as the resolution of a conflict, the manner in which it is performed reveals distinctive strands in its complex etiology. Character virtues express reason in the bone and muscles of action.[3]

It is, surprisingly enough, Aquinas who transforms substantive *phronēsis* as a fusion of intellectual-and-moral virtue into the intellectual virtue of *prudentia*. Although *prudentia* is listed among the moral virtues, it is a purely cognitive condition, an active capacity for deliberating well, with forethought. As a purely calculative faculty, it no longer plays the perceptive and end-specifying roles that Aristotle assigned to *phronēsis;* in order to form actions well and appropriately, *prudentia* must be accompanied by *synderesis,* which directs desire to its proper ends (*appetitus rectus*) (ST 2a2ae. 47,5–7).

But *prudentia* is itself complex: it has components and it has varieties. The varieties of *prudentia* demarcate distinctive domains: lawmaking, political prudence, military prudence, economic or domestic prudence, and private or individual prudence each has distinctive interests and priorities. They command the development of distinctive subvirtues (ibid. 47,11; 50,1). Further, prudence is itself composed of distinct "parts" which are "quasi integralibus": memory, insight or intelligence, receptivity or teachableness, acumen, reasoned judgment *(ratione),* foresight, circumspection, caution (ibid. 49,1). The range of skills and virtues of prudence has its allies—*eubulia* (being well-advised), *synesis* (sound judgment), *gnome* (special insight), and the gift of counsel (*consilium*) (ibid. 51; 52)—as well as a range of opposed vices (haste, thoughtlessness, inconstancy, imprudence, negligence).[4]

Although the ends of Hobbesian and Thomistic prudential reasoning are radically different, it is, ironically, Aquinas who prepares for Hobbesian practical reason as an inferential or calculative activity that traces causes and effects, and evaluates the effectiveness of means to ends. It has become an instrument whose utility derives in part from its neutrality to the content and context of judgments, as well as from its independence from other psychological and intellectual capacities and traits. Although *prudentia* constructs as well as judges action solutions, the emphasis is no longer on the improvisatory gifts for designing well-formed actions; *prudentia* moves toward becoming an evaluative judge with a commanding voice. Hobbes and post-Hobbesians construe the question, What should I do? as the question, What do I have most reason to do? And they construe that question as, What are the best supportive grounds for selecting among the preformed determinate alternative actions?

Assuming only the worst of times and the worst—or at any rate, the least civil—of men, Hobbes tried to show that first the polity, and after that, civic society and even civility might be created from nothing more than fear and a handful of reason, just that calculative reason required for the determination of self-interest. For Hobbes these—a healthy sense of fear and a sound capacity for calculation—are the foundation of all the virtues. Indeed, his hope was that there could be a science of right, that is, of instrumentally rational conduct so simple that it relies on nothing more than the crudest forms of self-interest. The program was meant to show that even the most churlish Everyman could and would move to the kind of tethered decency that would assure a modicum of civic and moral virtue, without having to appeal to the refinements of Aristotelian *arētē*, the kind of excellence of character and mind that can only be expected from a few, even in a well-established peaceable kingdom. Strangely, it is Hobbes who carries Christian egalitarianism to its secular, political application. The marks are all there: the egalitarianism of the Hobbesian civic subject is, like the Christian egalitarianism of souls, twin-bedded with the absolute centralization of absolute power. (Kant's attempt to retain an egalitarianism without an absolute sovereign had to be relegated to the postulate of an apolitical Kingdom of Ends.)

Thomistic *prudentia* is directed to select the means appropriate to realizing the ends God structured for practical and political life; Hobbesian rational prudence is directed to the calculation of losses and gains, initially in the interest of self-preservation and then, by extension, to the satisfaction of ego-oriented desires. Instrumental reason does not infuse, but directs the forces that determine actions, as vectorial outcomes of particular beliefs and desires. Because it is capable of corrective reflection on its own operations, and because its rules and activities are not affected by the content of ends and desires, rational inference can coordinate radically distinct and even opposed individual aims.

The primary problem for social planners as well as for individual agents is to persuade rational individuals intent on maximizing their own interests to cooperate beyond a calculation of their immediate utilities. For this persuasion to work, they must introduce long-range considerations to modify short-sighted satisfactions. The function of reason is not to erase or transcend, but to coordinate fear and desire, to give them perspective, to inform them by memory and calculation. It is, in Hobbes's view, our good fortune, the good fortune of the physiology of the species, that the rationality required for self-preservation and the satisfaction of desire is not only relatively simple but also relatively equally distributed.

While Hobbes himself thought that there was no conflict between egoistic prudence and morality—indeed, he argued that rational egoism provides the only motivation and ground for morality—his successors thought the primary moral problem was that of locating an independent set of altruistic motives that could counterbalance the standard-issue equipment of ego-directed desires that he charted. Following Butler—who attempted to fuse a divinely assured innate conscience with the natural psychology of benevolence—such natural philosophers as Hume attempted to describe a set of motives and sentiments that, though rooted in self-interest, could operate autonomously. In principle, the altruistic virtues—the sense of justice, along with other artificial social virtues—can, when they have been properly developed, outweigh primitive self-interest, functioning independently of their ego-oriented benefits. But though most post-Hobbesian moral theorists attack what they see as narrow Hobbesian egoism, they retain Hobbes's conception of practical rationality, an instrument without any independent motivational power or direction.

While post-Hobbesian moral theorists held that effective morality depends on proper psychological development, they prepared the ground for distinguishing the domain and operations of morality from those of mere psychology.[5] Some moral theorists—Shaftesbury and Hume, for instance—argue that we are naturally equipped with, and prone to acquire, sentiments whose effective application can be disinterested. Others—Adam Smith and Mandeville—argue that the free development of informed individual self-interest produces a system of checks and balances that ensures the benefits of traditional morality. Hobbes's immediate successors divide: there are those who, like Mandeville, thought that the systematic development of self-interest would, without further ado, work to the common good; and there are those who thought that the system of private self-interest would naturally lead to the further ado that *is* required, the development of a set of artificial virtues which can function independently of the consideration of narrow self-interest. While both parties retain Hobbes's conception of the operations of practical rationality, they misread him as claiming that actions are motivated by the general sentiment of self-interest. Butler, for instance, argues that there is a set of independent altruistic sentiments whose exercise is as natural as the exercise of the sentiment of self-interest. This attack on Hobbes has a double misreading. Nothing as diffuse or unquantifiable as sentiment could serve Hobbes's mechanistic construal of desires as quanta of forces with a direction of motion; and nothing as general as self-interest could serve his nominalist insistence on the particularity of beliefs and desires. The double misreading of Hobbes led to a double transformation: first, a whole new set of specifically altruistic virtues such as sympathy and benevolence was introduced. Second, what would have been literally incomprehensible to Aristotle or the medievals, these virtues—the sense of justice, for instance—were introduced as *sentiments*, modes of feeling. A whole new psychological category was introduced: while sentiments are reactive attitudes, they are not passions because they are formed and informed by thought and character; while sentiments are felt, they are not perceptions because they do not refer to, and are not attributes of, their causes; and while they are motives, they are not reducible to specific desires.

Having characterized reason as itself incapable of motivating or preventing action, and as concerned with discovering relations among ideas or inferring matters of fact, Hume nevertheless accords it the power of judgment and reflection, or reportive evaluation. He places practical wisdom in the hands of the reflective historians, who diagnose the character traits and the institutional practices that serve us, that is, those whose utility and admirability have consistently evoked the pleasurable approval of learned and experienced judges. There is no distinction between the operations of theoretical and practical reasoning: the primary contrast is that between reason and the passions, which, suitably enlarged by the sympathetic imagination, and transformed into sentiments by their double association with considered educated judgments, provide the basis of, and the grounds for, morality. Because we are so constructed that we are affected by the judgment of our fellows, the reflective judgments of historians' evaluations can affect our own reactions, our preferences. That influence is, however, a distinctively psychological connection, explicitly contrasted rather than merged with the logical and primarily inferential functions of reason. With Hume the transformation of *phronēsis* is complete: practical wisdom has moved from the character of the *phronimos* to the mind of the historically informed judge.

The train of thought that began with Hobbes finds its fullest development—and its sharpest critic—in Kant. The fullest development is the formality of pure practical reason: its position as judge and evaluator of the validity of inference. The sharpest critique is the separation of practical reason from psychological motivation in the establishment of a wholly independent domain of morality. Kant begins by making autonomy the precondition for morality, distinguishing the domain of moral obligation from all considerations of prudence or aesthetic delight. Indeed, he argues that the phenomena of morality are preserved only if a rational agent is capable of acting solely from the conception of the moral law, a conception which requires that the maxims that determine actions pass the court of reason, justified by the law of universalizability. The test of universalizability formalizes the moral law: its validity does not depend on any particular theory of human nature, let alone on the content of any particular social practices or institutions. The three formulations of the categorical imperative—act so that you can universalize the maxim of your action; treat each rational being as an end in himself and never as a means only; act from the conception of duty, out of respect for the law—explicate the conditions which make it possible for reason to be practical, that is, for it to determine the will. But if the will is to be free, it must be identical with, rather than externally constrained or directed by, practical rationality. So the conditions that assure the consistent practical employment of rationality are the conditions that define the operations of the will; and they are, in the first instance, formal conditions, that is, conditions that determine the logical forms of those maxims of action which have claim to be moral.

Kant attempts to recapture the pre-Hobbesian fusion of the conditions for rationality and morality, but he is committed to assuring that fusion without any teleological considerations. The moral agent can be unconditionally free and yet act from the requirements of rationality only if practical reason and the will are identical. But the identity of practical reason and the will does not, and cannot, assure that what is willed is performed. A rational person would, according to Kant, recognize her duty to develop a moral character, to acquire the individual virtues, but, as he is the first to acknowledge, that recognition is not necessarily sufficient to develop, let alone exercise, the appropriate dutiful habits. While Kant assures us that the rational course is the moral course, and that a rational moral being wills itself to develop whatever psychology morality requires, he gives no account of how pure practical reason can acquire the empirical psychology appropriate to it. To be sure, he recognizes that it is necessary for the moral agent to develop a good character—a set of habits—that assures that the maxims of his actions are automatically well formed, without each having to be tested for its rational conformity to the categorical imperative. But there is not—nor can there be—an account of how to move from the contingent psychology of prudence to rational morality, or from a recognition of duty to its well-formed successful performance. Indeed, Kant shows that no such accounts can be given: pure practical reason, the reason that is postulated as the condition that makes morality possible, operates in a domain wholly distinct from that of empirical psychology, from the particular contingent conditions required for the development of the intellectual virtues and talents. These are not different sectors of the same terrain; they represent entirely different domains. But while there is no continuity between pure and empirical practical reason, pure practical reason must, in all consistency, will its empirical application. It must therefore will to develop the range of intellectual and character virtues that assure the proper enactment of the intentions that judicial rationality has underwritten. The range of skills and habits that composed *phronēsis* reappear within the Kantian frame, as willed by a morally consistent reflective practical rationality. There is, then, within Kant, a double use of practical rationality: the primary sense is critical, formal, and unconditioned, a postulate whose realization is necessary to explain the possibility of morality. While the realization of pure practical reason dictates the acquisition of the virtue of prudence, along with other forms of empirical practical reason, the model of rationality remains regulative and judicial.[6]

Even anti-Kantian philosophy retains the judicial model of practical reason: utilitarian theories that attempt to break down the distinction between morality and prudence by defining *moral right* in terms of the *experienceable good*, locate the capacities for morality in the capacities for forming sound judgments about what is desirable. Even though Mill conjoined morality and prudence, the emphasis remains epistemological: What methods or rules select the best action? The primary virtues are those exercised in utilitarian calculation: all others must be justified by their utility in maximizing happiness. Of course Mill recognizes the role that the formation of appropriate habits, habits of perception, and sentiments, as well as habits of action and reasoning, play in the realization of a society based on utilitarian principles. But the development of any particular habit or type of habit—even those that might be constitutive of happiness, as well as instrumental to it—is itself to be evaluated and justified by instrumental reasoning. The emphasis remains judicial.

Hegel and Marx attempt to recover substantive *phronēsis,* located within a system of political (social, economic) practices. Hegel follows Kant in linking rationality with universality. The rational person autonomously wills what can be universally willed, treating every other being as an end in himself, a fellow citizen in the Kingdom of Ends. But Hegel reverses Kant's emphasis: rationality is itself constituted by what necessarily elicits universal consent or agreement. Instead of being presupposed by the possibility of universal consent, rational necessity emerges from the process of achieving it. Hegel and Marx make practical reason constructive and constitutive as well as critical and judicial. Instead of willing the rational alternative (and implicitly rejecting the others), Hegelian practical reason attempts to integrate apparently conflicting alternatives. It is directed to finding/forging reconciliations and resolutions in situations of conflict.[7]

The kinds of conflict that Hegel envisages as a natural part of social and political life contain, but also transform, Hobbes's view of the

inevitable conflicts between individuals engaged in self-preservation and
the satisfaction of their desires. Because each individual is in part formed
by his social and political relations, Hobbesian conflicts have become
intrapsychic. Since Hegel treats perception, imagination, understanding,
and rationality as aspects of, or abstractions from, complex psychological
and intellectual activities rather than as distinctive and independent
powers, he fuses the functions of inventive imagination with those of
critical reason in the processes of resolving conflicts by integration rather
than by selective choice.

If rationality emerges from the processes of communitarian reconcil-
iation, the formal structure of rationality is no longer separable from its
substantive content. Although agreement on procedural principles, on
content-neutral rules governing communication and debate, is desirable,
agreement on those principles itself reflects the resolution of substantive
conflicts.[8] The two—the rationality of procedural principles and the
rationality that emerges from substantive integrative resolutions of conflicts—are coordinate; they are different ways of expressing the same
emergent harmony.

Marx accepts Hegel's historicist and substantive account of the development of practical reason. Although he disagreed with Hegel about
the motivating forces of that development, he also accepted Hegel's
account of the emergence of rationality from the resolution of conflicts.
Marx was, of course, skeptical about Hegel's optimistic account of the
smooth progressive development of practical rationality. As Marx saw
the matter, such progress required stages of exclusivist struggle between
economic classes as well as inclusivist integration of opposing perspectives. Dramatic as those differences are, they do not affect the account
of practical reason.

It would be pretty—much too pretty—to end this brief historical
sketch by arguing that the Hobbesian theory of action is mistaken and
that post-Hobbesian moralism is arbitrary. It would be too great a sim-
plification to argue that an agent's actions cannot be fully characterized
or individuated independently of their etiology; that practical reason
cannot be characterized or individuated independently of its role in a
person's character; that character cannot be described or individuated
independently of its history and its place in a social narrative, a political
structure at a time, in a place. But our situation is more complex: for
one thing, we are post-Hobbesian rationalists, committed to a rational,
critical, judicial evaluation of our practices. These commitments have
become ingredient in our practices: they form our actions as well as our
understanding of action. For another, the distinction between private
interests and considerations of justice and the common good have become
constitutive of the social practices that form our motivational structures.

We have institutionalized the contrast between psychology and morality in such a way as to form a self-realizing practice. No critique of the limitations of formal and judicial practical reason can simply recommend that we abandon our conceptions of practical reason, selective choice, and morality so as to return to *phronēsis, proairesis,* and *praxis*. We need to find a way of retaining the integral benefits of critical practical rationality, while also preserving the psychological and political richness of *phronēsis*.

II. The Three Myths of Moral Theory

One familiar direction of moral theory is the attempt to formulate the criteria for—and the directions of—rational choice: this enterprise is guided by *the myth of justificatory judicialism (judicialism* for short). It treats the moral agent as a judge attempting to select the best action by determining which is the most justified. Because the emphasis is on the evaluation of actions by an evaluation of the reasons that support them, judicialism is often, though not necessarily, conjoined with a variety of formalism. Formalism requires that justificatory reasons be identifiable independently of the practices they justify. Further: the criteria for evaluating or ranking those reasons must also be neutral to such practices.

Another focus of moral theory is directed to the analysis of the distinctive character of moral principles and moral considerations, or of moral virtues and moral ideals. This enterprise is guided by *the myth of eminent domain,* which tells us that moral considerations and obligations are distinguishable from, and claim dominance over, those arising from personal commitments and loyalties, or from aesthetic and religious activity. The enterprises of morality are enshrined in—or as it may be exiled to—a distinctive domain defined by its ends, or its mode of reasoning, or its scope.

A third enterprise of moral theory is directed to articulating the principles that should guide individual action. It is guided by *the myth of apolitical individualism,* which claims that individuals are the ultimate subject of moral evaluation because they are the units of agency and responsibility.

Although they are often combined, and treated as mutually supportive, the three myths are independent of one another. Like most myths, they are schematic, capable of further specification and determination; like most myths, their significance emerges in the course of a narrative of action; and like most myths, they carry primitive belief. Let us examine them one by one.

The myth of judicialism: the first myth locates the focus of moral theory and moral action in the processes and rules for justification, as if the primary problem of an agent is that of resolving uncertainty about what to do, and her primary task is that of forming a judgment about what is best to do.[9] Even when the emphasis is on the first-person singular, as an agent, the focus is epistemological: What should I do? is interpreted as What alternative have I most reason to follow? Which is most justified? It is as if the model of justification serves as the model of deliberation. The virtuoso agent is a virtuoso deliberator, with the capacity to choose well by reasoning well, selecting the best alternative for the best reasons. The best position for an agent in determining what to do, is the position she would take as judge advocate in justifying the action to a skeptical but rational observer, forming her action by internalizing the deliberations of an impartial judge. It is as if the wise agent attempts to form her action by playing God the judge *in foro interno*.

There is, of course, a difference between smart-aleck justification and substantive justification. An action might be logically justified by considerations that do not genuinely illuminate what makes it worth performing. A piece of practical reasoning is not only logically valid but also well constructed when the reasons it presents are also the appropriate and relevant specification of what is valuable. The determination of what is substantively rational cannot precede but rather is coordinate with the determination of what is good. The motto *erst kommt die Rationalität, und denn kommt die Morale* is misguided: there is no royal road to rationality.

But even if an agent has a well-formed, relevant, and appropriate justification for what she does, her actions may have their sources in, and been formed by, a wholly different and perhaps even opposed set of reasons and causes. The rationality of an action (in contrast to the rationality of its justification) is at least in part a function of the reasons that have actually caused it, the reasons that form its effective intentional description. Because the actual etiology of an action affects the way in which the action is performed—because it affects the action itself—the rationality of an action is determined by its actual derivation and not merely by the validity and perspicacity of the agent's co-incidental justification.

Even if the reasons that prompt an action are appropriately justified, they usually underdescribe and underdetermine the detailed thoughtfulness required for appropriate action. The manner in which actions are performed is often as essential to acting well as the selection of the appropriate action. To act well, in accordance with, if not actually from, our judgments about what is best, we also need to be able to connect cognitive dispositions with habits of behavior, to assure that the smallest gestures, tonal expressions, lifted eyebrow, express, or at least conform to, our thoughts and reasons. The task for the moral agent is to connect the rationale of relevant, substantively appropriate justification of a practice or action with its rational etiological formation: to integrate the reasons of the articulate mind with the articulation of habits, the habits of bones, sinews, and muscles.

These are metaphors. How can they be substantiated?

Sometimes, but only rarely, we act by deciding to perform an extensionally described action, identified by what Ryle and Geertz call a thin social description: leaving the room, bringing elderly parents home to live with us. But we do not just open doors, leave rooms: we leave them ceremoniously, contemptuously, or expectantly. We do not just tend our elderly parents: we do so tenderly or exasperatedly, respectfully or resentfully. Of course we sometimes select an act from a range of alternatives identified and described by culturally standard norms, by the same criteria that we would use to explain or justify what we have done. More commonly, the processes of articulating the point of what we are doing, forming the thick intentional description of our actions, and justifying them by aligning them with our more general purposes and directions, are all interwoven. The full descriptions of our actions connect them with our reasons, intentions, and character. Though they set constraining boundaries, our ends or purposes—or principles or rules, for that matter—are too general, too indeterminate to specify all that is required for thought to be action-guiding. But on the other side, the processes of articulating intentions, formulating the detailed descriptions of the alternatives, further specify our ends or principles.

Sometimes, to be sure, the thin culturally fixed description of an action—"going to the bank to cash a check," "fleeing a tyrant"—implicitly identifies and forms the agent's intentions, and sometimes even her motives. In such cases, an action is formed by selecting among preformulated determinate action alternatives: the manner is not a significant part of the action. Usually when we decide to go to a bank to cash a check rather than to use a credit card, it doesn't matter whether we drag our feet or stride confidently. Of course sometimes—as when a tyrant must be stopped from injustice—the primary issue is simply that of what to do. In such cases attention to the subtle tonalities of the manner cannot only be irrelevant but distracting.

Nevertheless, the processes of formulating an intention—processes that involve imagining fragments of possible scenarios—often further specify general ends (or principles). General ends set a range of possibilities; but they are crystalized, further determined, by the ways we imagine or envisage the details of what we shall do. In deciding to live with elderly parents or an autistic child, a person might be acting out of love; or to save money; or from general principles about filial obligations; or from an idealized image of himself. But each of these general aims might have been realized by a different decision: had he been concerned about costs, he might have taken on extra work to cover institutional care; had he been interested in honoring his parents, he might have built a hospice in their name. The etiology of decisions is manifest in the *petites actions,* in the manner—the gestures, intonation patterns, and postures—of behavior. The grounds and sources of a person's decision characterize and specify the intentional description of what he does in bringing his parents or child home: they individuate and form the action. When actions conform to their typical etiology, the standard rationale—even the standard motivation—is presumptively built into the identification of the action (cashing checks, buying groceries). When an action is individuated by its typical etiology, the manner in which the action is performed (impatiently or languorously) usually connects the action to tangential features of the person's habits and character, not immediately relevant to the rationale of performing the action.

Judicialism needs to be expanded, supplemented with an account of the immanence of reason within character and habits, the role of thought in forming the delicate tonality of *petites actions,* in at least three ways. First, a person's characteristic guiding conceptions of herself, her ideals and aspirations, form a thick layer in the description of what she does. A generous gesture that flows *from* self-respect is different, and looks different, from a superficially similar gesture directed *toward* an aspired ideal of self-respect. The same action, thinly identified—going to a museum with a friend—can come from a person's primary identification as an intellectual with passion for understanding, or it can express a primary aesthetic sensibility, or it can be the expression of a person's primary commitment to friendship. These differences in thought—differences in a person's primary self-identifications—are manifest in the action: they are expressed in the thick, fine-grain descriptions of actions.

Second, characteristic dispositions—such as trustfulness, cheerfulness or melancholy, asceticism or aestheticism, irritability or imperturbability, sociability or solitariness, a literal or an associative cast of mind—affect the expression of practical reasoning in action. Because these cognitive traits form perceptions and interpretations of situations, they affect the ways thought is expressed and realized. Such traits need not express a person's ideals or her primary identifications: they can indeed sometimes be at odds with such ideals and self-definitions: a characteristically abrupt and ill-organized person might have an active idealized self-image of herself as serenely composed.

There are, finally, a set of interconnected scenarios that place minute habits of perception and organization within a network of culturally formed narratives. Such structures set expectations which elicit predictable reactions that then elicit further habits. Characteristically, as we say, a person's friendships or her relation to power and authority involve a certain rhythm or pattern of—as it may be—approach, reaction and avoidance, or intensity, exhaustion, and blankness. The typical scenarios and narratives of a person's habits have an impetus and direction that is often, though not solely or always, modeled on central cultural texts. The Bible, the *Iliad*, the blues, and blue-grass songs give such habits their typical patterning, criteria for their relevance, their rationale, and at least one measure of intelligibility within a reconstructed rational framework. Rationality does not leave off where habits begin. The influence goes in both directions: on the one hand, a person's rationality is expressed in and through just those habits of perception, of categorization, of tempo that are central to character. And on the other, the cultural norms implicit in the socialization of habits, and the basic narrative scenarios that constitutively define normality, provide some (though of course not the only) measures of the rationality of a plan of action.

A sophisticated and modest form of judicialism recognizes that the justificatory model of rational action is not sufficient to explain, let alone to generate, the delicate tonalities of the *petites actions* that constitute a large part of acting well. Such a suitably hedged form of judicialism can acknowledge that reasons individuate as well as justify actions. Judicialism is—and is acknowledged to be—radically incomplete. It is incomplete as a moral theory because it does not by itself provide a substantive theory of virtue, or principles and criteria, for what is good and right. And however essential the judicial model may be to a rationally constructed practical life, it is incomplete as a psychological theory because it does not exhaust, nor can it serve as the model for, the many functions of thought in forming appropriate actions.

But even when it is suitably and modestly hedged, judicialism tends to distinguish the judicial function of rationality from (what gets relegated to) the craftsmanly imagination exercised in constructing integrative solutions.[10] Emphasis on judicialism unfortunately tends to focus on the moment of radical, selective choice, rather than on the delicate and difficult processes that precede choice, the processes of generating and articulating the range of alternatives. Think how easily we are drawn into thinking of Gauguin as having to choose between becoming a painter or remaining a married bourgeois, or to thinking of Sartre's resistance fighter as having to choose between staying with his mother or joining his comrades in exile. Why suppose that Gauguin couldn't persuade his wife to join him in a new way of life? Or that the resistance fighter couldn't imitate Aeneas' taking Anchises with him into exile, by bringing his mother with him to Casablanca?

Judicialism tends to separate the task of rational selection and evaluation from its imaginative and integrative function in restructuring and reconciling apparently incompatible alternatives. But imagining is itself fused with reasoning, and reasoning well—reasoning fruitfully—is itself fused with imagining well. It is here that the contrast between Aristotelian *phronēsis* and the judicial model of practical rationality is most dramatic. Since *phronēsis* includes *deinotēs*, a kind of well-formed cleverness and inventiveness, it brings imaginativeness within the scope of active reason, simultaneously enriching rationality and providing directions for imagining. The immanence of thought in action affects the thick description of the ways the action is performed: subdominant or recessive alternatives can be expressed in voice, gesture, timing, without being denied or rejected. The etiology of an action—its rejected alternatives as well as its direct derivations, the psychological processes that articulated its intentional description—are expressed in the *petites actions* that form its tonality. In principle, of course, the justificatory model can include such thickly and finely described nuances, but it does so by justifying one nuance in contrast to another. When inventiveness, discovery, and articulation are included within a full model of practical rationality—when *phronēsis* is the model of practical reason—the etiology of an intention or decision becomes manifest in the thick action description. The etiology of an action—including the etiology of its justification—modifies its performance.

What is right but misunderstood and misrepresented in judicialism is that our actions are specified in, and individuated through, our explanations to our fellows, our addressing their questions and criticisms. Such explanations and justifications are not merely—though they are also—expressions of fallibility and respect. They are not only appropriate but also necessary to acting well. Because our individual actions are moments in the larger dramas of shared practices, what we do has its place in a social setting that requires cooperative interaction. Actions are specified, their sense and rationale are articulated, in dynamic social dramas. This conception of *justification* brings it closer to its use in printing and carpentry: to justify a page is to align its margins; to justify a wall is to assure its stability by integrating it with its surrounding corners. So understood, it is true that to act well is to justify well: unless we clearly connect our actions with common practice, we cannot actualize even our vaguest intentions. At a minimum, our actions would fail if we did not situate and articulate them to our community. More dramatically, the structure of our plans presupposes our having internalized the justifications that provide the norm of reasonable expectations. The justificational mode of rationality is not only an ideal or a norm to which we are committed in a certain kind of liberal society of mutually respectful persons, although it is also at least that. Nor is it only a matter of practical calculation that if we want cooperation, we need to explain and justify those enterprises in publicly acceptable terms. It is also a constitutive feature of our actions that they are individuated within a socially structured system of justification.

The myth of judicialism is, and rightly is, a temptation, because we want—we need—a relatively neutral way to evaluate and re-form actions, to reconcile competing habits. Judicialism is an excellent model for those cases where what matters most is doing the right thing, cases where the etiology of one's decision and the manner of performance matter not at all. When we are strongly conflicted, habits as well as judgments are conflicted. The agony of choice is at least sometimes an internal struggle for the primacy of certain habits, certain ways of seeing and imagining, as well as ways of thinking. Unless our integrative improvisations are also capable of being evaluated from a relatively neutral and independent capacity, we are simply left to power politics, psychologically to the power politics of the relative strength of competing habits, or politically to the power politics of the relative strengths of interests and institutions.

What is right about judicialism, but misunderstood and misstated by it, is that reasons do not end with embeddedness. The permanent possibility of sheerly formal improvisation on immanent substantive reasons, the permanent possibility of an external critique, and sometimes of playful improvisation, the permanent possibility of visionary—and sometimes only partially understood—reforms shows that practical reason can stand outside as well as within practices. Sometimes, even when practices and reasons are fused in a system of mutual support, it is possible to break the deadlock and to provide a critique, a reform, a formal improvisation, a substitution, based on reasons that are not intrinsic to the practices they criticize or reform.[11] Because this core of Enlightenment truth has played such an important role in our political history, because it is so central to our sense of ourselves as agents, it is tempting to take it as the whole truth about practical reason.

The myth of eminent domain: there is a domain, the domain of morality, and a class of actions, principles, considerations, or motives, that are distinguishable from those which govern the rest of practical life.

Significant disagreements about the criteria that distinguish morality should signal grounds for suspicion about its separation, particularly as the various characterizations define quite different domains. All versions of the myth appear to be subject to an accordion movement: when the view is interpreted broadly and widely, it appears to make morality ubiquitous. When it is interpreted strictly and narrowly, membership in the domain is at best indeterminate: the domain of morality may be empty.

The *strong version* of this myth makes morality not only distinctive, but normatively dominant.

1. Some versions of the dominance myth rest the primacy of the claims of morality on the superiority of its ends. Because they are higher or nobler than those of the rest of practical life, they take precedence over personal, prudential, or aesthetic concerns, for example. But what are the ends of morality, and in what does their superiority consist? Setting aside the epistemological problems of adjudicating among competing claimants for primary ends, there are serious problems about characterizing the ends of morality. If they are the general ends of thriving, there is nothing distinctive about them; indeed, they include the large varieties of subsidiary ends that are the substance of practical life. If the dominance of morality is a function of its comprehensiveness, then it is ubiquitous. Embarrassingly, then, the wise man and the fool, the villain and the saint can have the same general ends, and sometimes even the same understanding of those ends. In principle, they could have the same general conceptions of thriving, as encompassing friendship, esteem, the important and self-sustaining pleasures of life. Sometimes the villain and the goodly citizen are only distinguished by *petites actions* that cannot be mapped on a dichotomous terrain separating the moral and nonmoral or immoral. It is often the delicate ways that their common general ends are realized and manifest in the smallest of actions that differentiate the many varieties of good and admirable folk from the many varieties of despicable bad folk.

Even if the ends of morality consist in some specific activity or condition (freely obeying God's will, achieving moral nobility, or serving humanity, for example), the realization or actualization of such ends requires a vast variety of subsidiary aims that encompass, or at the very least overlap, with the ends of general practical life. (She who would conform to God's will must will whatever is necessary to his purpose; she who would serve humanity must set herself other directives.) But if the ends of morality are *sui generis*, requiring no further specification, no subsidiary aims, morality may have no particular connection with acting well or living well. If obeying God's will or achieving the highest and noblest of human glories are set apart, disconnected from other practical goods and ends, the significance of morality does not illuminate, nor does it serve, the significance of the rest of our lives.[12]

2. Another version of the myth accords dominance to moral claims on the ground that its principles are universally and unconditionally justified. This view is subject to the accordion principle: generously interpreted, it makes morality ubiquitous. Notoriously, an interpretation of the universalizability condition that is open to specification—that permits moral obligations to be regionalized and qualified by the agent's circumstances—is too generous. Every rational being wills to act from maxims that conform to duty, from a conception of what is right. But these are not abstract general motives: the overriding obligation of morality is that each action be performed from an intention to do what is right about *that* action. The obligations of morality also apply to imperfect duties and to permissible actions and intentions. Every action should be formed by a maxim that suitably directs and defines its rational or appropriate ends, whether those ends be categorical or hypothetical, universally binding or conditional. Conceived as the domain of conduct or intention open to critical evaluation as required, abjured or permissible, the domain of morality is ubiquitous. The obligation to be moral applies to any behavior that qualifies as an action.

On a narrow interpretation, however, the universalizability criterion remains agnostic about whether any particular action or intention has met the requirements. Morality is a pure postulate: whether an agent has acted from, and because of, the appropriate duty, rather than from the host of other intentions and maxims that are always with us, remains unknown.

3. Another version of the myth distinguishes morality by a distinctive motivating attitude—respectful impartiality according to one version, love and concern according to another—that is centrally linked to a conception of what is important to human interaction. The accordion movement again appears: on a broad interpretation of the respect or concern condition, morality requires that we treat landscapes and cityscapes, scholarly commentaries, works of art, mathematical proofs, machines, and even university committees with respect or love. Indeed, the general obligation to act with respect—to treat each thing with an appropriately attentive attitude—makes morality ubiquitous. But on a narrow interpretation of the respect or concern requirement, it is indeterminate whether any particular attitude conforms to the conditions. Psychological attitudes are overdetermined: since we can never know whether we have acted from proper impartial respect, rather than pride, desire, or fear, we must be agnostic about whether any given attitude

is appropriately impartial or respectful. Even if there is good evidence that an action is self-serving, or motivated by revenge or fear, it may nevertheless be both impartial and respectful. (The Capulets and the Montagues can kill each other with utmost respect; and they can be quite impartial about the particular individuals whom they are obliged to attack, dutifully setting aside personal affections and interests. The Grand Inquisitor may well have acted from a loving concern for the souls of unbelievers.)

In any case, *respect* and *loving concern* are umbrella terms covering a wide range of attitudes. Their individuation, function, and etiology vary with their intentional objects. There are as many types of respect and love as there are types of objects and activities: what is required in order to respect or love a child is different from what is required to respect or love a family homestead. What are the specifically *moral* varieties of appropriate respect or love? The special condition turns out to generate a general motto: act well and appropriately.

4. Another version of the myth distinguishes the moral domain by its scope: actions and attitudes whose consequences affect welfare or thriving are subject to moral evaluation. This makes the distinction between moral and nonmoral considerations one of degree. Since everything can in principle affect thriving, morality is everywhere, or nowhere in particular. In its application, this version of the myth of eminent domain needs further demographic specification. The scope of moral demography must be set: Just how is the welfare of future generations to be evaluated? Does morality require counting the welfare of every possible individual equally? Is it universal in its scope, or can its weighting be relativized to a political or cultural community, or to friends and relations?

While this version of the myth has the advantage of not drawing a sharp line between moral and nonmoral considerations, it suffers from single-mindedness in introducing just one set of considerations in expanding narrow self-interest to the larger, encompassing moral domain. But the kinds of considerations that direct a person away from the follies of narrow self-interest are extremely various: they do not form a single continuously expanding line. There is no real distinction between specifically moral virtues and the wide range of admirable and beneficial traits that guide action appropriately and well. To be sure, the virtues lie roughly in the domain of the voluntary, in that their development and exercise require a large range of discriminating abilities to regulate actions. But the range of traits that enable a person to refrain from, to initiate, or to modify action are varied and heterogeneous: they are not perspicuously located in *the will*, even when it is broadly conceived to cover the range of a person's motives.[13] Sometimes it is not a person's motives or understanding of what is good and right but rather her habits and heroines that reliably and appropriately guide her actions.

A much weaker version of this myth distinguishes the domain of morality but denies its claims to eminence. It allows that some kinds of considerations—those arising from commitments to some special vision of excellence, or from personal affection or loyalty, for example—can outweigh or override stringent moral considerations.[14] But whether it makes morality dominant and overriding, inclusive or sometimes capable of being overridden, the myth of eminent domain nevertheless characterizes a distinctive set of considerations as specifically *moral*. Even those who dispute its claims to dominance accept this characterization of morality: indeed, their complaints about the presumptions of morality depend on their characterizing it as a distinctive domain.

However it is defined or graded on a continuum, the contrast between morality and the rest of practical life distorts and simplifies the basic and familiar conflicts that are the substance of ordinary life. For instance, the contrast between the morality of objective impartiality and the amorality of a subjective, ego-oriented point of view forces our ordinary conflicts onto a simplified grid. To be sure, there are times when our dilemmas do take the form we've inherited from a parody of Hobbesian thinking: "It's me against them-who-falsely-claim-to-be-*us*." When that happens, it seems as if there are certain kinds of concerns that expand the boundaries of the self, radically extend its interests, or command assent beyond interest. In such cases—when the psychology of the self has become hopelessly narrow—it is sometimes psychologically appropriate to appeal to broader *moral* concerns. But real as the conflict between the perspective of an amoral self (even one whose interests include the interests of others) and the perspective of a self-oriented to a morality of impartiality or altruism may sometimes be, that conflict is not our only moral problem, nor does it serve as the source or model for the others. Usually what serves an individual interests well—good humor, ingenuity, a delicate balance between detachment and dedication, the wide range of intellectual and character excellences—also serves morality well, and vice versa. They equally express individual and general ideals. The interests and needs of *self* and *other*, of private and public are usually to be found on all sides of our major conflicts. Sartre's resistance fighter torn between taking care of his mother and joining the underground finds *self* and *others* on both sides. The conflict between Antigone and Creon is not a conflict between interest and morality, the private and the public realms, affection and duty, but between two worlds, two conceptions of the self, the family and the state, two conceptions of *philia* and duty.

The contrast between the psychology of amoralism and the rationality or impartiality of morality is, like the contrast between the private and public domains with which it is sometimes linked, based on a mistaken view of the structure of the self. To begin with, the individual person is formed by, and essentially linked with a widening and intersecting set of, groups. The welfare and intentions of a person's family, her intimate friends, the neighborhood, working partners, all enter into her own welfare. Does public altruism begin at the skin? At the lintel of the family homestead? The boundaries of a religious community? Unfortunately, the movement from 'the' private to 'the' public, or from narrow self-interest to objectivity or universality, is not assured by expanding the interest of the limited self to (a well-formed nestled taxonomy of) ever more inclusive groups. The complexities of the multiple identifications and interests of the self arise from intersecting and sometimes opposed groups.

The traits that are required for resolving the varieties of conflicts that face us—between attending to the needs of our families and those of our colleagues or workshop unions, between our commitments to intimate friends and to our professions—are extremely heterogeneous. There are no specifically *moral* virtues—no specifically moral act of will—that enable us to resolve—or even just survive—these conflicts successfully.[15] The traits we need, the excellences we require, are everywhere and anywhere. The virtue of a resistance fighter with an ailing mother may be an inventive imagination which can construct a solution that bypasses his dilemma. To be sure, just that sort of imagination may also serve a Mafioso with similar conflicts. Those traits that serve human thriving or moral nobility, that enable a robust expression of respect or love, can also be harmfully used.

Actions, motives, dispositions, considerations, and reasons are fruitful or sterile, brilliantly improvisatory or mechanical, heartening or discouraging, sustaining or diminishing, visionary or rigorous, noble or small-minded, generous or cautious, overrefined or crude. This richness and precision of direction and evaluation extends to the modes and styles of thought and reasoning that are necessary to acting well. Such reasoning is elegant or deep; it is ramified or regional, perspicuous, robust. Beyond the basic requirements of truth-orientation and validity, thinking is inventive or repetitive, disingenuous or frank, subtle, generous, or small-minded, skimpy or obsessive, rigorously consequential or associational. Such evaluations significantly introduce a wide range of factors that include aesthetic style and utilitarian benefits along with purely moral considerations.[16] To be sure, along some of the many dimensions of the claims for a distinction between moral and nonmoral domains—particularly those that contrast narrow with broader self-interest—there may be continuum. But for the many and various concerns that govern practical activity, that direct it toward what is admirable or well achieved or beneficial, the contrast(s) between moral and nonmoral dimensions are impoverished, even if they are conceived as distinctions of degree.

Nevertheless, the myth of eminent domain is a natural and real temptation. For us, amoralism is a case of theory becoming embedded in practical life. Because many of our practices do set even the most enlightened and enlarged interests, including personal loyalties, at odds with general disinterested or impersonal judgments about what is best, it is natural—and sometimes pragmatically wise—to dramatize these as the difference between prudence and the moral point of view. When amoralism has made itself true, when it has become constitutive as well as explanatory of institutions and practices, much of practical life rotates around problems that involve conflicts of interests. But these are the problems of all practical life, the problems of balancing numerous and varied values, attachments, and obligations.

The myth of apolitical individualism has three separable but standardly interconnected strands: (1) The individual is the autonomous source of action (or at any rate of her morally significant intentional attitudes) and the ultimate unit of moral liability and responsibility. (2) The focus of moral attention is primarily directed to the formation and reformation of individual attitudes and actions. (3) Social practices and institutions are evaluated primarily by their effects on individual thriving, on the ways they develop and satisfy the best potentialities of individuals. Let's examine the viability and vulnerability of these claims, to see what is tempting and what is misleading about them.

1. Interpreted as a psychological and social thesis, the first strand of the myth of apolitical individualism is untenable. Perhaps, under unusual circumstances, it is possible for individuals to regulate their motives and actions relatively autonomously. But there is no reason to take those cases as models for the more common cases in which character traits—a person's values, habits, beliefs, and motives—are culturally formed and socially exercised. A person forms her thoughts and motives—and her critical evaluation of those thoughts and motives—through subtle and minute social interactions, in improvisatory responses to interlocutors, their incredulity or incomprehension, the directions of their enthusiasms and interests, even their facial expressions. To be sure, sometimes those interlocutors are idealized figures, and the re-

sponses occur *in foro interno;* but they are no less social for that. Even the last imaginary moment of decision—the last yea or nay that accepts or denies the propriety of any given lower level intention or action— has its sources and conditions in the complex nexus of the individual's biological inheritance and social interactions. If there were such a thing as the autonomous individual it would, in the etymological sense of the term, be an *idiōtēs,* an individual living in its own isolated world. In any case, even an *idiōtēs* cannot act in a vacuum: he acts against the background of social institutions and practices, with the cooperation of normal social interaction.

The capacities for independent critical rationality are socially formed; the criteria for evaluating a community's assumptions are themselves expressions of cultural values. The directions of the most imaginative visionary critiques have their sources within the reformer's culture. It is a matter of moral luck—of the fortunes of an individual's social situation—that an individual develops the capacities for "autonomous" action or judgment; if she has those capacities, their exercise is, at any given time, at least partly a function of her circumstances.

When it is set in the familiar mechanistic context of explaining actions as outcomes of beliefs and desires, the view that individuals are the proper units of liability and responsibility improperly detaches the proximal differentiating cause of an event from the ramified network of necessary contributory causes. Even when an individual produces the differential effect on a course of events—when her beliefs and desires provide the distinctive causal contribution that makes the difference to a course of events—the proximate differential cause is not, on that account, the ultimate controlling cause. The belief-desire explanatory model is borrowed from mechanics: 'the cause' of motion is last moving force before impact.

In physics and mechanics, 'the' cause is identified as that which explains a particular change in the force and direction of motion, against the background of *ceteris paribus* assumptions about inertia and the normal direction and force of motion in a field of interactive forces. Locating the onus of responsibility and liability in an individual's capacity for autonomy—her capacity for being an uncaused cause—is a paradoxical extension of the mechanistic explanatory model. It projects explanations of extensionally identified behavior to intentionally identified actions. But once we go beyond the project of explaining changes in behavioral motion, 'the' proximal differential cause cannot be identified without specifying the intentional description of the action. (We can now better understand and sympathize with Kant's dilemma, with his belief that the possibility of morality depends on the possibility of individual autonomy. He fully recognized that if the explanation of intentional action is assimilated to that of mechanical causation, then the attribution of moral liability and responsibility is questionable, precisely because the explanation of behavior ramifies beyond a person's control. It is because he had accepted Hobbes's mechanistic causal theory of behavior that Kant thought it necessary to take the extreme measure of locating unconditioned self-legislative intentional morality in a wholly different domain.)

But what serves as the background against which an individual's differentiating contribution is made? Presumably cultural assumptions about standard action descriptions and standard motivational patterns—the material of folk social psychology—fill that role. Intentional actions are individuated by a complex and varied set of descriptions, each of which carries culturally laden assumptions about standard motivational patterns, normal ideals and values. When the attribution of differential causation carries the onus, bonus, and penalty of legal and moral liability and responsibility, applying the mechanistic model of explanation to intentional actions carries hidden political implications.

The attraction of the myth of apolitical individualism rests, ironically enough, on the recognition that cultural and political norms are implicit in the individuation and identification of standard action descriptions. The possibility of an independent and effectively motivating critique of the social and political practices that are implicit in standard action descriptions seems to depend on the possibility that individuals somehow have access to the grounds that can provide the basis for such a critique. The temptation of apolitical individualism is revealed more clearly in the thought that the individual can provide an apolitical critique of the political, than it is in the thought that there is an apolitical basis for judging the morality of the individual. This suggests that the myth is most viably interpreted as a second-order pragmatic claim about the appropriate and effective location for the primary onus of responsibility. So interpreted, the view is overstated and misleading, but not unsound. It is misleading because it is presented as a psychological or metaphysical claim, rather than as a politically charged pragmatic commitment. It is overstated because it does not distinguish the conditions for individual critiques of political and cultural practices from the conditions for the liability and responsibility of individuals.

2. The individual and her attitudes are the primary focus of moral education and moral formation. To use a medical phrase, those attitudes are the "points of positive intervention." The claim is that because the influence of social structures and institutions is mediated by individual psychology—by the individual's interpretations and preferences—such institutions and practices are only secondarily significant in influencing

individual actions. The great variety of individual reactions and choices is taken to provide evidence of the fact that social practices and institutions do not themselves determine intentions and actions: what matters is the individual's construal of these institutions and practices.

Certainly social practices and institutions 'act' only through individual psychologies: they are, as it were, filtered through an individual's cognitive and psychological structures, through the distinctions and categories that determine what is salient and significant to a person. But individual psychology is formed by and expresses a ramified etiology that includes a particular physical constitution and intellectual and social history. It is, so to say, the complex mediating field through which extremely diverse influences are filtered. Perhaps an image can help: individuals are like crystalline structures through which a large variety of sources are refracted and reemitted. While social and political structures do indeed have markedly different effects on individual psychology, those differences reflect differences in the ramified and socially structured etiologies of individual psychology. The variables within an individual's psychology—variables which differentiate individuals from one another—are formed by their distinctive social and institutional history.

Apolitical individualism is, however, right in its insistence that institutions act—and are designed to act—by affecting the actions of individuals. The details of social and political institutions are designed in such a way as to produce specific effects on individual psychology. Changes in those structures are introduced in order to effect specific changes in individual psychology. But this only reinforces the point that the most effective access to the formation and reformation of individual psychology is through the formation and reformation of social practices and institutions. Even though the purpose of intervening in social structures is to affect individual action, the actual point at which intervention normally takes place is social and institutional.

3. The evaluation of social and political structures—the ultimate direction of their functions—is ultimately set by the welfare and thriving of individuals, the full development of their lives. Formulated so baldly, this strand of the myth is evasive about the extent to which conceptions of thriving and of well-formed lives are socially formed, and the extent to which an individual's thriving is a function of her conception of her thriving. Even if there is a core preintentional direction of individual thriving, evaluating a person's thriving is not neatly separable from evaluating the political ideals that are implicit in social practices.

This strand of the myth of apolitical individualism is radically incomplete. As it stands, the claim fails to specify the generational range of its application; even more significantly, it is compatible with extreme egalitarianism and with Aristotelian or Nietzschean elitism. Ironically, the difficulties in the application of this view reveal its hidden political force. Those difficulties lead to the recognition that according priority to individual thriving expresses, rather than bypasses, a political ideal. Closely examined, the myth of apolitical individualism reveals the interdependence of ethics and political theory. A serious attempt to apply the principles of apolitical individualism requires a choice between egalitarianism or (some presumptively moral versions of) elitist individualism. Even after that commitment has been made, the problems of *weighting compossibilities* remain. When the thriving of individuals (with assigned weightings reflecting egalitarian or elitist political ideals, as well as a bias to present or to future generations) is both competitive and interdependent, evaluating social arrangements by their effects on individual thriving presupposes some way of weighing considerations for *combined* thriving. (The thriving of A and B can, for example, often be so interrelated that [1] each can only thrive if the other thrives and [2] the maximal thriving of each is incompatible with their equal thriving. They might choose a lesser overall thriving to retain their equality; or they might choose a slight differential in order to assure that each thrives at a higher level than they would under an equal distribution.) Whatever alternative they prefer—an egalitarian distribution, or a higher level of (differential) thriving for both—expresses a political ideal. It is not a preference that is dictated by considerations of pure rationality.

Still, for all its incompleteness, and for all its hidden political implications, the myth of apolitical individualism is right: in the end, the welfare of individuals—however they are weighted, however that welfare is measured—is the ground base for the evaluation of social and political institutions. Differences about how to measure the measurers of thriving reflect disagreements about political ideals: this reveals the irony, but not the falsity, of the myth of apolitical individualism.

And what—as all good Aesopians ask after a shockingly perfunctory survey of nearly every important topic in moral theory—is the moral of this myth of three myths? It is both more and less radical than an invitation to give up moral theory. It is more radical in denying that there is a domain of morality about which to theorize; it is less radical in retaining the propriety of psychological and political theory. The moral is this: practical reason without habit is empty; habit without practical wisdom is blind. Individuals without political communities are idiots; political communities without genuine individuals are nightmares. And if not now, when?[17]

15   The Two Faces of Courage

Beware of the virtues of your friends: they create the occasions
for their use.

Courage can be dangerous. If it is defined in traditional ways, as a set
of dispositions to overcome fear, to oppose obstacles, to perform difficult
or dangerous actions, its claim to be a virtue is questionable. If we
retain the traditional conception of courage and its military connotations—overcoming and combat—we should be suspicious of it. Instead
of automatically classifying it as a virtue, attempting to develop and
exercise it, we should become alert to its dangers. Yet there is an aspect
of traditional courage that serves us: we require the capacities and traits
that enable us to persist in acting well under stress, to endure hardships
when following our judgments about what is best is difficult or dangerous.
If courage is checked, redefined as the virtue that enables virtue, then
we need not fear its dangers. But redefined as the dispositions, whatever
they may be, that make us resolute in worthy, difficult action, courage
evaporates: it covers a diverse, heterogeneous variety of traits, dispositions, and skills. We have a choice: if we retain traditional courage
in its combative forms, we should toxify it, recognizing that its addictive
and expansive dangers disqualify it as a presumptive virtue. If we retain
courage as a virtue, we need to reform it by restructuring its cognitive
set and relocating it within a complex, counterbalanced system of dispositions and traits, to assure that it is not only locally but globally
beneficial. We need to make sure that the habits of courageous thought
and action do not threaten other prized goods, all things considered.

Reevaluating courage will lead us to touch on some of the largest and
some of the murkiest questions central to the analysis of the virtues:
When does a cluster of dispositions qualify as a virtue? Under what
conditions can virtue be attributed to a person, rather than to specific
sets of dispositions or actions? What cognitive components or presup-

positions are embedded in, or associated with, the virtues? What tasks—
and therefore what virtues—are required of the moral philosopher?

I

> When they start talking about courage, it is time to emigrate.

First, let's toxify courage. A person disposed to traditional courage is
set to oppose obstacles: she tends to set aside the normal fear of pain
and harm, taking risks and persistently enduring hardships for the sake
of a perceived good.[1] Even when soldierly *andreia* has become moral
fortitudo, and the courageous face ostracism or exile, or the inner enemies of disease, flaws of character, or the lure of certain trains of thought,
the position is still confrontational and combative: the objects requiring
courage are treated as external others, to be overcome or endured.[2] Even
when courage acts for something or moves to something, it is defined as
persistence against what is conceived as a resisting opponent. The person
gathers her forces against her natural tendencies to self-protection, inertia, or enjoyment. Even when she combats what she recognizes as
hers, part of herself, she identifies with the motives or forces that she
musters, and detaches herself from what she opposes. The echoes of
military campaigns and strategies remain.

The thoughts and habits of courage tend to expand and to generalize.
After all, the virtues are identified as the dispositions that typically
produce prized goods. Besides the internal rewards that each virtue
brings as an excellence that assures its specific good and that is pleasurable in its exercise, the traditional virtues are presumptively also
rewarded with the prizes of a culture: with wealth, social advantage,
important marriages, sometimes political power. For all these reasons,
the virtuous are rarely content to wait for occasions to produce the
situations that elicit their virtues. They form a life that sustains and
enlarges their particular excellences, creating situations in which their
virtues can be given the fullest play.

When a virtue is central to a person's character—when its exercise
is organizationally dominant—the thoughts and categorial preoccupations that are central to that virtue form interpretations of situations:
they focus attention and define what is salient. It is not enough that the
virtuous person acts and reacts in specific ways when the occasion arises.
She must also have a certain cast of mind.[3] This is not primarily a matter
of purity of heart or intention, not a matter of nobility or disinterest: it
is the very practical matter of seeing situations in such a way as to elicit
relevant actions and reactions. A virtue of action is worthless without

sensitivity to the conditions that require it. Cognitive dispositions—
habits of salient focusing, habits of association, the primacy of categorial
structures—affect action by affecting perception. The courageous cannot
be all readiness for danger and yet perceptively and interpretively dense
to the occasions that require facing difficulties, taking risks.

But the cognitive dispositions that partly constitute the virtues do
more than alert us to the occasions appropriate to their exercise. They
are magnetizing in that they promote and even construct and create the
occasions that require their exercise, just as the man with a chip on his
shoulder not only interprets but gravitates toward and actively creates
the confrontations he expects.

(1) *Dispositions of interpretation* categorize and organize situations to
focus on what is salient and important. A painter does not wait for a
scenic landscape to unfold before her: she organizes what she sees as
a composition, a configuration of forms and colors. A soldier characteristically sees landscapes as strongholds to defend, exposed flanks to
attack. (2) *Gravitating* or *tropic dispositions* lead a person to the sorts of
situations that predictably elicit valued character traits. A generous
person is not only generous and kindly when the occasion arises: she
seeks out occasions to be helpful, gravitates to those sorts of occasions
where her contributions are required. (3) *Self-activating dispositions* promote or produce the occasions that require their exercise. The prudent
merchant creates a self-reinforcing world: foreign policy, family relations, and friendships are structured and motivated by gain-maximizing
cost-accounting calculations.

Psychologically, the magnetizing dispositions of courage typically diminish the force of other highly desirable categorial dispositions. The
courageous are normally not magnetized to aesthetic delight in the ludicrous, to leisurely wonder, or empathic identification. The confidence
that is part of courage tends to diminish dispositions that are directed
to avoiding oppositional confrontation: imaginative foresight or tactful
humor. Perceiving actions as victories or defeats, seeing compromise as
a partial loss, the centrally courageous do not usually promote, and often
resist cooperative, compromising attitudes. Of course in the midst of
war, it takes courage to propose a critical reevaluation of national aims
or cooperative negotiation with the enemy. Though it often takes courage
to question one's ends, still the courageous normally accept the goods
they serve without question. Even veterans of moral wars rarely set
themselves the farsighted statesmanly task of assuring the peaceful conditions that would make their particular virtues obsolete.

Besides the attractions of all the virtues, courage has its own distinctive magnetizing and expansionist features: unless it is externally

checked, it appears to drift naturally into its excessive forms. Because the uncertainties and risks associated with traditional courage are often addictively intense and exciting, the cognitive magnetizing dispositions of courage tend to escalate and generalize. Activities originally prized for other reasons often lose their luster unless they also become dangerous. The attractions of courage are introduced into activities that do not or did not originally require it: romantic love, professional work. But the dispositions that constitute courage are rarely strongly correlated with the happy outcome of such activities. On the contrary, they deflect attention from their primary directions and purposes. Risk and uncertainty form habits that jade the courageous: they appear to require increasingly higher levels of excitement and intensity.[4] Having cast doubt on courage, our question now is, What conditions can assure its appropriate exercise, to prevent its sliding into its addictive, excessive forms? And how can it be balanced with the claims of other virtues?[5]

One might think that all this talk of toxifying courage is tendentious. After all, none of this is news, and most of it is rank speculation about empirical matters. Not only courage, but all the virtues are shadowed by their defective forms: the dispositions that constitute them can be wildly or inappropriately exercised. Virtue theorists have always known the prima facie or presumptive virtues must be secured: internally bound to prevent their sliding to their excessive forms and to assure their specific goods, and externally balanced with other claims.

One might think that the problems of courage simply set the stage for the traditional problem of assuring not only the virtuosity but the virtue of admirable, beneficent dispositions. And indeed this is true. But before turning to our central problem—analyzing the appropriate exercise of the dispositions that constitute the virtues—I want to complicate our problems still further.

II

Without courage, there is no active virtue.

Even if we manage to control the excessive forms of courage, we still have the even more fundamental and radical problem of identifying the dispositions that constitute it. There seem to be no specific set of dispositions that enable a person to overcome natural fears or reluctances, to take risks on behalf of a perceived good. The attribution of courage neither describes nor explains the dispositions, skills, or traits that assure the performance of fearful, difficult, risk-filled actions.

Courage is identified against the background of beliefs about what is objectively difficult, risky, or dangerous; its attribution rests on as-

sumptions about what is normally feared or found difficult. Yet attributions of courage are withdrawn when someone fails to recognize danger
or is especially qualified by constitution or training to minimize risk.
While courage can be attributed to enemies and even villains, some
motives and enabling attitudes make its attribution suspect: the attribution of courage is usually withdrawn if the action was performed under
the influence of hypnosis or drugs, or from a sense of the ludicrous, a
taste for the ironic, a sudden suicidal self-contempt. The action can be
typically courageous, the person not.

Still, while some enabling attitudes suspend the attribution of courage,
no particular attitudes assure it. A sense of urgency, indignation, fe-
rocious hope, admiration, contempt, disgust, love, curiosity, and loyalty
can serve as sources of exceptional action. Even the desire for gain and
fame can elicit the *petites actions* that are the behavioral beginning of
courageous action: the straightened back, the deep breath, the tightening
of the muscles. The skills and dispositions that enable someone to
overcome fear and to perform risky, dangerous actions are as various as
the actions they perform and the fears they face.

Modesty aside, the courageous themselves standardly cannot find what
the world calls courage among their enabling dispositions.[6] Even in the
dramatic cases that involve risking life rather than livelihood, the courageous generally say that they were able to do what they did because
they saw that it had to be done. Sometimes their fear seemed unreal to
them, as if they observed it taking place outside themselves; sometimes
the fascination for the task was so great they hardly felt their fear;
sometimes they were so angry or moved by solidarity or love that they
hardly focused on their fear. Sometimes they deflected fear by pride, or
more commonly, by a revulsion against what seemed shameful.

The best preparation for courageous action is the preparation for
action: competence and confidence in competence. Dangerous and fearful actions form a heterogeneous class, with distinctive problems of
attention and competence. But competence is always specific and confidence without competence is folly. Often the skills of the courageous
are those of proper focusing, cognitive habits specific to the actions they
must perform. Those who overcome acrophobia acquire such specific
techniques as looking at the horizon rather than straight down. Even
when the enterprises that require courage are not well-defined, when
they are not contained by a beginning, middle, and end—emigrating,
undertaking to live with a senile parent, preparing for chemotherapy—
encouraging maneuvres are highly specific. They characteristically involve the definition of small and easily performed actions that compose
the complex enterprise. Attempting to gather courage as such, in a
general way, gives no direction for the *petites actions* that carry persistent,

difficult action. Without overwhelming someone with anxiety-provoking attention, the more the encourager—and this can be the self-reformer—attends the details of actions and the details of dispositions required to perform them, the more useful the encouragement. Sometimes encouragement requires correcting the false beliefs that generate fear; sometimes it involves drawing a helpful analogy, assimilating the unfamiliar to the familiar; sometimes what assures courage is the evocation of an archaic anger or a significant fantasy. Perhaps some, but certainly not all, are heartened by the thought of mustering forces for combating, overcoming, or resisting. But often it is just the thought of such combat that is threatening.

And yet and yet . . . Sometimes there is a chasm in action: someone who is appropriately skilled and empowered to do what she judges desirable and good is not always set to act when she suffers the natural fears of harm and danger. And in those cases we admire courage in others and long for it in ourselves. Then, indeed, the dispositions that assure virtuous action in the face of fear, danger, and difficulty constitute courage. But if courage is the set of enabling dispositions, it is a wide open set.

III

> The virtue of a free man is as great in avoiding dangers as in overcoming them.
>
> Spinoza, *Ethics* 4.69

If courage evaporates as a set of specific dispositions exercised in performing dangerous, difficult, fearful actions, it also disappears when we trace its historical transformation. While the virtues can be characterized—even universally characterized—at a very general level, their typical realization in action varies with paradigmatically prized, difficult actions. The traits that a society prizes—its virtues—are those it takes to assure the performance of admirable or beneficial actions. But as political and social concerns change, and as conditions that make action difficult vary, so do the range of admirable virtuous actions. And therefore so do the dispositions that substantively enable the practice of the virtues. Even if virtue were at a general level everywhere the same, it is one thing to face Achilles in battle, another to defy Nero, or to publish a scientific treatise defying orthodoxy, or to set forth to explore the North Pole, or to undertake to raise a child with Down's syndrome.

Courage began as *andreia*, as military manliness, the specific dispositions necessary for hand-to-hand physical combat, to stand one's

ground or to advance against a powerful opponent. Its allies were shame
and pride; its opposites, cowardice and bravado. When the actions of
andreia were highly specific, the dispositions—the excellences—required to carry them were equally specific. The appropriateness conditions that corrected the addictive features of risk and excitement were
built into the characterization of the ends of the action-type. *Andreia*
consists just in this, in advancing or retreating appropriately. Because
the soldier's task is highly specific, his excellences, and their excesses,
are clearly delimited and defined. It is not the soldier who must assign
the appropriate weight to military action in relation to other relevant
goods. When the virtues are distributed with the division of labor, each
contains its localized or regionalized but not its global or all-things
considered appropriateness condition.

But when political and moral courage replace military courage as the
focus of action, the paradigm examples, the narrative stories that define
courage, also change. The definition that Plato proposed in *The Republic*
(429c)—the ability to remember what (one has been taught) is worth
prizing and worth fearing—has moved far from characterizing the particular dispositions exercised in courage. Even more soberly, it leaves
the determination of the appropriate knowledge in the hands of the
philosopher-kings who must educate or train the other classes to follow
rational justice, to assure the appropriate weight and distribution of the
varieties of virtue. Whatever remnants of the Socratic unity thesis survive
the division of labor in *The Republic* are abandoned in *The Statesman*,
where courage is openly acknowledged to conflict with other virtues
(Statesman 311b–c).

Aristotle's definition of *andreia* as the disposition to act and react
appropriately in situations that involve fear and confidence—a rationally
determined mean between cowardice and foolhardiness—moves toward
transforming it to a generalized enabling virtue. Although he retains
physical courage as the primary case, Aristotle extends its exercise to
political and moral contexts, as well as to those that, like the traits
involved in facing disease and loss, require endurance and fortitude.
Because the virtues are independently identifiable and exercised, they
can in principle conflict. It is sometimes possible for *andreia* and gentle-
ness *(praotēs)* to determine distinctive and competing actions, actions
that would undermine the realization of one another's goods. The condition that assures the internal appropriate exercise of each virtue, taken
separately—the condition that it consists in acting in a mean defined
by *logos*—does not automatically assure the appropriate exercise of that
virtue, in relation to all the others, all things considered. An external
appropriateness condition is also required. *Phronēsis* is the master virtue,

the practical and intellectual *hexis* that determines the priority and balance among the goods to be realized by the virtues.

In the best of times, Stoic *fortitudo* requires intelligence and the ability to speak and act effectively; in the worst of times, it requires endurance to live in exile. Its ally is detachment and imperturbability; its contrasts are servility and erratic impulse. For those Christians for whom the central tasks of life center around the struggles against original sin, Stoic *fortitudo* is transformed into the power to resist the natural inclination to pride and vice. Still carrying defensive, military connotations, Christian *fortitudo* is exercised in the battle against one's fallen condition. The primary contrary of this kind of *fortitudo* is not cowardice but *melancholia*. Because the coward still has an energetic attachment to himself, his self-protective actions can be bold and even daring. But *melancholia* and *accidie*, despair and dispiritedness, are the discouraged attitudes that the world affords nothing worth the effort of striving. The excessive form of *fortitudo* is also reinterpreted: rashness arises from false pride, to act for one's own glory rather than for God's law. With this new location on the map of traits and dispositions, the allies of *fortitudo* have also been changed: good faith and stout-heartedness, faith in God's benevolence, rather than an appropriate sense of glory and honor.

Aquinas characterizes *fortitudo* as "steadfastness of mind, . . . general virtue, or rather the condition of each and every virtue. *Virtus* can mean strength or courage, or virtue in general. Indeed *virtus* is a more literal translation of *andreia* than is *fortitudo*." *Fortitudo* as the general condition for active virtue is distinguished from the narrower capacity to overcome the natural difficulties of soldierly action, the risk of physical pain and death: "In another sense [it is] firmness of mind in enduring or repulsing whatever makes steadfastness outstandingly difficult, that is, particularly serious dangers, primarily sustaining action to overcome fears of bodily harm and death and secondarily in persevering in attacking" (*Summa Theologica* 2a2ae.123, 2–10).

For Machiavelli, the primary activities of courage are those of the Prince assuring the glory of his *città*. Quick, bold action, a sense of timing in grand enterprises, and a deft ability to calculate risks are the dispositions of *animatio, audacio,* and *coraggio*. A sense of style and elegant form are their allies; small-mindedness and hesitating caution are their opposites. When the primary activities of the *città* become mercantile, courage requires bold investment. Machiavellian *animatio, audacio,* and adventuresomeness shift from the domain of statecraft to that of mercantile enterprise. In such circumstances, eliciting courage requires radically different dispositions from those required on the battlefield: an energetic, inventive, bold imagination, a capacity to envision a distant benefit and unexpected means—a whole set of entrepreneurial capacities are required to carry out the exercise of courage. Its contraries become stinginess on one side and flamboyant improvidence on the other. Its new allies are the dispositions exercised in clear calculation and in ingenious imagination.[7]

The English word *courage* derives from *coeur*, "heart." But in its initial appearance, its connotations linked it to *thymos*, signifying energy and manly power. The horse's mane and the rooster's comb were called their *courage* because they were thought to be indications of aggression and sexual energy. In the physiological psychology that associated it to vigorous persistence, the heart was not the seat of feeling or of sentiment, but the source of energy. Heartiness was primarily a power of action, and only secondarily an attitude toward the world. To be heartened was to be emboldened, rather than to be cheered.

But it was precisely because the physiological theories associated with the etymology of courage marked it as raw and often mindless energy, that Hobbes, focusing on the dangers of individual aggression, classified courage as a passion rather than as virtue. He defines it as "the contempt of wounds and violent death. It inclines men to private revenges, and sometimes to endeavor the unsettling of the public peace."[8] Thinking peace necessary to civility and civilization, and believing that fear is its surest safeguard, Hobbes cast suspicion on courage: the habits of overcoming fear endanger peace.

Kant returns to Aquinas's characterization, distinguishing generalized courage as the condition for all virtuous action from the specific kind of courage that overcomes the fear of pain and death. He takes the general attitude to be the central form: "*Fortitudo* is the capacity and resolved purpose to resist a strong but unjust opponent; and with regard to the opponent of the moral disposition within us [he means wayward inclinations and desires], such fortitude *is* virtue [*virtus, fortitudo moralis*, that is, moral strength]." And, he adds, "*Fortitudo moralis* constitutes the greatest and only true martial glory of man: it is also called true wisdom, namely practical [wisdom]" (*Metaphysical Principles of Virtue* 11a37 65).

But once courage has become a generalized attitude, identical with practical wisdom, the prized constituent of reliably active virtue, it no longer designates a set of dispositions to specific sorts of actions. If the problem is to encourage action—to begin the *petites actions* that are the realization of virtue—the generalized attitude is insufficient. A generalized attitude has exactly the same problems that courage was invented to solve: since it does not by itself provide substantive directions for what to do, it is not the beginning of action. If justice and virtue do not as such assure their realization under difficult or dangerous circumstances, neither do generalized second-order attitudes of persistence and endurance devoid of any particular directions or dispositions for action. The determination of action that courage was invented to assure will again be required.

One might think: If courage evaporates, there is no need to fear or reform it, no need to toxify it or to assure conditions for its appropriate exercise. But we are the inheritors of a history of the transformations of *andreia:* the courage we have been taught to admire and to acquire is a generalized attitude, the descendant of traditional *andreia,* still carrying addictively combative, magnetizing cognitive dispositions.

IV

> Those who are careful, fair, and conservative—those of a moderate temperament—are not keen; they lack a certain sort of quick, active boldness. The courageous, on the other hand, are far less just and cautious, but they are excellent at getting things done. A community can never function well . . . unless both of these are present and active . . . woven together by the ruler.
>
> Plato, *The Statesman*

Recognizing the utility of traditional courage, let us turn to considering the conditions that would secure its appropriate use. Inheritors of all these definitions, how are we to assure the appropriate exercise of the vast array of enabling dispositions that constitute courage? There is a set of traditional solutions.

1. There is the flick-of-the-wrist solution that simply disqualifies inappropriate exercises of putatively courageous dispositions as bona fide instances of courage, or as genuine cases of virtuous courage.[9] Elegant, perhaps even true, but uninformative. Just what is it that needs to be built into bravado to qualify it as virtuous courage?

2. The unity-of-the-virtues solution builds the appropriateness-securing condition into the cognitive component of the various dispositions that define and identify the virtues. Only those who act from their judgments of what is best, all things considered, qualify as courageous. Since knowledge is the essential qualifying condition of the individual virtues, it is virtue.[10] Philosophers from Aristotle on have given us a rich variety of arguments against this solution. I don't want to diagnose just which of these arguments is most telling—the argument from akrasia, or the argument from the manifest independent variability of the contributory virtues. In any case, the unity solution is formulaic: it does

not specify the appropriate character traits exercised in virtuous, wisely formed action. Being assured that the virtues ultimately consist in knowing what needs to be done, and that such knowledge straightway moves to the appropriate action, is about as comforting and as informative to those of us who don't know what to do as being assured that in the long run we'll all be dead.

3. The harmonic-cooperation solution to the problem of securing the appropriate exercise of virtuous dispositions allows for the independent identification and variation of the individual virtues but requires their cooperative conjunction—at least at some modicum level—in genuinely virtuous action. The active cooperation of (MacDowell's) moral sensitivity, (Watson's) due concern, and a prudential descendant of *phronēsis* are centrally required.[11] Like the first two solutions, this view has the merits of elegance and simplicity. But like the others, it leaves the substantive questions unanswered. Just how does prudence—or as it may be, *caritas*, faithfulness, or respect—integrate with the dispositions to undertake naturally fearful dangers, particularly when the initial specialized direction for *caritas* or prudence can be opposed to that of courage?

This stand-together-fall-together account of the ways in which the virtues mutually assure their respective appropriate exercise glosses over the harsh question of whether these contributory virtues always support each other, each providing dispositions and skills that all go in the same direction, each independently moving toward the same action. The tensions between prudence and courage should sober the happy thought that cooperation among the virtues is always achieved harmoniously. Certainly prudence can serve as the internal direction for courage when it enters into the determination and selection, the formation of courageous action. Not only soldiers but also moral heroes can rationally choose to risk their lives for what they consider of the greatest importance. While considerations of prudence can coincide with those of global rationality, and while it might be both prudent and rational to extend local prudence toward global rationality, personal prudence—even when it is exercised in the service of enlightened interest and long-range welfare—may still conflict with disinterested judgment about what is best overall. A definitional extension of prudence—identifying it with generalized rationality—glosses over the possibility that prudence, exercised in a person's own larger interests, might conflict with an all-things-considered disinterested judgment about what is best. There may be weighty moral and psychological considerations that argue for a regulative principle connecting the two: but those considerations will be all the more weighty for not being introduced definitionally. In any case, defining the outcomes of prudential and global rationality begs the question at issue: Can the virtues conflict? And, more interesting, can that very conflict at least sometimes help assure the appropriate exercise of the various dispositions that constitute the virtues?

4. There is a sober, dark, and therefore probably more correct version of the cooperation solution. The checks-and-balances solution openly acknowledges rather than glosses over the possibility that the appropriate exercise of individual virtues might sometimes be secured by their conflicting with each other.[12] This view does not assume that all the virtues are cooperatively present and moving in the same direction to secure one another's appropriate and successful exercise.[13] The addictive and expansionist tendencies of courage can often be constrained and contained by independent dispositions that direct, check, and sometimes counterbalance its exercise. Sometimes prudence and its related cognitive dispositions do indeed inform and direct the exercise of courageous dispositions, nonoppositionally, by determining and specifying the appropriate action. For example, they may counsel the courageous to oppose the tyrant by mockery rather than by direct confrontation, or to establish a newspaper rather than run for public office. Not only prudence but other virtues can direct and channel the exercise of courageous dispositions by specifying their inappropriate exercise. Loyalty, friendship, and love can constrain the expansion and addictiveness of courage by directing its exercise toward the welfare of friends, fellow citizens, family.

But sometimes the appropriateness condition is assured by counterbalancing, opposed, or tensed dispositions. It is rare that two dispositions are tensed in opposition because their cognitive components are direct contraries. More frequently, they are opposed when they are typically exercised in actions whose standard outcomes undermine one another. For instance, the actions of patriotism often frustrate those of internationalism; the attitude of detachment tends to undermine that of active hopefulness; trust and caution can readily undo each other. Virtues are also opposed when the development of one set typically inhibits the development of another. For instance, the dispositions exercised in meticulous and precise rule-defined action typically inhibit the development of those exercised in free-ranging imaginative exploration; those exercised in adaptability to community consensus typically inhibit those exercised in decisively independent action.

But has the dark truth brought us anywhere useful? The checks-and-balances solution seems to have brought us full circle. It is as formulaic as the other solutions; even worse, it seems to eventuate in an unfortunate regress. Is there just one balancing capacity, one condition that identifies and assures the balance among tensed and opposed virtues? Are we back with *phronēsis?* Or can *caritas*, faithfulness, or Kantian respect also serve as the master virtue, assuring the proper checks and balances? If there are several candidates for the master virtue, can these sometimes conflict? Again these difficulties could be solved by definition, by characterizing *phronēsis* (or prudence) in such a way that it substantively assures virtue. But this solution assumes that competing criteria for determining the appropriate balance among virtues are themselves commensurable and balanceable. We are back with the first, definitional solution, with a fiat answer to the unresolved substantive question: can criteria for virtue conflict?

I do not think that there is one answer to these questions. The virtues are secured in different ways by different types of people, whose dispositions form quite different types of structures. For most of us, the balance between opposed dispositions is not automatically secured by their relative strengths, each virtue internally regulated and appropriately externally related to the other virtues. Most of us are not even assured of a master virtue to regulate conflicts among individual virtues. The happy few who have realized virtue by the fortune of their constitutions, upbringing, and political and social circumstances cannot always show the less fortunate how to secure the appropriate exercise of our traits. When the situations and tasks of virtue are radically heterogeneous, when a political system balances genuinely opposed interests, or when social and political situations undergo rapid and dramatic changes, a person's habits and experience—her magnetizing cognitive dispositions—cannot assure her realizing appropriate ends. In those circumstances, when *phronēsis* is itself jeopardized, virtue can sometimes be assured by rules and principles: "Quand on n'a pas du caractère, il faut bien se donner une méthode."[14] But sometimes there is no single appropriate resolution for conflicts among qualified criteria for balance among the virtues. Whatever conflicts arise among individual virtues is sometimes reproduced among the counsels of *phronēsis*, or among competing criteria for appropriateness, or among rules and principles.

V

> Principles without habits are empty; habits without principles are blind; and both without a systematic balance are dangerous.

But where are we now? Should we expose the dangers of traditional courage, by investigating its addictive and expansionist character, locating its oppositional excellences in their historical contexts, as directed to achieving the ends of warring or of competitively expansive cultures? Or should we attempt to reform courage, detaching it from its military history as the descendant of *andreia*, treating it as a set of diverse dispositions serving the civil virtues of empathic understanding, tact, inventive foresight, cooperativeness? How can appropriate dispositions best be developed and socialized within a system of checks and balances? Can moral philosophy provide the master virtue, philosophic analysis assure the proper balance among the virtues? To answer those questions substantively rather than formulaically, we need to answer the question, "What should be done?" Only when we are clear about the sorts of actions we should now prize can we determine which traits and dispositions can best assure the excellent performance of such actions. The question, "How can the appropriate exercise of courage be assured?" cannot be answered abstractly, independently of the particular contexts in which it occurs. To be sure, the contexts do not themselves dictate the resolution of the moral conflicts that arise from them, or within them. If principles without dispositions are empty, then habits and dispositions without principles are blind, and both without systematic balance are dangerous.

Once moral philosophy is in the practical realm, practical constraints apply to it. Central among those constraints is the working psychological structure of the agents whose practical problems set the question, "What is to be done?" We should not assume the active cooperation of idealized rational moral agents, especially when the reform of cognitive dispositions, habits, and motives is at issue. The outcome of reforms should not be presupposed to be effective in bringing them about.

But who is this "we" who should determine what should be done, and how should the virtues be reformed and balanced? Unless she explicitly distances herself as a historian or as an ethnographer reporting the practices of the natives, the moral philosopher implicitly endorses and valorizes the character traits and the dispositions she defines as constituting the various virtues. The implicit force, if not the explicit stance, of the moral philosopher is normative. The analysis of the virtues presupposes an answer to the question, "What is to be done?"; the identification of beneficial, worthy, and admirable actions has normative assumptions and practical action-guiding consequences.

Traditional moral philosophy was practical, educative, and political: the analysis of the virtues and their mutual correction was inseparable from the analysis of the psychology of moral development and the political structures that could (at that time, in that place) best support and sustain moral life. Wittingly or unwittingly, naively or selfconsciously, philosophers have always been policymakers; their theories always combined normative and empirical moral psychology. Even at its most speculative, the philosophy of mind embedded within and presupposed by normative ethics carries the stamp, the assumptions, of its time. A moral theory that makes no attempt to conjoin with psychology might define the ethics of rational Martians. Unless it can also apply to us, demonstrably apply to us, it can make no claims on us.

We now separate the didactic and political writings of traditional moral philosophers from what we take to be their central philosophic work. We read Spinoza's *Ethics* without reading his *Theological-Political Treatise;* Hume's *Treatise* and *Enquiry* without his *History* and his *Essays;* Aristotle's *Ethics* without his *Politics;* Kant's ethical writings without his *Lectures on the Virtues* or his essays on education, history, and politics; Hegel's theoretical philosophy without his political essays. Such an artificial separation leads us to suppose our enterprises to have been far more methodological, analytic, and less normative than they were.

What, then, of our initial problem concerning courage? Of course we need to do all these things, to examine the dangers of traditional courage, to reform our conceptions of its enabling dispositions, and to locate those dispositions in a system of checks and balances. To be sure, as the philosophic virtues are presently defined and developed, there is absolutely no reason to suppose that we are, by virtue of our professional training as philosophers, well equipped to have sound, let alone profound, answers to the question "What should be done?" But the analysis and reassessment of the virtues must include the reevaluation of the dispositions that constitute philosophic virtue. Like other virtues, philosophic virtues secure their appropriate exercise by being located in a system of checks and balances. We might fear that, in openly becoming normative persuaders, we might endanger other opposed philosophic virtues. But just now, the fear that philosophers will become mere popular demagogues seems premature. When philosophers run the risk of becoming rabble rousers, the question "What should be done in philosophy?" will of course again have to be raised. We shall then have to reassess and reevaluate the philosophic virtues. One reform at a time, one opposition of virtues at a time.

In becoming practical and particular, moral philosophy must take men as we find them, the problems as they are given, and the virtues as we can safely hope to elicit them.[15]

16   Virtues and Their Vicissitudes

When does a set of character traits qualify as a virtue? What assures—
or could assure—that such traits are well and appropriately exercised?

The somber answer to the first question is that dispositions—habits,
skills, and capacities—that can be voluntarily and discriminatingly exercised are classified as virtues when they are admired or when they are
thought socially beneficial, and when acquiring them is thought to involve
some initial effort. There is considerable pressure to acquire and exercise
virtues, despite the fact that they are not always directly rewarding or
rewarded, and often fail to secure individual thriving. Some of the virtues
are identified against the background of theories about ideal exemplars
of human excellence: such virtues represent the realization of what a
culture prizes as expressing what is highest or best in us. Other virtues
are identified against the background of theories about the pathologies
inherent in natural and functional movements to self-protection, or pleasure, or fame and honor: such virtues are beneficial instruments that
protect us against the excesses and misdirections of natural tendencies.
Still other virtues are traits that are believed to serve beneficial civic
functions, particularly when their exercise involves some cost to oneself.
Complex cultures cast a wide net: they valorize and promote a large
number of virtues without distinguishing those that cluster in a mutually
supportive system, from those that undermine one another. The traits
that protect, perpetuate, and enhance a society, that promote its harmony
and forward its enterprises, that are thought to conduce to its thriving,
form an extremely heterogeneous set. Some—like varieties of intelligence—are natural endowments; others—like tact—are culturally
formed and developed. Some—like patience—can be eroded under
harsh circumstances; others—like inventiveness—are more stable. Most
can be used well or ill.

Because the grounds on which traits are classified as virtues are
extremely heterogeneous, it is not surprising that the virtues sometimes
conflict, producing actions whose typical outcomes undermine one an-

314

other. It is also not surprising that the canonic list of virtues varies historically and subculturally, and that such lists retain traits that no longer express cultural ideals or serve social and political functions. A culture can, of course, be mistaken about the traits that serve its thriving, failing to identify some that are beneficial and admiring others that damage its (own conceptions of) thriving. It can idealize traits that its institutions no longer develop or promote.[1]

But at least sometimes the dark answer has a bright side: there is some relation between virtues and individual flourishing, if only because at least some virtues are esteemed and esteem is one of the goods of life. With moral and political luck, the connection is stronger: traits that are socially prized are often—though certainly not necessarily—connected to at least some aspects of both social and individual flourishing. That connection is sufficiently strong so that both moral philosophers and those who on the whole want to live well can at least initially and provisionally be guided by social conceptions of virtues. But where there is good luck, there is also bad luck: individual and social thriving can conflict even though individual conceptions of thriving are largely socially formed, and individual thriving is socially controlled. The connection between socially recognized virtue and flourishing is generally sufficiently weak to allow the indignant and the visionary good grounds for reformist proposals.[2]

The somber answer to the second question is that nothing can assure that the traits constituting the virtues are always well and appropriately used, except by the strategic unilluminating maneuver of not counting typically virtuous traits as *virtues* in a person unless they are well and appropriately exercised by that person.[3] But the merit of such a strategy is largely limited to the benefits of elegant theory construction: it leaves us in the dark about what assures or even conduces to the appropriate use of such traits.

However skeptical we are about the pretensions of a purely philosophical ethical theory to serve as a guide for action, we nevertheless do want a philosophic ethics that does more than propose a general theory of *right, good, duty, virtue*. There are implicit practical constraints and directives on normative ethical theories, even when they confine themselves to articulating ideals. Since such ideals are, after all, ideals *for us*, they should be capable of being psychologically action-guiding—or at least action-directing—in structuring and restructuring social practices and political institutions. And, since failure is nearly as common as success in this area, ethical theories should also explain why it is so difficult for even the most well intentioned to manage to live well.

I. Character and the Context of Virtue

> The virtues hunt in packs.

Before moving to the large and difficult problems we've set for ourselves, we first need to describe how virtues—or more generally, how character traits—function in forming actions. The thoughts and categorial preoccupations that are central to a virtue form interpretations of situations: they focus attention and define what is salient, placing other concerns in the background. To act well, and to do so reliably, a person must perceive and interpret situations appropriately, and do so reliably. Good will is empty unless it has appropriate cognitive structures—habits of salient focusing that are corrigible without being distractible, imaginative habits of association that elicit a wide range of relevant material without being volatile, thresholds that are sensitive without being hypersensitive.

The cognitive dispositions that partly constitute the virtues are tropic or magnetizing: they organize perceptions and interpretations of situations in such a way as to elicit appropriate habits and actions. Such cognitive dispositions sometimes generate appropriate actions by first eliciting appropriate motives: but they can also promote actions independently of—and indeed sometimes even contrary to—immediate desires. Significantly, they are also self-reinforcing and self-perpetuating. Virtuous actions tend to generate scenarios—sequences of events—that require their continued exercise. *Dispositions of interpretation* structure patterns of salience and importance: they organize the dominant proper descriptions of situations. Without waiting to be called upon, a generous person is perceptively and interpretively sensitive to needs, even when the needy are unaware of their condition. Where others standardly focus on ambition or relations of power, a strongly generous person notices how she can correct what is wanting. *Tropic dispositions* lead a person to gravitate to the sort of situations that predictably elicit prized traits. Often avoiding situations where she might herself require help, a strongly generous person tends to move toward situations in which her contributions might be useful, even when she has no desire to find herself in such situations. *Self-activating dispositions* promote or create the occasions that require their exercise. A highly charismatic figure can sometimes so structure situations—define decision-making processes, for example, or design a foreign policy, or even form her personal relationships—in such a way that others predictably come to depend upon, and even to require, her bold, imaginative leadership.

When the virtues are rewarded, they are expansive. They ramify to develop and exercise associated supportive traits, while inhibiting other, often highly beneficial traits. In situations of conflict, publicly recognized virtues tend to determine priorities, sometimes at the cost of highly functional, but socially unacknowledged, traits. The magnetizing dispositions of centrally organizing virtues are focal and expansive in a person's character: focusing on what is salient blurs what is in the background.[4] (The persistent and tenacious are not, for example, normally sensitive to the ironies of the contingencies of practical life; rarely delighting in ludicrous turns of chance, they are often so intent on their purposes that they are not responsive to a tangential, but highly beneficial, serendipity.)

Traits do not, of course, form actions in isolation. Individual virtues underdetermine appropriate actions. They only function within a supportive, directing, and sometimes oppositional network. The attribution of any trait is made against the background of *ceteris paribus* assumptions about an interrelated network of standard operating functions. Some of the interrelations among the virtues arise primarily from their cognitive components, others from the consequences of the actions they standardly generate. Artificially, solely for the purpose of exposition, and not because they are psychologically separable, we can distinguish the cognitive combinatorial properties of the virtues from those that are normally formed by the dynamics of their habitual exercise in action.

The cognitive components of the virtues carry the whole range of combinatorial logical and psychological properties: logically, their cognitive contents presuppose and entail one another; complex virtues contain simpler virtues as ingredients; they can be contraries. Psychologically, their associations can be lawlike; the development of the cognitive components of one virtue can presuppose, enhance, or block another; they can reinforce or inhibit each other; they can combine in new virtues and form cyclical patterns of vacillation and ambivalence.

The virtues are also narratively connected in dynamic, unfolding patterns.[5] There are culturally fixed, and institutionally controlled, structures that promote, inhibit, and then replace the sequence of virtues, as appropriate to gender, age, and role. The virtues of adolescence are sometimes dangerous to the middle-aged, those of age grotesque in youth. Sometimes the successes of one virtue generate situations that require not only the replacement, but also the checking of, the original virtue. The bold inventive entrepreneurial traits of an early mercantile society can, for instance, so change material and social conditions that the original virtues are reclassified as vices unless they are restrained by prudential and sometimes even cautious calculation. Obviously, these relations and changes do not necessarily occur smoothly or automatically. Strongly entrenched virtues continue to operate long after they are judged inappropriate; when that happens counterpoised virtues do not always adjust to achieve an appropriate balance.

II. Virtue and Virtues

> No virtues without virtue; no virtue without virtues.

With this characterization of the structures and relations of the virtues in mind, we are better equipped to return to our original question: What assures the virtue of the virtues?

1. The most radical solution is that of *contextualizing* attributions of virtue: since the same set of dispositions can sometimes be appropriately, and sometimes inappropriately exercised, even by the same person, traits qualify as virtues only when they have been appropriately exercised. While this solution is elegant, it appears to make the attribution of virtue redundant, reiterating—in the form of a pseudo-explanation—the judgment that the action is meritorious. In any case, this is a solution provided for, and by a problem in theory construction: it sets the conditions for the attribution of virtue without providing the analysis of those conditions.

2. The strictest solution is the introduction of a condition for *self-modulation:* no set of dispositions qualifies as a virtue unless it includes its own appropriateness-assuring conditions. To qualify as a virtue, a set of traits must be, first of all, discriminatingly *internally* self-regulating in order to determine the appropriate occasion, extent, and manner for its exercise (true courage doesn't lapse into bravado, generosity into wastefulness). Significantly, it must also be *externally* self-regulating in order to determine how it is to be appropriately balanced with other, sometimes competing, sets of traits.

While this solution is philosophically ingenious in defining conditions for identifying the virtues, it is not psychologically illuminating or, for that matter, psychologically convincing. In practice, while the individual virtues, characterized as a set of intellectual and practical dispositions to typical actions, are internally self-regulating, they are rarely in themselves externally self-regulating. When the action claims of various virtues compete, individual virtues do not themselves determine the appropriate balance. Kindness is self-regulating in situations in which no other virtues compete with its action-claims: kindness would not kill with kindness. But what is it about kindness that checks its exercise when it competes with the requirement of truthfulness? The claim that the requirements of kindness and those of truthfulness must in the end always coincide has all the air of denying the phenomena to save the theory.

3. The most familiar and the most thoroughly explored solution is the *master virtue* solution. Since definitions of the various individual virtues do not by themselves give rules for determining their appropriate relative priority, an independent external condition, a regulative master virtue such as *phronēsis* or *caritas* or Kantian good will—virtues that unite the practical and intellectual traits required to determine the priority and balance among the several virtues—seems also to be necessary. Since the master virtue solution has been developed in some detail, we should look at some of its most refined presentations.

It was because he thought that wisdom provides the necessary and sufficient condition for the development and the proper exercise of the various virtues that Socrates argued for the unity of the virtues in knowledge. The traditional virtues fail to qualify as *virtues* without knowledge; indeed, properly understood, virtue *is* knowledge. To defend this intellectualist account of virtue, Socrates had to introduce nonintellectualist conditions on wisdom: the wise must not only apply what they know in argument and discussion, but also in the minutiae of action and practice.[6] Notoriously, the Socratic condition is circular: the various traits that assure wisdom are both intellectual and practical. The wise are both good and clever: besides giving each dialectical inquirer the *logos* appropriate to his understanding, they must also act from that understanding. None but the wise are virtuous; yet none but the virtuous qualify as wise. A good formula, perhaps also informative, but not really helpful for those of us who do not yet know how to become either wise or good.

It was because he thought that the proper exercise of presumptively virtuous traits requires both cognitive and character dispositions—well-formed, discriminating habits directed to good ends, appropriately understood—that Aristotle has been interpreted as having located the master virtue in *phronēsis*. Since the internal self-regulation assured by locating each of the virtues in a mean defined by *logos* does not automatically assure the appropriate exercise of *that* virtue in relation to all others, all things considered, something else—*phronēsis*—is needed. But *phronēsis* is an umbrella term for a wide range of independent traits that enable a person to see and to actualize the goods that can best be realized in extremely varied, particular contexts. While Aristotle avoids some of the problems of the Socratic solution, he only postpones others. Since *phronēsis* combines a range of independent intellectual and character traits—ingenuity, insight, perceptual sensitivity, acuity in inference, a sound sense of relevance, an active understanding of the relative importance of heterogeneous and sometimes incommensurable ends, allocating different priorities to the various components of *phronēsis* could sometimes lead to different action outcomes. A *phronimos* whose ingenuity is more acute than his sense of relevance might form different actions from those performed by a *phronimos* whose acuity of inference dominated his insight. How does *phronēsis* assure that the individual virtues—including those that compose and constitute it—are appropriately exercised, in the right way, at the right time? *Phronēsis* includes a range of well-formed, well-balanced traits.

It was because he thought that only a good will could assure that the various virtues would be rightly exercised, that Kant held that the only thing good in itself, without qualification, is a good will, that is, an autonomous, rational will. Kant hoped to avoid Aristotle's difficulties in determining the priority among the various traits that compose *phronēsis* by showing the unity of the rational good will. While in principle the conditions that assure the will's freedom can be distinguished from those that assure its goodness, Kant attempts to secure the autonomy of the will by identifying its operations with those of practical rationality. Because the will *is* reason in its practical employment, it is self-legislative, free of external determination when it conforms to the requirements of rationality. And since rationality requires self-legislated impartiality, practical reason assures both the freedom and the goodness of the will. Because Kant proposed to give an analysis of the conditions that make morality possible, he was concerned to locate the unconditioned origin of action, the absolute locus of responsibility. While his preoccupations were quite different from those of Socrates, his solution to the problem of assuring the virtues is nevertheless a variant of the Socratic solution. Kant's claim that the commands of practical rationality *are* the claims of morality is parallel to Socrates' identification of knowledge with virtue. The analogue of the Socratic solution inherits an analogue to the Socratic problem: as Kant himself was the first to acknowledge, the condition that assures morality is judicial rather than generative. Acting from a good will requires testing the rationality, the universalizability, of maxims of action; but practical rationality neither develops the motives nor discovers the appropriate empirical maxims for any given action. While a good will assures the possibility of acting purely from a conception of the moral law, it does not by itself determine actions or, for that matter, empirical motives.

Both Socrates and Kant must perforce include the individual virtues within virtue. As the Socratically wise are also necessarily temperate, courageous, and just, so too Kant's person of good will must, in all consistency, command himself to possess the individual virtues. In doing his duty for its own sake, the moral agent does what each duty rationally commands. Consistent rationality recognizes that in order for moral intentions to issue in well-formed actions, the will must be supported by the virtues. Since Kantian morality commands the acquisition of the several virtues, Aristotle's problems reappear within the Kantian frame: something like *phronēsis* is required to assure the appropriate connection between the purity of the moral intention and the appropriateness of a particular action.

It is because she hopes to combine the advantages of Aristotle's complex psychology with Kant's strict account of responsibility that Philippa Foot distinguishes the virtues from other practical dispositions and skills: they are, she says, controlled by the will, directed toward what is good. With a keen understanding of the ways in which psychological and intellectual attitudes are ingredient in virtues, she recognizes a wide range of civic and character virtues (tact and generosity, for example). Although she has a latitudinarian understanding of the will that extends to "what is wished for as well as what is sought," she nevertheless makes a "good will" a necessary condition for moral virtue, in contrast to morally neutral practical skills and habits. [7]

But the virtuous can't assure the appropriate use of their traits by willing good ends. A villain and a good citizen can, and often do, will the same ends. To begin with, they have the same species-defined ends: they are constituted so as to have at least some of the same central needs and desires whose satisfaction constitute thriving. Besides the necessities and comforts of life, they want esteem and friendship, and want their friends and families to thrive. The virtuous and the vicious can be ambitious for fame, respect, and fortune; they can even sometimes have virtually identical intentional descriptions of their general aims; and both can be prudently courageous in pursuing their ambitions. Nor is the difference that the good citizen is reliable while the cad is not: they can both be counted on to behave in character. Sometimes it is just their *petites habitudes*—the configuration of their ends and traits, the *way* they are courageous, prudent, tactful in pursuit of their common ends— that differentiate the cad and the good citizen.

Other candidates for the master virtue—*caritas* or justice, for example—fare no better. Although each of the familiar versions of the master-virtue solution encounters somewhat different difficulties, we can generalize: there are roughly three major problems with all the candidates for that solution. There is, first, the problem of selecting among the serious candidates for the master virtue, particularly since each can, in principle, command different patterns of dominance and recessiveness among the various virtues. When there is uncertainty and conflict in action, *phronēsis* might well form different priorities from those proposed by *caritas*, envisaged by magnanimity, commanded by the good will, or assured by justice. Is there a master master virtue?

Second, there is the problem of downward regression: If the master virtue is to be action-guiding in particular, variable, contingency-ridden contexts, it does not act from, nor is it characterizable by, a set of rules. But then just how does the master virtue regulate or check competing first-level virtues? How does it fuse intellectual and practical traits to guide its determinations? Just identifying the will as reason in its practical application does not help us understand how that identity works, particularly if the will could in principle fail to affirm what rationality commands. Even if there are some very general principles that define *right* or *good*, what determines the appropriate application of these principles through the contingencies and vagaries of particular situations?

Third, there is the problem of upward regression, of determining the appropriate balance among the component dispositions that themselves constitute the master virtue. *Phronēsis*—or good sense, magnanimity, *caritas*, or justice—is composed of a complex set of skills, capacities, traits. The primary candidates for the master virtue involve an appropriate level of acuteness and precision in perception, the ability to focus—and stay focused—on what is important, despite irrelevant attractions; impartiality; a capacity to form well-structured, valid inferences; ingenuity and tact; the open-minded traits required for corrigibility combined with firmness of purpose. Because the master virtue itself encompasses a wide variety of potentially counterpoised intellectual and character traits required to coordinate first-order virtues, all the problems about the appropriate coordination of virtue-assuring dispositions reappear. The regulative intellectual and character virtues also function as first-level action-forming traits; and first-order virtues— tact or ironic detachment—can sometimes also function as regulative master master virtues. The distinction between first- and second-order virtues appears to be a context-dependent difference in functional role rather than a distinction between types of traits.

Indeed, it seems as if the master virtue is not one trait, not even one way of appropriately coordinating capacities, dispositions, traits: it is nothing in particular, over and above having a well-constructed character that tends to act well and appropriately. If excellence of character is assured by anything, it is assured by an appropriate configuration of traits rather than by a single trait or by a conjunction of traits. But since each situation requires a slightly different configuration of traits to produce an appropriate action, and since different people might require different configurations in different situations, the appropriate configuration of virtue-assuring traits cannot be specified.

The difficulties with the master-virtue solution suggest another, less familiar solution to the problem of assuring the virtues.

4. The next solution might be described as a checks-and-balances solution, for it locates the virtues in a system of supportive and tensed traits. This solution proposes that a set of traits qualifies as a virtue only when it is supported and balanced against other traits in an appropriate pattern or configuration. The traits that constitute the virtues hunt in role-differentiated packs, not only requiring one another to determine particular actions, but also, darkly and significantly, to modify, to check and balance one another's exercise. Long after moral philosophers abandoned Socratic theories of the unity of the virtues, they still retained the Platonic assumption that the various virtues form a harmonious system directed to the same general ends. However differentiated in function, the virtues were assumed either to coincide in forming the same extensionally identified action or—more frequently—typically to coordinate and support one another's exercise and action-outcomes.

By contrast, the checks-and-balances solution does not assume that the virtues form a mutually supportive, harmonious system directed toward realizing compatible ends. On the contrary, according to this solution at least some of the virtues are assured because their typical cognitions and actions are dynamically opposed to one another.[8]

Virtues can check one another in a number of different ways. (1) They constrain each other when their cognitive components are contraries. (The cognitive set of a particular devoted commitment can, for instance, sometimes be contrary to that of impartiality.) (2) Virtues can check each other when the traits that compose them are typically exercised in actions whose outcomes standardly undermine or frustrate one another's intention, direction, or satisfaction. (The habits of trust are, for instance, tensed against those of caution, consensual sociability against strong independence.) (3) The development of one virtue can typically inhibit the development of another. (Meticulously rule-respecting traits tend to block those of playful or improvisatory resourcefulness.) (4) The exercise of one set of traits can produce conditions that require the exercise of an opposed set. (The combative soldierly virtues that sometimes bring peace can endanger the fragile trust on which the preservation of peace depends.)

It is of course not possible to give a general rule or principle to determine the proper measure of any particular balance among tensed or opposed virtues. Sometimes one virtue might appropriately suppress another; sometimes two virtues combine to modulate or diminish one another's force; sometimes one virtue appears recessively within the action determined by another, modifying the way the dominant virtue is expressed, hesitantly or ambivalently, as a compassionate manner can modify the harshness of strict justice. The whole range of cognitive and habitual combinatorial properties of traits are brought into play.

Unfortunately, despite the advantages of its dark and rare truthfulness, the checks-and-balances solution seems as regressive as the master-virtue solution and nearly, but not quite, as uninformative as the contextualizing solution. Since there is no general rule or principle to determine it, what assures the *appropriate* balance in each situation? To make matters worse, there are competing criteria for what qualifies as a well-ordered appropriate configuration, each criterion expressing a different weighting for the various virtues. It seems that the difficulties of the checks-and-balances solution force us back to the master virtue in order to evaluate competing criteria for appropriate balance. But that solution in turn requires a system of checks and balances among the various components of the master virtue. Some circles are expansive and illuminating; this one seems small and frustrating.

While there are undeniably problems for the checks-and-balances solution, I believe that it nevertheless presents an advance over the other solutions. For one thing, it is psychologically truthful; for another, it presents some rudimentary heuristic guidance for maintaining the virtue of their virtues by locating them in a logical and psychologically dynamic field.

But here we are, once again, very close to where we started. Nothing in particular seems to assure virtue . . . nothing less than the whole of a virtuous character, well formed in a system of checks and balances, so as to assure its proper activity, acting appropriately as the situation requires, that is, acting virtuously. Where can we go from nowhere?

III. Community as the Context of Character

No action without interaction; no interaction without politics.

But perhaps our somber reflections are premature. Perhaps we've been looking at the wrong place. Virtue is, after all, primarily and fundamentally an attribute of persons rather than of actions or sets of traits. It is the man, Aristotle remarks, who is the source of action: the regression of traits that assures the appropriate balance of the virtues stops at the *person*, the total configuration of character, rather than at a master regulatory virtue or principle.[9] But if the man is the source of action, we need to understand what forms the man, what conduces to his being the sort of person who is capable of virtue. According to Aristotle, a certain sort of psychophysical constitution is required, as well as appropriate economic and sociopolitical conditions and the good fortune of a person's early models. The assurance of a person's virtues cannot occur in a social or political vacuum.

Action takes place in a social world. It is, in the end, our social and political relation to others that keeps our virtues in whatever precariously appropriate balance they have. Minimally, the cooperation and esteem we require from our fellows elicit the appropriate balance among supporting and opposing virtues. Significantly, our actions have their sense, their meaning, and their directions in a public, interactive world. This is not just a consequence of the fact that political institutions shape our attitudes and social structures form our views, although that is of course true. Nor is it solely a consequence of the fact that our actions often so change our social and political circumstances that they in turn require us to change, although that is of course also true. In addition, we are formed by a cultural ideal of mutual respect that requires our holding ourselves responsible for giving—or at any rate for having—a socially oriented justification for the principles that guide our actions.

More to the point of the assurance of the virtues, our actions are dramatically and substantively formed by our minute interactions with others. The details of most of our actions are determined through a subtle process of interaction. Think of the way in which a conversation, a real conversation, a common investigation rather than a comforting ritual or an exchange of monologues, takes place. In a real conversation the participants do not know, ahead of time, what they will say, or even sometimes what they think. To be sure, there are constraints: interlocutors want (among many other things) to arrive at what is true, and they are guided by what they presently believe is true.[10] But at any moment in the conversation there are an indefinite number of relevant, consecutive true things they could say and think. Closure is given by the minutiae of interactions: the look of puzzlement on an interlocutor's face, the excitement of common pursuit, an ironic remark. The more subtly partners in a conversation understand each other—the more they are familiar with one another's gestures, facial expressions, and reactions—the more condensed and improvisatory their conversation is likely to be. Like improvisatory jazz musicians, they sometimes lapse into a familiar riff for a little rest, finding something in that riff which will lead them in a new direction. It is not only conversations and music-making, but many of our central actions—designing a curriculum or a playground, teaching a seminar, choosing a restaurant or planning a meal, selecting a Supreme Court justice, hanging paintings for an exhibition—take this form. Even when we act in solitude or in character, from our deeply entrenched traits, the actions we perform emerge from an interactive process that sometimes takes place *in foro interno*, with familiar and usually idealized figures. Some of our interactive partners elicit our (very own) boldness, others elicit our (very own) caution. The configuration of a person's traits—the patterns of dominance and recessiveness—that emerges in any given situation is affected by her interactive company.[11]

We characteristically respond to a skeptical interlocutor in one way, to a confirming interlocutor in another, to a coexplorer in yet another. The views we form as a result of our common investigations—views that each interlocutor genuinely holds as her own—are, in their fine-grain details, coproduced, even when the interlocutors end with markedly different views.[12] As with views, so with the balanced pattern of our virtues. Character, in all its constitutional and sociopolitical configuration, regulates the particular virtues; and community regulates character. It is these that, taken together, hold the virtues in check. But then it is these that, taken together, can also lead to folly and vice.

Obviously, the interactive context of the formation of action cannot assure virtue, cannot determine the appropriate configuration of our typically virtuous traits. Even a virtuoso among the virtuous is sometimes corrupted rather than supported by the company he keeps. Nevertheless, once we know the patterns of our interactions, we can—bearing in mind our patterns of contrariness—strengthen an appropriate configuration of traits by being careful of the company we keep. But since we can also voluntarily erode what we take to be a relatively virtuous configuration, all the problems of assuring the virtues are again postponed. What determines the company we choose to keep? Have we returned to *phronēsis* and its cohort? Or to a checked-and-balanced cycle of dominance and recessiveness in the configuration of traits, this time extended to the company to which we gravitate, a characteristic cycle of high-minded and low-life company, or of solitude and random sociability? More soberly, does the interactive social determination of the checks and balances of the virtues throw us into the power politics of the control of the virtues? Aren't we playthings of the moral luck of our political and social situations, the luck of the draw of our interactive community? After all, we are subject to the power of charisma and of interest groups all contending to define the dominance and recessiveness of their prime candidates for our virtues: there is no assurance that the outcome of such struggles issues in an appropriate balance.

It is indeed just for this reason that some moral philosophers attempted to replace theories of virtue with theories of rules and principles. Complex, pluralistic, and dynamic societies with genuinely opposed needs, values, and interests are likely to have competing models of virtue. Acknowledging the motto "No virtues without virtue," they add: "No virtue without rules and principles." Sometimes, when such societies recognize that they require a variety of opposed models, they succeed in formulating general procedural rules and principles to adjudicate among the claims of competing models by placing them in a system of checks and balances. But there is no guarantee that there will be agreement on such procedural principles: when there are competing models for the proper balance of the virtues, there is also usually disagreement about principles, including those procedural principles regulating the adjudication of disagreement.[13] Attempts to find an overlapping consensus on rules for arbitrating disagreements introduces procedural justice as the master virtue. A set of principles governing procedures for adjudicating disagreements appears to have the special advantages of being self-referentially capable of arbitrating competing claims about its own formulation. But the self-referential closure of procedural rules and principles is broken when there are competing claims about their priority and formulation, particularly when differences in formulation and priority among procedural principles would issue in distinctive policies and actions. Such disagreements about priorities among procedural principles are most dramatic when they focus on issues that effectively define the boundaries of community membership, especially when that membership entitles or excludes access to respect, political participation, to rights and privileges. Although it seems initially to bypass the familiar problems of virtue theories, the attempt to provide procedural rules and principles for resolving conflicts has all the advantages and disadvantages of other versions of the master-virtue solution. The problems we've found for the virtues reappear in any complex, viable ethics of principle. Like virtues, principles hunt in packs; like virtues, they can—and probably usefully do—conflict with one another; like candidates for the master virtue, candidates for a master principle suffer problems of upward and downward regression. A system of checks and balances seems required; but its proper self-regulation cannot be assured.

It seems that we have, despite everything, returned full circle to the somber answers to our original questions. Traits are called virtues when they are culturally regarded as admirable or beneficial, when there is social pressure to develop and exercise them. When—as is normally the case in complex and dynamic societies—there are competing and sometimes conflicting models of benefit and admirability, we can attempt to find or form a consensus on procedural principles of justice, or develop a solidly operating dynamic system of checks and balances among the contending models of virtue. Nothing can assure that competing models of virtue in a polity will be appropriately balanced, rather than merely determined by the accidental play of power politics. We can try to characterize the master virtue and the particular system of checks and balances among the virtues that, given existing conditions and dominant motivational structures, are most likely to assure the appropriate exercise of the various virtues. The proposal to make procedural justice the master virtue is just such an attempt.

But sometimes there just *is* no appropriate way to assure the balance among virtues. At worst, the emergent balance is determined by the power of charisma and the power of interest groups. With luck, the distribution of power is so structured as to produce a cycle rotating the benefits of each model of virtue. But there is no guarantee that the cycles of fortune—the cycles that replace criteria for appropriate checks and balances—will bring some period of flourishing to each type of life.

All along we've been talking about the *appropriate* exercise of the virtues. Isn't that what ethics is supposed to be about, to define *appropriateness?* Indeed, it is just these dark conclusions—and the recognition that practicable ethical theories presuppose criteria for appropriateness (good, right, value)—that have led many moral theorists to elect to do programmatically normative moral theory, arguing that before we can direct operative psychological processes for assuring the appropriate balance of the virtues, we must determine the most general conditions of appropriateness. But there is no escape. Unfortunately, the constraints fixed by social and psychological processes—the lawlike effects of various relations of power, for instance—are directly relevant to defining criteria for appropriateness. The constraints of applicability—of psychological and political realizability—appear within the definition of what is appropriate. The difficulties of defining the appropriate balance among competing virtues reappear as difficulties in arbitrating among competing normative moral theories. The joys of constructing normative theories—they are great joys of course—are those of science fiction. Absolutely normative theories wear their poverty of their willful faces. The richness of such writing—and its utility—in part depends on the psychological and political constraints it accepts. Its power in part depends on its playfulness, and its visionary indignation. But here we are back again to a system of checks of checks and balances, this time a system of checks and balances among the virtues of moral theorists.

Reconstructivist moral philosophers who propose to assure virtue by offering either rules for, or an imitable model of, acting well must bracket the contingencies that affect moral luck: the luck of a person's constitutional and intellectual traits; the luck of having appropriate formative models to imitate; the luck of living in historical, economic, and sociopolitical conditions that are consonant with one's own dispositional directions; the luck of good company. But it is just the strength of practical, descriptively oriented theories of virtue that they acknowledge the pervasive presence of moral luck. The virtues are, among other things, the range of skills that enable a person to cope with luck, to deal with the contingencies and vagaries of the particular situations.

It seems we end where we began, recognizing that although there is much to be said about the details of the appropriate balance of checked and opposed traits, there is nothing in particular that assures virtue in general. Another, equally sober, reflection emerges from our investigation. Even action-guiding practical theories cannot—and indeed should not—provide moral solutions where virtuous moral agents have moral problems. The more practical an ethical theory, the more it reflects the sorts of difficulties that virtuous agents have, and the more clearly it locates and explains our failures. Ethical theories designed to be practical and action-guiding cannot reasonably be expected to provide salvation where none is to be had.[14]

17   Imagination and Power

Like freedom, power is most acutely perceived by those who lack it.

One man has another in his power when he holds him in bonds; when he has disarmed him and deprived him of the means of self-defense or escape; when he has inspired him with fear; or when he has bound him so closely by a service that he would rather please his benefactor than himself, and rather be guided by his benefactor's judgment than by his own. The man who has another in his power in the first or second way holds his body only, not his mind; whereas he who controls another in the third or fourth way has made the mind as well as the body of the other subject; but only while the fear or hope remain.

Spinoza, Tractatus-Politicus

"Power," Hobbes says, "is a person's means to obtain some apparent good." He goes on to distinguish natural powers (strength, prudence, eloquence, intelligence) from instrumental powers (wealth, reputation, friends), which can be acquired by natural powers, and then, as he says, invested to acquire yet more power. Each person inevitably tries to increase his power, not simply for the sake of having it, but because power, and more significantly, marginal power over others in competition for scarce goods, is necessary to assure the satisfaction of desires. "Because [we] cannot assure the power and means to live well . . . without the acquisition of more, . . . there is," he adds, "in all mankind, a perpetual and restless desire of power after power, that ceaseth only in death. . . ."

Shelley claims the poets as the unacknowledged legislators of the world; it is they, he intimates, who have the ultimate power, they who have the fullest rule. And Milton was acclaimed as a more powerful moralist than Aquinas.

I propose to show how, if we follow the logic of Hobbes's view, we shall be brought to that of Shelley, to see that if there is such a thing as power (and I doubt there is), it consists in the various capacities that are exercised by the imagination. If this is true, then to control someone is to control his imagination. But we must show, step by step, how this transition takes place. We follow the argument Hegel develops in his discussion of the relations between the Master and the Slave, in *The Phenomenology of the Spirit*.

There are four important and contentious implications of Hobbes's definition. (1) It follows from his view that it is always to someone's interest to have power, and to have as much of it as possible. (2) He is talking about power as the means, the capacities to assure an apparent good, which he defines as the object of a person's desire. Nothing is said about forms of satisfaction and dissatisfaction that might correct a person's desires. In Hobbes's view, if a person realizes what he takes to be his desires, and yet is still dissatisfied, it is because he has made a mistake about the properties of the objects meant to satisfy them. That he is dissatisfied, does not show a limitation on his power, but on his knowledge. Of course knowledge is a form of power: but the kind of knowledge that is included within natural knowledge is knowledge of how to get what one takes oneself to want; it is not yet a critique of one's wants, not knowledge of how to stop wanting what might be harmful. Hobbes's assumption is that people normally cease wanting what they believe to be bad, except as it may bring them what they take to be a greater good. It was the brunt of Plato's argument in *The Republic* that contentions 1 and 2 are at odds, that is, that if power is always desirable, then it is directed to real and not merely to apparent goods; but if it is directed to apparent goods, then it is not always desirable. Knowledge is a form of power in Plato's view only if it includes knowledge of what is worth desiring, as well as knowledge of what desires are nominally and normally satisfiable. (3) In Hobbes's view we cannot avoid the quest for power by limiting our desires. One might have thought that one way of avoiding the unending search for power, would be to have radically few desires. Hobbes closes the Stoic alternative: that road is not open to us because every chance satisfactory experience creates a desire for its repetition or enhancement.

Finally, (4) it follows from Hobbes' view that power is always relational: it is exercised in a field of counterforces and attributed against the background of expectations about the normal course of events in the absence of intervention. The intervening cause—the cause to which power is attributed—could not make its distinctive, differentiating contribution without the background of standard operating causes, which remain unmarked because they are presumed to be constant. In a political system as in physics, the attribution of power to an individual or group is elliptical for an analysis of a specific comparison in a specific context. The claim that X has power is a claim that X has marginal power in comparison to Y (or over Y) to do Z, at time t, in a situation where M, N, and O, are also contributory causes. If X has marginal power over Y to do A at t, nothing follows about whether X will have power to do A at $t + 1$, with a different set of contributory causes; nor does anything follow about whether X has power in relation to W to do A at t, or power over Y to do B at t. Even when the issue of a power relation is that of structuring situations in such a way as to increase the probability that desires will be satisfied, marginal power is always specific, relative to a particular aim in a particular situation.

Our situation being what it is—a situation of natural scarcity—we are in direct competition with one another for goods. More interesting than the fact of competition is the fact of dependency. Let us suppose that someone, let's call him the Boss, follows Hobbes's story: he endeavors to secure power. Now what does this mean and how does he do it? By strength or by wit, he tries to control the course of events so as to assure that he gets what he wants. The means he tries to control are, as Hobbes says, wealth or status, legal, religious, or military sanctions—whatever in that particular society or context will provide what he desires. Since we live where we do, let's take money and status as examples of this sort of instrumental power.

Hobbes himself thought all power resides initially in individuals, and secondarily through the social contract, in the Sovereign who is then empowered to delegate some of his power to institutions over which he still retains control. But one can be a Hobbesian in the analysis of power, and accord independent power to classes or institutions as well as to individuals and the Sovereign. The Boss could be an individual, an economic or social class, an institution, an employer, part of the complex self, a nation. Although some of the details will differ in the various applications, the analysis is quite general.

The exercise of instrumental power characteristically requires either the cooperation or the compliance of others in order to be used successfully in exchange for whatever goods the Boss wants. Someone must be willing to exchange goods for money; others must acknowledge status and be willing to grant it privilege and service. Let us call those who accept or acknowledge the Boss's power the Subjects.

The power of the Boss depends on his relation to the Subject, whose services he must compel, coerce, or secure by compliant cooperation.

If the Subjects refuse to acknowledge the wealth or status of the Boss, services can rarely be coerced. Hegel himself suggests that it is the Subject's acknowledgement of the Boss that initiates the relationship. In principle, of course, the Boss can effect compliance by the extremity of killing or maiming some representative Subjects, or by so limiting the means to survival that the Subject has no viable options. But there are internal constraints on the Boss's exercise of power, constraints set by the Boss's own interests. The dead, the maimed, and the starved are of little use except as examples. Even then, others must take themselves to be threatened by those examples. The Boss's coercion generally works through the Subject's fear of harm rather than through the actual exercise of deprivation. The threat of danger is more powerful than the exercise of that threat: once used, coercive power is diminished. In any case, if the Subjects gathered to resist or oppose the Boss, the Boss's resources have to be reallocated to force or coerce their efforts. This is usually an inefficient way of assuring the labor and services to actualize the Boss's ends. This is one reason that the Boss tries to disperse the Subjects, disorganizing them in order to prevent effective opposition, and to promote and feed the sort of fear that isolation and deprivation bring.

Of course Bosses do go amok, and act against their own interests, having become addicted to the exercise of power for its own sake, rather than for the satisfaction of desires. This is a problem that Hobbes did not face straightforwardly: he and his modern counterparts, rational decision theorists, concentrate on rational self-interest without considering the varieties of waywardness that stand in the way of the rational promotion of interests, except as these affect the probabilities of various rational alternatives. Perhaps he did not consider forms of insane power because going berserk is not a privilege of the Sovereign or Boss: anyone can do it. Indeed the power of destruction is more readily available to the Subject who has little to lose. When he regards his desires as unsatisfiable, he can at least have the pleasure of seeing the Alexandrian Library burn or New York's water supply poisoned. On a Hobbesian view, the power of the insane falls outside the structure of power relations: anyone who has access to this sort of power—and these days that is anyone—has this sort of power. Bosses and Subjects alike are subject to the power of the maniac who will not, or cannot, act on his own behalf. But another reason that Hobbes does not seriously consider the power of those who are simply intent on destruction is that such energies are not, by his definition, genuine exercises of power. They are not directed to the satisfaction of desires, but are rather expressions of the frustration of desires, signs of powerlessness rather than of power.

A more serious limitation of Hobbesian analysis, one that we shall also temporarily set aside, is that he does not consider the ways in which people become attached to habits that are pleasurable or satisfying simply because they are easy and familiar, even when they no longer satisfy desires. Hobbes was certainly aware of the momentum of desires. But he considered only one form of that momentum, the multiplication and replacement of desires. He did not consider that certain desires and the forms of thought associated with them might become habitual in ways that motivate independently of satisfaction. So, for instance, people might pursue power for its own sake, and not because it is a means to satisfying other desires. On Hobbes's view the power of the Boss would be directed to satisfying the Boss's desires; and that fact would provide certain rational constraints on its exercise. But when having power can come to be an independent satisfaction and desire, the rational constraints that Hobbes considered cannot be weighed as simply as he proposes. On his view when such power is not used to serve interest, when it is merely exercised rather than used, it is no longer strictly speaking *power*. We shall return to this problem when we sketch the place of the imagination in defining needs.

But now let us consider how the Boss can most effectively satisfy his desires, assuring the cooperation of the Subjects by limiting options, effecting cooperation without enforcing coercion. While fear can be sometimes effective to assure compliance in the last resort, it is not effective in the middle resort, especially when the Boss requires skilled tasks involving improvisation, initiative, and inventiveness.

A somewhat more efficient way of limiting the Subject's options is to make him easily replaceable, an advantage said to accrue to owning slaves or controlling an empire. But limiting the Subject's options or creating conditions that make Subjects replaceable can often direct the Boss's natural and instrumental powers inefficiently in ways that do not directly satisfy his desires. The Boss's own options characteristically become limited by the project of assuring that Subjects are easily replaceable. What was originally a project of building an empire to satisfy desires becomes a crippling yoke. Often such costs are difficult to discern: nevertheless, the hidden costs of assuring the services of Subjects often quite outweigh the benefits that were initially presumed to be gained by the power relation.

But of course even if the Boss controls the situation in ways that really allow the Subject no option save to render service, he does not necessarily secure the advantages of that service. In some cases, it might even be more rational for the Boss to secure his own desires than to assure cooperation of potentially dissatisfied Subjects, whose control over the Boss's projects in principle give them enormous potential power. Unfortunately, such countercontrol does not generally enlarge the options of the Subject: generally, his manipulation of the Boss reinstates, if not actually reinforces the terms of the original relation. A servant class can dominate, control, and subvert the interests of presumed Bosses (the British servant classes, the servant in Roman comedy, subservient wives to domineering husbands, sometimes a bureaucracy to a dictator). Even when the Boss has limited the Subject's options, the Subject who recognizes his situation can effectively rule the Boss to control his satisfactions. There is no point in having money to buy shoes if the cobbler is unwilling to make or sell them, or consistently makes shoes that leak in the first rain. No point in having the trappings of Pooh Bah if the insignia of majesty are treated as a clown costume.

The most efficient way for the Boss to secure the cooperative compliance of the Subject is to bring it about that the Subject wants to supply the labor or the goods that the Boss desires. One way of doing this is to make it objectively to the Subject's interest to do so, and to make that knowledge of the objective gains available. If the Boss takes this road, he is no longer simply the Boss: the relation is transformed into a partnership, a trade relation between two agents mutually satisfying one another's wants. We shall return to this relation later. Often, however, the Boss does not believe that it is to his interest to make the relation really benefit the Subjects. So he attempts to secure cooperative compliance by causing the Subject to believe, as it happens falsely, that he will benefit from the relation. This can be an extremely efficient way for the Boss to secure the cooperative compliance of the Subject. But there are two important constraints on this method. One is that even if the Subject is unable to diagnose the cause of his discomfort, his feebleness, his misery, still his services may not be useful to the Boss if his real interests are too grossly violated by the relation. (But this may depend on the sort of work that the Subject performs. There are many tasks where the Subject's psychological, and even to some extent, physical health, are indifferent to the satisfactions of the Boss.) Perhaps the more important constraint is that a good deal of the Boss's energy and power needs to be expended in the complex processes of successful brainwashing. The problem of efficiency arises again. If the Subject is marginally aware that he has been manipulated, then even if he has no clear diagnosis of preferable options, he is in a position to control and undermine the Boss. On the other hand, if the Boss really succeeds in controlling the Subjects' wants, there is the danger that the Boss may be taken in by his own cunning, and thus put himself in the position of eventually being forced to render the services that he has falsely promised.

These sorts of situations reveal the strong latent power of the Subject. As Hegel showed, the power relation between the Boss and the Subject is not one-directional.

Every power carries a hidden powerlessness, that of being dependent on cooperation. Every powerlessness carries a hidden power, that of withholding cooperation. Sullenness, silence, ridicule, and destruction are the Subject's hidden power. Since powerlessness is a function of desire, the powerless can, in principle and within severe limits, overcome their powerlessness by detaching themselves from their desires. But the Subject can only realize his hidden powers if he has insight, if he is imaginatively and intellectually enabled. The true latent power of the Boss is therefore that of forming the mentality of his Subjects, his being in a position to control their capacity to recognize their situation and the possibilities it holds.

Let us call a power relation malign (1) if it is asymmetrical, so that the Boss on the whole gains more than loses by the relation, and the Subject loses more than he gains within the relation; and (2) if the goods are subject to a zero-sum economy such that the Boss's gains are always made at the cost of the Subject and vice versa; and (3) if the Boss has closed the Subject's options in such a way that the Subject believes (often falsely) that despite his losing more than he gains in the relation, he would lose even more by leaving the relation than by staying in it. Malign power relations can be quite stable as long as no outside forces change the distribution of options available to the Subject. But often the services rendered by the Subject have the incidental consequences of actually increasing his options. (For instance, the centralization of industry that increases efficiency also increases the Subjects' opportunities to organize against the Boss.) In such cases a malign power relation becomes unstable. An inherently unstable relation is one in which the Subject's options are—in relation to those of the Boss—increased by some aspect of his service or productivity. Such changes are often unforeseeable by-products of the intentions of the original relation. But it is not always only the Subject's power that is so increased. Sometimes the Subject's productivity also increases the Boss's power to control the Subject and to do so in indirect, disguised, and more subtle ways. The deception and often self-deception that is involved in making the Subject believe that it is to his interest to serve the Boss may lead to situations in which it is very difficult for either party to assess respective losses and gains. In principle there are constraints on how much the Boss's interests can be secured by deception: it cannot be so great as to undermine the performance of the Subject's services. But this undermining can be very gradual, only marginally increasing. In the case of ongoing institutions, the damages of the relation—and what is required to maintain it—may not be realized for a very long time. Often the deceptions practiced by the Boss will prevent his own calculations of his interests. In the case of relations between individuals, it may, of course, never be realized.

It is of course possible for two parties to be in a power relation without either of them being responsible for being in that relation, both unable to change it, often both unaware of its structure. Not every Boss is boss of the situation. In fact it is very rare that the Boss has put himself in that situation: often he is not even conscious of his role. Sometimes in nonmalign power relations the Subject may be relatively more empowered than the Boss to change the relation. For instance the Boss may want what he wants more than the Subject fears the consequences of breaking the relation. Then even though the Boss may be getting more out of the relation than the Subject, and be more empowered within the relation, still the Subject is more empowered to shift the relation than the Boss, because although his options are more limited, they are more available to him, given his preferences, than the Boss's larger field of operations and options are available to him, given his preferences. (This leads directly to the Stoic's conception of power: the Stoic reads the equation between power and the satisfaction of desires to argue that the person who has few easily satisfiable desires is empowered by virtue of his freedom. This kind of freedom, and the wholly different sense of power that it brings, is equally available to Subject and to Boss. It falls outside Hobbes's discussion.)

What sorts of events can change the relation between Boss and the Subject? Obviously, first of all, technological changes can satisfy the Boss's desires more efficiently without costly dependence on the Subjects. Changes initiated by the Boss in this way generally leave former Subjects worse off than before, because alternative structures for viable independence do not yet exist. Sometimes exposure to other cultural and social examples can create desires and sometimes open new opinions. In strongly transitional periods it is often difficult to distinguish the Subject from the Boss without a program. Sometimes visionary leaders, poets, and reformers also open possibilities.

Let us look at some crucial patterns in a Subject's liberation from a malign power relation. Let us suppose that the Subject is on the verge of realizing that his losses outweigh his gains and that he can affect the options open to him. After all, options are not just open or closed. They are essentially *seen* to be open or closed, and crucially seen so under particular descriptions, descriptions that can themselves motivate or inhibit action. One crucial way that a Subject moves out of a power relation is to revise his conceptions of his gains and his losses, his sense of his presumed needs.

Of course this is also one of the most efficient ways that the Boss controls the Subject's wants, by controlling the Subject's imagination (that is, directing his conceptions of satisfactions, the terms in which he thinks of his losses and gains). Often the Subject willingly remains in a malign power relation because he cannot conceive doing without the gains that are presented to him in the relation, and because he cannot conceive accepting what he perceives as the losses he would endure by leaving the relation. Company towns control the Subject, not only because the Subjects must spend their earnings at the company store, but because the company provides a complete environment: the Subject cannot envisage living any other way. What one cannot envisage is difficult to choose.

Gains and losses need not of course be conceived merely in crudely utilitarian terms. The losses and gains of intrinsic and incommensurable goods such as dignity, self-respect, love, and integrity can outweigh what are normally taken to be utilitarian considerations. Sometimes— but not always—the realization that one can open or redefine options is itself a benefit. But not every expansion of options is automatically on that account beneficial. Generating costly or improbable options—mere possibilities—can produce a debilitating depression.

How and when is liberation—especially when it is the realization that one can define at least some of one's options—beneficial to the Subject? The answer to that question partly depends on the person of the liberator. Rarely can a Subject whose options have been deeply limited achieve his own liberation, and of course this is especially true when his options have been limited by constraining and directing his capacity to formulate or imagine his alternatives. So whether a liberation is beneficial to a Subject sometimes depends on the ends and the character of the liberator. Whether an intervention is benign often depends on whether the liberator has something to gain by the Subject's new priorities: the liberator can— sometimes all unknowingly—merely become the new Boss. The prognosis is more benign if the liberator does not stand in an immediate power relation to the Subject. But sometimes the liberator's imagination has been as severely constrained as that of the Subject. Unfortunately, the simplest operation of the imagination in defining options is simply to reverse the order of dependency. Such reactive moves are frequently as malign for both parties as the original relation. Even though there is no doubt a temporarily welcome, and importantly rectifying, change of personnel in the halls of power, the gains of each party still are achieved by exacting losses from the other. The terms of the original relation are retained even when the goods are temporarily beneficially redistributed and some new desires are introduced. Sometimes it is possible to transform a power relation to one of mutual trade, where the services are mutually esteemed and reciprocated, both parties realizing their mutual reliance. It is then no longer a power relation between Boss and Subject, but some form of partnership. Standardly such partnerships involve complementarity rather than identity of services exchanged. Standardly even fair partnerships—those that involve mutual and interdependent gains—do not assure equality of gains. Even when both gain, one party gains more than another. Such gains often put one party in a position where he has more control, and can exact more gains at the cost of the other. It requires a great deal of alert good will from both parties to prevent such a partnership from degenerating into power relations.

Now what sorts of traits are desirable in a Subject who wishes to transform a malign power relation? What sorts of traits are desirable for a Boss who wishes to retain that relationship? What sorts of traits are required to maintain stable, mutually beneficial partnerships? It now should be clear that the one power that it is fatal to lack is the imagination. After all, presumably what is wanted is the realization of one's options. Often what holds Subjects in damaging power relations is that they are unable to realize the options that are in principle open to them, or are unable to conceive ways of changing the options that are open to the Boss. It is not power as such, then, that holds Subjects in bondage. Indeed our analysis suggests that there is no such thing as power as such: there are only parties in relative positions of being able to conceive or control conceptions of options. Subjects render services willingly or unwillingly because they believe the gains of doing so are greater than the losses they would incur by not doing so. But gains and losses are so in the eyes of the believer. Characteristically, the options of both the Subject and the Boss are at least in part critically fixed by their beliefs about their needs, about what they must have and what they cannot lose. If this is right, then being empowered critically rests on being in a position to define needs, either one's own or someone else's to serve one's own.

I have been stressing the fact that the Boss can also be imprisoned by his attempts to control the Subject. But of course that does not obviate the asymmetry of the relation between the Boss and the Subject: the Boss commands, as the Subject cannot, the instruments that form the Subject's life by forming his imagination. He can control the media that structure and direct the beliefs and images of alternatives. A Subject can in principle become a countercultural force—a street poet, a cabaret satirist, a religious visionary, a popular musician. But though the power of such forces can be enormous, they are usually both politically and psychologically limited. Politically, they are limited by the control that the Boss has over the cultural market; psychologically, they are limited by the tragically damaging effects of rage and frustration on the powers of imagination. Nevertheless, sometimes the accidents of birth and subculture can nourish a relatively innocent visionary. Usually, however, the voice and ideas of such a visionary take some time to be heard and understood, precisely because he provides genuinely new perspectives on needs. His best hopes lie in following the tactics of those Christians who tried to convert the Byzantine emperors: to try to capture the imagination of the children of the Bosses. But of course success has its own costs. The children of the Bosses are still their fathers' children: their understanding of the visionary message will bear the stamp of their fathers.

The faculty that envisages possibilities, that works them out in detail, that formulates them in such ways as to make them viable and available options is the imagination. It is not one single faculty; its exercise involves many different sorts of skills, many of them acquired through practice and imitation. It involves separating variables, recombining them, defining and redescribing situations, tracing possible consequences, drawing inferences from hypothetical considerations, constructing ramified counterfactual alternatives.

There is a continuum between (1) adding details in preexisting options, filling out a schema, (2) describing the variables that might vary within a relatively indeterminate value system, (3) improvising variations, (4) reconstructing priorities, (5) revising priorities, and (6) completely transforming and transcending values. Developing, improvising, reconstructing, revising, and creating slide subtly into one another. And it is not always possible to determine the function and force of an investigation by its form. Indeed, sometimes the most startling inventions take the form of announced returns, myths of Golden Ages. For dark reasons to which we shall return later—reasons fixed by the deeply conservative character of the species—disguising novelty in the form of archaic myth often prevents mobilizing the defensive resistance that meets presumptuous bold innovators. But the exercise of the imagination also crucially involves those Rube Goldberg constructions with a wealth of visualizable details, so that the person can connect them to himself, to habits he might possibly acquire, so that he not only sees alternatives as possible in principle, but possible for him. Now it becomes clear that in potentially liberating situations, it is important to distinguish fantasy from the imagination. One of the ways of binding a Subject is to entice his imagination to futile exercises, either to envisaging options that he cannot obtain or to seducing his passive fantasy. Unfortunately the constructions of a fantasy cannot be distinguished by their content alone: it is their functional roles that distinguish them. Fantasy takes the forms it does precisely because the person does not treat the envisaged options as genuine action-options. The fantasy is the substitute for the actions, its gratification remains within the act of fantasizing. As we are considering them, however, the constructions of the imagination have a minimum prima facie motivational force. To conceive of an option as genuinely available, rather than merely possible, endows it with a prima facie attraction. That attraction can of course be overridden by many other considerations. To the extent that what is imagined is distant, unfamiliar, it is easily overridden.

Inventing and opening alternatives does not by any means entail choosing those options. Making a choice viable does not by itself make that the best choice. A Subject may discover that his having invented options, redefined his losses and gains, by itself transforms his position in a power relation; it may take him from a malignant power relation to a trade-off partnership. It is sometimes just the exercise of the Subject's liberating imagination that forces the Boss to improve the trade-off in such a way that the Subject may rationally prefer to remain in what is no longer a malign power relation. The same sort of development may occur for the Boss. He can come to realize that even though he gains more than he loses within a specific power relation, he would gain more by redescribing his needs so that he does not require the cooperation of a Subject to satisfy them.

The attempts to control a malign power relation that involve crippling the Subject's imagination or directing it to unprofitable channels carry dangers for the Boss. When the Boss and the Subject are in the same culture, the Boss may suffer from the side effects of the processes that were meant to paralyze the Subject's imagination. Or he may himself come to believe what was meant for the Subjects, while the Subject adopts ruling-class attitudes. The convergent cultural system may be extremely stable—even though it serves no one well—because there is no independent point within the system that provides an assessment of losses and gains. Sometimes this happens cross-generationally: the Boss's children become believing Subjects. Of course, if the Subject's services are primarily menial, crippling the Subject's imagination may be functional for the Boss. But if he requires improvisation, adaptive inventive thinking, such crippling is likely to subvert his own interests.

For instance, a Subject-Wife whose imagination has been controlled may turn out to be incapacitated as a partner, as a wife and mother, damaging her Husband-Boss's real interests. Certainly, controlling the imagination is the most effective way of maintaining malign ascendancy; but it is also the most dangerous because it may keep both parties from realizing their losses, making them unable to move to their real interests. When the Boss's losses are as great as those of the Subject, and when his devices prevent his being able to diagnose his own losses, it is no longer clear that dominant power is always a desirable good.

In fact, by this time it is clear that we have moved from Hobbes to both Plato and Shelley, have realized why poets are the unacknowledged legislators of the world. The move from identifying power as the means to obtaining what a person desires leads directly to seeing that the imagination is among the greatest of these powers, and the control of the imagination gives the greatest control over power.

But who has the greatest power? One might think, as Hobbes did, that it is the Sovereign. As Hobbes described him, the Sovereign is completely autonomous: he not only controls the terms in which his Subjects come to think of their expanded interests, but he has the rational capacities for self-legislation, self-legislation of the most thoroughgoing sort, that forms not only actions, but his thoughts and language, especially those that define losses and gains. But in fact in modern societies, the Sovereign rarely forms his own conceptions of the options open to him and to his society, and rarely forms his own conceptions of his needs and his political interests. In a modern society, the Sovereign's imagination is formed by the same powers as form the imagination of the Subject: the hidden Bosses are the formers of public opinion, the TV script writers, the mass media, the public relations industry. But as long as these people are dependent on others believing them, they too enter into dialectical relation with their publics. The modern rhetorician and demagogue depends on the public for acceptance. He needs opinion polls to tell him what to say, and they often get it wrong. Whoever can make the demagogue appear ridiculous or impoverished or hysterical or vile in the eyes of the Subjects has power over the Boss. This is the point of Meredith's claim that the ultimate and consummate social moral critic is the satirist. To the extent that it is possible for the poets and the ironists, the Shelleys on the one hand and the Charlie Chaplins on the other, to imagine options or to announce that the emperors have no clothes, they are the unacknowledged legislators of the world. There is one important respect in which the poets and satirists differ from industrialists and ad men: even when they want appreciation and fame, they are not in a power relation to their audience. They do not undertake their imaginative activities for the sake of the benefits they get from binding their audience to one rather than to another image of options, to one or another conception of needs, losses, and gains. Naturally poets wish to be honored in their own lifetimes, and in their own countries; and they need to live. But rarely are they in the poetry business for the usual gains. This means that they, unlike some liberating politicians, and unlike all ad men, are not Bosses in a new guise. Even when, like their audiences, they are the children of their time, they are less their Subject's Subjects than the usual Boss.

But if it is all so easy, if malign power relations are rarely beneficial to either party in the long run, the hidden cost of maintaining ascendancy too great, and if all it takes is poetic imagination to envisage options, why do malign power relations remain stable for so long? The answer is dark. We are an odd and ill-constructed species, essentially conservative in our psychological structures. We suffer from our benefits: we learn from experience, and that simple fact has devastating effects on us. Our early experiences form expectations not only of what is real, expectations of what is actual: they also form expectations of what is possible. Our capacities for imagining alternatives are strongly limited by early experiences. Despite the amazingly constructed, intricate, and subtle changes we have invented, we have moved only a few steps at a time. Since we are also a fairly stupid species, this may also be a blessing. We are generally unable to see the long-range consequences and the side effects of our most impassioned improvements. One of the simplest and most basic imaginative permutations is, after all, the move of reversal. We tend to believe that we can improve our lots by reversing one set of details within an unsatisfactory pattern. We focus on what harms us. Unfortunately focusing entails blurring. We leave the consequences of our harms and of our improvements in the background, as if they could remain constant throughout our imaginative reversals. In the end the simplest and most basic moves of the imagination tend to lead us to zigzag repetitive patterns, replacing negative after-images for the originals, and then doubling back to the double negative.

The optimism as well as the pessimism of the argument that moves from Hobbes to Shelley rests on the power of individual action to recognize and in principle to change malign power relations. But the power of individuals—whether they be persons, classes, institutions, or subcultures—inevitably fragments and disperses. It fragments because individuals are compound and complex: their powers are functions of many independent factors, each of which is affected by changes around it. (An individual's social power, for instance, is a function of his family's social standing, his wealth, his intelligence, the vicissitudes of his abilities and opportunities. The power of a university is a function of its wealth, its history, the prestige of its faculty and alumni.) Each of these factors itself operates in a dynamic and unstable field of comparisons, in a system of interactive forces. Furthermore, individuals are themselves identified and partly constituted by sociopolitical structures that constrain and direct interactions. (Universities became independent secular institutions, detached from the religious orders, that originally formed and controlled them, as a result of changes in the distribution of political power.) One of the reasons that power is often invisible is that it is not lodged in any individual person or group, but is exercised through a system of institutions that allocate authority. Because economic systems determine access to goods and services, they profoundly affect the distribution of power, without anyone actually making decisions about that distribution. Social systems determine the legitimacy of voice—the power of women or alien poets to be heard—without anyone in particular being in control of such determination. It is often through such hidden processes, and not through the marginal power of any particular group, that enabling or limiting power is exercised. Because processes of this kind form a culture's conceptions of its own interests—as well as its ability to hear visionary poets—interests tend to be self-perpetuating, difficult to recognize, and even more difficult to change.

But there is a darker reflection still. The structures of power have an astonishing stability. In the large range of constructive imagining of options we turn again and again to archetypal patterns, to the Charismatic Leader, to the Band of the Brotherhood Committee, to the Pure Young Hero, to the Good-Bad Earth Mother. Why are our imaginations of power structures so fixed? It is because we learn from experience; and our most formative experiences of power, and of power relations, are those we have during our prolonged and wholly dependent infancy. While this prolonged infancy makes empathy and psychological complexity possible, it exacts a cost. We are formed not only by what we have learned from experience, but by the ways we learn. As long as we are in complex and often highly benign compliance to those who nurtured and sustained us as infants, we associate security and well-being with dependence on power figures. It is to these beginnings that our imaginations return when we are discomforted, depleted, in need. Even though we eventually chafed at the restrictions of our nurturing figures, even though, if we were lucky, we developed sympathy and autonomy, we still have as part of our expectations our early experiences of childhood where reality meant dependency, being Subject to a Boss. If that relation was a benign one, we are all the more subject to gravitate to reconstructing it when we are troubled; but if it was a malign relation, then we are all the more incapacitated. For then a malign power relation is what we expect of the world. It is what defined normality. And of course if it was malign, then we are crippled in our abilities to envisage alternative structures.

With luck, we might discover some clarity about these constraints and relations. Even when we see that there is no such thing as power that binds us, but only complex and usually dynamic relations of trade-offs, with closed options and hidden routes for redefining options, our clarity does not by itself help develop those capacities of the imagination that transform needs. Utopias, there are none.

Notes

Mind in Action, Action in Context

1. "Reply to Gassendi's 'Objections to the Meditations,' " in *The Philosophical Writings of Descartes*, ed. John Cottingham, Robert Stoothoff, and Donald Murdoch (Cambridge: Cambridge University Press, 1984), 2:246.

2. We are caught in the flypaper of the terminology we have inherited from traditional philosophy of mind. Those of us who are suspicious of an ontology of substances or of minds nevertheless are drawn into talking of mental activities as if they form a natural class; those of us who are suspicious of faculty psychology nevertheless speak of beliefs and desires as if they were distinct kinds of psychological activities. I must ask for a combination of indulgence and care in reading: indulgence to let me use the only available vocabulary at hand, without the cumbersome set of shudder quotes that should distance us from the apparent ontological implications of our inherited vocabulary; care to fill in the equally cumbersome qualifications that must attend the free use of such tainted terms. The context-dependent approach of these essays emphasizes the primacy of the particular and favors description over reconstruction. Its motto is: No cross-contextual exportation without fruitful cross-fertilization. Such an ontologically liberal stance is compatible with context-specific realism, and is hospitable to any entities that do serious explanatory work, on condition that they be contextually subscripted. It countenances explanatory cross-contextual classification and the unification of theories whenever doing so is illuminating. Because its contextualist bent tends to locate problems and issues within the historical contexts in which they originally appeared, it is especially suited to the analysis of social and cultural variations. But at least some fears of relativism should be allayed: once the context of questions and issues is specified, there are facts of the matter that set constraints on permissible classifications.

3. Some perceptual functioning might, for example, be coalesced with such neurological phenomena as reflex actions, while other kinds of perception might be classified with some types of higher thought processes . . . which might themselves be distinguished from other, more primitive types of cognitive activities . . . some of which were classified with . . . etc.

4. See Frederick C. Beiser's *The Fate of Reason* (Cambridge, Mass.: Harvard University Press, 1987) gives an excellent account of part of that history. I

attempt to give a very brief and schematic sketch of other parts of that history in several of the papers included in this book: "Characters, Persons, Selves, and Individuals," "Moralism and the Judicial Model of Practical Reason," "The Two Faces of Courage," "Virtues and Their Vicissitudes."

5. An analogy might be helpful: because maps are constructed for specific purposes (to chart mountain passes, or to facilitate navigation, for example), it is sometimes difficult to identify topographical locations across maps. The system of latitudinal and longitudinal designations serves the purpose for which it was constructed: to permit the identification or projection of geographical locations across maps. That system of coordination is constructed from a perspective that is independent of any particular terrestrial map; but it is nevertheless still a particular perspective, selected to serve a particular function. It cannot, for example, be used to resolve disputes about the relative merits of various definitions of absolute space.

6. The question of whether there are several independent concepts of belief (desire, emotion) or one concept with distinctive criteria for its attribution can safely be left to the delights of theories of theory construction. The answer to that question does not affect us here.

7. *Treatise of Human Nature*, ed. L. A. Selby-Bigge and P. H. Nidditch (Oxford: Oxford University Press, 1978), 385.

8. To be sure, an emphasis on the complex composition of psychological activities that relativizes the distinction between state-defined dispositions and activities appears to generate a regress that must end by postulating something like the basic states of traditional faculty psychology. But an explanatory strategy that begins with discrete determinate states has difficulty accounting for activities whose functional roles are not reducible to those of their component states. The standard advantages and disadvantages of the two explanatory strategies— one that begins with complex activities vs. one that begins with discrete states— are general. They do not present special problems for a contextualized. In any case, the contextualized approach has the advantages of hospitality: it can acknowledge the localized utility of the constructivist approach without being committed to its generalized exportation.

9. Cf. Spinoza, *Ethics*, 2.49S; also W. Lycan, *Consciousness* (Cambridge, Mass.: MIT Press, 1987).

10. In principle, such processes can be reconstructed on a causal model, but because such a model presupposes interactions between determinate entities, it tends to set aside an investigation of the structured rationale of continuous determination of fears, hopes, resentments, indignations. See Tyler Burge, "Intellectual Norms and the Foundations of Mind," *Journal of Philosophy* (1986); Ronald de Sousa, *The Rationality of Emotions* (Cambridge, Mass.: MIT Press, 1987), chap. 7; and Alasdair MacIntyre, "The Intelligibility of Action"; and Rom Harré, "Mind as Social Formation," both in *Rationality, Relativism and the Human Sciences*, ed. J. Margolis, M. Krausz, and R. M. Buridan (Boston: Nijhoff, 1986).

11. To be sure, we are sometimes able to work against the grain. But while sculpting against the grain can produce remarkable, beautiful statues, it also

tends to produce splinters. There is no one more obsessed with eating than dieters, no one more obsessed with power than those with an ideal of humility, no one more obsessed with sexuality than ascetics. Moralists might, of course, admit that such psychological or political redirections have their costs, but argue that the cost is worth paying. And indeed this might sometimes be true. But determining whether a particular direction presents a genuine rather than a notional ideal must respect the particularity and the holism of practice. Powerful as they often are, the attractions of any psychological or political reform cannot be measured abstractly, or independently of the details of its consequences in particular historical contexts.

12. See Stuart Hampshire, "Morality and Conflict," in *Morality and Conflict* (Cambridge, Mass.: Harvard University Press, 1983); Charles Taylor, "The Diversity of Goods," in *Philosophical Papers* (Cambridge, Cambridge University Press, 1982), Vol. 2; Bas van Fraassen, "Values and the Heart's Commands," *Journal of Philosophy* (1973); Michael Walzer, "Political Action: The Problem of Dirty Hands," *Philosophy and Public Affairs* (1973).

13. See Alasdair MacIntyre, *After Virtue* (Notre Dame, Ind.: Notre Dame University Press, 1981).

14. Bernard Williams observed (in *Morality* [New York: Harper and Row, 1972]) that the telling considerations against a determined, consistent psychological egoist are those that demonstrate the poverty rather than the incoherence of such a life.

15. Those who are uncomfortable with Aristotle's elitism fear that it may mark him as an apologist for the mores of his culture rather than as a genuine moral theorist. This methodological discomfort also expresses a political commitment. Nietzsche is often excluded from the canon for similar reasons. Rejections of the political import of his views are expressed as charges against his method.

16. At a time when they were themselves pressed by the necessities of their own work, Françoise Balibar, Rüdiger Bittner, J. Thomas Cook, Owen Flanagan, Brian McLaughlin, Georges Rey, William Ruddick, Ronald de Sousa, Jerry Samet, Michael Slote, Willem deVries, Norma Ware, and Rex Welshon went far beyond the usual offices of friendship in responding to my urgent request for their comments.

Chapter 1: Persons and Personae

1. See Charles Baron, "The Concept of Person in the Law: Defining Human Life," in *Medical, Legal and Ethical Implications*, ed. M. W. Shaw and A. E. Doudera (Ann Arbor, Mich.: AUPHA Press, 1983); and Richard Tur, "The 'Person' in Law," in *Persons and Personality*, ed. Arthur Peacocke and Grant Gillett (Oxford: Basil Blackwell, 1987).

2. See Karl Capek, *War with the Newts* (London: Allen Unwin, 1985); and Peter Singer, *Animal Liberation* (New York: Avon Books, 1977).

3. See H. Kohut, *The Restoration of the Self* (New York: International Universities Press, 1977).

4. See Jerome Bruner, *Actual Minds, Possible Worlds* (Cambridge: Harvard University Press, 1986).

5. See Thomas Nagel, *The View from Nowhere* (New York: Oxford University Press, 1986).

6. I am grateful to Christopher Gill, Adam Morton, and other participants in a conference held at Aberystwyth in June 1985. The title of this essay derives from a chapter in Dorothy Emmet's *Rules, Roles and Relations* (New York: Macmillan, 1966).

Chapter 2: The Transformations of Persons

1. See B. A. O. Williams, "Personal Identity and Individuation," *Proceedings of the Aristotelian Society* 57 (1956–57), and "Are Persons Bodies?" in *The Philosophy of Body*, ed. Stuart Spiker (Chicago, 1970); A. J. Ayer, "The Concept of a Person," in *The Concept of a Person and Other Essays* (New York, 1963); S. Shoemaker, *Self-Knowledge and Self-Identity* (Ithaca: Cornell University Press, 1963); T. Penelhum, *Survival and Disembodied Existence* (London: Routledge and Kegan Paul, 1970).

2. Locke, *Essay concerning Human Understanding*, book 2, chap. 27. Butler, *The Analogy of Religion*, appendix 1. For an excellent analysis of what can be said in Locke's defense, see David Wiggins, "Locke, Butler and the Stream of Consciousness: and Men as Natural Kind", in *The Identities of Persons* ed. A. O. Rorty (Berkeley: University of California Press, 1976).

3. See C. B. Martin and Max Deutscher, "Remembering," *Philosophical Review* 65 (1966), and S. Shoemaker, "Persons and Their Pasts," *American Philosophical Quarterly* (1970).

4. The richest documentation of this is, of course, *Remembrance of Things Past*. Even when Marcel recaptures the very taste of the *madeleine*, the memory carries resonances his experiences did not have: the resonance of all the intermediate experiences and the mediating search for the original. When he recaptures it, it is embedded at the core of the crystal that has grown around it; in a sense he has the original at the core, but he can never see or savor it without the crystalline structure that has formed around it. See also F. H. Bradley, *Appearance and Reality* (Oxford, 1920), 71–73, and Stuart Hampshire, "Dispositions and Memory," in *Freedom of Mind* (Princeton: Princeton University Press, 1971), 160–82.

5. See J. M. Shorter, "Personal Identity, Personal Relationships, and Criteria," *Proceedings of the Aristotelian Society* 71 (1970–71):165–66; and Dorothy Emmet, "Persons and Personae," in her *Rules, Roles, and Relations* (New York: Macmillan, 1966).

6. Hume, *Treatise*, book 2, part 4, chap. 6; D. Parfit, "Personal Identity," *Philosophical Review* (January 1970); John Perry, "Can the Self Divide?" *Journal of Philosophy* 69 (1972).

7. See David Wiggins, *Identity and Spatio-Temporal Continuity* (Oxford: Basil Blackwell, 1967), especially 43–58.

8. I have tried to develop this argument in "Essential Possibilities in the Actual World," *Review of Metaphysics* (1972).

9. For a firm and careful attempt to distinguish various types of criteria for identification, and to discuss their relationships, see M. J. Woods, "Identity and Individuation," in *Analytical Philosophy*, second series, ed. R. Butler (Oxford: Basil Blackwell, 1965).

10. See Wiggins, *Identity and Spatio-Temporal Continuity*, and P. T. Geach, "Identity," *Review of Metaphysics* 21 (1967):3–12. Since the serious differences between Wiggins and Geach do not affect my analysis, I shall not discuss them here.

11. For an excellent analysis of Leibniz's position on identity, see Ian Hacking, "Individual Substance," in *Leibniz: A Collection of Critical Essays*, ed. Harry Frankfurt (New York, 1972). Saul Kripke develops a closely related view in "Naming and Necessity," in *Semantics of Natural Language*, ed. D. Davidson and G. Harman (Dordrecht: Reidel, 1972). Kripke shows how identity statements are corrigible.

12. It might be thought that the criteria for individual differentiation and reidentification would exhaust individual identification. But the characteristics that distinguish and reidentify individuals may be criteria that are not considered significant in identifying a person as the *sort* of person he essentially is. For instance, fingerprints may successfully differentiate and reidentify persons for some purposes, and yet an individual might consider himself, and be considered by others, as essentially unchanged even if we found some way of changing his fingerprints without scars.

13. See E. Durkheim, *The Rules of Sociological Method* (Chicago, 1938).

14. See Harry Frankfurt, "Freedom of the Will and the Concept of a Person," *Journal of Philosophy* 68 (1971):5–20.

15. I have argued a similar point in "Naturalism, Paradigms, and Ideology," *Review of Metaphysics* (1971).

16. K. Read, "Morality and the Concept of the Person among the Gahuku-Gama," in *Myth and Cosmos*, ed. John Middleton (New York: Doubleday, 1967).

17. The literature on this subject is vast. An excellent source is *Magic, Witchcraft, and Healing*, ed. John Middleton (New York, 1967). For a subtle and brilliant analysis of the ramifications of such practices, see Caroline Humphrey, "Magical Drawings in the Religion of the Buryat" (Ph.D. diss., University of Cambridge, 1972).

18. See Read, "Morality and the Concept of the Person"; and Meyer Fortes, "Totem and Taboo," *Proceedings of the Royal Anthropological Institute* (1966).

19. See Williams, "Personal Identity and Individuation."

20. This paper was originally read at meetings of the Moral Sciences Club at the University of Cambridge and the Philosophy Society of the University of Sussex. I am grateful to participants at these meetings for lively discussion and trenchant criticism.

Chapter 3: Persons, Policies, and Bodies

1. This view of what distinguishes persons has ancient origins: the Stoics developed it, and Augustine accepted and transformed Stoic doctrine. Descartes and Kant are, in very different ways, committed to the theory. Harry Frankfurt

has revived a version of it in "Freedom of the Will and the Concept of a Person," *Journal of Philosophy* 68 (1971):5–20.

2. While the view that persons are rational agents was originally developed to provide criteria for species differentiation, it is often treated as though it could be extended to provide criteria for differentiating individuals from one another and for reidentifying the same individual. (But see M. J. Woods, "Identity and Individuation," *Analytical Philosophy*, second series, ed. R. Butler [Oxford: Basil Blackwell, 1965], for a discussion of the relation between individuation and identification.) Even more ambitious versions of the theory would use it to sketch the essential character of individual persons.

3. The legal concept is linked to a dramatic one. *Personae* were originally masks that identified actors' roles, rather than the characteristic traits associated with those roles. Though still linked to action and agency, *personae* came to be identified by the capacity to choose roles, rather than the characteristic traits determined by a fixed role. See Dorothy Emmet, "Persons and Personae," in *Rules, Roles, and Relationships* (New York: Macmillan, 1966); and J. M. Shorter, "Personal Identity, Relationships, and Criteria," *Proceedings of the Aristotelian Society* 71 (1970–71):165–86.

4. See Clifford Geertz, *Person, Time, and Conduct in Bali*, Southeast Asia Studies no. 14 (New Haven: Yale University Press, 1966); Kenneth Read, "Morality and the Concept of the Person among the Gahuku-Gama," in *Myth and Cosmos*, ed. John Middleton (New York: Doubleday, 1967), 185–230; C. Lévy-Bruhl, *The "Soul" of the Primitive* (London: Allen Unwin, 1965), 86–95; Meyer Fortes, "Totem and Taboo," *Proceedings of the Royal Anthropological Society* (1966). See also the collection of articles in *Magic, Witchcraft, and Curing*, ed. John Middleton (New York: Doubleday, 1967).

5. Locke, for example, tries to distinguish the identities of person, man, and substance (*Essay concerning Human Understanding*, book 2, chap. 27, 7–26).

6. PRAT generally assumes, but rarely explicates, a range of "normal" needs, wants, and desires, as well as a "normal" range of actions attending those desires. For one might imagine a robot programmed to have conflicts and a higher level set of principles or policies that come into play whenever such conflicts arise. The presumption is that the wants of *persons* characteristically arise in certain sorts of situations and are expressed in certain sorts of actions.

7. I shall, following Frankfurt, talk about "desires" and ignore, for the time being, the differences between wants, needs, and desires.

8. Some versions of PRAT—Descartes's and Kant's, for example—are perfectly content with this consequence. Those which are not must find some way to connect the principle of individuation (usually defined in terms of physical or spatio-temporal continuity) to an individual's identifications, or to his capacities to form desires by rational policies. See David Wiggins's discussion, *Identity and Spatio-Temporal Continuity* (Oxford: Basil Blackwell, 1967). Talk of an "individual's identifications" of course introduces a significant shift in terminology; it raises issues that are tangential to a discussion of PRAT. See D. Schechter, "Identification and Individuation," *Journal of the American Psy-*

choanalytic Association 16 (1968):48–80, for a discussion of some of the problems involved in the shift of terminology and for a bibliography. See also R. Wollheim, "The Mind and the Mind's Image of Itself," *International Journal of Psycho-Analysis* 50 (1969):209–20.

9. For a discussion of this strategy, see T. Penelhum, "The Importance of Self-Identity," *Journal of Philosophy* 68 (1971):667–77.

10. See B. A. O. Williams, *Morality* (New York: Harper, 1972), 79–107.

11. Frankfurt, "Freedom of the Will," 16.

12. See E. Hildegard, "Human Motives and the Concept of Self," in *Personality*, ed. R. S. Lazarus and E. O. Opton, Jr. (Baltimore: Penguin Books, 1967), 255–58; Oliver Sacks, *Awakenings* (New York: Vintage, 1976).

13. Frankfurt, "Freedom of the Will," 16.

14. See G. H. Mead, *Mind, Self, and Society* (Chicago: University of Chicago Press, 1934), esp. 144–45, 149–52; H. Hartman, *Ego Psychology and the Problem of Adaptation* (New York, 1939). The literature on this subject is too rich and too well known to be sampled here.

15. PRAT should perhaps not be devastated by this objection, since it might very well give criteria for identifying persons without giving criteria that are easy to apply. Theoretical difficulties in applying the criterion should reflect the difficulties we actually do have in identifying responsible persons. On the other hand, if PRAT forces us to reduce the population of persons far beyond the practice that it was designed to explain, we may well conclude that something has gone wrong somewhere.

16. For a discussion of the balance between the policies of strict rationality and adaptivity, see my "Belief and Self-Deception," *Inquiry* 15 (1972):387–410.

17. Butler, "Of Personal Identity," in *The Analogy of Religion;* B. A. O. Williams, "Personal Identity and Individuation," *Proceedings of the Aristotelian Society* 57 (1956–57):229–52; S. Shoemaker, *Self-Knowledge and Self-Identity* (Ithaca: Cornell University Press, 1963), chap. 1; T. Penelhum, *Survival and Disembodied Existence* (London: Routledge and Kegan Paul, 1970).

18. See D. Wiggins, "Locke, Butler and the Stream of Consciousness: and Men as Natural Kind" in *The Identities of Persons* (Berkeley: University of California Press, 1976).

19. See B. A. O. Williams, "Are Persons Bodies?" in *The Philosophy of the Body*, ed. S. Spiker (Chicago: University of Chicago Press, 1970), 137–56; and P. Strawson, *Individuals* (London: Methuen, 1959), chaps. 1–3. Williams defends the view that persons *are* bodies, against the Cartesian view and against Strawson's view that persons are irreducible subjects of mental and physical predicates. Since these differences do not affect my general analysis, I shall speak indifferently of persons having bodies or being embodied. All this leaves open the determination of what sort of body a person must have or be.

20. Read, "Morality and the Concept of the Person."

21. Geertz, *Person, Time, and Conduct in Bali*.

22. See B. A. O. Williams, "The Self and the Future," *Philosophical Review* 78 (1970):161–80.

23. This is not to say that identity-statements are relativized to contexts. See Wiggins, *Identity and Spatio-Temporal Continuity*, esp. 45–46, 55; and P. T. Geach, "Identity," *Review of Metaphysics* 21 (1967):3–12.

24. There is a huge literature on this subject, ranging from commentators on the Platonic tripartite soul, to neo-Freudian analyses of the psychodynamics of ego development. See the bibliography in Schechter, "Identification and Individuation," and *Magic, Witchcraft, and Curing*. See also C. Humphrey, "Magical Drawings in the Religion of the Buryat" (Ph.D. diss., University of Cambridge, 1972).

25. This "is" can be interpreted referentially, rather than descriptively. See K. Donellan, "Proper Names and Identifying Descriptions," in *Semantics of Natural Language*, ed. D. Davidson and G. Harman (Dordrecht: Reidel, 1972), 356–79.

26. See Wiggins, *Identity and Spatio-Temporal Continuity*.

27. See A. J. Ayer, "Individuals," *Mind* 61 (1952).

28. See D. Parfit, "Personal Identity," *Philosophical Review* 79 (1971): 3–27.

29. See S. Alexander, "The Self as Subject and Person," *Proceedings of the Aristotelian Society* 11 (1910–11).

30. H. P. Grice, "The Causal Theory of Perception," *Aristotelian Society Supplement* 35 (1961); C. B. Martin and M. Deutscher, "Remembering," *Philosophical Review* 75 (1966):161–96; and A. Goldman, "A Causal Theory of Knowing," *Journal of Philosophy* 64 (1967):357–72. We may expect a series of such papers: "A Causal Theory of Emotion," "A Causal Theory of Imagining," "A Causal Theory of Referring," etc.

31. With respect to this point, S. Shoemaker, in "Persons and Their Pasts," *American Philosophical Quarterly* 7 (1970):283, analyzes quasi-remembering, causal connections to someone else's experience.

32. See Williams, "Are Persons Bodies?" 152–53.

33. Shoemaker, "Persons and Their Pasts," 269–85, does try to give his analysis some psychological substance.

34. See A. Schutz, *Collected Papers* (The Hague: Nijhoff, 1962), 16–18, 221–22; Mead, *Mind, Self, and Society*, 152–63; H. Hartman, E. Kris, and R. M. Lowenstein, "Comments on the Formation of Psychic Structure," in *The Psychoanalytic Study of the Child* (New York: International Universities Press, 1947), 2:11–38.

35. One could imagine a society, probably relatively small and homogeneous, in which corrective or retributive punishment were directed to offending traits, leaving other character traits relatively unchanged. If someone's passion for art led him to steal a painting, he might, instead of being jailed, be refused entry to a museum, or made apprentice to a public arts program.

Chapter 5: Explaining Emotions

Many people contributed to the writing of this essay. It grew out of conversations with Kathryn Morgan and Ronald de Sousa; Ernest Loevinsohn and Adam

Morton helped shape an early draft. Jonathan Bennett and Georges Rey showed me how to eliminate some unnecessarily Baroque elaborations; Mark Johnson and Graeme Marshall gave me some distinctions when I needed them most. I am also grateful to the participants of a number of seminars where I have read this paper.

1. The contract between voluntary actions and involuntary passions is generally too sharply drawn. For an account of the degrees in the voluntary control and redirection of the emotions, see Iris Murdoch, "The Idea of Perfection," in *The Sovereignty of the Good* (London: Routledge and Kegan Paul; New York: Schocken Books, 1970).

2. As Russell Dancy and Nancy Cartwright have pointed out to me, an emotion need not be irrational or inappropriate to be anomalous: it may simply be out of character. Identifying an emotion as anomalous can, but need not, presuppose a normative judgment. Michael Stocker convinced me that even apparently appropriate and rational responses can be baffling: "Why did he do *that*?" always has a purchase.

3. A person's emotion is irrational if correcting the false belief presupposed by the emotion fails to change it appropriately or if the person uncharacteristically resists considerations that would standardly move him or her to correct the belief. But an emotion can be irrational even if the presupposed belief is true; for the true belief presupposed by the emotion need not be its cause, even when the person does genuinely hold it. The emotion may be caused by beliefs or attitudes that bear no relation to the true belief that would rationalize it. An emotion can be inappropriate when there is no irrationality: the emotion may be too strong or too weak, out of balance with other emotions that are appropriate. Irrational emotions can sometimes be perfectly appropriate to the situations in which they occur. The rationality or irrationality of an emotion is a reflection of the relation between its causes and the beliefs that are taken to justify them: judging the rationality of an emotion requires knowing its etiology. Both judgments of rationality and of appropriateness involve conceptions of normality that have normative force. Disagreements about the classification of an emotion often disguise disagreements about what is wholesome or right.

4. See W. V. Quine, *Word and Object* (Cambridge, Mass.: MIT Press, 1960), 57–61; and Donald Davidson, "Belief and the Basis of Meaning," *Synthese* 27 (1974):309–23. For some modifications of the principle, see Richard E. Grandy, "Reference, Meaning, and Belief," *Journal of Philosophy* 70 (1973):439–52; and Colin McGinn, "Charity, Interpretation, and Belief," *Journal of Philosophy* 74 (1977):521–35.

5. See William P. Alston, "Feelings," *Philosophical Review* 78 (1969):3–34; and "Emotion and Feeling," in *Encyclopedia of Philosophy*, ed. Paul Edwards (New York: Macmillan, 1967). See also R. E. Lazarus, "Emotions and Adaptation: Conceptual and Empirical Relations," (paper read at the Nebraska Symposium on Motivation, 1968); P. T. Young, *Motivation and Emotions* (New York: Wiley, 1961); and Magda Arnold and J. A. Gasson, "Feelings and Emotions as Dynamic Factors in Personality Integration," in *The Nature of Emotion*, ed. Magda Arnold (New York: Penguin Books, 1968). This anthol-

ogy—as well as Arnold's *Emotion and Personality* (New York: Columbia University Press, 1960)—contains an excellent selection of papers, surveying current psychological theories of the emotions.

6. But see Michael Tanner, "Sentimentality," *Proceedings of the Aristotelian Society* 77 (1977):127–47, who describes a range of objectless (and sometimes pointless) emotions.

7. J. de Rivera, *A Structural Theory of the Emotions* (New York: International Universities Press, 1977).

8. For discussions of genetic and physiological determinants of emotions, see Charles Darwin, *The Expression of the Emotions in Man and Animals* (New York: Appleton, 1869); and D. Hamburg, "Emotions in the Perspective of Human Evolution," in *Expression of the Emotions in Man*, ed. Peter Knapp (New York: International Press, 1963). See also Paul Ekman, "Darwin and Cross-Cultural Studies of Facial Expression," in his *Darwin and Facial Expression: A Century of Research in Review* (New York: Academic Press, 1973); P. Ekman, W. Friesen, and P. Ellsworth, *Emotion in the Human Face* (New York: Pergamon Press, 1972); Ekman, *Unmasking the Face* (Englewood Cliffs, N.J.: Prentice-Hall, 1975); Silvan A. Tomkins, *Affect, Imagery, and Consciousness*, vols. 1 and 2 (New York: Springer, 1962–63); and C. E. Izard, *The Face of Emotion* (New York: Appleton-Century-Crofts, 1971). For a discussion of cultural and social factors, see *From Child to Adult: Studies in the Anthropology of Education*, ed. John Middleton (New York: Natural History Press, 1970). The essays by Margaret Mead, Meyer Fortes, and Dorothy Eggan are especially useful for an account of the socialization of the emotions. See also Hildred Geertz, "The Vocabulary of the Emotions," *Psychiatry* 21 (1959); and Jean Briggs, *Never in Anger* (Cambridge, Mass.: Harvard University Press, 1970). For a controversy about the priority of social structure and "basic" human sentiments, see Rodney Needham, *Structure and Sentiment* (Chicago: University of Chicago Press 1962); and George Homans, *Sentiments and Activities* (New York: Free Press, 1962). For a general discussion of the genetic and the social determinants of emotions, see James Averill, "Emotions and Anxiety," in *Emotions and Anxiety*, ed. M. Zuckerman and C. D. Spielberger (New York: Wiley, 1976).

9. This terminology is meant to be neutral between competing analyses of causality and of the logic of dispositional terms. I shall speak of dispositions and habits interchangeably; but I want to examine the relation between the cause of a disposition and its triggering conditions, and to alert us to the possibility that the component "elements" of a disposition may be quite heterogeneous. I would hope that the account of dispositions—as it finally emerges from the specialists concentrating on that issue—will show us why and how some dispositions have a magnetizing momentum of their own: the more they are acted upon, the more likely it is, the easier it becomes, to fall into that way of responding.

10. For an excellent account of how traits dispose a person to have characteristic *sorts* of beliefs and desires, see N. Hirschberg, "A Correct Treatment of Traits" (manuscript).

11. See G. E. M. Anscombe, "On the Grammar of 'Enjoy,'" *Journal of Philosophy* 64 (1967):607–14; Anthony Kenny, *Action, Emotion, and Will* (New York: Humanities Press, 1963), chaps. 1–3; D. F. Pears, "The Causes and Objects of Some Feelings and Psychological Reactions," *Ratio* 4 (1962):91–111; George Pitcher, "Emotion," *Mind* 74 (1965):326–46; Irving Thalberg, "Constituents and Causes of Emotion and Action," *Philosophical Quarterly* 23 (1973):1–14.

12. See Gilbert H. Harman, "Knowledge, Reason, and Causes," *Journal of Philosophy* 67 (1970):841–55. Harman's solution to the Gettier problem provides an analogue to my account of the conservation of the emotions. But as Brian Skyrms pointed out to me, and as Bas C. van Frassen has shown in "The Pragmatics of Explanation," *American Philosophical Quarterly* 14 (1977):143–50, the phrase "inference to the best explanation" is incomplete: apparently competing claims are sometimes compatible because there are different questions at issue. For instance, sometimes we want to know why a person has that emotion (is resentful rather than hurt) and sometimes we want to know why his emotion is directed to that object (why he is angry with his son rather than his boss).

13. See Keith S. Donellan, "Reference and Definite Descriptions," *Philosophical Review* 75 (1966):281–304; and Saul Kripke, "Naming and Necessity," in *Semantics of Natural Language,* ed. D. Davidson and G. Harman (Boston: Reidel, 1972), esp. 269–72, 301–3.

14. See H. Hartman, "Ego Psychology and the Problem of Adaptation," in *Essays on Ego Psychology* (London: Hogarth, 1964); and H. Hartman, E. Kris, and R. M. Lowenstein, *Papers on Psychoanalytic Psychology* (New York: International Universities Press, 1964).

15. One might worry that this involves the sort of circularity that is supposed to trouble claims that the reasons that sometimes cause actions also identify them. But Davidson, among others, has made headway in answering these objections by distinguishing action-types and action-events. These solutions can be transposed to emotion contexts. See D. Davidson, "Actions, Reasons, and Causes," *Journal of Philosophy* 60 (1963):685–700; and G. E. M. Anscombe, *Intention* (Ithaca, N.Y.: Cornell University Press), 11, 45–46. A different solution is proposed by Alvin Goldman, *A Theory of Human Action* (Englewood Cliffs, N.J.: Prentice-Hall, 1970).

16. See J.-J. Rousseau, *Fragments pour "Emile"*: "Nos passions sont des instruments spirituels dont la nature arme nôtre coeur pour la défense de nôtre personne et de tout ce qui est nécessaire à nôtre bien être. Plus donc nous avons besoin de choses étrangères, plus d'obstacles peuvent nous nuire, plus aussi nos passions sont nombreuses et éxaltées; elles se mesurent naturellement sur les besoins de nôtre coeur."

17. See Stephen Stich, "Beliefs and Subdoxastic States," *Philosophy of Science* 45 (1978). Stich gives excellent arguments for the necessity of postulating intentional states that are not beliefs. Though he is primarily concerned with perception, the argument can be generalized.

18. See Robert C. Solomon, "The Logic of Emotion," *Noûs* 11 (1977):41–

48. For an excellent discussion of ambivalence, see P. S. Greenspan, "A Case of Mixed Feelings: Ambivalence and the Logic of Emotion," in my *Explaining Emotions* (Berkeley: University of California Press, 1980).

19. As part of his general program of mapping the facial configurations characteristic of particular emotions, Paul Ekman has begun to specify the configuation of facial muscles associated with various forms of deception. See P. Ekman, W. Friesen, and Schever, "Body Movement and Voice Pitch in Deceptive Interaction," *Semiotica* 16 (1976).

20. It is common in such circumstances to deny the attribution, saying of an adrenally charged person, "Oh, he isn't angry; it's just glands." Sometimes, at any rate, we shy away from attributing an emotion because the person's condition hasn't got the right sort of causal history.

21. See Jerome Singer and Stanley Schacter, "Cognitive, Social, and Physiological Determinants of Emotional States," *Psychological Review* 69 (1962):379–99. Following Cannon, they argue that, as the same visceral changes occur both in a variety of emotional states and in nonemotional states, our perception of these changes cannot identify distinctive emotions. They also hold that "cognitions arising from the immediate situation as interpreted by past experience provide the framework within which one understands and labels feelings" (380). It is, they argue, the cognition that determines whether the state of psychological arousal will be labeled "anger," "exuberance," "fear." Their experiments led them to conclude that "emotional states may be considered a function of a state of physiological arousal and a cognition appropriate to that arousal." But "given a state of physiological arousal, for which an individual has no immediate explanation, he will label that state and describe his feelings in terms of the cognitions available to him" (398). The subject's reports of his emotions, and sometimes his behavior, can be manipulated by exposing him to modeling behavior or by misinforming him about the drugs administered to him. These classical experiments have been subjected to a variety of criticism, ranging from criticisms of experimental design to criticisms that the data do not warrant the conclusions. In any case, Singer and Schacter do not discuss whether the psychological factors they introduce can be redescribed in physical terms.

22. William James, *The Principles of Psychology* (New York: Holt, 1893), 2:499: "The bodily changes follow directly the perception of the exciting fact . . . and our feeling of the same changes as they occur *is* the emotion." It is very difficult to establish whether or to what extent James can be called a physicalist. On the one hand, he seems to hold that particular perceptions can be distinguished from one another by their felt qualities. On the other, he does not reduce the content of propositional attitudes to extensionally described brain states.

23. Cf. the controversy in John O'Connor, ed., *Modern Materialism: Readings on Mind-Body Identity* (New York: Harcourt, Brace and World, 1969).

24. See Paul MacLean, "Sensory and Perceptive Factors in the Emotional Functions of the Triune Brain," in *Emotions, Their Parameters and Measurement*, ed. L. Levi (New York: Raven Press, 1975), and "The Triune Brain,

Emotion, and Scientific Bias," in *The Neurosciences: Second Study Program*, ed. F. O. Schmitt (New York: Rockefeller University Press, 1970). See also P. Black, ed., *Physiological Correlates of Emotion* (New York: Academic Press, 1970).

25. See Clifford Geertz, "Deep Play: Notes on the Balinese Cockfight," in his *The Interpretation of Culture* (New York: Basic Books, 1973), 448–53.

26. See Adam Morton, *Frames of Mind* (Oxford: Oxford University Press, 1980), for an illuminating account of how we attribute and explain psychological states in ordinary contexts.

27. See Graeme Marshall, "Overdetermination and the Emotions," in my *Explaining Emotions*.

28. See Robert C. Solomon, "Emotions and Choices," *Review of Metaphysics* 27 (1973):20–41; and Jean-Paul Sartre, "Bad Faith," in *Being and Nothingness* (New York: Philosophical Library, 1956). Of course it might also be useful to think of choices and voluntary judgments as the expressions of certain sorts of habits, and so as also evincing the problems of conservation. Sartre constructs an ontological explanation for the conservation of habits of choice: the evasion by consciousness of its own nonbeing. More naturalistic explanations are given by Melanie Klein, "On the Development of Mental Functioning," in *Envy and Gratitude* (New York: Delta, 1975), 236–46; and by John Dewey, *Human Nature and Conduct* (New York: Modern Library, 1930), part 3, 172–210.

29. The distinction that Harry Frankfurt has made between first-order desires and their second-order evaluations can be applied to the emotions. See "Freedom of the Will and the Concept of a Person," *Journal of Philosophy* 58 (1971):5–20. There is, however, much more latitude in second-order emotions than there is in second-order attitudes toward desires. A person can enjoy being afraid, be angry at being afraid, regret being afraid, fear being afraid, etc.

30. I am grateful to Jerome Neu for his discussion of this issue in "Jealous Thoughts," in *Explaining Emotions*.

Chapter 6: The Historicity of Psychological Attitudes: Love Is Not Love Which Alters Not When It Alteration Finds

1. An earlier, shorter version of this paper was presented as a commentary to Robert Kraut's "Love *De Re*" (*Midwest Studies in Philosophy* 10, ed. P. French, T. Uehling, and H. Wettstein [Minneapolis: University of Minnesota Press, 1986]) at a meeting of the Eastern Division of the American Philosophical Association. In that paper, Kraut examined an account of love as a *de re*, rather than a *de dicto* attitude; he also analyzed it on the model of naming, as a rigidly designating relation. In a later paper, he proposed an account of love as defined by a series of specific counterfactuals: if the beloved were to die, the lover would grieve, etc.

2. The feeling or affective tone of psychological attitudes is, as Stocker has argued, a central feature of their motivating force. Often the effects of psychological attitudes are a consequence of what it feels like to have them.

3. The analysis of the constancy of love rests on an account of the criteria for personal identity, as well as the criterion for the identity of psychological attitudes whose functional roles change over time.

4. See Kraut, "Love *De Re*."

5. See my article "Jealousy, Attention, and Loss," printed as chapter 7 in this volume.

6. But friends who are not equally wise also have special problems. Perhaps this is why Aristotle thought true friendship could only exist among *phronimoi*.

7. Not all lovers want all this Proustian-Jamesian sensibility from their loves. If Ella is strongly autonomous, so that the details of Louis's love for her do not affect the person she becomes, if his perceptions of her do not further individuate her, she may not care whether Louis's love is historical: appropriate, not-too-rigid constancy may be all she wants, and indeed all she prefers. Ella might be the sort of person who finds an acutely historical love too demanding and time-consuming, preventing her from getting on with other things to which she wants to attend. It is just this sort of difference about preferences for historicity or for mere decent, not-too-rigid general constancy that leads lovers to be baffled by one another's disappointments in what seems to each of them a perfectly adequate fidelity.

A set of observations of prudence seems to follow from this analysis. (1) A friendship between a person who hopes that the constancy of love comes from its historicity and one for whom constancy is a matter of rigidity is likely to lead to deep misunderstanding. But such friends might reach an agreement about asymmetry: one of the friends might want to receive, but be disinclined to give, historical sensitivity; the other might have the appropriate corresponding desire, to give a historical sensitivity but be reassured by a rigid constancy rather than a dynamic permeability. Such a love might be very stable, even though there was considerable asymmetry of understanding between the pair. (2) Although a friendship between two constant, nonhistorical lovers is not likely to lead to misunderstanding, it is also not likely to assure very deep understanding. But both people might prefer to get on with other things in their lives. (3) A friendship between two strongly historical types might phase itself out. It is a difficult empirical question, one that we are not now in any position to answer, whether such differences—differences between a desire for dynamic permeability and a desire for rigidity—are associated with gender or with socioeconomic dependency.

8. See my article "Characters, Persons, Selves, Individuals," printed as chapter 4 of this volume.

9. The early version of this paper was expanded and presented to a colloquium on the emotions sponsored by La Maison des Sciences de l'Homme, 23–25 March 1984. Because organizers of that conference asked participants to address issues concerning the rationality of the emotions, I argued that evaluating psychological attitudes for their rationality is not a particularly perspicuous way of evaluating their appropriateness, their utility, or their soundness. See "Varieties of Rationality, Varieties of Emotions" *Social Science Information* (1985).

Chapter 7: Jealousy, Attention, and Loss

1. See G. Foster, "The Anatomy of Envy," *Current Anthropology* 13 (1972). H. Schoeck, *Envy: A Theory of Social Behavior* (New York: Harcourt, Brace and World, 1969); and D. W. Winnicott, "Transitional Objects and Transitional Phenomena," *Collected Papers* (London: Tavistock Publications, 1958).

Margaret Gilbert and Gareth Matthews have pointed out that my analysis focuses on what might be called dark and heavy cases. They produced many convincing examples of light and passing jealousy that do not require strong fears at all, let alone fears of abandonment. A woman might be jealous that her partner spends too much time with someone else at a party; a child might be jealous that someone else gets a slightly larger piece of cake. These cases need not be disqualified as bona fide instances of jealousy because there is nothing strong enough to be called *fear* that provokes them. I think that is right: and yet, in such cases, we are generally puzzled about why the person should be *jealous* at all. Often, it is a serious question whether a person is jealous, rather than piqued or angry. Following the suggestions developed by Jerry Neu, I think that if a person is *disposed* to passing light jealousy, when the occasions seem to present no threat, it is because the conditions for dark and heavy jealousy obtain in the background. A child prone to passing jealous outbursts is one who generally fears some losses, even though he does not fear a particular loss on a particular occasion. A woman need not fear the loss of her husband to this, that, or the other acquaintance made at a party; but if she characteristically requires her husband's attentions at social gatherings, she suffers an underlying fear.

2. Stanley Cavell, *The Claim of Reason*, (New York: Oxford University Press, 1979), part 4, chap. 13.

3. See Selma Fraiberg; *Insights from the Blind* (New York: Basic Books, 1977); Margaret Mahler, *On Human Symbiosis and the Vicissitudes of Individuation* (New York: International Universities Press, 1968); and René Spitz, *The First Year of Life* (New York: International Universities Press, 1965).

4. See Jerome Neu, "Jealous Thoughts," in my *Explaining Emotions* (Berkeley: University of California Press, 1980). I found Neu's paper enormously useful and stimulating: indeed much of my paper is a development of ideas and suggestions contained in his essay.

5. Melanie Klein, "Some Theoretical Considerations Regarding the Emotional Life of the Infant," *Envy and Gratitude* (New York: Delta, 1977); Rudolph Schaffer, *Mothering* (Cambridge, Mass.: Harvard University Press, 1977); Daniel Stern, *The Developing Child* (Cambridge: Harvard University Press, 1977); Judy Dunn, *Distress and Comfort* (Cambridge: Harvard University Press, 1977); T. Alloway, L. Krames, P. Pliner, eds., *Attachment Behavior* (New York: Plenum Press, 1975).

6. Erving Goffman, *Interaction Behavior* (New York, Anchor Books, 1967), and *Strategic Interaction* (Oxford: Basil Blackwell, 1970); T. Alloway, L. Krames, P. Pliner, eds., *Communication and Affect* (New York: Academic Press, 1972).

7. See Ronald de Sousa, "Self-Deceptive Emotions," in *Explaining Emotions*.

8. Freud, "Some Neurotic Mechanisms in Jealousy, Paranoia, and Homosexuality" (1922), *Standard Edition*, vol. 28; Freud, "On Narcissism" (1914), *Standard Edition*, vol. 22; Michael Lewis and Leonard Rosenblum, eds., *The Origins of Fear* (New York: Wiley, 1974).

9. Sartre, *The Emotions: Outline of a Theory* (New York: The Philosophical Library, 1948).

10. See Michael Stocker, "Intellectual Desire, Emotion, and Action," in *Explaining Emotions*.

11. Anna Freud, *The Ego and the Mechanisms of Defense* (New York: International Universities Press, 1946).

12. See my article "Explaining Emotions," chapter 5 of this volume.

13. Cf. Spinoza, *The Ethics*, parts 2–4, and Kant, *The Critique of Pure Reason*, The Antinomies and Paralogisms.

14. Discussions with Marcia Aufhauser and Margaret Gilbert were helpful in the writing of this paper; Genevieve Lloyd contributed many substantive and organizational suggestions for which I am very grateful. Correspondence with Liam Hudson provoked the section on Oedipal jealousy. As always in such matters, literary sources are the richest, not only *Othello* and *Remembrance of Things Past* but also novels by Henry James, Ivy Compton-Burnett, and the Brontë sisters.

Chapter 8: Unconscious Affects, Mourning, and the Erotic Mind

1. *The Unconscious* (1915), vol. 14 of the *Standard Edition of the Complete Works of Sigmund Freud*, ed. James Strachey, 23 vols. (London: Hogarth Press, 1966–74). Henceforth all references to this edition will be given in the text as "SE." Freud's use of the term *Affekt* derives from Spinoza's *affectus*, a reactive modification contrasted to the active expression of *conatus*.

2. Ibid., 110. Without systematically distinguishing them, Freud sometimes speaks of the *idea* (*Idee*), sometimes the *concept* (*Begriff*) or *content* (*Inhalt*), sometimes the *presentation* or *representation* (*Vorstellung*), sometimes the *object* (*Objekt*) of psychological states. In all cases, he is referring to intentional objects.

3. Since Freud sometimes suggests that drives are themselves *felt*, and that their being felt is part of their operation, he owes us an account of the difference between the felt experience of the expression of a drive and the felt experience of its frustration.

4. The Talmudic strand that Freud shares with Spinoza is central here: a mechanistic account of behavior is compatible with an open-ended and revisionist intentional, ideational, or cognitive description of that behavior.

5. Freud is greatly indebted to Rousseau's account of the effects of dependence: it produces a kind of anxiety that in turn generates a cycle of vulnerability to, and defiance of, the powers and opinions of others.

6. Brian McLaughlin has suggested this formulation for the difference between the two strands in Freud's theory: "A given state is an affect in virtue of having a functional role F [that of releasing the energy of a blocked drive]; that state is a state of *love* in virtue of having a functional role, F′; it is a state of *loving one's mother* by virtue of having a functional role F″. Being in an affective state is essentially open to consciousness. Any F″ state is also F′; and any F′ state is also F. But an F state need not be F′; nor need an F′ state be F″. So while being in an affective state F is essentially open to consciousness, a person might be in F′ or F″, without being aware of being in a certain type of affective state and without being aware of the particular content of that state." (Though essentially aware of being in some sort of affective state, a person can mistake his anger for love, and his anger for his father as an anger for his boss.)

Ronald de Sousa has suggested that there might be interesting parallels between this aspect of Freud's theory—the view that affects are sensed experiences of physiological changes—and the James-Lange account of emotions as the sensations of bodily states.

7. Mourning at death is, of course, not the only kind of mourning. There are losses in separation, alienation, the death of affection, even in the perception of dramatic or radical change in the objects central to a person's identity. There are even losses of fantasy objects and losses of fantasy relations. Whatever is perceived or experienced as the kind of loss that affects a person's conception of what is essential to her sense of herself presents an occasion for mourning.

8. Clearly it is not necessary that a person loves what she mourns or that she loves what she takes to be centrally identificational. Someone can, for instance, mourn the transformation of a family home or neighborhood which, in childhood, brought pain and misery; or she can mourn the loss of a hated enemy. Her sense of herself, her identity, had been bound up with him, or with her hatred of him, even though she not only hated the villain but hated hating him.

9. This interpretation of the gender-linked asymmetry of mourning is borne out by the differences between the mourning of widowers and that of widows: widowers who have lost their primary nurturers, as well as their friends and partners, often suffer affective debility and disorientation, while widows who must learn how to manage their financial affairs appear to suffer in more straightforwardly practical, less affect-ridden ways. Of course when such practical difficulties are symbolically highly charged—as often they are—they become affectively laden.

10. Freud took marriage to be the central model of the kind of bonding he described. But of course the phenomena are more general: even men and women who form relatively bracketed and short-lived alliances exemplify the patterns Freud characterizes as marital. It is not always the woman who follows the pattern Freud describes: it can be Marcel in relation to Albertine, one male homosexual to another, or a nurturing man to a narcissistic woman. But even such variations on the standard type exemplify the plot Freud sketches, when the suitable substitutions are made.

11. Cf. Anne Thompson, "Affects and Ideas in Freud's Early Writings" (unpublished paper).

12. Ronald de Sousa, Lawrence Friedman, Brian McLaughlin, and Ruth Nevo contributed useful comments on this paper. An earlier and shortened version of the paper appeared in *Hebrew University Studies in Literature and the Arts* (1987), ed. R. Nevo and A. Besserman, under the title "Mixing Memory and Desire: Freud on Unconscious Mourning."

Chapter 9: Adaptivity and Self-Knowledge

1. 'Focus' and 'attention' suggest an active, perhaps even a deliberate process. But of course it is only rarely that attentiveness involves work; it is a selective (not always selecting) response to what is salient in the sensory field.

2. *Contra* R. Rorty's subtle argument in "Incorrigibility as the Mark of the Mental," *Journal of Philosophy*, 67 (1970).

3. An integrated organization is systematically unified, without autonomous separable subsystems. When there is possible conflict between the dominance of various functions, the order of precedence is defined.

4. I shall use 'feeling' to refer to sensations, pains, and emotional feelings, realizing, of course, that there are important differences between these.

5. See G. Pitcher, "Pain Perception," *Philosophical Review*, 79 (1970) and his "The Awfulness of Pain," *Journal of Philosophy*, 67 (1970).

6. But not *all* the time, or he'd be avoided as a dreadful bore.

7. Of course I do not mean to imply that all emotions are feelings, or even that emotions that are associated with particular somatic states (e.g., anger or fear) are reducible to sensations. I am here only talking about the felt quality of some emotions, usually simple ones, primitive in the development of our emotional repertoire, without at all claiming that these emotions can be identified by their felt qualities.

8. Whether we shall call our sensations and feelings a type of noninferential knowledge and so complicate our criteria for knowledge, or keep our criteria tidy and exclude them, is a matter of costs and benefits accounting rather than an occasion for heavy philosophical polemics. The question of whether there is noninferential knowledge is partly a neurophysiological question, and partly a matter of the economics of theory construction.

9. For our purposes, the important differences between wants and desires can be neglected. I shall use 'wants' and 'desires' interchangeably.

10. See my "Belief and Self-Deception," *Inquiry*, 15 (1972).

11. See W. Alston, "Varieties of Privileged Access," *American Philosophical Quarterly*, 8 (1971), for distinctions between 'incorrigibility', 'infallibility', 'self-warranted', and his "Self-Warrant: A Neglected Form of Privileged Access", (manuscript).

12. See H. Frankfurt, "Freedom of the Will and the Concept of a Person," *Journal of Philosophy*, 68 (1971).

13. See J.-P. Sartre, *Being and Nothingness*, trans. Hazel Barnes (New York: Philosophical Library, 1956); 303–51; and his *Baudelaire* (New York:

New Directions, 1950); *Essays in Aesthetics*, particularly the essays on Calder and Giacometti, (New York: Washington Square Press, 1966); and *Saint Genet: Actor and Martyr* (New York: Braziller, 1963).

Chapter 10: Fearing Death

1. E.g., Epicurus and Spinoza.

2. Thomas Nagel, "Death," in *Mortal Questions* (Cambridge: Cambridge University Press, 1979).

3. See Robert Gordon, "Fear," *Philosophical Review* (October 1980), and my "Explaining Emotions," which appears as chapter 5 of this volume.

4. Kant notoriously did not apply the arguments of the first antinomy to the substantiality of the soul (conceived as a unified object) as he had applied them to the world (conceived as a totality). The reasons for his failure to extend those arguments lie in his ethics: although moral action is performed solely as a duty to what is right, the moral agent should in principle receive benefits from morality. As it seems evident that such benefits do not always accrue in life, Kant postulated an immortal soul to receive them. Despite this lapse, however, it seems clear that the arguments of the necessity *and* the impropriety of certain metaphysical inference patterns should consistently apply to the soul as well as to the world considered as a totality.

Chapter 11: The Deceptive Self: Liars, Layers, and Lairs

1. A first, rough characterization of self-deception, as it applies to that subclass of propositional beliefs, meets the following conditions:

1. The person believes that p.
2. Either (a) the person believes not-p (standardly this involves the person believing what, given her beliefs and her strongly entrenched habits of inference, she ought to recognize as equivalent to not-p) or (b) the person denies that she believes p.
3. If self-deception does not reduce to error, the person must on some level recognize that she has conflicting beliefs. Standardly, attributing such recognition is an inference to the best explanation of the person's behavior or inferences.
4. If self-deception does not reduce to conflict, the person must on some level deny that her beliefs conflict. Sometimes this is achieved by an ad hoc strategy for reconciling the apparent conflict. The self-deceiver usually makes no attempt to suspend judgment or to determine which of her beliefs are defective.
5. The attribution of self-deception presupposes an account of what the person would normally believe, perceive, notice, infer; it presupposes that she accepts canons of rationality and that she is alert to the sort of evidence that weighs against her belief.

There appears to be an interesting difference in the focus of the discussion of the family of cases: philosophers in England and the United States have largely focused on cases of self-deception, cases where an individual adopts a complex strategy in the face of a conflict of specific belief of which she is presumptively aware. While such cases have not been neglected in France and Germany, philosophers there have focused primarily on *mauvaise foi* as a general condition in which consciousness denies its condition as nothing-but-the-reflection-of-some-arbitrary-content-before-it. Or they have focused on false consciousness as a condition of a class of people whose beliefs and desires have been manipulated and directed in such a way as to violate their natural latent awareness of their real condition.

2. Straightway, then, self-deception seems problematic. For a start, its attribution seems to require a suspicious regression. Because I want to concentrate on other issues, I shall set aside at least some of the familiar puzzles about the attribution of self-deception. Certainly the general difficulties of identifying and attributing beliefs in opaque contexts make it difficult to demonstrate that there are bona fide cases of strict self-deception that do not reduce to error or to conflict. But since these difficulties attend any attribution of belief—let alone the attribution of conflict of belief—they should not by themselves cast doubt on the existence of cases of bona fide self-deception.

3. Donald Davidson, "The Paradoxes of Irrationality," in *The Multiple Self*, ed. Jon Elster (Cambridge: Cambridge University Press, 1986).

4. Daniel Dennett, "The Self as a Center of Narrative Gravity," in *Consciousness and Self*, ed. T. Cole, D. Johnson, and F. Kessel (New York, 1987). Dennett is referring to the work of M. S. Gazzinga and Joseph Le Doux, *The Integrated Mind* (New York: Plenum, 1978). See also Howard Gardner, *The Shattered Mind: The Person after Brain Damage* (New York: Knopf, 1975); and E. R. Hilgard, *Divided Consciousness* (New York: Wiley, 1977).

5. See Ronald de Sousa, "What Computers Will Need to Feel: Emotion and Cognitive Science" (manuscript).

6. See Gilbert Harman, "Coherence and Foundations: Positive vs. Negative Undermining," in his *Change in View* (Cambridge: MIT Press, 1985).

7. See David Pears, *Motivated Irrationality* (Oxford: Oxford University Press, 1984); M. S. Haight, *A Study in Self-Deception* (Sussex, 1980); and Herbert Fingarette, *Self-Deception* (New York: Humanities Press, 1969). See also my "Self-Deception, Akrasia, and Irrationality," *Social Science Information* 19 (1980): 905–22, reprinted in Elster's *The Multiple Self*; "Akratic Believers," *American Philosophical Quarterly* 20 (1983): 175–83; "Belief and Self-Deception," *Inquiry* 15 (1975): 387–410; "Adaptivity and Self-Knowledge" and "Akrasia and Conflict," printed as chapters 9 and 13 in this volume; and Shelly Taylor and Jonathan Brown, "Illusion and Well-Being: A Social Psychological Perspective on Mental Health," *Psychological Bulletin* (1988).

8. Adam Morton, *Frames of Mind* (Oxford: Oxford University Press, 1980). See also Harman, "Coherence and Foundations."

9. The second picture of the mind is a schema that is realized in distinctive ways by a larger variety of theories:

a. Evolutionary accounts of the structure of the brain. See P. D. MacLean, *A Triune Concept of Brain and Behavior: The Hincks Memorial Lectures,* ed. T. Boag and D. Cambell (Toronto, 1973); and Eliot Sober, "Evolution of Rationality," *Synthese* 46 (1981): 95–120.

b. Psychological studies of the compartmentalization and confabulations of inference. See R. Nisbet and T. Wilson, "Telling More Than We Can Now: Verbal Reports on Mental Processes," *Psychological Review* 84 (1977): 321–59; R. Nisbet and L. Ross, *Human Inference: Strategies and Shortcomings of Social Judgment* (Englewood Cliffs, N.J.: Prentice-Hall, 1980); L. Ross, M. R. Leper, and M. Hubbard, "Perserverance in Self-Perception and Social Perception" *Journal of Personality and Social Psychology* 32 (1975): 880–92; A. Tversky, D. Kahnemann, and P. Slovic, *Judgement under Uncertainty* (Cambridge: Cambridge University Press, 1982); U. Neisser, *Cognition and Reality* (New York: W. H. Freeman, 1976); and Alvin Goldman, "Varieties of Cognitive Appraisal," *Nous* 13:22–38.

c. Neuroanatomy and brain physiology. See G. E. Schwartz annd D. Shapiro, eds., *Consciousness and Self-Regulation* (New York: Plenum, 1976), especially A. R. Luria, "The Human Brain and Conscious Activity." See also Patricia Churchland, "A Perspective on Mind-Brain Research," *Journal of Philosophy* 77 (1980): 185–207; A. R. Luria, *The Working Brain* (New York: Basic Books, 1973).

d. Cognitive and functionalist theories in philosophical psychology. See the following works by Daniel Dennett: *Brainstorms* (Montgomery Vt.: Bradford Books, 1978); "Making Sense of Ourselves," *Philosophical Topics: Functionalism and the Philosophy of Mind* 12 (1):63–81; "Three Kinds of Intentional Psychology," in *Reduction, Time, and Reality,* ed. Richard Healy (Cambridge, 1981); "Consciousness," in *Oxford Companion to the Mind,* ed. Richard Gregory (Oxford: Oxford University Press, 1987); and *Elbow Room* (Cambridge: MIT Press, 1985). See also William Lycan, *Logical Form and Natural Language* (Cambridge: MIT Press, 1985); and Hilary Kornblith, ed., *Naturalizing Epistemology* (Cambridge: MIT Press, 1985), especially the articles by Nisbett and Ross, Stich, and Harman. Also useful are the following articles by Stephen Stich: "Dennett on Intentional Systems," *Philosophical Topics: Functionalism and the Philosophy of Mind* 12 (1):39–62; "On the Ascription of Content," in *Thought and Object,* ed. Andrew Woodfield (Oxford: Oxford University Press, 1982); "Beliefs and Subdoxastic Systems," *Philosophy of Science* 45 (1978): 499–518; *From Folk Psychology to Cognitive Science* (Cambridge: Cambridge University Press, 1983); "On Genetic Engineering, the Epistemology of Risk, and the Valuation of Life," in *Logic Methodology and the Philosophy of Science,* vol. 6, ed. J. L. Cohen et al. (New York: North Holland Publishing Company, 1982).

e. Freudian theory on internalization and introjection. See H. Kohut and Ernest S. Wolf, "The Disorders of the Self and Their Treatment: An Outline,"

International Journal of Psychoanalysis 59 (1978): 413–25; H. Kohut, *The Restoration of the Self* (New York: International Universities Press, 1977); and Roy Schafer, "Concepts of Self and Identity and the Experience of Separation-Individuation in Adolescence," *Psychoanalytic Quarterly* 42 (1973): 42–59.

f. Social psychology and the internationalization of social norms and models. See J. Aaronfreed, *Conduct and Consciousness: The Socialization of Internalized Control over Behavior* (New York: Academic Press, 1968); also selections from Durkheim, Weber, Freud, Mead, Cooley, and Schutz in *Theories of Society*, vol. 2, ed. Talcott Parsons, Edward Shils, Kaspar Naegele, and Jesse Pitts (Glencoe, Ill.: Free Press, 1961).

g. Last, and by no means least, see the history developed by Julian Jaynes, *The Origin of Consciousness in the Breakdown of the Bicameral Mind* (Boston: Houghton Mifflin, 1976).

10. See de Sousa, "What Computers Will Need to Feel," and my "Moving Magnets of the Mind" (papers read at a meeting of the Boston Colloquium for the Philosophy of Science, 1986).

11. Eleanor Rosch, "Principles of Categorization," in *Cognition and Categorization*, ed. E. Rosch and B. Lloyd (New York: Wiley, 1978).

12. See Stich, "Beliefs and Subdoxastic Systems," and Robert van Gulick, "Mental Representations: A Functionalist View," *Pacific Philosophical Quarterly* 63 (1982): 3–19.

13. This is of course the view developed by the philosophic tradition that runs from Descartes to Kant: it has also been presented by Harry Frankfurt, "Freedom of the Will and the Concept of a Person," *Journal of Philosophy* 68 (1971): 5–20.

14. I am grateful to Rudiger Bittner, Martin Bunzl, Owen Flanagan, Jens Kulenkampff, Brian McLaughlin, Michael Martin, and Richard Schmitt for their constructive criticisms of earlier drafts of this chapter. Discussions at colloquia at CUNY-Brooklyn and SUNY-Albany were also illuminating and helpful.

Chapter 12: Where Does the Akratic Break Take Place?

1. My preference for retaining the Greek term *akrasia* is not an arcane taste for the esoteric; it arises from my conviction that the other expressions for the phenomena—"weakness of will" and "moral weakness"—are, as we shall see, profoundly misleading.

2. See Michael Stocker, "Desiring the Bad: An Essay in Moral Psychology," *Journal of Philosophy* 76 (1979): 738–53.

3. Harry Frankfurt, "Freedom of the Will and the Concept of a Person," *Journal of Philosophy* 68 (1971): 5–20.

4. Charles Taylor, "Responsibility for the Self," in *The Identities of Persons*, ed. A.O. Rorty (Berkeley: University of California Press, 1976), 281–99.

5. William Alston, "Self-Intervention and the Structure of Motivation," in *The Self*, ed. T. Mischel (London: Basil Blackwell, 1977), 65–102.

6. The Socratic formulation is to be found in the *Protagoras* 352a–358d; the Platonic account is advanced in the *Republic* 439a–441c. While Aristotle

modifies the Platonic account, he accepts at least part of the motivational theory. See book 7 of the *Nicomachean Ethics*.

7. Donald Davidson, "How Is Weakness of the Will Possible?" in *Moral Concepts*, ed. Joel Feinberg (Oxford: Oxford University Press, 1970), 93–113.

8. Daniel Dennett, "How to Change Your Mind," in *Brainstorms* (Montgomery, Vt.: Bradford Books, 1978), 300–9.

9. See my "Jealousy, Attention, and Loss," printed as chapter 7 of this volume.

10. See David Wiggins, "Weakness of Will, Commensurability, and the Objects of Deliberation and Desire," *Proceedings of the Aristotelian Society* 79 (1978–79): 251–77.

11. See my "Akrasia and Conflict," chapter 13 of this volume; there I discuss the attractions of several strategies that pull an agent toward the akratic side.

12. This chapter was delivered as an invited address at the December 1979 meetings of the APA. I am greatly indebted to the commentator, Georges Rey, for extremely valuable suggestions. I also benefited from discussions with Robin Jackson, Mark Johnston, Graeme Marshall, Michael Stocker, and Genevieve Lloyd.

Chapter 13: Akrasia and Conflict

1. *Protagoras* 352a–358d.
2. *The Republic* 439a–441c.
3. *Nicomachean Ethics*, book 7, 3.
4. 1151a, 20–28; 1114a, 25ff.; *Nicomachean Ethics*, book 7, 3. See my "Akrasia and Pleasure: NE Book 7," in *Essays on Aristotle's Ethics* (Berkeley: University of California Press, 1980).
5. *Summa Theologica* 1.11.Q.77, art. 3.
6. Michael Walzer, "Political Action: The Problem of Dirty Hands," *Philosophy and Public Affairs* 2 (1973), reprinted in *War and Moral Responsibility*, ed. M. Cohen, T. Nagel, and T. Scanlon (Princeton: Princeton University Press, 1974).
7. Donald Davidson, "How Is Weakness of the Will Possible?" in *Moral Concepts*, ed. Joel Feinberg (London: Oxford University Press, 1970).
8. See Jon Elster, "Negation Active and Negation Passive" (Lecture d'Alexandre Zinoviev).
9. See my "Belief and Self-Deception," *Inquiry* 15 (1972): 387–410; and "Adaptivity and Self-Knowledge," printed as chapter 9 in this volume.
10. A habit is a second-order habit when it can take other habits as its object. But such habits are functionally defined: a habit that normally operates on events can in some circumstances be directed to other habits. For instance, a person may have certain emotional habits of fear or resentment that are characteristically exercised on relatively specific sorts of objects. But it is possible for someone to exercise those emotional habits, fearing to be resentful or being resentful at fearing. See my "Explaining Emotions," printed as chapter 5 of this volume.

11. H. Frankfurt, "Freedom of the Will and the Concept of a Person," *Journal of Philosophy* 68 (1971): 5–20.

12. Charles Taylor, "What is Human Agency?" in *The Self*, ed. T. Mischel (Oxford: Basil Blackwell, 1977); and William Alston, "Self-Intervention and the Structure of Motivation," in ibid. But reflexive identification need not always favor evaluative judgments. A person might consider that some of his evaluative attitudes—specific regrets or guilt—are not to be underwritten because they are the products of inappropriate and harmful socialization. In such cases, the reflexive identification might underwrite first-level motives rather than evaluative attitudes.

13. See Jon Elster, *Logic and Society: Contradictions and Possible Worlds* (New York: Wiley, 1978), chaps. 5 and 6; and my "Imagination and Power," printed as chapter 17 of this volume.

Chapter 14: Three Myths of Moral Theory

1. See Gary Watson, "Recent Work on the Will," *Mind* (April 1987).

2. See "The Place of Contemplation in Aristotle's Ethics," *Essays on Aristotle's Ethics* (Berkeley: University of California Press, 1980).

3. John McDowell, Iris Murdoch, and David Wiggins have characterized Aristotelian *phronēsis* in such a way as to show its connection to perception and habit. For the most part, however, they have concentrated on individual actions, without locating them within the larger frame of social and political practices. Alasdair MacIntyre and Martha Nussbaum have extended that analysis to an appropriately Aristotelian understanding of socially formed *praxis*. And indeed, one may put it more strongly: the recognition of the role of *phronēsis* and its appropriate formation may require a certain sort of self-conscious polity. There are, of course, *phronimoi* even among post-Hobbesians; and even we ordinary post-Hobbesian agents form our actions more subtly than our theories explain. But we are, to some extent at least, formed, and limited, by our moral theories, even when they are inadequate to account for the full richness of our practices.

4. Henry Richardson has suggested (in private correspondence) that the reason Aquinas did not include perceptive and end-specifying functions within *prudentia* is that the ultimate ends of humans are those of achieving a proper relation to divinity. Practical and theoretical virtues are ultimately at the service of fulfilling that primary end.

5. See Alasdair MacIntyre, "Why Moral Agents Became Ghosts," *Synthese* (1982).

6. Kant, *Doctrine of the Virtues*. Barbara Hermann and Onora O'Niell, among others, have argued that Kant not only accommodates, but insists on, the benefits of virtue-oriented theories.

7. See Charles Taylor, "Responsibility for Self," in *Identities of Persons*, ed. A. O. Rorty (Berkeley: University of California Press, 1976).

8. See Jürgen Habermas, *The Theory of Communicative Action*, 2 vols. (Boston: Beacon Press, 1981/87) and John Rawls, "The Ideas of an Overlapping Consensus" and "The Priority of Right and Ideas of Good in Justice as Fairness."

9. Even those who, like Bernard Williams, are most determined to preserve the position of the agent, and who deny that there is a special moral sense of "ought" or "should" seem committed to some form of judicialism. He remarks, " 'What should I do?' simply means 'What have I most reason to do?' " "Formal and Substantial Individualism," *Aristotelian Society Proceedings* (1984–85): 120.

10. By contrast, these tasks are fused in Aristotelian *phronēsis*, which includes *deinotēta*, a kind of well-formed cleverness, structured habits of relevant inventiveness. Aristotle's emphasis on the manner in which actions are performed sets the possibility for resolving apparently conflicting alternatives: subdominant or recessive alternatives can be preserved and expressed in voice, gesture, timing, without being denied or rejected. See Maurice Catani and Suzanne Mazé, *Tante Suzanne: Une Histoire de Vie Sociale* (Paris, 1982), for a subtle description of an immigrant woman who retained, integrated, and expressed alternatives that, on a judicial account, she might be thought to have rejected.

11. See "How to Interpret Actions" in *Rationality, Relativism and the Human Sciences*, ed. J. Margolis, M. Krausz, and R. M. Buridan (Dordrecht: Nijhoff, 1986).

12. The tensions within Aristotelian and Kantian ethical theory—their commitment to what is highest and best on the one hand, and their commitment to a comprehensive life on the other—are symptomatic of this problem. Commentators are familiar with the tension in Aristotle's thought, the tension between living a life that actualizes the best and highest of human potentialities. (Never mind how we are supposed to know what these "highest and best" things are, or why an autonomous and independent activity is better than one which is communal and mutually reliant). Commentators are now beginning to find a similar tension in Kant's thought, a tension between a strict conception of the formal conditions of morality, and a broader conception which includes whatever is encompassed and required to actualize or realize the formal commands of morality. The first fixes on the purity of the will; the second on actualizing what the will commands.

13. "Virtue must actually engage the will." *Virtues and Vices* (Berkeley: University of California Press, 1978), 7ff.

14. See Bernard Williams, *Ethics and the Limits of Philosophy* (Cambridge, Mass.: Harvard University Press, 1987), and Susan Wolf, "Moral Saints," *Journal of Philosophy* (1982) and "Above and Below the Line of Duty," *Philosophical Topics* (1986).

15. See Watson, "Recent Work on the Will" and "The Two Faces of Courage," *Philosophy* (1986).

16. See Tom Nagel, "The Fragmentation of Value," in *Mortal Questions* (Cambridge: Cambridge University Press, 1979), 128–41; Elizabeth Anderson,

Value in Ethics and Economics, unpublished Ph.D. dissertation, Harvard University, 1987; and Charles Taylor, "The Diversity of Goods," in *Philosophical Papers*, vol. 2 (Cambridge: Cambridge University Press, 1985).

17. I am grateful to Larry Blum, Sissela Bok, Sarah Waterlow Broadie, Ronald de Sousa, Owen Flanagan, Eugene Garver, Michael Hardimon, Henry Richardson, Richard Schmitt, Michael Slote, Georges Rey, Greg Trianowski, Stephen White, and David Wong for detailed and helpful comments. I also benefited from colloquia discussions at the New School for Social Research, North Carolina State University at Raleigh, St. John's University, the University of California at Davis, the University of California at Santa Cruz, and Western Washington University at Bellingham.

Chapter 15: The Two Faces of Courage

1. Although the terminology of "dispositions," "character traits," and "habits" is meant to be neutral between competing analyses of the causal force of intentionality and the logic of dispositional terms, I believe that the account of psychological dispositions—as it finally emerges from the variety of specialists concentrating on those issues—will explain how some dispositions have a magnetizing and expansionist momentum: the more they are exercised, the more likely it is that they will be elicited. In his *Virtues and Vices* (Ithaca, N.Y.: Cornell University Press, 1978), 78ff., James Wallace gives a typical formulation of the conditions that define traditional courage. An action, *y*, is courageous just when:

1. *A* believes that it is dangerous for him to do an action *y*.
2. *A* believes that doing *y* is worth the risk it involves.
3. *A* believes that it is possible for him to do *y*.
4. The danger *A* sees in *y* is sufficiently formidable that most people would find it difficult to do *y*.

This characterization has the consequence of making the attribution of courage comparative, set against a background of expectations about normal fears and desires. Moreover, without further modification, this definition does not assure that the exercise of courage is always beneficial, admirable, or virtuous. An action need not be worth the risk the agent takes, even in her own system of priorities, just because she believes that it is.

2. See Kant, *The Metaphysical Doctrine of Virtue*: "Fortitude is the capacity and resolved purpose to resist a strong but unjust opponent; and with regard to the opponent of the moral disposition within us, such fortitude is virtue *(fortitudo moralis)*."

3. See Philippa Foot, "Virtues and Vices," in her *Virtues and Vices* (Berkeley: University of California Press, 1978); John MacDowell, "Virtue and Reason," *The Monist* 62 (1979); Gary Watson, "Virtues in Excess," *Philo-*

sophical Studies 46 (1984); and Iris Murdoch, "The Idea of Perfection," in *The Sovereignty of Good* (London: Routledge and Kegan Paul, 1970).

4. Charles Ferster and B. F. Skinner, *Schedules of Reinforcement* (New York: Appleton-Century-Crofts, 1957).

5. Cf. Watson, "Virtues in Excess," *Philosophical Studies* 46 (1984), and Susan Wolf, "Moral Saints," *Journal of Philosophy* (1982). See Peter Railton, "Alienation, Consequentialism, and the Demands of Morality," *Philosophy and Public Affairs* 13 (1984).

6. The best examples are always from literary and autobiographical sources: Emma Goldman, *Living My Life*; Sophocles, *Antigone*; Nadezhda Mandelstam, *Hope against Hope*; Hugh Walpole, *Fortitude*; Thomas Keneally, *Schindler's List*. See Simone Weil, *The Iliad: A Poem of Force*, for a discussion of Homeric criticisms of traditional *andreia*. For the debunking of courage, see Brecht, *Mother Courage*, and Stephen Crane, *The Red Badge of Courage*.

7. See Albert Hirschman, *The Passions and the Interests* (Princeton: Princeton University Press, 1981).

8. Hobbes, *Leviathan*, "A Review and Conclusion."

9. See Aristotle's discussion of actions that appear to be courageous without really being so, and actions that are courageous without the agent being so (1116a, 16–1117a, 28); see also Aquinas on sham prudence (St 2.2ae.47.13).

10. See my "The Limits of Socratic Intellectualism," *Proceedings of the Boston Area Colloquium in Classical Philosophy*, ed. John J. Cleary, (New York: University Press of America, 1987).

11. See McDowell, "Virtue and Reason," and Watson, "Virtues in Excess."

12. See Henry Moore, *An Account of the Virtues* (1690; reprint ed., New York: Facsimile Text Society, 1930), book 2, 92. See also Chaucer, "The Parson's Tale," *The Canterbury Tales*; *Summa Virtutum de Remediis Animae*, ed. S. Wenzel (Chicago: University of Chicago Press, 1984); Benjamin Schwarz, "On Polarity in Confucian Thought," in *Confucianism in Action*, ed. David Nivison and Arthur Wright (Stanford: Stanford University Press, 1959); Arthur Wright, ed., *Studies in Chinese Thought* (Chicago: University of Chicago Press, 1953).

13. Michael Walzer, "Political Action: The Problem of Dirty Hands," *Philosophy and Public Affairs* 1 (1972); Charles Taylor, "The Diversity of Goods," in *Utilitarianism and Beyond*, ed. Amartya Sen and Bernard Williams (Cambridge: Cambridge University Press, 1982); Stuart Hampshire, "Morality and Conflict," in his *Morality and Conflict* (Cambridge, Mass.: Harvard University Press, 1983); Bernard Williams, "Ethical Consistency," in his *Problems of the Self* (Cambridge: Cambridge University Press, 1973).

14. Camus, *The Fall*, quoted by Bernard Williams in *Ethics and the Limits of Philosophy* (London: Fontana Press/Collins, 1985).

15. I am grateful to Rüdiger Bittner, Sissela Bok, Jens Kulenkampff, Jerrold Katz, Michael Martin, and Virginia Valian for their critical comments, and to participants in discussions at colloquia held at Mount Holyoke College, Union College, and Yale University.

Chapter 16: Virtues and Their Vicissitudes

1. Entrepreneurial traits might, for instance, be valued in the mistaken belief that they tend to improve the standard of living, which itself might erroneously be believed essential to a culture's (conception of its) thriving.

2. Cf. Michael Walzer, *Interpretation and Social Criticism* (Cambridge, Mass.: Harvard University Press, 1987), and Jonathan Lear, "Moral Objectivity," in *Objectivity and Cultural Divergence*, ed. S. C. Brown (Cambridge: Cambridge University Press, 1984).

3. Philippa Foot, "Virtues and Vices," in her *Virtues and Vices* (Berkeley: University of California Press, 1978), 7ff. Following this strategy, Foot says, "The villain's courage is not a virtue in him."

4. See my "Two Faces of Courage," chapter 15 of this volume.

5. See Michael Slote, *Goods and Virtues* (Ithaca, N.Y.: Cornell University Press, 1983), chap. 2; Alasdair MacIntyre, "How Virtues Become Vices," in *Evaluation and Explanation in the Biomedical Sciences*, ed. H. T. Engelheardt and S. F. Spicker (The Hague: Mouton, 1982).

6. See my "The Limits of Socrates' Intellectualism: Did Socrates Teach Virtue?" in *Proceedings of the Boston Area Colloquium in Ancient Philosophy*, ed. John Cleary (New York: University Press of America, 1987).

7. Foot, "Virtues and Vices."

8. There is a tradition according to which virtue is assured by the balance among opposed virtues. That tradition is represented by Plato, in *The Statesman* (311 B–C): "Those who are careful, fair and conservative—those of a moderate temperament—are not keen; they lack a certain sort of quick, active boldness. The courageous on the other hand are far less just and cautious, but they are excellent at getting things done. A community can never function well . . . unless both of these are present and active . . . woven together by the ruler." The opposition of virtues is explored in book 3 of *The Faerie Queen* where Spenser describes a duel between the Knight of Temperance against the Knight of Chastity. See also Hume, *Treatise of Human Nature*, book 2, part 2, secs. 1–12, and Spinoza, *Ethics*, part 3, Scholia and Definitions, for detailed accounts of the ways in which the passions function within a dynamic system of support and opposition.

9. I am grateful to Alasdair MacIntyre for stressing this point.

10. Cf. Tyler Burge, "Individualism and Psychology," *The Philosophical Review* (1986), and "Intellectual Norms and Foundations of Mind," *Journal of Philosophy* (1987). Burge argues that the individuation of intentional states essentially refers to social practices.

11. Stephen White pointed out to me that it might seem that interactive action formation could be analyzed as a sequence of microactions. M says x in manner f, which serves as a stimulus for N to say y in manner g, which serves as a stimulus for M to say z in manner h. While a conversation or an improvisation could be analyzed in that way, such an analysis would miss the formation of the action as a whole. Of course any action can be broken down into a series of microactions: not only such complex actions as emigrating, undertaking to

follow a course of study, but also swimming across a pond or walking can be decomposed into micromovements. But while such an analysis might explain the details of each micromovement, it would not explain the form of the sequence, taken as a whole, in relation to other action sequences, taken as wholes. To understand the structured sequence of microactions as forming a complex whole, we refer to a shared general intention that integrally encompasses the interactive process: partners making music together, or having a conversation.

12. David Wong pointed out to me that it might seem as if the greater the role assigned to the interactive structuring of actions, the less of a role does the configuration of character play in acting well. It is true that we often not only have different types of conversations with different interlocutors, but even different types of conversations on the same subject. The emergent details of a person's views on a topic are strongly influenced by the views and the characters of her interlocutors. But both are required: a particular interactive response is drawn from a person's repertoire of character traits: it is, as we say, characteristic. See Jonathan Adler, "Moral Development and the Personal Point of View," in *Women and Moral Theory*, ed. Eva Kittay and Diane Meyers (Totowa, N.J.: Rowman and Allenheld, 1986).

13. See John Rawls, "The Idea of an Overlapping Consensus" and "The Priority of Right and Ideas of the Good in Justice as Fairness." See also Jürgen Habermas, *The Theory of Communicative Action*, 2 vols. (Boston: Beacon Press, 1981/87).

14. This paper grew out of many conversations, held over a long period of time: Rüdiger Bittner, Larry Blum, Sissela Bok, Owen Flanagan, Genevieve Lloyd, Alasdair MacIntyre, Georges Rey, William Ruddick, Michael Slote, Stephen White, and David Wong have helped shape it, as did the participants in colloquia at the University of Maryland, the University of Washington, and the University of British Columbia.

Acknowledgments

An earlier version of "Persons and Personae" appeared under the title "Persons as Rhetorical Categories," in *Social Research* 54 (1987):55–72. Other versions are in *Persons and Human Beings*, ed. Christopher Gill (Oxford: Oxford University Press, 1988) and in *Relativism: Interpretation and Confrontation*, ed. Michael Krausz (Notre Dame, Ind.: Notre Dame University Press, 1988). This essay also contains material excerpted from the introduction to *The Identities of Persons* (Berkeley: University of California Press, 1976), © 1976 by The Regents of the University of California and reprinted here by arrangement with the University of California Press.

"The Transformation of Persons" first appeared in *Philosophy* 48 (1973):261–75.

"Persons, Policies, and Bodies" first appeared in the *International Philosophical Quarterly* (1973):63–80.

"Characters, Persons, Selves, Individuals" first appeared in *The Identities of Persons* (see above).

"Explaining Emotions" was originally published in the *Journal of Philosophy* (1978):139–61, and reprinted in *Explaining Emotions*, ed. A. O. Rorty (Berkeley: University of California Press, 1980), © 1980 by The Regents of the University of California and reprinted here by arrangement with the University of California Press.

"The Historicity of Psychological Attitudes: Love Is Not Love Which Alters Not When It Alteration Finds" first appeared in *Midwest Studies in Philosophy*, ed. P. French, T. Uehling, Jr., and H. Wettstein (Minneapolis: University of Minnesota Press, 1986), 399–411.

"Jealousy, Attention, and Loss" was first published under the pseudonym of Leila Tov-Ruach in *Explaining Emotions*, 465–87 (see above).

"Unconscious Affects, Mourning, and the Erotic Mind" was published under the pseudonym of Leila Tov-Ruach in *Perspectives on Self-Deception*, ed. Brian McLaughlin and A. O. Rorty (Berkeley: University of California Press, 1988), © 1988 by The Regents of the University of California and reprinted here by arrangement with the University of California Press. An earlier version appeared in *Hebrew University Studies in Literature and the Arts* 14 (1987), ed. R. Nevo and B. Besserman.

"Fearing Death" first appeared in *Philosophy* 58 (1983):175–88.

"The Deceptive Self: Liars, Layers, and Lairs" appeared in *Perspectives on Self-Deception* (see above). An earlier version appeared in *Analyse und Kritik* 7 (1985):141–61.

"Where Does the Akratic Break Take Place?" appeared in *The Australian Journal of Philosophy* 58 (1980):333–46. It also contains material excerpted from "Akratic Believers," *American Philosophical Quarterly* (1983).

"Adaptivity and Self-Knowledge" first appeared in *Inquiry* 18 (1975):1–22.

"Akrasia and Conflict" appeared in *Inquiry* 23 (1981):193–212. It also contains material excerpted from "Self-Deception, Akrasia, and Irrationality," *Social Sciences Information* 19 (London, Beverly Hills, and New Delhi: SAGE, 1980).

An earlier version of "The Two Faces of Courage" appeared in *Philosophy* 61 (1986):151–71.

"Virtues and Their Vicissitudes" will appear in *Midwest Studies in Philosophy*, ed. P. French (Minneapolis: University of Minnesota Press, 1988).

"Imagination and Power" first appeared in *Social Sciences Information* 22 (London, Beverly Hills, and New Delhi, 1983), 801–16.

The illustration to part 1 is taken from Franciszka Themerson, *Traces of Living* (London: Gaberbocchus Press, 1969); © 1969 by Franciszka Themerson.

Illustration to part 2 © 1988 by Jacob Kosman, who drew it when he was ten years old.

Illustrations to parts 3 and 4 © 1988 by Shelly Errington.